LENIN'S LEGACY

HISTORIES OF RULING COMMUNIST PARTIES

Richard F. Staar, editor

Korean Workers' Party: A Short History, Chong-Sik Lee

History of Vietnamese Communism, 1925–1976, Douglas Pike

Lenin's Legacy: The Story of the CPSU, Robert G. Wesson

LENIN'S LEGACY
THE STORY OF THE CPSU

Robert G. Wesson

HOOVER INSTITUTION PRESS
Stanford University • Stanford, California

Hoover Institution Publication 192

Contents

Editor's Foreword

This is the third book in a series on the histories of the sixteen ruling communist parties from their organization to the present time. The studies were initiated to fill an important gap in the modern English-language historiography on communism in Albania, Bulgaria, Cambodia, China, Cuba, Czechoslovakia, (East) Germany, Hungary, (North) Korea, Laos, Mongolia, Poland, Romania, the Soviet Union, Vietnam, and Yugoslavia.

This particular volume in the series covers the following aspects of the ruling party in the Soviet Union:

- Social and political background of the revolutionary movement in Russia.
- Founding of the Leninist party, its early struggles, important personalities, polemics, and difficulties.
- Accession to power because of special conditions toward the end of World War I.
- Development of the party from a revolutionary to a governing organization in and after the civil war.
- Stalinist succession; transformation and purge of the party under Stalin.
- The party as an instrument of totalitarian rule, 1930–1953.
- Succession after Stalin; the Khrushchev interlude of de-Stalinization and qualified liberalization.
- Stabilization of party rule under Brezhnev's leadership, problems in the late 1970s, with an overview of the role and nature of the CPSU, and its relationship to the world communist movement.

As general editor of this series, I am pleased that such a distinguished scholar as Professor Robert G. Wesson accepted our invitation to prepare this monograph.

RICHARD F. STAAR
Coordinator of International Studies

Hoover Institution
Stanford University

Preface

The Russian Revolution, the interwar period wracked by the struggles between conflicting ideologies, the passions of the Second World War, and the following cold war lose the vividness of living memory with the passing years. As distance grows, the rise of Bolshevism and the Soviet experiment gain clarity, or become less obscure, against the broad horizons of history. It has become easier to see through some of the mystification and to view the party of Lenin, its seizure of power in the world's largest state, and the subsequent dramatic events in objective focus. The onetime fiery revolutionary state has settled down to sedate maturity, and our view of it should likewise be on the way to settling down.

Detachment is still difficult, because the Soviet state and the Communist movement still base their legitimacy to a large extent on their idealized interpretation of the rise of Lenin's party. But at the distance of sixty years the Russian Revolution has lost much of its apocalyptic aura, diabolical or saintly; we can now see it as it has always been in reality, an episode of Russian history, an eruption not of wholly new forces but of old forces in new shapes, not a total overthrow and renewal but a remaking of the Russian polity under the impact of modernization and the strains of maladjustment and war, a result of the long-term abrasive interaction of Russia and the West. The new Russia has always contained much of the old Russia, and Lenin's men were Russian revolutionaries far more than they were Marxist radicals. This obvious but frequently neglected fact forces itself ever more strongly on the student as the postrevolutionary government, with its fondness for stability, its modest growth rate, flagging technology, discontented intellectuals, and reliance on pressure more than terror, comes to look more like the prerevolutionary state.

It is consequently appropriate at this time to take a new look at the Leninist party as it rose from a minor radical movement torn by factional squabbles to a governing power, presided over the remaking and industrialization of Russia, fought its way to victory in Russia's greatest war, and accommodated to stability. On the one hand, the present history continues the story from where the able accounts of such scholars as Leonard Schapiro and John S. Reshetar, Jr., left it some years ago to cover the Brezhnev period. On the other hand, the perspective of the present day seems to require some shifts of emphasis. This work offers no new discoveries but sees many things differently from previous depictions.

Much is still mysterious, largely because those in a position to publish the truth have frequently preferred persuasion to objectivity, and because one can make only surmises about many important matters. But the story that emerges is a tremendous dark epic, a tale of magnificent achievement and horrible suffering, of nobility and crime; to convey its dramatic grandeur requires the sweep of a Tolstoy plus the psychological insight of a Dostoyevsky. It is of a piece with Russian history, in which the vast success of four hundred years of empire building was shadowed by the sufferings of the people and the misdeeds of the rulers. Peter not only built monumentally but murdered on a scale almost worthy of Stalin, and the shiny new capital of St. Petersburg cost the lives of tens of thousands of serfs. Whether under tsars or general secretaries, Russia has never been a land of moderation.

As we attend to the details of the story of Lenin's party, which in 1917 became practically the story of Russia, the follies, cynicism, deceit, and cruelty stand out more than the idealistic dedication and heroism. It seems in many ways a sordid tale of collective egotism, of narrow self-seeking and the self-centered use of power, of false and consequently broken promises, and of the crushing of all who seemed potential dangers to the monopoly of the party. By the moral standards of the Western world, the history of the Communist Party of the Soviet Union has been by no means pretty; its ugliness stands out even more in contrast with the lofty proclamations and exalted self-appraisals. But if we children of the West take satisfaction in ethical superiority, we can hardly deny some ethnocentrism. Lenin was entirely within the Russian tradition, in which what a Westerner might call cruelty and deceit was fully justified by the purposes of absolutism.

In its own terms, the Bolshevik party has been a paragon of virtue—indeed the chief expression and essence of virtue. This is not merely to note the trite fact that it has indulged in considerable self-congratulation, which we do not have to take at face value. A more important indication is that when Lenin and his followers and successors have done things that might be considered immoral—made and broken promises, trampled on the rights of others, used and discarded allies—they have been acting in the name of what they considered a higher morality, the strength and welfare of the political movement. The advancement of the cause (usually, in effect, the strength and unity of the party) has been the supreme rule. In dedication to this cause, very many persons, both leaders and led, have shown exemplary loyalty, courage, and self-sacrifice. In this context, it might be held a sin not to lie or murder if the well-being of the party required it. As Dostoyevsky put it, Russia should be judged not by its villainies, but by its lofty ideals.*

We should recognize that the conduct of persons who have given their lives to the party has not been amoral—although it is not easy to refrain from harsh judgments of some Stalinists—but guided by a morality of their own, the sense of which we can penetrate only partially. Whatever we may think of it, it has proved itself effective. Against competitive philosophies, it gained power and held it when few thought this possible. It made a new, and in many ways path-breaking, government, won the civil war, and transformed its great realm socially and economically according to preconceived ideas to an extent never before attempted by any state. The party could acquire the status it did only because it genuinely fulfilled important functions and did not operate solely for its members and direct beneficiaries. If success pragmatically proves virtue, Bolshevism has been more virtuous than other movements that are of more traditional outlook or that have been more influenced by the Western world view.

Ethnocentrism, however, is not to be wished away, and we are as entitled to examine the warts and ulcers of Communism as the Communists are to point to the shortcomings of our more open and liberal society—something they do with great vigor and self-righteousness. We are also justified in recalling that Lenin's party has not necessarily expressed accurately the feelings of the Russian or Soviet peoples as a whole. To a large majority of Russians in the relatively tranquil years preceding World War I, Bolshevism was morally and intellectually outrageous; since 1917 they have never really had an opportunity to express their preferences. Finally, we may remember that the fates have not yet decided whether the organizational morality of Communism will outlast the less coherent and often less effective philosophy of the Western world.

Santa Barbara, California   Robert G. Wesson

*Cited in Alexander Kerensky, *Russia and History's Turning Point*, p. 38.

Name	Age	Total Years Tenure (In full years)		Present Position (Date of Election or Appointment)
		As Voting Member	As Nonvoting Member	

Politburo Voting Members

Name	Age	As Voting Member	As Nonvoting Member	Present Position
Yu. V. Andropov	63	4	6	Chmn, KGB (May 67)
L.I. Brezhnev	70	20	2	General Secretary (Oct 64) Chmn, USSR Supreme Soviet Presidium (Jun 77)
V.V. Grishin	63	6	10	Moscow City First Secretary (Jun 67)
A.A. Gromyko	68	4	0	USSR Minister of Foreign Affairs (Feb 57)
A.P. Kirilenko	71	15	4	Party Secretary (Apr 66)
A.N. Kosygin	73	21	5	USSR Premier (Oct 64)
F.D. Kulakov	59	6	0	Party Secretary (Sep 65)
D.A. Kunayev	65	6	5	Kazakh First Secretary (Dec 64)*
K.T. Mazurov	63	12	8	USSR First Deputy Premier (Mar 65)
A. Ya. Pel'she	78	11	0	Chmn, Party Control Committee (Apr 66)
G.V. Romanov	54	1	3	Leningrad Oblast' First Secretary (Sep 70)
V.V. Shcherbitskiy	59	6	7	Ukrainian First Secretary (May 72)
M.A. Suslov	74	22	0	Party Secretary (Mar 47)
D.F. Ustinov	68	1	11	USSR Minister of Defense (Apr 76)

Politburo Nonvoting Members

Name	Age	As Voting Member	As Nonvoting Member	Present Position
G.A. Aliyev	54		1	Azerbaydzhan First Secretary (Jul 69)
K.U. Chernenko	65		0	Party Secretary (Mar 76)
V.V. Kuznetsov	76		0	First Deputy Chmn, USSR Supreme Soviet Presidium
P.N. Demichev	59		12	USSR Minister of Culture (Nov 74)
P.M. Masherov	59		11	Belorussian First Secretary (Mar 65)
B.N. Ponomarev	72		5	Party Secretary (Oct 61)
Sh. R. Rashidov	59		16	Uzbek First Secretary (Mar 59)
M.S. Solomentsev	63		5	RSFSR Premier (Jul 71)

Secretariat (Members who are not in Politburo)

Name	Age	Present Position
V.I. Dolgikh	52	Party Secretary (Dec 76)
I.V. Kapitonov	62	Party Secretary (Dec 65)
K.V. Rusakov	67	Party Secretary (May 77)
Ya. P. Ryabov	49	Party Secretary (Oct 76)
M.V. Zimyanin	62	Party Secretary (Mar 76)

*General policy responsibilities have been assumed on the basis of public activities as well as the public career background of the leaders. (There are overlapping responsibilities among

Responsibilities xiii

General Policy Responsibilities**	
Domestic	Foreign

Security, Intelligence
General Supervision, Defense,
   Security, Legislature
	Intelligence
	General Supervision, General Foreign
	   Relations

Moscow Party Supervision	
	General Foreign Relations

Party Organization, Industrial Mgmt.
   Economic Administration, Finance,
   Defense Agriculture
Agriculture
Kazakh Party Supervision
Economic Administration, Industry
Party Discipline
	Communist Bloc Economy
	General Foreign Relations, Trade
	
	Economic Aid Programs

Leningrad Oblast' Party Supervision	
Ukrainian Party Supervision Ideology, Culture	International Communism (Including PRC)
Defense, Space	Military Aid, Foreign Military Support
Azerbaydzhan Party Supervision Politburo Staff Work Legislative Agencies	General State Relations
Culture Belorussian Party Supervision	
	Relations with Non-Ruling Communist Parties, Foreign Relations
Uzbek Party Supervision RSFSR Economic Admin., Finance	
Heavy Industry Party Staffing	
	Communist Bloc Liaison
Defense Industry Culture	

several leaders and there are responsibilities not attributable to any one leader that should be taken into account when using this table.)
**Excludes a previous stint in this position.

Vladimir Ilich Lenin

Introduction

It is easy to define the Communist Party of the Soviet Union as an organization composed of recognized members and candidate members, who officially totaled 16,203,446 in November 1977. However, this definition is hardly satisfactory. The membership never acts as a body, and the ordinary members have slight influence or initiative; very little is known of them beyond a few unreliable statistics. For most political purposes, the party consists of the apparatus, the professional party people, a self-selected and fairly clearly set-off group consisting of about 1.5 percent of the membership, that directs and guides the entirety and through it Soviet society. If these members form the elite, the essential nucleus is what Lenin called the "Old Guard" of the party, the oligarchy currently composed of about twenty-five men at the summit of power—the Politburo plus the Secretaries of the Central Committee. In his time Lenin was equated with the party in the minds of many; and in Stalin's day, the dictator with his coterie was almost equivalent to the party.

On the other hand, there is no real reason to draw a line at formal membership in the CPSU. The Komsomol, the youth auxiliary of the party, is a kindred organization through which young people normally pass on the way to party careers. Members, especially leaders, of trade unions, and activists in local councils or soviets and many other organizations, are *ipso facto* affiliated with the party. In a sense, all Soviet citizens are party-bound in that they are expected to respect and serve the party, the sovereign institution of their lives. In Lenin's words, which are frequently cited in the contemporary Soviet press, "The Party is the intelligence, honor, and conscience of our era." It is the focus of the Soviet world, around which nearly everything revolves.

The Communist Party of the Soviet Union also has branch parties, such as the Ukrainian, Tadzhik, and Lithuanian parties, that are integrated into its structure. Nearly a hundred offspring are informally joined to it. All non-Soviet Communist parties are directly related to Lenin's party; most of them were formed by Comintern or Soviet agents and shaped in accordance with Lenin's conditions and in imitation of his example. Some of these, the parties of Mongolia, North Korea, Poland, East Germany, Czechoslovakia, Hungary, Romania, and Bulgaria, were lifted to power by Soviet forces; with the partial exception of the Romanian party, they remain relatively faithful to the wishes and policies of the CPSU. Parties that came to power largely or entirely on their own, those of Yugoslavia, Albania, China, and Indochina, are independent or hostile, but they continue to revere the founder, Lenin. The Cuban party, too, was a child of the Leninist family before Castro adopted it as a vehicle of his rule. The many non-ruling parties are mostly loyal to the Soviet Fatherland of the Workers; many of them amount to branches of the Soviet party.

The influence of Lenin's party is much broader still. Many parties that avoid overt identification with the Soviet-led Communist movement, and a large fraction of intellectuals, especially of Third World countries, are Communist, or leftist, oriented. The Marxism of most of the world is not Social Democratic but Leninist in inspiration. The Leninist party is the predecessor and to a large extent the model for innumerable leadership parties of this age. Fascism, too, borrowed much from Communism; Mussolini renounced the Marxism of his youth but kept Lenin's additions to Marxism. Lenin was unable to ignite the world revolution, but his brand of doctrine, equalitarian elitism, and political action have phenomenally influenced the modern mode of protest and revolution coupled with authoritarianism.

How all this has come to pass is nearly equivalent to the history of our times. The present book can cover only a tiny fraction of the story, but it deals with perhaps the most crucial thread of all, the growth and vicissitudes of Lenin's party. This has been the central, or at least a key, element, the generator of trends, movements, and reactions; understanding it should carry us far toward understanding many of the travails of this age.

We can make only a beginning toward this understanding, however. Russia is too alien, facts are too few or uncertain, and obfuscation is too great. Perhaps because of a deficiency in our understanding, much in the story of the party's ascent seems more or less accidental, almost miraculous. Paradoxically, while the philosophy of Leninism dealt with social forces, classes, and historical determinism, nowhere have personalities and extraneous events been more determinant. In 1914 nothing could have seemed less inevitable than the triumph of Lenin's obscure faction. The Bolshevik party clearly owed its existence and character to a single individual and his at times apparently irrational insistence on having his own way. It probably could not have emerged on top without the unsuccessful war, Rasputin and the tsarina, German financing, the abortive rightist coup of General Kornilov, and various other contingencies. The untimely demise of Lenin (the victim of a stroke at age fifty-two) and the improbable rise to supremacy of the Georgian Stalin over the essentially Russian party set the stage for the totalitarian party-state. The Stalinist party escaped defeat in the Second World War thanks in part to the delusions and cruelty of the Hitlerites. The postwar evolution of the party was again strongly marked by the personality of the virtually deified leader and by the somewhat capricious character of his onetime lieutenant and subsequent derogator, Nikita Khrushchev. Only in the latest period has the party seemed to follow a logical and comprehensible course, on the basis of which one may venture, perhaps rashly, to project a future.

Chapter 1

The Russian Discontent

The Soviet Communist party has shown remarkable institutional continuity over a long period; it has experienced no organizational break from its beginnings to the present. However, the party had no clear beginning. The most crucial turning point was 1917, when it rapidly evolved from a radical sect to a mass movement and then a governing elite; the vast majority of the Bolsheviks who made the October Revolution entered the party in the six months preceding that event. But the central core of the party, except Trotsky and his adherents, had been working with Lenin for many years, and much in the history of Bolshevik Russia (as it was commonly called in its first decades) is more comprehensible in the light of the traditions that were built up in the prewar period. Lenin set the seal upon the existence of his group as an independent party in a meeting in Prague in January 1912. However, in the official chronicle, this gathering is called the Sixth Congress. A Bolshevik faction first formed at the Second Congress, held in Brussels-London in July – August 1903, when Lenin endeavored to muster his adherents to make of the new Marxist party a political instrument such as he (almost alone) envisaged. This was, for all practical purposes, the founding congress of the Russian Social Democratic party, but Lenin had already gathered a following, a protoparty, in the preceding two years. The official First Congress had been held in Minsk in 1898, but it had been broken up by police and left nothing but a memory for the subsequent party to build upon.

Possibly the party should be considered as originating in 1893, the date of Lenin's entry into Marxist circles in St. Petersburg and the date to which he ascribed his entry into the party. Or one might find the beginnings of the Russian Social Democratic party, which produced Lenin's group by fission, in the European Social Democratic movement, or in the inception of Marxism with the *Communist Manifesto,* which was put out by Marx and Engels in 1848.

Yet the Russian Marxism of the 1890s was not only the theoretical offspring of Marxist philosophy, but also, perhaps more strongly, the heir to a long tradition of radical protest against the injustices and failures of the old Russian empire. Before Lenin, such would-be revolutionaries as Nechaev and Tkachev were Leninists in their hopes for a party that would overturn society for but not with the people. These and other publicists of the 1870s to the 1890s, who were loosely called "Populists," were in turn the successors of the Slavophils of the 1860s, who stressed the communal virtues of Russia in contrast to the perversion of the commercialized West, while blending with their nativism some of the insistence of the Westernizers on improving Russia by adapting Western ideas.

The radical intellectuals of the nineteenth century were too few to trouble the government very much, except when they succeeded in making points by assassination. They were not the cause but the symptom of secular maladjustment, the origins of which, like the origins of Leninism, must be sought in the fundamental Russian situation. The essence of this situation was the irritation of the huge, proud, and powerful, but relatively poor and technologically backward, autocratic, and semi-Asiatic empire at its inferiority to the richer, more rapidly modernizing, less harshly governed, and more pluralistic states of Europe.[1] This antithesis of cultures came about originally by virtue of the conquest of nearly all Russian lands by the Tatars of Central Asia in the thirteenth century and the incorporation of these lands (somewhat loosely, to be sure) into the immense Tatar empire. Previously Russia, which was centered on Kiev, had been politically akin to the West and approximately up to its cultural level. But by the time Tatar power receded in the fifteenth and sixteenth centuries, Russia had become politically alien to the West.

The Moscow-centered realm that emerged as the unifier of the Russian lands took over many of the Tatar traditions of imperial rulership that, along with military skills, had enabled the horsemen of the steppes to build the largest contiguous empire ever known. Moreover, the Russians were able to make themselves practically the heirs to the Tatar domain. Steadily and systematically advancing, especially to the east and south, they came to rule, by the time of Peter (the early eighteenth century), the greater part of the lands once held by Kublai Khan.

The Russians began their monumental expansion at roughly the same time that Western Europeans were undertaking the voyages of discovery that led to the Portuguese, Spanish, French, Dutch, and British empires. In both cases the basic cause was the technological and consequently military superiority arising from the intellectual upsurge of the West, leading into the later scientific and industrial revolutions. Although Russia was a borrower and hence lagged somewhat, it was sufficiently capable of assimilating Western invention to overcome Asian resistance and at the same time defend itself against its European neighbors.

If the basis for Russian and Western European imperialism was the same, the effects were very different for a simple reason: European empire building occurred overseas, but the Russian-conquered lands were contiguous. Although profitable colonies strengthened kings and contributed to monarchic authoritarianism in Spain and other countries, the Western European empire-holding nations remained nation-states, and kingship was never elevated to total domination of society. The colonies were external holdings, not expansions of the state.

For Russia, on the other hand, there was no sharp division between old and new territories, and expansion swelled an already autocratically inclined state. It gave a mission to rulership and made the total power of the monarch seemingly, and probably in fact, indispensable to prevent dissolution and chaos (much as the power of the monolithic party is accepted today by many Russians as the only guarantee against breakup and disorder). Rulership over the boundless territories and countless peoples became a necessity, therefore a holy vocation with overtones of universalism and messianism. Far more than in the West even in the so-called Age of Absolutism, the Russian state, as maker and holder of the continental empire, became an entity superior to society, standing above it, taking its own directions, and imposing them on society. The Russian empire became and remained characterized by the idea of rulership that does not ask but commands, the use of law as a political instrument instead of an impartial regulator, indoctrination and censorship, an obligatory official philosophy, control of movement and exclusion (so far as was practicable) of alien influences, lack of independent standing for either wealth or nobility, and government by a self-chosen elite of political administrators—a political tradition that was continued and intensified after the October Revolution.[2]

But it did not suffice for imperial tsarist Russia to rule in absolutist fashion. It had to maintain its technological level in competition with rapidly progressing Western Europe. It had continually to borrow ideas and inventions from the West because of the uninventiveness and difficulty in innovation that are part of the price of any tightly governed society. The Russians, being Christian in background and culturally and racially akin to Europe, found it much easier than did other empires, such as Turkey or China, to put to use the technological, economic, and organizational attainments of the modernizing Western community. From the days of Ivan the Terrible (who reigned 1547–84), Russia was importing not only Western artillery and artillerymen, mechanics, architects, and so on, but also many Western laws and social patterns.

Hence tsarist Russia was—and Soviet Russia remains—a compromise between Eastern and Western, European and Asiatic, wherein the autocratic society, making good use of the achievements of more liberal societies, has inevitably taken on some Western institutions or at least their appearances. Russia had to govern autocratically to exist as a multinational empire, yet it always had to import the achievements of more liberal states to sustain its auto-cracy. These two aspects coexisted in abiding ambivalence—an ambivalence that was made only more acute by the Bolshevik revolution and the assertion of total power by the political party in the name of a Western ideology of total liberation.

This ambivalence and the antithesis of Western ideas and Eastern political modes began to trouble Russians as soon as they were able to give it thought. From the days of Ivan the Terrible, some became aware of the greater liberties of Western lands and wondered why they should not enjoy similar liberties. The desire for greater freedom was limited to a few nobles, however; discontent rising from comparisons between Russia and the West was of no great importance until near the end of the eighteenth century. The number of persons who were acquainted with conditions abroad or sufficiently educated to think about the differences was very small; the prevailing style of government in the West was monarchy, as in Russia; and change in the West was slow enough that Russia could keep fairly well abreast of military and productive technologies.

But these conditions began breaking down in the last decades of the eigh-teenth century. "Enlightened Despotism" lost standing and became intellec-tually enfeebled under philosophic criticism even before the French Revolution. Tsarina Catherine II felt compelled, in the interest of modernity, to correspond with such skeptical thinkers as Voltaire and Diderot, to make pretenses of implementing some of their liberal political ideas, and to employ a republican, Frédéric-César La Harpe, as tutor for her grandson, the future Alexander I. The French Revolution then came to topple the leading monarchy of Europe and to exalt rationalism, liberty, democracy, and the rights of man, concepts that were wholly subversive of the Russian way of rule. Although France was ultimately defeated and the Bourbons returned, the ideals of the great libertarian revolu-tion could never again be laid to rest. At the same time, economic development was quickening, fueled by increasing technological progress. The industrial revolution that took shape in England in the eighteenth century was not quick to spread to the continent; but especially after the end of the wars in 1815, the pace of change began visibly to accelerate. The West continued to move forward ever more rapidly, and Russia was increasingly pressed to avoid falling too far behind. Pressure to keep pace required more education and more travel, both of foreigners to Russia and of Russians abroad, compounding the difficulties of the empire.

The patriotic feelings aroused by the Napoleonic invasion and the exhilaration of victory in 1814–1815, when Russian troops paraded down the boulevards of Paris, subdued potential discontent for a few years. But it came to the surface at the death of the victorious tsar, Alexander I, on December 23, 1825. In the confusion surrounding the succession, which the oldest son, Constantine, had privately renounced, a group of officers (called the "Decembrists" after the date) attempted a coup d'état. Having learned something of the relative freedom of Bourbon France from their service in that country, they sought not merely to determine the person of the ruler, as in previous palace coups, but to remodel the state according to ideological preconceptions. Some dreamed of a constitutional monarchy, others aspired to a republic (to be inaugurated by military dictatorship). Their insurgency met only incomprehension among the people and failed quickly, but it began the radical oppositionist movement that led to 1917. Soviet histories claim that the Decembrists were precursors of the Leninist party.

The immediate effect of the Decembrists' failure, however, was repressive reaction on the part of the threatened tsar. Nicholas I tried to rule his land like a drill-sergeant and to cut it off, so far as possible, from subversive Western influences. No Russian was permitted to go abroad except by special permit; an official ideology of "orthodoxy, autocracy, and nationality" was proclaimed (1833); a political police was charged with controlling the subjects; and reform was banned in all sensitive areas. Nicholas thus succeeded in imposing a few decades of relative quiet.

But the small Russian intellectual movement continued to grow, led by the earliest of the well-known Russian writers, including Pushkin, Lermontov, Gogol, and Griboyedov. Art is inherently disposed to criticism, and voices of protest began to be heard. In the 1830s German idealist philosophy became the mode.[3] By the 1840s a new radicalism was stirring, deriving (like Marxism) from Hegel, Proudhon, and other prophets of socialism. Herzen and Bakunin, both of whom sought freedom in exile, represented respectively moderate socialism and anarchism. The French revolution of 1848, which spread to most of the countries of Europe, provoked some excitement among Russian intellectuals and raised the idea of revolution to the level of a general aspiration.

Voices of change in Russia were few and subdued, however, until humiliation in the Crimean War (1854–56) showed that the proud, stiff, militarized Russian state was inwardly rotten. The price of shutting out the West and suffocating dissent was evidently weakness. Nicholas having appropriately died in the shambles of his lifework, the new tsar, Alexander II, instituted a series of reforms in the Russian tradition of reaction to defeat. He ended the serfdom that had degraded the majority of the population, relaxed censorship, improved higher education, established noble-dominated agencies of local self-administration, modernized army service, and instituted a model court system.

Russia's problems were not, of course, solved thereby, and critics were not satisfied but were encouraged to increase their demands. The intellectuals became only the more vocal when, after a few years, a conservative reaction led to restrictions and the partial withdrawal of concessions. In the process, the Russian mind was opened and stimulated, and the great debate began on the meaning and future of Russia that went on until the victory of Lenin's party imposed an answer, or at least silenced opposing views.

The passionate and far-ranging debate was carried on by a class that was at that time new to history, the intelligentsia (a Russian word).* Its members were primarily students and journalists whose distinguishing characteristic was that by virtue of Western-style education and outlook they no longer fitted into traditional Russian society and could not find the employment for which they believed themselves qualified. Of diverse social backgrounds (many came from the nobility, which was demoralized by its loss of functions after the emancipation of the serfs), they had little in common except profound alienation. They were generally quite young, as were the radicals of Lenin's day; in maturity they usually found places in the bureaucracy and became faithful cogs in the tsarist apparatus. Their chief vehicle was essays in fat journals, usually rambling discourses posing as literary criticism. The tsarist government practically cultivated their extremist opposition by imposing capricious and irritating, yet ineffective, restrictions. Somewhat unpredictable censorship served mostly to make critical writings, with their Aesopian language, more interesting. Lacking any tradition of objectivity or of tempered, rational discourse, and with no responsibility for policies, the intellectuals were fond of indefinite, often incoherent theorizing and of striking statements advocating unachievable ends. They were amateur philosophers with a dilettantist passion for the latest theory. They saw the world in black and white and hoped for quick and total change, that is, revolution. They had something in common with modern youth protests; the nihilists of the 1860s, finding virtue in the rejection of conventional values ranging from cleanliness to orthodox religion, were akin to the hippies of a century later.

In the intellectual ferment, many currents interacted. Some themes, however, were general. The basic preoccupation of young people in their shabby quarters and of studious journalists alike was Russia's relations with the West; the question of questions was how Russia should measure up to modern values and preserve its virtues and its power against the challenge of the West. In the background lurked a sense of injured pride. Russia was inordinately larger than the Western states, and thus plausibly appointed to rule the world; the intellectuals could not and would not renounce the deep pride of Russia in its magnificent destiny. Yet Russia was relatively impotent, poorer and more backward than small Western neighbors. The enlightened world seemed to regard Russians as unwashed barbarians who slurped cabbage soup from a common pot. Russian intellectuals regarded themselves as the equals if not the superiors of their counterparts in France or Germany; it was bitter to be treated as inferiors both in Russia and abroad. It was necessary to learn from the West, hence to admire its achievement. But the West caused trouble and humiliation, and so was to be hated.

---

*Such a class appeared first in Russia as a by-product of Westernization; in our day, however, nearly every Third World country that does not repress it has a similar class of unhappy uprooted intellectuals.

The radicals thus revolted against both Russian autocracy, at least in the form in which they saw it, and the Western liberalism[4] that they did not try to understand.

The only obvious explanation of Russia's difficulties was its backward system of autocratic government; hence, and also because there was no way to work for reform within the system, the radicals became revolutionaries. Revolution was for very many or most of the educated young, an incontestable value, something virtually holy that was worthy of every sacrifice, to the neglect of serious thought about what was to follow the revolution. The vague value to be achieved was "socialism," as incontestably a good thing for the intellectuals of nineteenth-century Russia as it is for many intellectuals of the less developed world today. It was easy to be anticapitalist because the West was capitalist; they expressed their horror of the obvious evils of early industrialization in the West and hoped that Russia, in its moral and political superiority, would avoid the troubles of the West even while making the most of its technology.

Happily, the intellectuals discovered in the Russian peasant communes a native "socialism" that made them morally superior to the factory-towns and commercialism of Europe. In a sense they were conservatives; the Populists wanted to make a revolution not so much to introduce socialism as to save it from encroaching capitalism.[5] Many Russians were, of course, procapitalist in practice, but since they made money instead of writing tracts, they were scorned by the intellectual elite. The business or commercial classes were always poorly esteemed in the tsarist empire, a situation that usually occurs in politically oriented societies; in the latter nineteenth century they suffered further discredit in that they were both regarded as agents of destabilizing change and frequently associated with foreign and presumably exploitative interests.

A closely related article of faith was the idealization of the people. This was inevitable because the popular masses were regarded as the antithesis of the tsarist government and democracy was the accepted mode of modern political thinking. But the people needed not individual freedom or formal justice, but social freedom and economic equalization. The passion for equality and general brotherhood merged into the passion for the greatness of Russia; by raising and uniting the people, Russia could obviously realize its proper strength and save itself from the dangers of Western corruption, as well as from military and political weakness.

Theoretical devotion to the cause of the people was qualified, however, by de facto elitism. The intelligentsia, who were of upper-class or upper-middle-class origins, could idealize the masses because they knew very little of them. Unlike Tolstoy at a slightly later date, the intelligentsia were concerned with peasants or workers not as real people but as instruments for the regeneration of Russia. There was no idea of learning from the people to work for the satisfaction of popular aspirations; at best the Populists sought to carry the word to them, to educate and uplift the ignorant folk who lived in a medieval universe.

Their overt goal could only be the welfare of the people; yet the people, who were either apathetic or loyal to church and state, repelled them. Hence they could only be elitist, counting on dedicated heroes to save the world from itself. Bakunin typically believed in revolution made by force by a minority for the unenlightened majority. Chernyshevsky, to whom Lenin owed very much, likewise looked to the action of the few for the benefit of the many and wanted a dictator to guarantee equality. In his novel *What is to be Done* (an unbearably dull book that captivated a generation), he proposed applying the principles of the peasant commune to manufacturing; his hero, Rakhmetov, was virtually a Nietzschean superman who hardened himself on a bed of nails and ate raw meat for strength. Of those who dedicated themselves to the socialist cause, Chernyshevsky wrote, "They are few in number but through them flourishes the life of all; without them it would die out and go sour. . . . They are the flower of the best people, the movers of the movers, the salt of the salt of the earth."[6]

The movement of criticism could not stand still, but continually changed in its waves and crosscurrents. As Marx wrote, the Russians "always run after the most extreme that the West can offer. . . ."[7] A set of ideas, a recipe for releasing Russia from its travails, would be brought up, elaborated, and tossed around for a few years, but nothing would happen, the revolutionary dawn would only flicker faintly on the horizon. Then a new generation would look for new prophets and fresh panaceas.

The first major tendency that was fairly coherent was the Slavophilism of the 1850s and 1860s. The Slavophils hoped for a revival of native virtues under a good ruler to restore Russia. Although they were romantic nationalists who were partly inspired by Herder, they were in some ways forerunners of the Bolsheviks. Basically authoritarian, they sought salvation not in freedom but in the rule of the enlightened. They saw moral superiority in poverty, looked for strength in collectivism, and rejected rationalism, individualism, and commercialism. The Slavophils were countered by the smaller company of Westernizers, who felt that Russia, swallowing its pride, should boldly take over Western institutions and philosophy, just as it had taken over Western material tools. It might be said that the Bolsheviks were outwardly intellectual heirs of the Westernizers, but inwardly and spiritually the heirs of the Slavophils.

As the post−Crimean War reform wave subsided in disillusionment, the intelligentsia became more bitter and turned more to the abused and silent masses as the true Russians and the means of salvation. It seemed necessary only to educate and arouse the people to assert their native virtues, destroy autocracy and oppression, and build a beautiful new order avoiding the anarchic and evil ways of the "bourgeois" West. Slavophilism merged into Populism, which took its name from the "going to the people" of 1873−74, when thousands of educated youth, caught up in an idealistic fever, undertook a mission of enlightening the uncomprehending peasantry. But a division soon arose between the moderates, who felt that it was necessary to win a democratic majority before a revolution could be made properly, and their radical opponents, the Jacobins, who thought an organized and dedicated minority could make the revolution—indeed, had to make it soon to prevent a capitalist subversion of peasant socialism.[8] (The argument and the division closely resembled those of the following generation between the Mensheviks and the Bolsheviks.) Ironically, both factions exalted the peasant commune, which the government maintained as a tax-collecting device and which conservatives esteemed as an antirevolutionary force.

The failure of the crusade and the realization that the dark masses were likely to remain faithful to church and tsar no matter how many students lectured them caused a reaction toward elitism; if the intellectuals could not convert, they could conspire. They had to think of themselves as acting on behalf of the masses, but they could not doubt their own right and ability to remake the world.[9]

A notorious figure of this generation was Sergei Nechaev, who, in his *Catechism of a Revolutionary,* called for total devotion to a revolutionary society, which should by its firmness qualify itself to govern all society. He was sufficiently convinced of the justice of his political approach to murder a disobedient member of his tiny group; morality consisted of the needs of the revolution as understood by the leader.

Nechaev entered literature only as the model for the chief character of Dostoyevsky's *The Possessed,* but Piotr Tkachev was an intelligent publicist who wrote somewhat as Nechaev acted. It is hardly an exaggeration to call Tkachev the first Bolshevik.[10] Lenin reportedly studied him closely and recommended him to his followers, and his importance was generally acknowledged by Soviet historians until Stalinist times. From Tkachev Lenin borrowed the title of his 1917 book *State and Revolution,* as he borrowed the title of his 1902 book from Chernyshevsky's *What is to be Done.* Like Lenin, Tkachev wanted a thoroughgoing revolution right away and considered Russia better suited for the making of revolution than Western Europe. Finding it reprehensible to wait for the concurrence of a majority, he presented a closely reasoned argument for minority dictatorship and urged that the state should not be destroyed but captured and used by the revolutionaries—an idea that foreshadowed the key Leninist concept of the dictatorship of the proletariat. Tkachev was one of the first Russian students of Marx, but he declined to apply Marxism to Russia.[11]

No one, in any case, managed to build up much of a revolutionary organization, and the would-be remakers of the world began looking for a more satisfying program. The answer nearest to hand, the means grasped by many desperate and frustrated groups of that day and this, was terrorism. If the chief villains could be struck down by the heroes of the organization, society would cave in and the great goals could somehow be clutched. This idea was derived partly from Bakunin, who wanted the sun of revolution to rise from a sea of blood. It was encouraged by the successful heroism of Vera Zasulich (women were conspicuous among the terrorists). After she murdered the abusive police chief of St. Petersburg, a sympathetic jury freed her, and she escaped abroad to become a leading figure of the nascent Marxist party. Assassination thereby came to seem both less dangerous and more romantic. In 1879 a revolutionary-terrorist organization, the "People's Will," was established; like Lenin's party, it demanded that its members be wholly revolutionaries, surrendering individual will to the society.[12] In 1881 it attained its great goal, the assassination of the tsar. The result was the only one possible, the enthronement of a more repressive tsar, whose police captured most of the leaders of the terrorist movement.

The revolutionary movement thus came to an impasse in the late 1880s. Those who had once believed so passionately in revolution, the virtues of the peasant, and scientific conspiracy[13] had seen their hopes come to nothing. At the same time, industrialization was making rapid progress; it no longer seemed obvious that Russia could do better than to follow in the path trodden by the West. The antiquated peasant commune was disintegrating, and the special virtues of the peasants no longer seemed to promise a special destiny for Russia. The old problems were drawing no nearer solution, perhaps even farther from it, as modern trends of thought undercut the legitimacy of the autocratic monarchy, the bond of empire and the capstone of the Russian edifice. More than ever, tsarism seemed outdated, a burden for Russia. Yet there was nothing with which to replace it.

At this time, however, a new social-political-economic philosophy was taking hold in Western Europe, especially Germany. Karl Marx had died in 1883, and Marxism, under the guiding hand of Friedrich Engels, was becoming an effective political ideology that was ready for the Russians to embrace.

Chapter 2

Lenin's Party: Formation and Waiting

THE MARXIST VOGUE

The anguished outcry of Populism was largely an effort to save Russian virtues and the Russian soul from the evils of capitalism. But by the 1890s, with the expansionist economics of Finance Minister Sergei Witte, it was becoming clear that capitalist industrialization and commercialization were coming to Russia willy-nilly, dragging it into modernization in the wake of the West, breaking up the glorified peasant communal institutions, disrupting old ways and semifeudal relations, corrupting society (in the view of many), turning towns into industrial slums, and bringing riches to some and insecurity or impoverishment to many others.

Hence it seemed increasingly necessary for intellectuals to find a new pattern of thought that would be consonant with the undeniable and apparently irresistible development of capitalism in Russia (Lenin's first major work was entitled *Development of Capitalism in Russia*). At the same time, journalism was expanding rapidly and increasing political awareness, ideas of nationalism and democracy were seeping in through a loosened censorship, and cultural Westernization was proceeding apace. Groping for an answer, a gradually growing number of Russians became outright Westernizers, or political liberals, seeing Russia's future in political development toward constitutionalism and freedom. This tendency grew steadily in importance up to World War I. Mostly, however, at least in the 1890s, the successors of the Populists turned to an emotionally more satisfying framework of reasoning, Marxism.[1]

Marxism appealed to newly industrializing Russia for reasons much like the ones that had given rise to it a few decades earlier in Western Europe. In

England, France, and Germany, modernization had been demoralizing and injurious to many since the first part of the nineteenth century. Most people accepted it as either good or inevitable, but some reacted in a new-old direction of thought that came to be called socialism, an endeavor to save values and remake society by emphasis on the human community. Pessimistic about the present and optimistic for the future, socialism above all told the world that the maladjustments and sufferings of the developing machine age were not inevitable and that dedicated and enlightened people could build an ideal future.

Most socialist writing was diffuse, if not incoherent, and decidely naive; the tendency would probably have dissipated in a few decades but for the systematization and philosophic underpinning provided by a German scholar who was resident most of his life in London, the heart of capitalist power. Karl Marx put together a general theory strongly supporting many ideas that were in the atmosphere in the middle part of the nineteenth century—a large number of them similar to concepts that were dear to the Russian Populists. Marx taught that capitalism was only a phase of history, to be succeeded by the far happier era of socialism which would grow into communism; that capitalism was associated with immorality and the destruction of traditional social values; and that the bourgeoisie, which held the power of the industrializing West, was exploitative and evil, and would soon be thrown down violently from its haughty eminence. Furthermore, present governments and churches were only instruments of the selfish ruling classes; true virtue lay with the workers, the poor and cheated of the earth, who would inevitably come to rule universally and inaugurate a new age of justice and happiness. Marxism also implied that power should not rest with owners or nobles but with the intellectuals who, thanks to their deeper understanding of society and its true underlying forces, could look behind the pretenses of class society and help guide the workers. Most of all, Marxism exalted revolution as a value in itself. Damning the West in scientific or seemingly scientific terms, Marxism offered a new faith that held the answers to all the vexing problems of economics, philosophy, ethics, and history.

Logically, however, Marxism did not apply very well to Russia. Marx dealt with developmental sequences in society, not with the relations of societies that were at different stages of development; but relations with the more advanced West were the crux of Russia's problem. Marxism assumed that all societies should pass through the same stages, attaining socialism after the overripening of capitalism. Yet Marx, who was above all a revolutionary at heart, looked hopefully to revolutionary upsurges practically anywhere, whether Ireland, preindustrial Italy, or even China; as prospects for revolution in the West dimmed after the suppression of the Paris Commune (1871), he took much interest in the Populists, who were conspiring and assassinating in Russia. Marx and Engels never really decided how to view Russia and its revolutionary movement, and they took somewhat contradictory positions at different times. Vera Zasulich, a Populist at heart who moved to Marxism not for its philosophy but because of her indignation at oppressive government, asked Marx's opinion regarding Russian prospects. He penned a famous reply (March 1881) in which he spoke of having "*expressly* limited the 'historical inevitability' of this process [of capitalist development] to the *countries of Western Europe*," and went on to express the conviction that the peasant commune could, given favorable conditions, discard its primitive features and turn into an element of the socialized economy.[2] Marx was thus prepared to do violence to his basic theories if that was necessary to encourage genuine revolutionary activists.

Many Russians were quite as ready to bend Marxist theory for application to Russia; and an intense interest quickly developed in Marx's theories, although they implied that socialist revolution was probably distant. The first translation of Marx's chief work, *Das Kapital*, appeared in Russia in 1872, fifteen years before an English version was published. It quickly became a big seller despite the small number of educated persons in Russia, and it was followed by many other Marxist works. If Marxism captured the labor movement in Germany, in Russia it captured the intelligentsia. In the West, Marxism followed industrialization; in Russia, industrial capitalism and Marxism arrived concurrently.

Logically, Marxism could promise Russia nothing better than a hope of following the West at a distance through the degradation of capitalism to the promised land of socialism; it deprived Russia of the special destiny that was dear to the Slavophils. Its appeal was nonetheless overwhelming. It was anticapitalist in a time and place in which capitalism was seen as essentially foreign; not only did capitalism represent an alien, Western way of life to Russians, but a large proportion of capitalists were in fact foreigners—German or British investors moving in to exploit the Russian market or raw materials. In attacking capitalism, Marxism was essentially attacking Britain, which was by far the leading industrial country; Britain was most irritating to the Russians not only because it was the land par excellence of liberalism, middle-class values, and commercial success, but also because it was the chief antagonist on the world stage, opposing Russian expansionism in the Balkans, Turkey, and Central Asia.

If capitalism was not to be avoided, Marxism at least said that it was necessary and temporary. It was a consolation to know that the peoples of the West were really exploited and miserable, despite the appearances of relative prosperity, and that the despised "bourgeois" society of the West was doomed. The idea that the masses were ground down and pitiful also nicely implied that the educated—who in Russia felt themselves especially superior—had the right and duty to lead these masses, who in their ignorance did not know their real needs. Where no legitimate political opposition was possible, change seemed attainable only by revolution, and many Russians had been dreaming of revolution for ages; it was a magic word meaning freedom, justice, creativity, and happiness. Now Marxism cherished revolution as its emotional heart and gave a "Western" and "scientific" rationalization for it.

There were more concrete reasons for the remarkable appeal of Marxism to the Russian intellectuals of the latter 1880s and 1890s. One was that it was favored by the police and censors, who saw it as a relatively harmless opponent of Populism. The Marxists engaged in erudite arguments instead of assassination, and they postponed revolution to a distant future. It was all too impractical to cause worries for the tsarist government, which saw agitation for a constitution as a nearer threat. Hence, a great deal of Marxist writing could be published quite openly.

Marxist emphasis on the industrial proletariat was also opportune. The peasantry had proved to be a disappointment, and the still small but rapidly growing class of factory workers was the only group showing any real responsiveness to revolutionary agitation. Neglected by the government, lacking legal protection (a factory law of 1886 to check the worst abuses was hardly enforced), forbidden to organize in regular unions, and often living in crowded dormitories, the workers were much more reachable for propaganda than the peasants and, in the strange and uncomfortable new milieu, readier to answer calls to action. At last, the intellectuals seemed to have found a real tool for the making of their revolution.

Marxism consequently came as a revelation to many intellectuals who were looking desperately for a way out of the unhappy condition of Russia. It was a rather strange creed, however, and gathered strength only slowly through the 1880s. The first outstanding Russian Marxist was Georgy Plekhanov, a onetime leader of the Populist Land and Freedom organization who had shifted his hopes from the peasants to the workers. Leaving Russia to avoid arrest, he settled in Geneva, which had long been a center of Russian radicalism. There, with a handful of other exiles, he founded in 1883 the Liberation of Labor, the first Russian Marxist organization. The group undertook to publish a little radical paper (it became *de rigueur* for any self-respecting radical faction to put out its weekly or monthly sheet; of the many appearing subsequently Lenin's *Iskra* was the most famed). Plekhanov was converted to the toned-down Marxism of Engels, with whom he corresponded (Engels lived until 1895), rather than to Marx's revolutionism, and he was a historical determinist who saw Russia taking the inevitable capitalist road—although he was quite willing to see a revolutionary party give history a shove.

At first, Plekhanov and his colleagues in Geneva were isolated and uninfluential. The 1880s, following the assassination of Alexander II in 1881, were a time of repression and reaction in which most intellectuals were still unwilling to accept the growing evidence of the capitalistic development of Russia. It was still heretical to contend that the factory workers should have the honor of making the socialist revolution in Russia[3]—not surprisingly, in view of the fact that the peasantry still comprised close to nine-tenths of the population. In the midst of generally increasing restlessness among land-hungry and overtaxed peasants, critical intellectuals, middle-class liberals, and discontented national minorities, however, a few Marxist groups were being formed in Russia; in the late 1880s, there were at least discussion circles in half a dozen cities.

Marxism caught on first among relatively cultured minorities who had been subjected to bad treatment, particularly Jews and Poles. The former had been turned against the regime by the pogroms, which conservatives began to encourage in the 1880s, and by sundry legal discriminations. The latter had been deprived of previously promised political rights by Russian overlords, who tried forcibly to russify them. A Marxist labor movement also got an early start in the Ukraine, where anti-Russian sentiments were added to economic dissatisfaction.

The famine of 1891 was a seminal event; the intellectuals and students were thereby made aware of the misery of the peasants and the incompetence of the government. Lenin typically welcomed it, holding the traditional Populist view: "The worse, the better." By calling on the public for help and permitting the establishment of relief committees, the monarchy allowed a stirring of freedom and of ideas of popular action that remained after the emergency had passed.[4] The leadership of the few small workers' circles that had existed here and there since the 1870s passed generally from the Populists to the Social Democrats, as the Russian Marxists called themselves in imitation of their comrades in the West. In 1895 the League for the Struggle for the Liberation of the Working Class was founded in St. Petersburg, only to be quickly scattered by the police. Strikes were becoming current reality and often took on a political character, climaxing with the big textile strikes in St. Petersburg in 1896. They were encouraged by articulate "society," which had no great enthusiasm for the economic demands of workers but saw labor troubles as a powerful means of attacking the autocracy. Marxism also mostly displaced Populism in the journals, aided by the complacency of the censors.[5] There was a flood of Marxist writing and discussion; at no other time and place has Marxism enjoyed an equal intellectual vogue.

There was naturally a strong desire to bring the numerous small Social Democratic groups together to form a powerful united organization on the model of the big German party, of which the Russian Marxists were uncritical admirers. Only in 1898, however, was it possible to assemble, on the initiative of Social Democrats of Kiev and the Jewish Bund, a tiny "congress" at Minsk in western Russia. Nine socialists, three of them from the Bund, issued a call for social revolution, laying on the tiny Russian proletariat the task of liberation, a task the allegedly weak and cowardly middle classes were incapable of carrying out.* The congress managed, however, to do little more than proclaim its existence, its purpose, and the name of the Social Democratic Workers' Party. The police broke up the meeting and arrested not only the participants but some five hundred activists. There was no attempt to reconstitute a committee, and organizational continuity was broken except for the name, which was borne by the Russian Marxist party and Lenin's Bolsheviks until March 1918.

Russian intellectual Marxism crested about this time. Its hegemony in the press declined, and the movement was much weakened by the end of the century. Its leading intellectual lights, such as Struve, Bulgakov, and Tugan-Baranovsky, had defected. There was a revival of religious philosophy; Tolstoyan passivity attracted many, and the attention of the intellectuals swung back toward the peasants, the bulk of the people of Russia. The Social Democrats tended somewhat to forget the workers as the presumptive makers of the obviously distant revolution, reverting instead to direct struggle against the police and the autocracy. As long as strict believers insisted that the bourgeois intellectuals were unreliable—they undoubtedly tended to waver—and thought the workers had to act on their own, they could easily conclude that revolution was a faint prospect. Russian Marxism was showing signs of the questioning of basic ideas under the impact of facts.

THE ADVENT OF LENIN

Marxism in the Soviet Union has become Marxism-Leninism; it was in reference to the Russian movement that Mayakovsky composed the lines that were to be a million times repeated in later days, "We say 'party'—we understand 'Lenin'; we say 'Lenin'—we understand 'party'."

Lenin (né Ulianov) was born April 22 (N.S.), 1870, in the sleepy provincial town of Simbirsk (now Ulyanovsk) on the Volga.[6] Although his birthplace was in the heart of Russia, Lenin had Tatar, German, and Swedish forebears, but little (or no) strictly Russian ancestry.[7] The family background was upper middle

---

*According to the manifesto, written by Peter Struve, who later turned moderate as a "legal Marxist" and became an opponent of Lenin,

> The further east one goes in Europe, the more cowardly, mean, and politically weak is the bourgeoisie, and the greater are the cultural and political tasks confronting the proletariat. The Russian working class must and will bear on its own sturdy shoulders the cause of winning political freedom. This is an essential, but only an initial step in discharging the great historic mission of the proletariat—creating a social order in which there will be no exploitation of man by man. The Russian proletariat will throw off the yoke of autocracy, and thus with greater energy will continue the struggle against capitalism and the bourgeoisie for the complete victory of socialism.

Resolutions and Decisions of the Communist Party of the Soviet Union 1898–1964, ed. Robert H. McNeal, vol. 1, p. 35.

class. Lenin's maternal grandfather was a self-owner, that is, he belonged to the nobility. The father served the tsarist state as a school inspector and built up the school system of his district ably enough to rise, under the administration of the reactionary minister of education Count Dmitry Tolstoy, to the class of hereditary nobility. In his last years, however, he came into official disfavor.[8] He may have transmitted his schoolmasterish ways to his second son, Vladimir, although he died when the future Lenin was nearing age sixteen. The family was given to the middle-class virtues of order, thrift, diligence, and respectability, and Lenin carried these with him throughout his life. Despite the early demise of the breadwinner (his widow received a handsome pension), the family estate was sufficient to allow Lenin's mother to furnish him until her death in 1916 with the funds requisite for life as a full-time political activist. Lenin always remained fairly close to his family. His sisters Anna and Maria were faithful helpers during his career.[9]

There has been much speculation regarding childhood influences that might have shaped the character of the future leader, but nothing is known of any experiences prior to age seventeen that would have implanted an overriding determination in him to turn society upside down, other than the usual discontents that afflicted the educated youth of his generation. In 1887, however, Vladimir's elder brother, Alexander, was caught up in a conspiracy to assassinate the tsar and was executed. His punishment was hardly excessive by Russian standards; he had written a manifesto and produced the bomb intended for the autocrat. But the tragedy seems to have had a strong effect on Vladimir. Alexander earned permanent admiration by assuming more than his share of guilt and refusing to beg for mercy. In the official Soviet interpretation, the adolescent Vladimir became a revolutionary upon learning of the hanging. Perhaps more important, as was emphasized by his widow, Krupskaya,[10] the Ulianovs found themselves ostracized by polite society; regicide was less respectable in 1887 than it had been in 1881. A few months later, after entering the University of Kazan, Vladimir Ulianov was expelled, ostensibly because of his trivial part in some student disorders, but actually because he was the brother of a hanged conspirator. Marked by the police and more or less barred from a normal career, he was almost driven to radicalism.

Retiring to the family estate, the future Lenin had ample time to brood bitterly on the injustices of the tsarist state and the narrow, hypocritical, and cruel society of those who considered themselves his betters. With the self-esteem that came from having been a brilliant student, Lenin saw himself wholly unjustly wronged and rejected. He also had ample opportunity to read radical writings that were circulating legally or illegally.

In 1889 Lenin was persuaded by his mother to try his hand at gentleman-farming. But this did not appeal to him, and he secured permission to pursue his law degree by independent study—political discrimination was not so harsh as it was to become. After a year of cramming what was normally a four-year course, Lenin passed the examinations with the top grade and was admitted to the bar in 1891 (for this he had to have a certificate of good character and loyalty). He went into practice briefly in Samara, where he apparently undertook to defend thieving peasants and other impoverished offenders.[11] But he soon began taking more interest in Marxist discussions and polemics with the Populists. His revolutionary outlook was sufficiently engrained by this time for him to oppose famine relief as pacification.[12]

In 1893 Lenin moved to St. Petersburg to join a law firm, but he soon turned to full-fledged revolutionary activity. In 1894 a genteel young radical, Nadezhda Krupskaya, was much impressed with "the learned Marxist from the Volga," whom she met at a revolutionary gathering disguised as a pancake party.[13] One year older than Lenin, she was a fellow revolutionary, like Lenin of petty-noble origin; her father had been deprived of his position because of his efforts to help Poles who were under his jurisdiction.[14] Lenin and Krupskaya seem to have been joined much less by romance than by shared devotion to revolution; she became and remained for the rest of his life his invaluable secretary and general aide. Together they diligently read and analyzed Marxist writings, tried to teach Marxism to workers, polemicized against non-Marxist radicals even more energetically than against the tsarist government, and went around St. Petersburg collecting contacts, setting up codes, and trying to put together the revolutionary organization that radicals had been talking about for thirty years.

In 1895 Lenin took a four-month tour in Western Europe to meet various exiled Marxist leaders. Upon his return, he joined in the first effort to establish something like a broad party uniting sundry Marxist groups, intellectuals, and workers; Lenin's principal associate in this "League of Struggle for the Liberation of Labor" was the future Menshevik leader Julius Martov (né Tsederbaum). However, the police easily kept tabs on these somewhat amateurish efforts. Lenin was arrested together with others, jailed a little over a year, and exiled to Siberia for three years.

The years of exile completed Lenin's development as a revolutionary. It was at this time that he took the name of Lenin, apparently from the Lena river. He lived fairly comfortably, being permitted as many books as friends and family cared to send him, and he corresponded with fellow thinkers. Krupskaya, who had also been arrested, asked to be sent to the same locale, and they were married so that they could remain together. During his confinement, Lenin wrote his longest and most scholarly work, *The Development of Capitalism in Russia,* which solidified the reputation as a Marxist that he had already gained in debates with the Populists. He also cogitated at length on the need for a new kind of party to overturn the tsardom that kept him under restraint.

While Lenin was in productive semi-isolation, Russian Marxism was undergoing an intellectual crisis. The hopelessness of expecting revolutionary action from the workers was becoming all too apparent. Lenin had experienced some of it in his efforts from 1893 through 1895 to teach Marxist theory to workers who had neither the time nor the education to assimilate it. In Germany the failure of the workers to advance toward revolution and the obvious growth of reformism led to a questioning, by Eduard Bernstein and others, of the movement's basic tenets: if, contrary to Marxist expectations, the workers were not becoming poorer, and if the middle classes, instead of being ground out of existence between the capitalists and the proletariat, were becoming more numerous and more influential, then it seemed fatuous to pursue the mirage of revolution. Instead, the workers might as well seek economic benefits, and the proletarian party should work with bourgeois liberals to secure concessions from the state. This logic of economism and revisionism was applicable also to Russia, and it led to what Lenin regarded as "a period of disunity, dissolution, and vacillation."[15]

Lenin was a self-confident young man; at age twenty-four he had not hesitated to attack boldly an outstanding figure of the radical movement, N. K. Mikhailovsky, in his pamphlet *Who are the Friends of the People?* Now (in 1899) he launched from Siberian exile a violent attack on what he regarded as disruptive tendencies in the Marxist movement, Bernsteinism and economism. Unwilling to accept the rather well-based conclusion that the party might review its assumptions and goals in the light of new circumstances, he denounced the thesis (especially as it was expressed in the *Credo* of K. Kuskova) that the workers should fight primarily for their material interests. If the workers failed to become more revolutionary, as Marxist theory predicted, Lenin's answer was not to accept this as reality and give up on the revolution but to organize the intellectuals to bring to the workers the necessary political views and dedication.

Lenin's call for the making of revolution by the party rather than the class was hardly novel. A generation earlier the Populists, disillusioned by the unresponsiveness of the peasantry, had retreated to a conspiratorial approach. The great intellectual question of Russian radicalism from 1875 on was the relation between "spontaneity," or natural growth, and "consciousness," or guidance by the enlightened—between the idea of working with the people and that of setting up a leadership to guide the people. The Populists saw "spontaneity" as the growth of detested capitalism and generally favored "consciousness." The Marxist theory of class struggle and economic determinism implied, to the contrary, that the basic forces must be spontaneous.

Yet the feeling was widespread in the 1890s that the workers, whatever their purity and virtue, needed bourgeois guidance, and the intellectuals called for "discipline" and "organization." There was a growing demand for an authoritative Central Committee to put order into the movement. The abortive Congress of 1898, with its nine delegates, decreed that a Central Committee (to be elected by a future congress) would have full powers over all except local questions.[16] Lenin consequently found substantial acceptance when he forcefully proposed a strong party that might have possibilities of actually achieving something. He advocated turning futile intellectuals into powerful shapers of the incoherent masses. He wanted to do away with amateurishness and localism; a Marxism that had outworn most of its intellectual fervor was ready to be organized. His activist revisionism was a refuge for many who had staked their emotions on Marxist revolutionism and were unhappy at seeing it undermined by the dull revisionism of economism; it was an attempt to save the radical view by substituting political will for failing Marxist determinism.

LENIN'S MOVEMENT

After his release from Siberia, Lenin prudently left the jurisdiction of the tsar and lived abroad (except for a time, 1905−07, when it was safe to be in Russia) from 1900 until April 1917. His stock of ideas was complete,[17] and he now set about trying to put them into practice.

The first move was to start a new (biweekly) paper, *Iskra*, in the West, in collaboration with Plekhanov, Martov, Potresov, and Zasulich. Lenin dominated the enterprise because he was more energetic than the others; he particularly controlled the organization by handling the correspondence.[18] The German Social Democratic party, which had a section for the Russian revolutionary movement, was helpful both in launching the paper and in arranging transportation into Russia, no easy task. Lenin's intention was to replace the rather irregular Social Democratic publications, to unite the Social Democrats in European exile, and to guide the movement in Russia. Lenin was influenced in this by the success of Herzen's *Bell*, which penetrated the border censorship to exercise great influence in mid-nineteenth-century Russia.

Lenin took his title, *Iskra* ("Spark"), from the Decembrists, implying that the little incendiary sheet should set Russia aflame. It hardly did so, but it was immediately very successful among the Russian Marxists, who were ready to welcome a call to action. It quickly gave Lenin standing as a major leader of the diffuse movement. The task of publishing and distributing *Iskra* provided a frame and center for Russian Marxist radicals. Lenin viewed party members as *Iskra* distributors and its readers as potential party members. Its professional style, militant tone, and broad political-ideological coverage gave it a powerful appeal.

However, the birth of Lenin's movement may more accurately be dated from the publication in 1902 of his most important writing, *What is to Be Done?* Intended to help organize the *Iskra* adherents, this work amounted to a statement of the principles that were to guide his followers from that day forward and that prefigured the Soviet government. In it he asserted the primacy of theory ("consciousness"): "Without a revolutionary theory there can be no revolutionary movement. . . . The *role of vanguard fighter can be fulfilled only by a party that is guided by the most advanced theory. . . .* " But the workers were not only lacking in theory; they had also failed to develop class consciousness:

> It could only be brought to them from without. The history of all countries shows that the working class, exclusively by its own effort, is able to develop only trade union consciousness, i.e., the conviction that is is necessary to combine in unions, fight the employers and strive to compel the government to pass necessary labour legislation, etc. The theory of Socialism, however, grew out of the philosophic, historical and economic theories that were elaborated by the educated representatives of the propertied class, the intellectuals. According to their social status, the founders of modern scientific Socialism, Marx and Engels, themselves belonged to the bourgeois intelligentsia. In the very same way, in Russia, the theoretical doctrine of Social-Democracy arose quite independently of the spontaneous growth of the working-class movement; it arose as a natural and inevitable outcome of the development of ideas among the revolutionary socialist intelligentsia. . . .

> This shows . . . that *all* worship of the spontaneity of the working-class movement, all belittling of the role of the conscious element, of the role of Social-Democracy, *means, quite irrespective of whether the belittler wants to or not, strengthening the influence of the bourgeois ideology over the workers.*[19]

It was necessary, moreover, to adhere strictly to correct theory:

> There is no middle course (for humanity has not created a third ideology, and, moreover, in a society torn by class antagonisms there can never be a non-class or above-class ideology). Hence, to belittle the socialist ideology *in any way,* to *turn away from it in the slightest degree,* means to strengthen bourgeois ideology. There is a lot of talk about spontaneity, but the *spontaneous* development of the working-class movement leads to its becoming subordinated to the bourgeois ideology, *leads to its developing according to the program* of the *Credo,* for the spontaneous working-class movement is trade unionism, and trade unionism means the ideological enslavement of the workers by the bourgeoisie.[20]

To incorporate the ideology, Lenin sketched an army-like corps of dedicated and disciplined followers:

> . . . a small, compact core of the most reliable, experienced and hardened workers, with responsible representatives in the principal districts and connected by all the rules of strict secrecy with the organization of revolutionaries, can, with the widest support of the masses and without any formal organization, perform *all* the functions of a trade union organization, and perform them, moreover, in a manner desirable to Social Democracy.

. . . I assert: 1) that no revolutionary movement can endure without a stable organization of leaders that maintains continuity; 2) that the wider the masses spontaneously drawn into the struggle, forming the basis of the movement and participating in it, the more urgent the need of such an organization, and the more solid this organization must be (for it is much easier for demagogues to sidetrack the more backward sections of the masses); 3) that such an organization must consist chiefly of people professionally engaged in revolutionary activity. . . .[21]

Actual workers, who had to toil for a living, were *ispo facto* excluded, and leadership was reserved for a sector of the bourgeoisie. This corresponded in fact with the makeup of the *Iskra* board at the time: Lenin, Plekhanov, and Vera Zasulich were of the nobility; Potresov was the son of an army officer; Martov was the son of a merchant; and Axelrod, humblest of all, of a tavern-keeper. Lenin's professional revolutionaries aspired to the Populist ideal of heroes deriving from the privileged classes who stepped down to save the multitude, sacrificing everything for the noble cause with a presumptive reward of power and glory.

The necessary result of this elitism was a party based on centralization and hierarchic control. Lenin wrote in *Iskra* shortly afterwards that the center conducted the revolution like an orchestra director commanding each fiddle and each note, not consulting but directing the workers, who were to be turned not to an economic struggle they could understand but to revolutionary theory handed down from above. The proletariat were like children who had to be protected from their own misguided inclinations. As Krupskaya put it, Lenin blueprinted "a broad plan of organization in which everyone would find a place for himself, become a cog in the revolutionary machine."[22] Representatives of the organization who were sent into the factories were, in Lenin's view, to be simply agents, dedicated solely to following orders and instructing workers, but not consulting with them. This presupposed an authoritative body at the heart of the organization, a Central Committee that would decide all general questions and direct the local bodies; it also implied a general who would be in command of the obedient soldiers of revolution.

What is to Be Done strikes the modern reader as verbose and somewhat incoherent. Its reasoning sometimes seems forced. For example, Lenin stated that "the more we *confine* the membership of such an organization to people who are professionally engaged in revolutionary activity and have been professionally trained . . . the *greater* will be the number of persons from the working class and from other social classes who will be able to join the movement and perform active work in it."[23] It was also shocking to some at the time. Populist conspiratorial ideas of revolution-mongering had been largely set aside by this date, replaced by the examples of the popular, open, and more or less democratically organized parties of Western Europe and the huge, trade-union-affiliated German party in particular. Many found it difficult to forget the clear implication of Marxist theory that the socialist revolution should be made by proletarians who had been hardened to class consciousness by the conditions of their existence. Axelrod, for example, characterized Leninism as "bourgeois radicalism."[24] But the message of action fitted the circumstances of the time— Lenin was explicitly adapting Marxism to Russian conditions—and it brought Lenin a personal following. Many felt moved to accept commissions in the new army to battle for the new world.

Lenin thus generated a division among Russian Marxists even before he had a well-defined faction. The corollary of his insistence on dedication was narrowness; all who failed to adhere were ipso facto opponents. Lenin was quite irate when *Iskra*'s presses in Russia were loaned to local papers that were in dire straits.[25] Any compromise with the aspirations of the workers was viewed as a concession to economism and consequently heresy, in the spirit of Lavrov, who had seen any assistance to the people as treason against the revolution.[26]

The depth and character of the division became evident, however, only when the leaders of Russian Social Democracy (except for the real moderates, who stayed away) gathered in a Second Congress. Forty-three voting delegates, including three or four workers, met in Brussels on July 30, 1903; finding themselves subject to the attentions of unfriendly police, they transferred the meeting to London and talked until August 23. In the course of bitter debates, Lenin's followers became the hard-line faction. Thus 1903 became the nearest thing to a birthdate for Bolshevism, and ultimately for the Soviet state and world Communism. A gathering that was unnoticed at the time hence became one of the most analyzed meetings of history.

Lenin looked to the congress to establish the kind of party he had been advocating for several years; and he used the *Iskra* network, which he dominated, to get as many reliable friends and supporters for it as possible. Perhaps three-quarters of the participants were *Iskra*-affiliated. At the outset Lenin pushed through a presidium composed only of *Iskra* men. Yet the sessions were heated, and Lenin's group was only occasionally in the majority. It gained firm control only at the end, for a reason that has served Communist parties and groups countless times since. Many of his faction's opponents left the field, the Jewish Bund because its demand for autonomy was rejected, and various others because they were weary or had business elsewhere. Perhaps the most important consequence of the qualified numerical predominance of the Leninists was that they took the name of "Bolsheviks," that is, "majorityites," while their opponents, with much less than Lenin's sagacity, cheerfully accepted the name of "Mensheviks," or "minorityites." The name was a major asset for Lenin through the years of contention with the Mensheviks, when he was always claiming to represent a majority of the party but usually was not doing so. It was doubtless also a plus in the hectic days of 1917, when the Bolsheviks tried to present themselves as the party of the popular majority. The name was discarded by Stalin in 1952 as a gesture of anti-Leninism.

It was not surprising that revolutionaries should squabble; there had always been many factions with varying visions of how Russia was to be saved and, even more, with varying opinions about who was appointed to take charge of the country's salvation. Moreover, since all of the factions agreed that the government was bad, they were likely to spend most of their energy attacking one another. But the split that materialized at the 1903 congress was remarkable for its consistency and persistence. It was perceived as a fundamental divide at the outset; and it lasted, continually deepening despite some waverings, fence-sittings, and secondary splits, until the last Mensheviks died or were politically exterminated by the Soviet state in 1920.

The first meetings of the congress, however, were devoted mostly to the party program and were fairly harmonious. The chief snag was Lenin's difficulty in including in the program the dictatorship of the proletariat (defined as "the conquest by the proletariat of such political power as to suppress any resistance on the part of the exploiters"[27]), which no Social Democratic party of the West had proposed.[28] The division came to the fore when the question of membership was brought up. In Lenin's draft, membership required, in addition to acceptance of the program and material support for the party, "personal participation in one of the party organs." Martov's draft required "regular personal cooperation under the direction of one of the party organizations." The difference was slight and it was of little practical importance for Russian conditions, since affiliation with the clandestine party usually had to be informal. But it was a matter of principle for Lenin, who wanted membership more restricted, the better to control it, and for those who would leave the door a little more open to recruit a larger party, more like the Western European mass parties. The moderates were in the majority in this case, twenty-eight to twenty-three (some delegates had double votes).

The division was between Leninist extremists, the "hards," who were more dedicated to immediate revolutionary action, and the moderates, the "softs," who were more concerned with following Marxist theory as it was generally understood. Even before the congress, Lenin had been drawing apart, on such grounds, from his old friend Martov, who was almost the only intimate friend Lenin ever had.[29] The Mensheviks, led by Martov, were less centralist-minded and were much more aware of the potentialities of abuse of power, which frightened Lenin and his close followers not at all. Trotsky at this time prognosticated presciently: "Lenin's methods lead to this: the party organization at first substitutes itself for the party as a whole, then the Central Committee substitutes itself for the organization, and finally a single 'dictator' substitutes himself for the Central Committee."[30] Plekhanov, following Engels, warned that a premature effort at proletarian revolution—the Leninists insisted that Russia was already ripe—could lead only to a new pseudosocialist autocracy.[31]

The question lurking behind the debates over dictatorship of the proletariat was really one of authority, specifically of Lenin's leadership; it was less a matter of theory than of organization and personality.[32] This became evident as a result of Lenin's motion to reduce the editorial board of *Iskra* to three, Lenin, Plekhanov, and Martov, thereby dropping Axelrod, Potresov, and Zasulich. There may have been reasons of efficiency, since the latter three were not very active, but it looked like a power play to strengthen the hand of Lenin, who counted on Plekhanov's acquiescence; it also seemed to be a ruthless blow against old comrades.

Lenin won this skirmish but lost the battle. After the congress Martov withdrew from the board, but Plekhanov brought him back and restored Axelrod, Potresov, and Zasulich. Thereupon Lenin quit and found himself excluded from the cherished instrument of his political ambitions. Generally, the much-anticipated congress represented a failure for Lenin. He failed to draw to his side a single intellectual leader of Russian Marxism and antagonized enough of them to turn victory into defeat. Lenin attracted the action-bent, but at this stage few wanted a party under his sole authority claiming exclusive orthodoxy.[33] Later Lenin regretted his performance at this time. After the revolution, on rereading his pronouncements (which have since been made canonical), he commented to Karl Radek, "Isn't it interesting to read what fools we were then!"[34]

At the end of the Second Congress, Plekhanov, the dean of Russian Marxists, broke bitterly with Lenin, accusing him of aspiring not to "dictatorship of the proletariat" but to "dictatorship over the proletariat" in the spirit of Nechaevism. Presumably as a result of his setback, Lenin was under severe strain, at times near nervous breakdown, and for about a year he accomplished little. In August 1904, however, he held a conference of twenty-two of his most faithful adherents, including such men as Lunacharsky, a longtime intimate and future Soviet Commissar of Education; Maxim Litvinov, future Commissar of Foreign Affairs; Bogdanov, Lenin's second-in-command for several years; and Rykov, Chairman of the Council of Commissars after Lenin. This conference marked the practical beginning of Bolshevism as a separately organized movement. It was supplemented by the issuance, beginning in December 1904, of a strictly Bolshevik paper to rival *Iskra*, which was now a Menshevik organ; it was called *Vperëd* ("Forward"), after a journal once produced by the Populist Lavrov.

Lenin thus had his own, albeit diminished, organized faction, a base on which to build. It was, however, still a long way from the obedient instrument of power he envisaged. Nearly all the Bolsheviks in exile wavered occasionally or differed on some issue with Lenin, who was only de facto leader, without any institutionalized special position to give him the highest authority. Lenin's stature grew over the years as those around him became accustomed to his primacy and as the more independent spirits dropped out and were replaced by unconditional adherents. But he was able to make a disciplined and tightly bound party of persons supposedly wholly dedicated to the cause only after the revolution, when persuasion was reinforced by coercion.

Lenin's group was decidely more authoritarian than the Mensheviks, but the theoretical difference should not be exaggerated. In theory, nearly everyone was in favor of democracy, and the program adopted by the Second Congress, which mentioned "dictatorship of the proletariat," called for a whole series of rights in the best democratic tradition, including elections by secret ballot, local autonomy, inviolability of the person and the home, freedom of conscience, of speech, of press, and association, and the right to strike.[35] At the congress Plekhanov asserted that election results might be overridden if they were contrary to the needs of the revolution, but only one other delegate supported this thesis;[36] indeed, it was not really characteristic of Plekhanov's thought and he later regretted it. On the other hand, democracy was a rather alien, if respectable, concept. Trotsky said at the congress that the dictatorship of the proletariat would be possible only when the proletariat formed "the majority of the nation."[37] In the Soviet view, "This was in reality a denial of the dictatorship of the proletariat." However, Trotsky, who was more or less a Menshevik, had previously argued for a Central Committee with powers of discipline and purge over the revolutionary movement.[38]

The radicals in general saw as good whatever favored their ambitions and looked to a reorganization of society led by themselves. There was little objection to an autocratic party. Not only Lenin but also the other *Iskra*ites were opposed to the electoral principle in the party even at the lowest level; they wanted the workers' leaders to be designated from above.[39] The Mensheviks were in theory more worker-oriented than the Bolsheviks, and they worked more with and for the workers,[40] but in practice they were about as ready to guide the benighted proletariat as was Lenin. The idea that the educated should know the true will of the workers better than the workers themselves was almost inevitable under Russian conditions and was in fact not alien to Marx. In *The Holy Family*, for example, Marx wrote, "The question is not what this or that proletarian, or even the proletariat as a whole, considers as its aim at any given moment. The question is *what the proletariat is*, and what, in accordance with its *being*, it will be historically obliged to do. Its aim and action in history is patently, irrevocably preordained, by its situation in life. . . . "[41] Lenin made a fetish of the idea; for Lenin, too, however, to act as the vanguard of the workers meant at this time not to coerce but to persuade.

Quite as important a cause for division was Lenin's personality. He scoffed and ridiculed as much as he argued, and treated those who had different opinions as villains or idiots. He particularly scorned and hated people of his own class and of the "bourgeois" intelligentsia who were not prepared to accept his leadership; the intensity of his revulsion for his own kind, despite their frequent dedication to social causes, is suggestive of self-hatred. Somewhat anomalously, the fervent advocate of the dictatorship of the proletariat was also totally skeptical of the ability of the workers to discern their own class interests. Regarding the "bourgeoisie" as treacherous, Lenin consistently rejected any compromise with Russian liberalism. The Mensheviks, to the contrary, had no strong feelings against intellectuals in general or political liberals, and favored joining forces with them to force concessions from the tsarist regime.

In this regard Lenin was much more the descendant of the Populists and Slavophils than were most Russian Marxists.[42] From his first active years Lenin had been insisting on the need to adapt Marxism to the special conditions of Russia. The Populists hoped to avoid capitalism; Lenin held it to be unavoidable, indeed exaggerated the extent to which it had developed, but wished to truncate it by revolution. For Lenin the development toward and through liberalism was anathema; most Marxists saw it as necessary and desirable. The Mensheviks reproached Lenin for turning his back on the international Social Democratic movement, which they admired and craved to imitate; they branded Bolshevism at the outset as a non-Western variant, "Slavophilizing Marxism."[43]

Lenin's haste to make a revolution implied that there could be no waiting for a slow growth of the masses from spontaneity to consciousness; he necessarily came down strongly for the absolute necessity of "consciousness," that is, the necessity for the intellectuals, who were endowed with superior knowledge and understanding, to take the lead over "spontaneity," that is, the dark masses. The party, somewhat mystically, was to be "the conscious expression of the process [of history]."[44] The whole idea of consciousness versus spontaneity came out of the almost unbridgeable distance between those with a more or less Western education and the ignorant people for whom they felt some responsibility; the dichotomy is alien to the Western political tradition, deeply elitist, and thoroughly Russian. This is perhaps the key element of Lenin's specialness; he was in vocabulary a Marxist, but at heart a thoroughly Russian revolutionary whose program and tactics had much less to do with Karl Marx than with the imperial ideal of rulership by the enlightened few. For Lenin history was not to be made by Marxist economic classes and forces but by leaders and ideas, Russian style. Lenin's "dictatorship of the proletariat" was not far, in essence, from the Slavophil ideal of government by a good tsar; the proletariat (or those who acted on its behalf) by Marxist canon had to be good and was hence entitled to unlimited power. Lenin was a revolutionary who, in the intellectual atmosphere of his milieu, saw in the proletariat a means of making the revolution and giving it meaning and direction.

To impose the rule of "consciousness" meant, however, that there had to be a single doctrine. This insistence on conformity was the most effective difference between the Bolsheviks and their rivals. On the Menshevik side there was room for a variety of opinions, some dictatorial-revolutionary and some more moderate, less conspiratorial, and more Western-oriented; the Mensheviks were more disposed to accept genuine collaboration with a broad labor movement. There was no recognized leader of Menshevism and, in consequence, no Menshevik orthodoxy. The Bolsheviks, on the contrary, grouped themselves around a leader who defined an orthodoxy. Lenin, with what seemed to many to be excessive presumption, held that only those who believed as he did could be good Marxist revolutionaries. From first to last Lenin insisted on organizational and ideological unity, even if this meant dividing his following; he never hesitated at the prospect of a split. He preferred a tight splinter to a loose agglomeration, however much larger the latter might be.

In consequence, the Leninist party (which remained formally a "fraction" until 1912) was to be essentially conspiratorial. Lenin had a great fondness for codes and secret methods.[45] He spoke often of the danger of police infiltration as an excuse for a narrow party and undemocratic leadership, but this was apparently more rationalization than reality. On the contrary, the centralization on which Lenin insisted facilitated the work of the Okhrana, the tsarist political police. The Bolshevik organization was perennially and thoroughly penetrated by police agents, as were other radical organizations; all the emphasis on secrecy kept little from the authorities.

In summary, the schism was between those who preferred a loose group, or no group at all, and those who were willing to engage themselves to a close-bound group under a hard-driving leader. The first alternative appealed more to the genuine intellectuals or thinkers; consequently Lenin enlisted none of the outstanding minds of Russian Marxism. The second appealed to the persons who were most eager to get on with revolutionary action and did not mind subordinating their opinions and personalities to the general in charge in return for the hope of being his lieutenants in the great action. Thus the Mensheviks tended to be debaters; the Bolsheviks lusted more for combat and power. It would hence be logical to assume that the Bolsheviks might repel more people than they attracted in tranquil times, but that in turbulent times their purposeful coherence might bring them to the top.

HOPE AND FAILURE

In 1904, as Lenin was making his following into a clear-cut fraction of the Social Democratic Workers' party, the tsarist government was injuring itself, showing up its weaknesses, and undermining its legitimacy by an ill-conceived and unsuccessful war against Japan. In peacetime the possibility of revolution had been trivial, but student unrest, peasant disorders, occasional strikes, and liberal calls for a constitution had alarmed the weak regime; in fact, it had decided upon war in hopes of distracting the people. But the war showed up the weakness of the government, emptied its treasury, and reduced the loyalty of the armed forces; revolution became a very real possibility.

Lenin welcomed the war and the defeats of the tsarist forces, but he and others who were supposedly entirely dedicated to revolution did little or nothing to prepare for it; instead, they continued to devote themselves mostly to bickering. Indeed, Marxist leadership of the expanding working class was flagging; the police, on the contrary, had demonstrated considerable success in organizing loyal unions, under the leadership of S. V. Zubatov, the head of the Moscow Okhrana (the so-called "police socialism"). The Mensheviks and Bolsheviks together had only about eighty-four hundred members in 1905, whereas the Jewish Bund had had twenty-four thousand a year earlier; at least in St. Petersburg the Mensheviks were five times as numerous as the Bolsheviks.[46]

Trouble was triggered by a stupid violent reaction of the nervous government.[47] On "Bloody Sunday," January 22, 1905, troops were ordered to fire on a crowd whose only offense was an attempt peacefully to petition the tsar (who happened to be away from the palace). Several hundred were killed. The tsarist government lacked the capacity either to hush up the story or to invent excuses; the biggest casualty was the lingering affection ordinary Russians still had for the Little Father, the uninspiring Nicholas II.

The demands for change multiplied and disorders mounted in city and countryside. The middle classes withdrew their support from the government. Strikes spread. The police went slack, and censorship flagged, until within a few months Russia became de facto a fairly free country. Workers, professionals, and businessmen organized unions to support reform. A leading role was taken by the union of railroad workers, which found and used its power virtually to paralyze the country. There was unrest in the armed forces, particularly mutinies in the navy. At the end of summer, the protest grew into a general strike; by that time the authority of the government seemed all but ended.

The professional architects of revolution had little to do with generating this largely spontaneous revolutionary wave—the "conscious" Bolsheviks even less than the Mensheviks. The situation also evoked a powerful institution of revolution, the workers' councils or soviets, quite without the benefit of revolutionary theory. The original move seems to have come as the result of a suggestion by tsarist officials that workers elect delegates to discuss their grievances;[48] from this beginning the soviets of workers' delegates took hold as strike coordinating committees, first in certain industries, then in whole cities.[49] The soviets spread all over Russia and found themselves becoming increasingly powerful as the government faltered and slipped. In the general strikes, the soviets, especially the one in St. Petersburg, took charge; for a time it seemed as though the soviet would become the ultimate source of power. However, in

1905, as in 1917, the soviets failed to see themselves as a potential government, but sought to promote the constitutional assembly that represented the general aspiration.

Much impetus for change came from non-Marxists. There had previously been a revival of the propeasant orientation, and in 1902 the Socialist Revolutionary party was founded, with a principal aim of land reform. In 1905 the Constitutional Democratic party, a liberal, middle-class, reformist party, was also founded; its major aim was to achieve constitutional government. Both of these organizations seemed more in keeping with Russian realities than the Marxist Social Democratic party, which supposedly represented the small working class.

The Social Democratic leadership was unprepared for the upsurge of the revolution that it had so long supposedly been working and preparing for. Many of the leaders had returned to Russia from exile soon after Bloody Sunday, but they seem to have been so dazed that they mostly stood on the sidelines. Trotsky, who had been more or less affiliated with the Mensheviks, was the only outstanding Social Democratic leader to play a prominent part in the action; he became vice chairman of the Petersburg Soviet and then chairman in its latter days, after the previous chairman was arrested. Lenin, who had been so avid for action, delayed returning until November, some nine months after it was reasonably safe; he remained a spectator, only writing a few tracts.

Having little influence in the soviets, Lenin was not enthusiastic about them. They might be useful, but he thought they should limit themselves to trade-union functions and not assume a political role in competition with the party. Lenin, like other Marxists, also had difficulty in handling the situation theoretically. By all the logic of Marxism, the revolution could be only a "bourgeois" one that would usher in the stage of capitalism; it was unclear what part the feebly developed proletariat could or should have in it. The best answer he could devise was that the proletariat and peasantry should mount an armed uprising and propel the revolution toward the creation of a democratic republic, since the "bourgeoisie" was too weak and reactionary to make its own revolution. The proletariat, with the help of the peasantry, should then hold power while capitalism developed the country in preparation for socialism. It was contrary to the basic axiom of Marxism that the owners of the means of production should necessarily form the ruling class, and it was contrary to common sense that either side, "bourgeoisie" or proletariat, should live with such an abnormal arrangement.

Trotsky furnished an answer that was more useful, both as applied Marxism and as a political program. In 1904 Trotsky had analyzed the revolutionary potentialities together with his close friend, Alexander Helphand, who was commonly known as Parvus, his pen name in the German socialist press; Helphand was an intriguing character of whom there is more to tell in connection with the events of 1917. Trotsky and Helphand-Parvus sketched out a theory, which Trotsky refined in 1905 and subsequently published, of "permanent revolution."[50] This theory, which was Trotsky's great contribution to the treasury of world Marxist thought, was designed specifically to justify socialist revolution in Russia. It contended that when the cowardly bourgeoisie deserted the cause of revolution, the workers and peasants could still carry it forward, thereby making it in a sense "permanent." The peasant majority, having received the land they longed for, would turn conservative, Trotsky acknowledged.[51] But the Russian revolution would (as Marx had once hoped) ignite revolution in Germany and other countries, thereby making the revolution permanent in another sense, and the foreign workers would come to the rescue of their Russian brothers. Trotsky's theory even postulated that this was the way the world socialist revolution had to come, because it was easier for the proletariat (supported by the peasant masses) to take power where capitalism was weak. This theory became important in 1917 when Lenin adopted it.

Despite the inadequacies of Lenin's theories and the failure of the Bolshevik leaders to come forward in the mass organizations, the party prospered in the chaotic situation. Early in 1905 the Socialist Revolutionaries could promise ten thousand workers for an uprising, whereas the Social Democrats (the Mensheviks and Bolsheviks working closely together in the real-life crisis) had only a few hundred worker followers capable of being mobilized, as a Bolshevik avowed. But a few months later the Bolshevik and Menshevik papers each had a circulation of about fifty thousand.[52] Lenin's elitist approach to party membership was set aside, and many workers, students, and intellectuals, including numerous persons of gentry background, were admitted.[53] The Bolsheviks' influence was reduced, however, by their distrust of organizations (trade unions, soviets, or whatever) they could not control. Lenin, for example, opposed the establishment of a workers' congress until he should have secured power.[54]

The wave of discontent crested even before Lenin returned to Russia. In the summer the government shed its greatest burden by ending the war with Japan. As the strike movement and the breakdown of order became a threat to the throne, Nicholas brought the sensible and realistic Witte back into the government and by his advice granted many of the oppositionists' demands through the issuance of the October Manifesto. This amounted to a semiconstitution that promised civil rights and an elected legislative assembly, the Duma. It had only restricted powers, and there was no assurance of a really representative government; nevertheless, many reformers, fearful of violence, were satisfied to call a halt to the agitation. Moreover, the Petersburg Soviet brought forward the workers' economic demands, trying in particular to impose an eight-hour working day, a radical claim the industrialists of the day were not prepared to accept. The movement was split and lost morale and enthusiasm. The government meanwhile recovered its will. In December it was able to arrest the Petersburg Soviet. The Moscow Soviet, in which the Bolsheviks played a more important role, called a general strike. To repress it, the government had to call in forces from Petersburg, but the quixotic insurrection lasted only a little more than a week. Subsequently, punitive expeditions taught both unruly peasants and insubordinate minority nationalities some of the dangers of opposing the imperial government.

It is the conventional Soviet interpretation that the 1905 revolution was a useful, perhaps necessary, "dress rehearsal" for the 1917 revolution. This reflects only ideological optimism; the failure to achieve very much in 1905 left the revolutionary forces exhausted and discouraged for many years. They had failed to gain anything but reforms that were pleasing to the despised liberals. However, the 1905 revolution did parallel that of 1917 in several ways, and a penetrating observer might have drawn useful lessons from it. Both uprisings were triggered by defeat in war and were essentially spontaneous in inception. In both cases, disorder deepened for about nine months. In both, the Mensheviks were stronger than the Bolsheviks at the outset, but the Bolsheviks gained strength more rapidly in the anarchic situation. Finally, in both, the outcome depended not on the workers but on the soldiers, who obeyed their commanders in 1905, but withheld their obedience in 1917. The Mensheviks were right in 1905 in their belief that the workers could press for change only in cooperation with the middle-class liberals. Nevertheless, Lenin seems to have learned much from the earlier attempt, as he showed by his actions in 1917.

DISILLUSION AND DECADENCE

The experience of 1905 represented a serious and demoralizing setback for the revolutionary forces, especially for Lenin and his cherished party. In the spring of 1905, the Bolsheviks held a separate congress. Lenin claimed that this splinter congress spoke for the entire party, but the desire for unity in the rising tide of revolution was so strong that he could not prevent a unity resolution. Lenin was unable to maintain a separate party organization in Russia because the people on the spot regarded any philosophic differences with Menshevik fellow Marxists as much less important than joint action against the tsarist regime in the crisis. The failure of the Bolshevik-led Moscow uprising in December further damaged Lenin's standing. In April 1906, the Bolsheviks and Mensheviks met together at a "unity" congress in Stockholm, the fourth such meeting of the party; thereafter Lenin had to observe the forms of a united Social Democratic party until 1911, at least pretending to collaborate with the execrated Mensheviks.[55]

Through 1906 it was possible to continue to believe in a new revolutionary upsurge, but the program adopted by the 1906 congress consisted of democratic and libertarian demands. By the middle of 1907 the government felt confident enough to dissolve the obstreperous Duma and to change illegally, that is, contrary to the promise of the tsar's manifesto, the terms of the electoral law to make the Duma highly unrepresentative and assuredly conservative. The indignant deputies of the dissolved Duma called upon the people to resist the government by refusing to pay taxes, but no one stirred. The energetic Prime Minister, Piotr Stolypin, thereupon instituted a period of repression together with a program of agrarian reform that was designed to stabilize the government. He proceeded to crack down on radicals and disturbers of order with a harshness that had been unknown in Russia for a century. According to Karl Liebknecht's tally, between 1825 and 1905, 625 political prisoners were condemned to death, but between 1906 and 1910, 3,741 suffered execution[56]—a total for the five years that would have been an ordinary day's work in Stalin's purges, but that was terrifying to prerevolutionary Russia.

Public opinion became subdued and apathetic. It seemed that the radical agitation of many years had been played out. Revolution ceased to be the general ideal of the intellectuals. The Populist (and Bolshevik) attitude of the elite guiding the people was becoming outmoded as a result of increasing literacy and the wider reach of journalism. Interest in Marxism, which had been gradually declining since the end of the 1890s, waned more markedly. The contrast between the intelligentsia and the people was becoming less acute,[57] and the leading intellectuals were now associated with the Cadet, or liberal, party. The country was prospering economically, modernization was creeping into the villages, the press was semifree, the Duma served as a political forum, and conspiratorial politics was worn out. The membership of the revolutionary parties, which had swollen in 1905–06, shrank to a small fraction even of the pre-1905 figures. Early in 1907 the Social Democrats claimed 150,000 members; by 1910 the estimate was 10,000. The number of Bolsheviks, which had risen more in the period of disorder, declined more afterwards. By 1909–10 the Bolsheviks had only some half-dozen committees in Russia.[58] Even this reduced party was far from Lenin's vision of a corps of full-time revolutionaries, since it consisted mostly of workers who occasionally attended to party duties. As Krupskaya saw it in 1908, "It became clearer every day that the Bolshevik group would soon come apart."[59]

The leadership in exile was equally demoralized. The revolutionaries abroad lived in disorderly fashion, mostly isolated from Western society and talking endlessly with one another. Polemics and bickering were their chief activities— theoretical, organizational, and personal quarrels that were often carried on as though for the sake of quarreling, a means of passing the dull years. Lenin's existence from 1907 to 1917 was rather desolate; his young manhood was slipping away with nothing accomplished. He moved frequently, to Finland, Geneva, Paris, Krakow, Berne, and Zurich. He produced nothing memorable between the 1905 revolution and First World War, which inspired his tract on *Imperialism*. He suffered psychosomatic illnesses from time to time when things went badly. It may be guessed that the unhappy years, especially 1907—12, had their effect on his personality.

The great magnetism and the organizational and leadership talents with which Lenin has been credited because of his ultimate success were not evident during the bad years in his divided and ineffective little following. In 1906—07 he took to holdups, which he dubbed ''expropriations,'' as a means of financing his party. In the aftermath of the breakdown of law and order in 1905 there was a good deal of brigandage, especially in the Caucasus with its traditions of banditry; Lenin saw armed robbery not merely as an unexceptional transfer of resources from exploiters to revolutionaries, but also as training for revolutionary violence. Lenin's chief assistant in this department (and the second or third man in the party) was Leonid Krassin, a capable and affluent engineer and business manager who made a hobby of revolutionary activism. He organized and supplied the bombs for the biggest operation, the expropriation of 341,000 rubles in Tiflis in June 1907. Stalin stood behind the exercise although he did not take part personally. Eminent Bolsheviks were subsequently arrested in Western Europe while trying to pass expropriated banknotes (the serial numbers of which were known to police). A scandal followed. The Mensheviks and other radicals had at one time condoned such adventurous ways of raising money, but they had turned away from them, and these practices were condemned by a large majority at the party congress of May 1907. Lenin was compelled by general sentiment, even within his own faction, to give up such spectacular means of procuring resources. But he was open-minded; in 1907, the Bolsheviks were scheming to counterfeit ruble notes.

Not long afterwards, the history of the party was enlivened by another curious and tangled affair. A soap manufacturer named Schmidt seems to have desired his estate to go to the Russian Social Democratic party, which the Bolsheviks interpreted to mean themselves. When he died intestate and the fortune went to his two unmarried sisters, the Bolsheviks sent two handsome fellows to give them love in return for a large part of the money. The Mensheviks demanded a proper share for themselves, and they exerted enough pressure to force Lenin to turn part of the money over to three leading German Social Democrats, Karl Kautsky, Franz Mehring, and Rosa Luxemburg, as trustees to adjudicate the dispute. A handsome sum, about five hundred thousand rubles, was at stake, and Lenin's special hatred for Kautsky may have been caused by his refusal in 1911 to return the money to the Bolsheviks.

The morale and cohesion of Lenin's faction were also severely tried by the difficulty of adjustment to nonconspiratorial politics, in particular to the presence of an elected assembly. All of the revolutionary parties boycotted the elections to the First Duma with the well-founded feeling that it was a hindrance to the further progress of the revolution. As the wave of violence receded, it became evident to many that there was no point in renouncing the opportunity to acquire a forum for their radical views and a chance of exerting some influence on the national stage. Most Bolsheviks still wanted to boycott the assembly, but on this question Lenin went over to the Menshevik side. His position was vindicated when the Mensheviks, who campaigned in the elections, gained sixty-five seats, while the Bolsheviks got only eighteen.[60] Lenin himself may have been an unsuccessful candidate in these elections.[61] When, after the dissolution of the Second Duma, the electoral law was changed to deprive the workers and peasants (and minority nationalities) of most of their representation, a large majority of the Bolsheviks again desired to boycott, but Lenin joined the Mensheviks to defeat this policy at the July—August 1907 party conference. Lenin declared that the Duma, like "bourgeois" constitutionalism in general, was a fraud, but he insisted that the party make every possible use of the opportunity presented by the class enemy. After the elections many Bolsheviks demanded that the Bolshevik deputies be withdrawn ("recalled") from the Duma in a defiant gesture, and these "Recallists" caused Lenin much trouble as he endeavored to keep control of restive organizations in Russia and abroad.

Because of differences over expropriations and tactics regarding the Duma, and general disillusionment, Lenin's faction nearly broke up in 1908—09. Attempts to rethink the basic principles resulted, and many Bolsheviks set off on philosophical adventurings, seeking, in line with the general trend of the Russian intelligentsia, to reconcile Marxism with spiritual values. According to Krupskaya, "those were years of the greatest confusion of ideas among the Social Democrats. Attempts were made to revise the very foundations of Marxism. . . . Those were dark days."[62] One of Lenin's closest lieutenants, A. A. Bogdanov, took the lead in "God-building," turning Marxism into a sort of religion. He also developed, with Maxim Gorky, Lunacharsky, and others, ideas that derived from the physicist-philosopher Ernst Mach. Bogdanov espoused a sort of positivism in which qualities were only a matter of perception. He had written in this vein in previous years, but only now did his views, which were not incompatible with Marxism, become the subject of bitter controversy. Lenin was sufficiently exercised to take time off to bone up on metaphysics and write a long, dull book, *Materialism and Empirio-Criticism*, to refute Bogdanov's theory.

Somewhat incongruously, the group of philosophical revisionists were at the same time political extremists, a Bolshevik left, who corresponded more or less to the Recallists. They set up a theoretical school in rivalry to Lenin on the island of Capri with money earned by the popular writings of Maxim Gorky, and attacked Lenin for his monarchic approach, which they termed "party tsarism." In elections to the January 1909 Social Democratic congress, they campaigned as a separate group under the leadership of Bogdanov. Lenin was infuriated, of course, by this insurgency; in June 1909 he secured a condemnation by a conference of Bolshevik leaders of God-building and Recallism as anti-Marxist movements. The leftists, claiming to be the true Bolsheviks, formed a separate faction and put out a paper of their own, turning the tables on Lenin by accusing him of softness and conciliation.[63] But they were revolutionary romantics, disdainful of organization and lacking a real leader and any philosophy or program except to take charge of the mass movement that should answer their call. The group soon dissolved, with most of the members drifting back to Lenin.

The idealists, those who wanted to modernize the movement's philosophy or who were restrained by scruples, came and went; the unconditionals, those who trusted neither the masses nor themselves but only the leader, stayed with Lenin. Because of growing habits of separate action, these years of formal unity between the Bolsheviks and the Mensheviks saw an actual drawing away of the Bolshevik faction and a hardening of its positions. Nearly all the Social Democrats wanted a united struggle—even united the party was pitifully small—but neither side was prepared to yield its positions for the sake of harmony. Typically, the Paris conference of January 1910 eagerly endorsed unity and approved measures to bring it about, including a new board of editors for the party paper, *Sotsial-Demokrat*, consisting of two Bolsheviks, Lenin and Zinoviev, two Mensheviks, Martov and Teodor Dan, plus a Polish Social Democrat. But neither side lived up to the agreements, the Bolsheviks in particular failing to desist from their irregular fund raising, and the two groups were soon at odds again.

A basic point of difference was the Mensheviks' greater inclination to move with the times. They were less hostile to liberalism and parliamentarism; their view that a period of capitalism must follow the "bourgeois" revolution meant that they saw less reason to drive for violent revolution and more reason to collaborate with middle-class reformers. This contradicted the Marxist fundamental of class struggle, yet it seemed the only reasonable way to work for political change in Russia. Lenin was, of course, passionately opposed to compromise with "bourgeois" elements.

The Mensheviks were likewise becoming uncomfortable with the idea of a conspiratorial, underground party and wished instead to take advantage of the half-freedom of Russia to build up a mass party in the Western style. Some wanted to end illegal work. Lenin used this tendency to brand the Mensheviks as a whole as "liquidationists," that is, proponents of a move to liquidate the party, and the conspiratorial tradition was still strong enough to make the charge effective. For Lenin, giving up illegal work would have been equivalent to surrender, because much of his authority in the party depended on his holding the keys to the underground network.[64]

If the Mensheviks retreated a little from dogma, Lenin's ideological line, despite some confusion, remained hard. He particularly insisted on the necessity of the dictatorship of the proletariat as the heart of Marxism, with the implication of indefinite party rule; the dictatorship should come to an end only at some distant date when the proletariat should form the overwhelming majority. The thesis that a revolutionary minority should go beyond or against the wishes of the majority was less acceptable to the Mensheviks in 1910 than it had been in 1903.

Lenin's antiliberalism meant that he remained in the older Russian tradition. Unlike many Russians, Lenin, in his seventeen years abroad, never became associated with anything that was Western European, and he regarded the moderation of the European proletariat and Marxist parties with pure disgust. Like Russian conservatives, Lenin regretted the agrarian measures of Stolypin, which were directed toward the breakup of the peasant commune and the promotion of private land ownership. Impressed by the importance of jacqueries in 1905, he shifted his hopes partly back toward the peasants as a revolutionary force, contrary to the Menshevik inclination to attribute greater importance to the more modern sectors of society. In some ways Lenin took positions that were similar to those of the reactionary Union of the Russian People, which hated bureaucrats, capitalism, and constitutionalism, and saw salvation in a mystical union of ruler and masses.[65]

The factor that made the split unbridgeable, however, was Lenin's own personality. He acted as harshly as he could without alienating his following, using labels for arguments and pouring ridicule and sarcasm over his opponents. He wrote and spoke with dogmatic certitude, careless about everything but the cause of socialism as interpreted by himself. In February 1907 the Mensheviks managed to summon Lenin before a party tribunal on charges of slander. With remarkable candor he admitted having chosen "obnoxious terms calculated to evoke hatred, aversion, contempt . . . calculated not to convince but to break up the ranks of the opponent, not to correct the opponent's mistake but to destroy him, to wipe his organization off the face of the earth."[66]

If the Mensheviks represented a rather ill-defined political tendency, the Bolsheviks were primarily the party of Lenin. He was dedicated to the party to the exclusion of almost all personal considerations. He never had children, and historians, searching for frailties of the flesh, have found only a romantic interest in the beautiful and talented Inessa Armand, who came to Bolshevism from an upper-class, largely Western background. The closeness of their relationship from 1909 to 1916 is uncertain. Lenin used even Inessa, like his wife, as an instrument of the party. It was one of Lenin's strengths, however, that he rewarded those who were loyal to him with warmth and generous attention.[67]

The party was Lenin's own, and no party discipline except his own ideas meant anything to him. He kept the organizational strings in his own hands so far as he could, handling the correspondence with Krupskaya, who was secretary of the Central Committee from 1905 through 1908. All major decisions were made by Lenin and by close associates whom he selected without the sanction of any regular party body. He wished to contend with no intellectual rivals; in a letter to Gorky of February 7, 1908, he expressed satisfaction that the intellectuals were abandoning the party.[68] Probably for the same reason, the Bolshevik leaders were considerably younger than the Menshevik ones. At the Fifth Congress, in 1907, the Bolshevik leaders averaged thirty-four years of age and the Menshevik leaders forty-two. The oldest Bolsheviks were Lenin and Krassin, who were both thirty-seven, and Krassin was strictly a man of action. Plekhanov and Axelrod were in their fifties. Bolshevik delegates to the congress averaged just twenty-seven.[69]

All these factors gave the Bolsheviks strength in 1917. Lenin gathered only a small group because he would have only unconditional followers. But he did have followers, whereas the Menshevik intellectuals had only sympathizers or adherents. With a leader who was able to set or change course and a hierarchy that could implement policy, the Bolsheviks had the advantage of flexibility to meet changing and unforeseen circumstances; thus Lenin could borrow the theory of Trotsky and the agrarian program of the Socialist Revolutionaries. The Leninists also lacked scruples about getting funds; consequently they were usually much better financed and able to support an organization than their rivals. In addition, the Bolsheviks could carry the attack to their opponents. The Mensheviks always hoped for reconciliation and tried to settle differences by discussion and compromise; Lenin rejected compromise in principle. The Mensheviks forgot that the issue was not really one of theory but of power; Lenin never neglected the main thing. For the Mensheviks the party was a means to a social end; for the Bolsheviks it was an end in itself, a meaning for life.

LENIN AND THE MINORITIES

Lenin was eager to exploit any discontent, not only the conflict of the industrial workers with the capitalists, but also the peasants' desire for more land, the unhappiness of the non-Orthodox at official discrimination against them, and the resentment of the minority nationalities at their rule or misrule by the Russians. In the latter regard, the situation became more favorable for the revolutionaries after 1905. Intellectual Marxism was ebbing, the workers were gradually improving their standard of living, and the villages were becoming more stable by virtue of the agrarian laws, but the minorities were becoming more resentful of alien domination.

The spirit of rebellion had long burned in the Ukraine and other minority areas; the uprisings of Stenka Razin in the seventeenth century and Pugachev in the eighteenth drew their strength from non-Russian areas. But early in the nineteenth century the Russian empire was a multinational state in which it was no great advantage to be Russian. Russification became official policy only in the reign of Alexander III; and modern ideas of freedom, equality of peoples, and self-determination of nations were concurrently seeping in from the West. The

Russians were becoming nationally prouder and more disposed to see the empire as theirs; the minorities were more resentful at being ruled not only by an oppressive autocracy but also by foreigners. The minority areas, particularly the Caucasus and the Baltic provinces, were especially rebellious in 1905–06. The establishment of the Duma aggravated the situation by calling attention to national demands, institutionalizing the principle of representation, and providing a forum for minority grievances; after the Second Duma was dissolved, the minorities were deprived of most or all of their mandates, increasing their sense of injustice. In the period of reaction, reprisals were especially ferocious in the Baltic and Caucasus regions. The Jews were also made scapegoats by the authorities to divert popular feelings away from the government to a vulnerable section of the population. Jewish intellectuals became embittered and were set free to engage in revolutionary politics by their exclusion from the chief employment of the educated, state service. For these reasons, the Marxist party was very popular with the minorities. In the Duma elections of 1906, the Social Democrats in the Caucasus, who were mostly Mensheviks, received twice as many votes as all the other parties together. At the party congress that year, less than half the delegates were Russian (a quarter were Jewish),[70] although it was ostensibly a Russian party (the "Russian Social Democratic Workers' party"); Jews and other minorities had their own organizations. The Mensheviks were as much a Georgian-Jewish party as a Russian one, since 28 percent of the delegates to the 1907 congress were Georgian and 22 percent were Jewish, while only 34 percent were Russian.[71] Although the Mensheviks dominated the Social Democratic party in the Caucasus, other minorities, particularly the Poles and Latvians, favored the action-oriented Bolsheviks (it was only with the help of the Polish and Latvian delegations that Lenin held a majority on the Central Committee in 1907). Lenin, on the other hand, subsidized Polish and Latvian Bolshevik subparties.[72] At a later date, the Latvian sharpshooters were Lenin's invaluable supporters in the making of the revolution, and at times in the first year of Bolshevik power they were almost the only reliable force at his disposal. Lenin welcomed the Jews as better revolutionaries than Russians, and his closest aide from 1910 on was Grigori Zinoviev, a Russian Jew.

With keen political insight, Lenin took a strong theoretical interest in the nationality question. He invited Stalin to compose an essay on the subject late in 1912, and in the next few years Lenin wrote extensively about the need to recognize the right of smaller nations to independence. His position was basically that under prevalent conditions it was necessary for the Social Democrats to promise and agitate for complete self-determination, including the right of secession, for minority peoples, with the qualification (which was not emphasized as long as the destruction of the tsarist empire was the aim) that the working class must remain united under the Bolshevik party, representative and guide of the proletariat. This position was hardly new for the Russian Social Democrats—

Russian intellectuals had long advocated freedom for oppressed peoples—but Lenin's emphasis on it was new. His stand was also in opposition to the more conventional Marxist position, which had been expressed most effectively by the Polish Social Democrat Rosa Luxemburg. Marx himself had been centralist in outlook, and he regarded nationalism as a bourgeois prejudice. From the logical Marxist viewpoint, national self-determination was meaningless under capitalism and needless under socialism; to make an issue of it was to threaten the international solidarity of the proletariat.

Many Social Democrats opposed Lenin on this issue, including Karl Radek (Polish-Jewish), Nikolai Bukharin, Georgi Piatakov (Ukrainian), Alexandra Kollontai, Feliks Dzerzhinski (Polish), and Trotsky (Jewish).[73] Lenin compensated by speaking also of internationalism and the world state, and he rightly argued that Marx himself and various socialist bodies had advocated self-determination. His nationality policy was dictated not by Marxist logic, however, but by an appreciation of the markedly growing revolutionary potential of the minority peoples of what Lenin called the "tsarist prisonhouse of nationalities."

It was an adept program for winning adherents while in reality giving away nothing. It promised freedom and equality to people who comprised over half the population of the empire, while telling Russians that their empire would, in effect, be converted into a glorious international movement.

Lenin's position should not be seen as purely opportunistic, however. The minorities, for the most part, desired independence less than equality, a fair share in the state, and this Lenin tried to deliver. He was a Russian antinationalist by temperament, and he fought relentlessly against Russian nationalism. His ethnic background was non-Russian and he had probably sympathized with non-Russians as a boy; his father had once espoused the cause of Tatar children.[74] Shortly before the outbreak of World War I, Lenin took up residence in Austrian Galicia, near the Russian border, so that he could be in direct contact with the Polish and Ukrainian movements; this move represented a shift of emphasis from the oppressed workers to the oppressed minorities. At the outbreak of the war, he did not merely withhold support for the Russian war effort but he seems positively to have desired a German victory. At that time he advocated cutting off from Russia most of its western acquisitions, including the Ukraine and the Baltic provinces.[75] This was a position very difficult for a Great Russian, even a socialist, to assume, and it was quite similar to the provisions of the Treaty of Brest Litovsk. After the tsar was overthrown, Lenin was at first almost alone in his sharp opposition to the defensist policy of the Provisional Government. In his last years and months in office Lenin distinguished himself by his opposition to "Great Russian chauvinism," when concessions to minorities meant infringement of the Bolshevik power that was so dear to him. Complete freedom from patriotic prejudices was a basic strength of Lenin's political character.

THE LAST YEARS OF WAITING

By 1912 radicalism was again stirring in Russia, strikes and demonstrations had reappeared, and the extremist parties were showing signs of revival. This was probably not the beginning of a great revolutionary wave that was just showing its promise when it was cut off by the world war, but the ebbing of the wave of reaction and repression that followed the revolution of 1905. Russia was getting back to its ineffectively governed normality.

At this time Lenin finally achieved his longtime aim, the establishment of a formally independent Bolshevik party. The preparatory intrigues revolved around the somewhat sordid affair of the Schmidt inheritance. Lenin seems to have been moved to separate his own following to form an independent party largely by his anger at the fact that his rivals had demanded a full share of the money and managed to get a little of it.

Instead of admitting that he was founding a new party, Lenin set up an organizing committee for a new congress in the name of the party as a whole. However, only fully committed Leninists came to the congress, which was held in Prague in January 1912. Lenin now gave up his efforts to collaborate with independent Social Democrats or to bring them under his influence. The leadership that emerged after the Prague congress was entirely new except for Lenin and Zinoviev; it included an exceptionally large proportion of Caucasians and underground workers, and many names that were to become celebrated in the Bolshevik state, such as Ordzhonikidze, Kamenev, Rykov, Tomsky, Kalinin, Sverdlov, and Koba (Stalin). Of the first seven full members of the Central Committee, three were Russians, and one of these, Roman Malinovsky, was a police spy.

The presence of a tsarist operative in the highest Bolshevik circles was not remarkable; the Bolsheviks, much more than the Mensheviks, were thoroughly riddled by the Okhrana. At Lenin's ideological "school" near Paris in 1911, for example, out of ten students, at least two, including Malinovsky, were agents; at a Bolshevik conference in Galicia in August 1913, five of the twenty-two persons present were agents.[76] Spies formed a majority of the Moscow committee and nearly half of the one in St. Petersburg.[77] Still, Lenin's relationship with Malinovsky was interesting and controversial.

Malinovsky was almost an ideal Bolshevik. Of commendably proletarian origin, unlike a large majority of the Bolshevik leaders, he was the secretary of the St. Petersburg metalworkers' union. A capable speaker and agitator, he became a Bolshevik representative in the Duma and the leader of the Bolshevik faction (of five deputies) from 1912 through 1913; during this time the Okhrana helped write his flaming speeches. He was for a time Lenin's chief deputy in

Russia, and he was charged with starting and managing *Pravda* in 1912 (the first editor, Chernomazov, was also in the tsar's service).

Rumors of Malinovsky's dual role began circulating chiefly because of the frequency of the arrests of persons on whom he could have informed; many, especially Mensheviks, demanded that he be expelled or called before a party tribunal. Lenin, however, steadfastly defended him against the alleged "slanderers" and arranged to whitewash him. Lenin's purposes coincided with Malinovsky's in large measure. Following the wishes of the police, who valued Lenin's splitting of the Social Democratic party and saw the moderates as more dangerous than the extremists, Malinovsky was among the most vehement denouncers of the "liquidators." He arranged for the arrests of many of these and of many Bolshevik "conciliators." It seems clear that Lenin was not greatly concerned with learning whether Malinovsky was affiliated with the police so long as he was useful; it is likely that Lenin was aware that he was a spy.[78] Early in 1914 Malinovsky resigned from the Duma on police instructions, his role having been made untenable by leaks, and went abroad, visiting Lenin in Cracow on the way to Germany. Although Malinovsky's Okhrana connection was almost public knowledge, Lenin continued to defend him and during the war sent him parcels and literature for distribution among Russian prisoners in Germany. After the war Malinovsky returned voluntarily to Russia, although he knew that the Okhrana records were available; apparently he expected Lenin to save him. He pleaded at his trial that Lenin must have known his situation,[79] but Lenin did nothing, and he was shot.

It is by no means unusual or surprising that a political police should work with radical extremists, since both groups operate somewhat within the same world and share an interest in tensions and threats to order. The Okhrana especially intermingled with Socialist Revolutionary terrorist groups, and it was often unclear whether a double agent belonged to the Okhrana and was infiltrating the revolutionary group or vice versa. The Okhrana cooperated with Bolshevik Duma deputies in inciting rebellion to furnish the tsar with an excuse for shutting down the Duma, an eventuality desired by both the Bolsheviks and the reactionaries. The Okhrana, as noted, favored the Bolsheviks, since they were more extreme, hence more useful and less dangerous than the Mensheviks. On the other hand, Lenin purchased some leniency for the Bolsheviks in Russia by his attacks on non-Bolshevik radicals, whether or not he thought in such terms.

Following the 1912 Prague congress, however, the Bolsheviks decided, in a rather sudden shift of policy, to come partly out of the underground in Russia. Censorship had been sufficiently loosened that it was possible to publish a rather radical paper, and in February 1912 Lenin decided to launch his own daily in St. Petersburg. He borrowed the name *Pravda* from a paper that had been founded by Trotsky in 1908 and published in Vienna. Bolshevik finances sufficed to make it a daily publication, for a time the only daily labor paper in Russia, and it enjoyed considerable success until it was closed upon the outbreak of the war. Stalin and Molotov were the chief editors, and *Pravda* was useful both in guiding the illegal organizations and in lashing out at the Menshevik "liquidators."

Nonetheless, Lenin's position was weak. There were continuing strong pressures for unity because of the basic similarity of the programs of the two wings of the Social Democratic party. By early 1914, the Bolsheviks were not far from bankruptcy, and the underground committees were languishing. The circulation of *Pravda* had fallen from a peak of about sixty thousand to only twenty thousand.[80] Sitting in a small town near the Russian frontier, Lenin was having trouble keeping his Bolsheviks in line and directing *Pravda* from afar. In an attempt to patch up the differences, the Socialist International sponsored a conference in Brussels in July 1914 of all the factions of the Russian Social Democrats. Lenin refused to attend but sent Inessa Armand with an uncompromising statement. Very few supported Lenin. A unity resolution was voted, and it seemed possible for Lenin to continue his separatist course only at the price of excluding himself from the international movement. The case was put over until August; meanwhile the war began.

The war gave Lenin and his party a new cause and new life; as Ulam stated, "Communism was born in Lenin's brain the day World War I erupted."[81] Yet it caught him unawares. Conscious as he was of war as the midwife of revolution, in Marx's phrase, he hardly noticed the mounting crisis and the advent of war;[82] at least he was silent on the subject. Austria declared war on Serbia on July 28, and Lenin was arrested as an enemy alien on August 7 by local officials. But he had originally come to Austria in cooperation with Austrian authorities who were interested in making trouble for Russia in the Ukraine, so the Vienna government moved to have him released. In the creaky bureaucracy, this required two weeks; he was then allowed to move to neutral Switzerland, where he spent the years remaining before the overthrow of the tsar permitted his return to Russia on April 16, 1917.

The ugly question that was forced upon the socialists of Europe was what attitude they should assume toward the conflagration. Prior to the war, socialism was universally assumed to imply pacifism, and one of the chief preoccupations of the Socialist (Second) International had been the prevention of war. It was widely believed that war would be impossible because the workers and trade unions, who were devoted to the international cause, would refuse to lend their support to warring governments.

The workers, however, turned out to be nationalists more than they were internationalists, and an overwhelming majority of the Marxist parties came out flatly in support of their own warring governments. In each case they found good reasons. The French socialists, for example, saw the war as the defense of democratic France against German-Prussian militarism. The German Social Democrats saw their country as the land of Social Democracy, which had to be defended against tsarist autocracy. In doing so they were following the injunctions of Marx and Engels, who regarded tsarism as the greatest enemy of progress. Only the Russian Social Democrats, who existed outside the political process, generally refused at the outset to lend their support to their embattled state.

Even for the Russians, however, an antiwar position was not easy to sustain. Defeatism had been socially acceptable a decade earlier in the war with Japan, when there had been no sense that the national existence was at stake. In 1914, however, there was an enormous wave of enthusiasm for the war. Deep-seated Slavic antagonism to the secular Teutonic enemy came to the fore. The conservatives wanted to fight for Russia and trusted that victory would solidify the regnant system; the liberals and democrats saw the struggle justified by the alliance with democratic France and England against authoritarian Germany and hoped that victory alongside such allies would lead to political reform. For the socialist leaders to oppose the war would have meant opposing the sentiments of the workers.

In these circumstances, at the beginning of the war the Menshevik and Bolshevik Duma factions made a joint declaration of pacifist defensism, much to Lenin's disgust. Some of the Mensheviks shifted to a defensist position; Plekhanov, the outstanding Marxist theoretician, turned strongly patriotic. Most Bolsheviks remained opposed to their government, but a few wavered and left the party. Many Bolsheviks abroad volunteered for military service with the Allies.[83] In any case, the Bolshevik organizations in Russia were almost entirely liquidated soon after the onset of the war by the police,[84] who no longer showed them mercy. Early in 1915 the Bolshevik Duma deputies were expelled as traitors and shipped off to Siberia, although they repudiated Lenin's extreme antiwar position.

Marxists thus rationalized attitudes toward the war to suit their intimate purposes. Lenin, the most determined opponent of participation in the "imperialist" war, went beyond refusal to lend support to the tsarist war effort and favored the German side—in contradiction to the general Marxist view that revolution in Germany was much more important than revolution in Russia, which would at best serve as a trigger. Lenin wrote, on October 17, 1914, "Tsarism is a hundred times worse than Kaiserism," a sentiment whose importance is underlined by Krupskaya's citation of it.[85] Lenin blamed the capitalists on both sides for the war, but he seemed to blame the Anglo-French imperialists more vehemently. He disseminated defeatist propaganda in France but not in Germany.[86]

It was contradictory to his assessment of the relative evils of the imperial Russian and German regimes that Lenin sharply blamed the German Social Democrats for their at first rather eager backing of their government. More broadly, he damned all the defensist parties composing the Second International, branded them "social chauvinists," and called for the formation of a new and purer revolutionary Third International (which was not to be founded until 1919) and a change of the party's name from "Social Democratic" to "Communist" (this was accomplished in March 1918). He was no doubt happier thus to condemn the Second International (which was in any case killed by the war) since it had probably been about to expel him.

The world war thus effectively separated Lenin and his followers from the broader socialist movement and marked another beginning point for the Soviet party and world Communism. In a world upset by war, revolution was again on the agenda, evoked not by the exploitation of workers by capitalists but by the follies of those who were supposedly dedicated to the security of their nations. It was no longer necessary to try to elucidate Marxist theory to uncomprehending workers; the anguish and evil of war were all too well known.

Yet Lenin could do little about it. In Switzerland for two and a half years, semi-isolated from friends and adherents, he struggled to hold together his following when many were dissatisfied with his defeatist stance. After his mother died in 1916 and support for her forty-six-year-old son from her official pension ceased, he became impoverished as well.[87] He had some company from fellow refugees from the war, from Russia and other nations, and a number of young evaders of military service in surrounding countries created an atmosphere of radicalism. However, Lenin seems to have built up no consequential following. He enjoyed the amenities of Swiss "bourgeois" culture; indeed, he was lavish in praise of it.[88] He lived to some extent in a dream world, wherein half a dozen men of no particular status could get together, call themselves a party conference, issue an antiwar manifesto, and change history. With no sense of the ridiculous he preached to the Swiss the absolute necessity for them to have an immediate socialist revolution.[89]

At this low ebb in Lenin's fortunes, a future Soviet police boss under Stalin, V. R. Menzhinsky, characterized Lenin and his group as follows in an emigré paper in Paris:

> Lenin is a political Jesuit who over the course of many years has molded Marxism to the aims of his movement. He has now become completely confused. . . . Lenin, this illegitimate child of Russian absolutism, considers himself not only the natural successor to the Russian throne when it becomes vacant, but also the sole heir of the Socialist International. . . . The Leninists are not even a faction, but a class of party gypsies, who swing their whips so affectionately and hope to drown the voice of the proletariat with their screams, imagining it to be their unchallengeable right to be the *drivers* of the proletariat.[90]

Lenin was, however, able to develop and expound his ideas of revolution in the war situation, ideas that served him well in Russia in 1917, and in this way he much increased his authority as a radical leader.

It was Lenin's strong point to give Marxist revolutionism a new and stronger basis by laying the blame for war, a venerable but newly horrible institution, on capitalism. While opposing the war, he refused, unlike other socialists, to urge pacifism and a negotiated settlement, but urged the soldiers to turn their guns on their officers and the warring peoples to convert the "imperialist" war into a civil war and make a socialist revolution. Only by ending capitalism, Lenin repeated, could war be ended. In this position Lenin stood on the left of the left wing of European socialism, and his stance was not at first popular.

To support his equation of war with capitalism, Lenin put together in 1916 his most widely influential book, *Imperialism, the Highest Stage of Capitalism*. For it he drew freely on the works of the British liberal journalist J. A. Hobson, and the German socialist Rudolf Hilferding, to whom he acknowledged indebtedness, and on the work of the somewhat independent Bolshevik Nikolai Bukharin, which Lenin did not acknowledge.[91] In the analysis of these authors, which was reworked by Lenin, capitalism had changed since the time of Marx by cartelization, the replacement of industrial capital by finance capital, and the inevitable outreaching of this monopolistic capital to markets and investments abroad. This led to the exploitation of weaker countries and to colony-grabbing; war was hence due to conflicts of financial interests. The people, as Lenin endlessly stated, were bleeding for the profits of the bankers.* Lenin also furnished an explanation for the failure of revolution to arrive in the capitalist countries as Marx had predicted: the capitalists could bribe their workers into passivity with a share of the profits gleaned from oppressed peoples.

The ideas of *Imperialism* were also useful for revolution in Russia. In the Leninist view, there were not only exploited classes but exploited nations. Although Russia was actually as imperialistic a nation as any, it could be claimed that it was exploited because of the large amount of foreign capital in its economy. Russia was semicolonial, and the chain of world capitalism was to be broken not where capitalism was most advanced but at its weakest link. The Russian workers could have the honor, which had been renounced by the cowardly Social Democrats of the West, of inaugurating the new age.

Lenin's call for civil war was decidedly impractical, since ordinary soldiers were too patriotic to desire to aid the enemy by attacking their own governments; thus he received little support. Even at a conference of dissident socialists who were rejecting the Second International, held at Zimmerwald, Switzerland in September 1915, out of thirty-eight participants only eight delegates, including Lenin, Zinoviev, and Radek, formed the leftist group. But Lenin's forthright

---

*The enormous contemporary influence of Lenin's work derives not, of course, from its explanation of war, but from its argument that the advanced industrial countries are inevitably exploitative of the weaker ones, whether they are formally colonies or not, and that some nations are rich because others are poor.

condemnation of the war became more attractive as the futility of the slaughter beset consciences. At a larger conference at Kienthal in April 1916, the radical formula drew much more support. Lenin was becoming a widely known and recognized spokesman.

Nonetheless, at the beginning of 1917 Lenin had little to show for his twenty-two years of political activity. He hardly had a party, either in Russia or abroad; the core of his movement was only a few score loyal friends. All of his talk and writing about revolution had apparently changed nothing at all. He pessimistically told the Swiss, "We of the older generation may not live to see the decisive battles of this coming revolution."[92] But the catastrophe of war was breaking down the barriers to radical change and to the seizure of power by such an organized and dedicated action group as Lenin dreamed of.

Chapter 3

The Conquest of Power

THE END OF TSARISM

Woes, not industrial development, prepared Russia for revolution.[1] The legitimacy of the tsarist government rested primarily on success and strength; it was accepted because Russia could be strong only (it was generally believed) under an autocratic government. But the war proved the tsarist government to be weak and a failure in the great national enterprise. The army suffered defeat after defeat, with painful losses of manpower and of territory; refugees for whom little or no provision had been made flooded into the cities, especially the capital. Mobilization created shortages at home without adequately supplying the soldiers, and inflation ran wild. Many people suffered a sharp drop in their living standards, while a few grew rich from profiteering. Transportation broke down. By late 1916 the police were warning of the danger of riots because of hunger. Strikes and lockouts multiplied to an epidemic by February 1917.

The autocratic government, which claimed to manage everything, was inevitably blamed when everything went wrong. Nicholas assumed command of the armies at the front and hence personal responsibility for their sufferings. Rumors floated around about pro-German circles at court, and there were suspicions about the unpopular German-born (but probably quite loyal) Tsarina Alexandra. The evil reputation of the eccentric monk Rasputin, who swayed the empress and through her the tsar, did more to discredit the monarchy than all the propaganda of the revolutionary parties. As early as 1915 there were schemes for getting rid of the tsar, who was regarded as an incubus on embattled Russia.[2]

The tsarist government fell, however, not so much because of its concrete failures as because of its inflexibility and inability to adapt its power structure. In the war the people were organizing, in business, industry, and civic groups,[3] while the tsarist government was becoming more fearful of its people. The liberals, convinced that the tsar and tsarina were obstacles to victory, wanted to use the emergency to bring constitutional government; the tsar, urged by his wife to demonstrate his masterful character, wanted to crush all opposition and restore the autocracy unimpaired. As the situation deteriorated, the court became more afraid of strong ministers. Latter-day appointees were far below the caliber of such capable servants of the crown as Witte and Stolypin. In February 1916 the tsar defied public opinion by appointing as Chief Minister, and later also as Foreign Minister, Boris Stürmer, who was known for his unsavory dealings, lack of enthusiasm for the war, and advocacy of total autocracy. Toward the end of the war the government, fearful of popular organizations to help the war effort, was fighting not defeatists but defensists.[4] Even princes and grand dukes separated themselves from the ruling clique and murdered Rasputin on December 17 (30), 1916.* The more calls were raised for a responsible ministry, however, the more stubbornly Nicholas resisted.

It should not have been surprising that when the government was tested, no one was prepared to defend it. Minor disorders beginning on February 24 (March 9) quickly mushroomed. The garrison was composed mainly of men who were unfit for the front, and included many sick and wounded, and unindoctrinated recruits. Ordered to suppress the riots, they hesitated, then refused to fire on the civilians. The tsar might still have saved the situation by naming a ministry that would have restored public confidence. Instead, the weak-willed but stubborn Nicholas dissolved the Duma, thereby removing a possible bulwark of order. The bulk of the army followed the Petrograd garrison in refusing to support the tsar. The leading generals saw no alternative to calling upon him to abdicate, and the three-hundred-year-old dynasty was at an end. The soldiers brought about the February revolution as they were to make the more celebrated one in October.

The tsar signed away all his precious powers without protest, his brother renounced the doubtful honor of assuming the crown, the ministers disappeared, and the officers absented themselves in fear of their mutinous troops. The stage was left to the radicals.

The radicals picked up the power that the old regime was not capable of holding. They had not won it. The organizations that had for so many years been plotting, scheming, and propagandizing to achieve the overthrow of autocracy—the Socialist Revolutionaries, Mensheviks, Bolsheviks, and others—had nothing to do with its demise. The end was so sudden that some historians have questioned whether there was not a hidden hand behind the quickly spreading disturbances. There is some possibility that tsarist circles incited the riots as a provocation that would provide an excuse for repressive measures.[5] On the other

---

*Dates of this period are given according to the old (Julian) calendar in use in Russia until January 1918 with Western (Gregorian) dates in parenthesis.

hand, George Katkov and Stefan Possony were convinced that the German government had promoted the uprising.[6] This is not impossible; there were German agents in Petrograd, and they had been helping to organize and finance strikes. Lenin, on the contrary, in a letter of March 20 from Switzerland, attributed the revolution to "the British and French embassies and their connections," which had been striving to keep Russia bleeding for imperialistic purposes.[7] Yet it may well be that the overthrow of Russian autocracy was one of history's greatest manifestations of the spontaneity Lenin hated.

LENIN TAKES CHARGE AND FAILS

The generals who removed the tsar decapitated the state, depriving it of its role as the focus of legitimacy and authority, without any thought about what was to be put in its place. They assumed that Russia would more or less follow the West toward more modern, constitutional government. It is not impossible that under more favorable conditions the shock of the world war might have brought Russia the free and stable political system the educated classes almost unanimously hoped for. But the liberals were too weak and uncertain to navigate the stormy seas of 1917. After the old autocracy was cut down, disorders increased month by month until Lenin was able to establish a new autocracy.

At first the country seemed bathed in the sunshine of the new freedom. As the first issue of *Izvestiia*, February 28 (March 13), put it, "the Russian people has shaken from itself the age-old slavery." To maintain order, however, the Duma, which had been disbanded on February 26 (March 11), remained informally in session and set up an ad hoc committee to take charge. It called itself the Provisional Government. Although this body had been elected by no one, it was considered democratic because of its general commitment to law, liberties, and free elections. Through it the Russian intelligentsia came to power. For the most part, the Provisional Government was composed of eminent public figures. Its Premier, Georgi Lvov, was a leader of the Cadet party; the Foreign Minister, Pavel Miliukov, was an outstanding historian as well as a liberal spokesman. Perhaps the most influential member of the Provisional Government, however, was Alexander Kerensky, a brilliant socialist lawyer and former leader of the Trudovik (Labor) party in the Duma.

Kerensky's special influence in the Provisional Government derived from the fact that he was also an important figure in the Petrograd Soviet; in effect, he was its representative in the government. The soviet was convened on February 27 (March 12), just as tsarist power in the capital was disintegrating (three days before the abdication of Nicholas). A Provisional Executive Committee was formed by members of the Menshevik-dominated Central Workers' Group who had been released from prison in the course of the disorders. The committee called for the election of delegates, one from each one hundred workers in factories and each armed company.[8] The soviets (others were rapidly established across Russia) were inspired by the powerful institutions that had been invented in 1905. But there was a critical difference. The soviets of 1905 had represented workers only. In 1917 Petrograd was crowded with soldiers, and they were included in the soviet for the conscious purpose of winning them to the side of the revolution. Indeed, because of the rule that one deputy would be elected for each unit, the soldiers were overrepresented; they composed perhaps two-thirds of the approximately twenty-five hundred members.[9]

The Petrograd Soviet also differed from its predecessor in that it was dominated from the first by radical parties and politically activist intellectuals. In the flux, partisan affiliations were at first unclear, but Mensheviks, led by the Georgians Irakli Tseretelli and Georgy Chkeidze, and the Socialist Revolutionaries, led by Viktor Chernov, predominated; initially there was only a sprinkling of Bolsheviks. The soviet, like traditional radical parties, immediately undertook to issue a paper, which it called *Izvestiia* ("Information").

The St. Petersburg Soviet of 1905 had tried to exercise considerable semi-governmental authority for a short time in direct competition and conflict with the government. In 1917, the leftists, Socialist Revolutionaries, Mensheviks, and members of various minor parties assembled in the soviet were prepared neither psychologically nor ideologically to call themselves a government nor to assume the responsibilities of rule. Yet the soviet represented the power that had cast down the tsar, and its leaders were politically conscious activists. Consequently it adopted an anomalous policy of working for socialist goals, protecting the rights and interests of its constituents, and controlling or checking the Provisional Government while renouncing formal sovereignty.

In its first proclamation,[10] the Petrograd Soviet called for a constituent assembly to be elected by universal suffrage, and two days later the Provisional Government promised to summon it. The soviet also practically claimed to be a government at the beginning of its existence:

> The Soviet, sitting in the Duma, has set for itself as its main task to organize the popular forces and to fight for the consolidation of political freedom and popular government.

> The Soviet has appointed commissars to establish the people's authority in the wards of Petrograd. We invite the entire population of the capital to rally at once to the Soviet, to organize local committees in their wards, and to take into their hands the management of local affairs.[11]

A little later *Izvestiia* was writing, "The Soviet of Workers' and Soldiers' Deputies will not resign what it regards as its right and duty—the control of the activities of the Government."[12]

Even more ominous for the Provisional Government was the soviet's claim to speak for the soldiers of the garrison and indeed for the army as a whole. The famous Order No. 1 of March 2 (15) gravely undercut the authority of the officers, decreed the election of committees throughout the forces, and reserved the right to countermand orders of the military authorities of the government, to control the issuance of arms, and to protect the Petrograd garrison from removal, on the grounds that it was needed to shield the revolution from counterrevolutionary movements.[13] The Provisional Government, on taking office, felt obliged to pledge no disarming or removal of the garrison.[14] It was thus saddled from its inception with a radical and politically organized military force that was irremovably occupying its capital. To make their revolution in October the Bolsheviks had only to reassert the claims of the soviet in March.

At first, however, Lenin's followers had no such purposes. The few Bolsheviks in Petrograd before the arrival of Lenin on April 3 (16) were divided and uncertain. They joined in the exultation of all the radical groups over the fulfillment of their old dreams, and they shared the almost universal assumption that the socialist revolution could follow the bourgeois one only after an extended preparatory period.[15] It was much too small a group to think seriously of taking power; its total membership across Russia was estimated, perhaps optimistically, at 23,600, with 60 percent of them workers and most of the rest white-collar employees, intelligentsia, and students.[16]

Immediately after the fall of the tsar, a group of leftist Bolsheviks in Petrograd wanted to follow Lenin's line in Switzerland and attack the Provisional Government and the war effort. But after a few days higher-ranking leaders arrived, those who had been of sufficient importance to have been exiled to Siberia. The most prominent of them, Stalin and Kamenev, took command and assumed the direction of *Pravda* from Shliapnikov, who was one of the very few workers among the higher Bolsheviks, and Molotov, then aged twenty-seven. These two had opposite destinies: Shliapnikov became spokesman for the Workers' Opposition and was eliminated; Molotov attached himself forthwith to Stalin and remained his faithful servant until the death of the dictator in 1953.

Under the guidance of Stalin and Kamenev, the Petrograd Bolsheviks went decidedly counter to Lenin's wishes, even refusing to print in *Pravda* three of his four "Letters from Afar."[17] At one time Stalin proposed an all-Russian government by soviets,[18] but the Bolsheviks took a qualified defensist position. Stalin wrote in *Pravda* on March 15 (28): "No, the free peoples will stand firmly at their posts, will reply bullet for bullet, shell for shell." A Bolshevik conference held on March 29 (April 11) asserted that a democratic revolution was enough for the time being and that the party should strive for a democratic workers'-peasants' republic, not the dictatorship of the proletariat. This was a position close to that of the Mensheviks, and there was strong sentiment for common action, if not complete unity, with the fellow Social Democrats. Without Lenin, the Bolsheviks would doubtless have rejoined the Mensheviks.

But Lenin dropped into their midst like a political bomb and gave Bolshevism the direction that led to the Soviet state. As soon as the news of the tsar's fall reached him in Zürich, he resolved to avoid the error of 1905 and plunged into the scramble for power. While sending off letter after letter urging the Bolsheviks in Petrograd to take a radical stance in favor of further revolution, he looked around for a means of travel from Switzerland, which was entirely surrounded by belligerent powers, to Russia. He had various schemes, such as disguising himself as a speechless Swede, but he apparently regarded travel through British-French-controlled territory as out of the question. At length it was arranged, through various intermediaries, for Lenin, Zinoviev, Krupskaya, Inessa Armand, and fifteen other Bolsheviks, plus six members of the Jewish Bund, three Mensheviks, and four others to travel by train through Germany. He went with visions; as Karl Radek said, "Vladimir Ilich is imagining himself Premier of the Revolutionary Government."[19]

Lenin's party crossed Germany and proceeded via Sweden and Finland to Petrograd. As an outspoken opponent of the Provisional Government who had been trafficking with the enemy, he feared arrest on his arrival. Instead, the broad-minded leaders of the revolution gave him a pompous reception befitting the return from exile of a major figure of Russian Socialism: a welcoming speech by Chkheidze, banners, a band, and an honor guard. Lenin promptly turned away from the official greetings to harangue the crowd about world revolution.

Within hours Lenin was telling his comrades that the Provisional Government must be destroyed, and in the next few days he shocked the party with his "April Theses." This outright revolutionary program called for a quick leap past capitalism into socialism, or something very near it, Populist style: governmental power to workers' and peasants' soviets, the abolition of the police, army, and bureaucracy, the election of all officials, the nationalization of all land and the conversion of estates to model farms, a change in the name of the party, and the establishment of a new international.[20] The day after these proposals were published in *Pravda*, April 8 (21), Kamenev labelled them "the personal opinion of Comrade Lenin," and wrote of Lenin's and everyone's duty "to submit to judgment of the revolutionary democracy his understanding of current events"— a sentiment quite alien to Lenin. Kamenev, who had renounced the party position on the war in 1915 when he, as a Bolshevik deputy, had been arrested for defeatism, urged cooperation with and "control" over the Provisional Government. Like Kamenev, most of the Bolsheviks at first found Lenin's activist program shocking. But he hammered away, and within a few weeks brought the party into line behind himself as an active claimant for revolutionary power.

Lenin's Theses were partly party program, partly mere demagoguery ("Abolition of the police, the army, and the bureaucracy," and so on); the Bolsheviks could propagate them freely because Russia was, as Lenin said at the time, "the freest of all the belligerent countries in the world."[21] At first many of the soldiers met Lenin's antiwar position with patriotic repugnance and were inclined to consider him a German agent. But as the war dragged on, opposition to it grew, and Bolshevik talk of an early peace began to appear more sensible and less treasonous.

Lenin's party rapidly became a strong alternative to the Provisional Government. Having made itself at home in the palace of a onetime ballerina mistress of the tsar, the party at its April conference elected a Central Committee of nine (smaller than the size the Politburo was to attain by 1924) that included Lenin, Zinoviev, Stalin, Kamenev, and Sverdlov, with the first three receiving votes in the order named. Membership rose quickly; in April it may have reached, by different estimates, forty-six thousand or seventy-nine thousand.[22] Lenin went around pounding his message into the masses of Petrograd, and Bolshevik slogans and catchwords were heard increasingly often.

The first demonstrations against the Provisional Government occurred on April 19 (May 2) in reaction to Foreign Minister Miliukov's promise to the Allies to keep up the war and his linking of Russia's fight to the acquisition of Constantinople ("Victory is Constantinople and Constantinople is victory—for this reason it is necessary to remind the people all the time of Constantinople.")[23] Nothing could have caused more doubts about the necessity of bleeding and suffering. Miliukov had to resign, and in the ensuing reorganization Socialist Revolutionary and Menshevik ministers joined the government. As a result they shared power, but they also shared responsibility and lost the ability to criticize the government effectively. That role was left to Lenin and his fellows, who equated the moderate socialists with the capitalist enemy, and to various loosely organized radicals, such as Trotsky, who was newly arrived from New York by courtesy of the Provisional Government.

Lenin's program was initially shocking not so much because of its specific proposals as because it was the first concerted attack on the generally accepted Provisional Government. The February 28 (March 13) proclamation of the Petrograd Soviet, for example, had used such strident language as the following:

> The provisional revolutionary government has the immediate and urgent task of entering into relations with the proletariat of the belligerent countries both for a revolutionary struggle of the peoples of all countries against their oppressors and enslavers, against royal governments and capitalist cliques, and also for an immediate end to the bloody human butchery which has been forced on the enslaved peoples.[24]

Ideas of workers' control and peasant land seizures were commonplace. But the Provisional Government was at first accepted as right and necessary, and the Bolsheviks gained respectability in the measure that its aura wore off.

By June Lenin had sufficiently asserted his authority to end the joint Bolshevik-Menshevik organizations.[25] The Bolsheviks gained much ground in the trade unions; at a June all-Russian trade-union conference, 36 percent of the delegates were Bolshevik.[26] The Bolsheviks were gaining popularity with the basically peasant masses by advocating not a Marxist-style nationalization of land, but what the peasants wanted—to grab land from richer neighbors.

In the First Congress of Soviets, which met on June 3 (16), Bolshevik representation was still not large, only 105 delegates, against 285 Social Revolutionaries and 298 Mensheviks (out of 882 in all),[27] but it was much more substantial than their representation in the Petrograd Soviet had been in March. Lenin was sufficiently emboldened to state a claim, for the first time, to Bolshevik rule. This congress, which brought together elected delegates from all Russia, might logically have asserted governmental power, as the soviet representing only Petrograd and its garrison could hardly do. But the Menshevik chairman, in an address to the meeting, rejected the idea and went on to say that no political party in Russia would assume power. Lenin jumped up to offer the services of the Bolsheviks. He was greeted with general laughter, but he proceeded to argue the Bolshevik capability to rule the great empire as the landlords and capitalists had ruled it.

With this confidence, the Bolsheviks made a bid for power, or at least tried to create revolutionary disturbances. They wished to call for a mass demonstration on June 10 (23), but pulled back when the Congress of Soviets forbade it; *Pravda* appeared with a large blank space in lieu of a manifesto. By decision of the congress, a general, nonrevolutionary demonstration was held on June 18 (July 1); it turned out to be a triumph for the Bolsheviks, whose followers were the most conspicuous and vocal.

The government brought the Leninists a better opportunity. Kerensky hoped to restore the morale of the army, which had been resting in the quiet the Germans had maintained on the front since the fall of the tsar, by sending it onto the offensive. Action began on June 16 (29), but the Germans were uncooperative and it was smashed in the first days of July. The government tried to cover up the extent of the disaster, but demoralization spread in the army and among the public. The government blamed the Bolsheviks and their defeatist propaganda for the defeat, but the public seems to have been readier to believe the Bolsheviks' contention that the war was futile and good only for the capitalists. Another crisis arose concurrently. On July 1 (14) the Provisional Government conceded broad autonomy to the Ukraine. Four Cadet ministers, who were better Russian nationalists than liberal democrats, resigned in protest next day. Disturbances began in the capital on July 3 and 4 (16 and 17), with the Bolsheviks in the lead. The mob became violent, if not revolutionary, shouting the Bolshevik slogan "All power to the soviets."

Just what part the Bolshevik leadership played in the riots and whether they seriously hoped to seize power in the crisis remain unclear. As in June, a revolutionary document was drafted on July 2 (15), but it was omitted from

Pravda at the last minute. If the leaders had such plans, they hesitated, the popular temper cooled, and loyal forces were brought into action. On July 4 (17) the government released documents purporting to prove that Lenin was a German agent. Two days later the Germans launched a new counterattack and routed the Russian army; it seemed that the riots must have been organized to coincide with the German push. The effect was electric. Loyal units went into action against the Bolsheviks, *Pravda* was smashed, and several leading Bolsheviks were arrested. Lenin hastened away, hid in the bushes, and slept in a haystack for two weeks before slipping across the border to Finland.[28] Trotsky, in contrast, asked to be arrested, saying that he was equally guilty of revolution making, and his request was granted.

The fiasco left the Bolsheviks weakened and discredited. They were isolated as never before, since the Mensheviks and Socialist Revolutionaries were supporting the repressions in the belief that the Bolsheviks had been engaging in disloyal activities. Nevertheless, the Provisional Government did not move decisively to crush Lenin's party. His organization remained largely intact, with Stalin the ranking officer at large. The Red Guard was not disbanded, and the Bolshevik network in the armed forces continued its work.

THE GERMAN CONNECTION

Many, including some Bolsheviks, thought that Lenin should face and disprove the charges of treasonous relations with Germany. But the Bolshevik party claimed that the leader of the revolutionary proletariat could not possibly place himself in the hands of class enemies. However, if Lenin fled while Trotsky defiantly asked to be arrested, this may have been because Lenin was guilty and Trotsky was not. The Provisional Government was in fact temperate in dealing with its opponents, and others who had been arrested had been fairly soon released unharmed. A trial might have been an excellent forum for the revolutionary leader, in the tradition of the heroic Populists turning their oratory on their oppressors. The rapidity with which Lenin disappeared as soon as the charges were publicized seemed hard to reconcile with his claims of innocence.

The Provisional Government produced affidavits and intercepted telegrams showing business between Lenin and a Pole named Ganetsky or Haniecki in Stockholm, who was an employee or partner of a known German agent, Helphand-Parvus, whom we have already encountered as the coauthor of the theory of permanent revolution. Anti-Bolsheviks willingly accepted the idea, which fitted their beliefs about the unscrupulousness of Lenin and his coterie; it became an article of anti-Communist faith, reinforced by Lenin's insistence on acceptance of the Treaty of Brest Litovsk in 1918, that Lenin was a German agent.

This attitude subsided, however. The evidence presented by the Provisional Government was circumstantial, somewhat ambiguous, and in part falsified. The government did not see fit to press the prosecution, partly because of mismanagement and partly because the leftist parties saw the affair playing into the hands of the conservatives;[29] and Bolshevik denials were loud and vehement. These denials were somewhat confused and not entirely plausible; for example, the Bolsheviks assured the world that Ganetsky just happened to be making an honest living working for Helphand.[30] The contention that Lenin was the victim of hostile slander, however, seemed not unreasonable, and with the passing of years and the growth in respectability of the Soviet state the idea dropped out of sight. To say that Lenin was financed by the kaiser's government seemed poor taste. But after World War II, German documents became available that showed that Lenin did receive funds from German sources on a large scale and over an extended period, particularly during the months when the Bolsheviks were clawing their way to power.[31] Why the Nazis never publicized this information remains a mystery.

It would have been most surprising if the Germans had not done whatever they could to promote Bolshevism in Russia. Subversion of the enemy and psychological warfare are as old as history, and Russia, with its social tensions, national minorities, sundry antitsarist movements, and ineffective government, was a tempting target. In the brief 1904–05 war, the Japanese gave support both to minority nationalities (for example, the Poles and Caucasians) and to antigovernmental parties, including the Socialist Revolutionaries. Even before the world war, Germany was making efforts to subvert tsarism by aiding national minorities, as was its alliance partner, Austria-Hungary. In the first years of the war, Germany was subsidizing labor unrest in Russia.[32] For a time, Germany tried to lure the tsar into a separate peace; when this policy seemed in December 1916 to have failed, however, the German Foreign Office turned its attention more definitely toward subversion. The removal in February of the unpopular tsar threatened to strengthen Russian patriotism and to make Russia a stronger enemy, but it also opened the gates to antiwar propaganda. The response of the Germans was to keep the front as inactive as possible; once they even practically apologized for a local victory.[33] They correspondingly increased their political warfare, hoping to win without fighting. In the general disorganization and relaxation, this was an easy way to conduct the war; in 1917 German agents were said to be everywhere in Petrograd.[34]

Of the many channels through which the Germans might operate, Lenin and his party were by far the most suitable. Lenin was the most thorough and emphatic opponent of defensism and the most capable organizer and propagandist, and was supported by a consequential party. The German authorities probably did not foresee, at least at first, that Lenin could gain control of the state, but they knew that he could hamper the Russian government in its prosecution of the war. Through his incitement to class warfare, he could disrupt Russian industry, especially munitions production. More important, he was able to spread defeatist propaganda and, through the Bolshevik agents, cells, and publications, to demoralize the armed forces. He had apparently already shown his willingness to do so in 1912 by negotiating with German authorities regarding propaganda in Russia in case of war.[35] He cooperated with the German government by propagandizing Russian prisoners while he was in Switzerland.

It would have been equally surprising if Lenin had refused to accept a German subsidy. He was aware of the implications of dealing with a power that was at war with Russia and was careful to minimize his role. For example, of the projected journey across Germany he wrote, "We cannot participate either directly or indirectly; our participation [in making arrangements] would *ruin* everything. But the plan itself is *very* good and *quite* right."[36] He was careful to have non-Bolsheviks accompany his party to reduce suspicions, and he dealt not directly with Helphand-Parvus but through intermediaries. But there is no reason to credit the Bolshevik assertions that Lenin would not have dirtied himself by taking money from a capitalist government; his party had received many contributions from Russian capitalists. Lenin wanted money and was not fussy about the source; he had relied heavily on "expropriations" (armed robbery) in 1906 and afterward, and he had resisted desisting even when the practice was condemned by a party congress. He seems to have been in contact with Japanese agents during the Russo-Japanese War and may have received money, as some other revolutionaries did.[37]

It would have been harder for Lenin to decline the kaiser's help because he needed money. This was inherent in the Bolshevik approach; organization requires monetary fuel to keep running. The professional revolutionaries Lenin wanted had to be paid revolutionaries, and contributions from Russian workers and the proceeds from the sale of newspapers and pamphlets were at the best skimpy—the sheets were usually given away. Moreover, Lenin was not at all reluctant to do what the Germans wanted. He regarded the military defeat of Russia, which was about the same as German victory, as desirable. He also had a great deal of admiration for German efficiency and organization, admiration that did not extend to Britain and France. German was his second language and came very easily to him. At the climactic moment, when he suddenly found himself atop a successful revolution, he used German to express himself. According to Trotsky, Lenin "pauses for the right word. 'Es schwindelt' ['It makes me dizzy'], he concludes."[38]

From the point of view of the dedicated revolutionary, of course, good and bad were to be measured by the effects of actions on the prospects of the revolution. This was the frank Bolshevik position, but the Bolsheviks were only somewhat more extreme than other parties. The Mensheviks and Socialist Revolutionaries also seem to have had some contacts with German agents; these contacts may have had something to do with the reluctance of these parties to press accusations against Lenin, either inside or outside the government. In sum, Lenin's conscience would probably have been troubled not by quietly receiving an invaluable assist from German sources, but by rejecting it for reasons of bourgeois sentimentality.

The details[39] are nonetheless of interest. Lenin probably received assistance through various sources in both the German Foreign Office and the general staff, but the principal mover and conduit was the shadowy figure of Alexander Israel Helphand, known also as Parvus. Born in White Russia of Jewish background, and once terrorized by a pogrom, he emigrated and became involved in the German Social Democratic movement. Around the turn of the century he aroused the admiration of Lenin and other Russians because of his assault on revisionism. From 1900 to 1905 he saw much of Russian exiles in Munich, aided in the printing of *Iskra*, and contributed articles to it. He and Trotsky met in 1904 and became very close friends. Helphand worked with Trotsky in the 1905 revolution, taking a radical position in favor of a "workers' democracy"; he viewed the Russian proletariat as better qualified than the German to lead the world to socialism.[40]

This revolutionary romantic in 1910 went to Turkey, gave up socialism in favor of personal capitalism, and became rich by obscure means. In 1914, however, on the eve of the war, he was machinating in the Balkans and indulging his lifelong aversion to the tsarist empire by assisting Ukrainian nationalists. After the war began, it became his firm purpose to break up the Russian empire and to bring revolution to Germany via Russia. He became a contractor for the German army and recruited Caucasian deserters.[41] In January 1915 he made a proposal to the German government for the partitioning of the tsarist realm into smaller states. He channelled money to the Romanian socialist leader Christian Rakovsky, who in 1917 joined Lenin's party and subsequently became Premier of the Ukraine and a purgee. Helphand also helped Karl Radek, who served the Soviet government as a publicist and diplomat, and David Riazanov, a Trotskyite and leading Soviet Marxologist.

Beginning in mid-March 1915, Helphand was probably the German government's chief advisor on revolutionary affairs in Russia. At the end of that month he received his first million marks.[42] Although he hoped for a union of revolutionary parties, he saw the Bolsheviks as the most effective group and hoped by generous application of money to make them a powerful tool of revolution. In May 1915 he went to consult with Lenin in Switzerland, but failed to reach agreement, probably because of a personality conflict; Lenin apparently received no money at this time, although Helphand was disbursing millions for propaganda in Russia.[43]

Helphand then went to neutral Copenhagen to set up, with German friends, a research institute to act as a cover for their activities in Russia. For this he recruited some Russian exiles, including M.S. Uritsky, who subsequently became the police boss of Petrograd. More effectively, he established a trading house for buying and selling goods from and to Russia, an operation that both added to Parvus's substantial wealth and provided channels for sending men, information, and funds. He laundered German money by using it to buy Western goods, then sold them in Russia and used the proceeds to finance subversion and strikes. In this business, Ganetsky, who had been a close associate of Lenin for several years and subsequently became the head of the Soviet State Bank, became his partner, almost certainly with Lenin's consent.[44]

Helphand managed to underwrite and organize some major strikes in Russia in January 1916 in the hope that they would grow into a revolution. When they failed to do so, the German Foreign Ministry cut back its support for revolution, largely limiting its activities to propaganda and leaflets; it hoped to negotiate a separate peace instead. Lenin, in Switzerland, was badly in need of funds at this time.

Subversion in Russia was very much on the agenda when the February revolution opened up indefinite possibilities, and the German government almost immediately allotted substantial sums to the cause. It became most urgent to help Lenin return to Russia. In this effort Helphand was joined by Alexander Keskeula, an Estonian nationalist and onetime member of the Bolshevik party who had gone to work for Germany, helped to organize support for Russian revolutionary groups, and supplied literature to the Bolshevik underground in Petrograd in 1916.[45] It was no novelty for Russians to traverse Germany; in 1915 several Russian exiles had been permitted to go through Germany to join Helphand's institute in Copenhagen. Helphand at first tactlessly tried to arrange for Lenin and Zinoviev to travel through Germany alone, but this Lenin refused. It was necessary to work out the arrangements for a larger group through intermediaries, including Swiss socialists. Ganetsky met Lenin and his party when they landed at Malmö, Sweden and accompanied them to Stockholm. Lenin, who a few weeks earlier had had trouble paying his landlady, had tele-graphed ahead a request for two to three thousand Swedish crowns for expenses.[46] Either from caution or personal distaste, Lenin did not have a personal meeting with Helphand, who went to Stockholm to confer with him, but let Ganetsky serve as go-between. Helphand also had a long discussion on April 13 with his old contact Radek.

Soon after Lenin's passage through Sweden, Helphand reported on it to the Foreign Ministry in Berlin. The ministry, Helphand, and Lenin shared the same objectives. The ministry saw the victory of the radical movement as the way to get a favorable peace with Russia; Helphand wanted to see socialism in Russia as a means of bringing socialism to Germany; and Lenin wanted the same things, but with himself as leader and with a slight change of emphasis.

During the months of Lenin's struggle for power, Helphand was a frequent traveller to Stockholm, where he maintained contact with the Bolshevik Foreign Mission stationed there. This mission consisted of Radek, Ganetsky, and V. V. Vorovski, all three of whom were of Polish origin. The Bolshevik Foreign Mission was also able to use the communications channels with Russia that Helphand had developed.[47]

How much money was transferred remains a secret that will probably never be revealed, but it was certainly many millions of dollars, a huge sum of money considering the times and Russia's poverty.[48] Helphand-Parvus seems to have been proud of his part in the affair. After the Bolshevik revolution he wished to join the triumph, his purposes having diverged from those of the German government. Presumably he expected to occupy an important position in the Soviet government, but Lenin would have no part of the corpulent bon vivant, socialist writer, financial manipulator, and intriguer. Rejected, Helphand turned bitterly against the Bolsheviks, whom he called ignorant, non-Marxist despots.[49]

The German government esteemed its success. State Secretary Kühlmann wrote to army headquarters on September 29, 1917: "Our work together [our support of the revolutionary movement together with the General Staff] has shown tangible results. The Bolshevik movement could never have attained the scale or the influence it has today without our continual support."[50] Not long after, on December 3, he restated this message: "It was not until the Bolsheviks had received from us a steady flow of funds through various channels and under different labels that they were able to build up their main organ, *Pravda*, to conduct energetic propaganda, and appreciably to extend the previously narrow base of their party."[51]

The Bolshevik seizure of power was a near thing, as several writers have pointed out and it is reasonable to assume that it would have been impossible without external material support. Thanks to a sound financial basis, the Leninists could publish in the summer of 1917 about 320,000 copies daily of forty-one newspapers and other periodicals, probably none of which was self-sustaining.[52] There was no revenue from advertising, and the workers could spend little for reading material even if they had desired to do so. The Bolsheviks also kept up a large organization of paid staff, armed a paramilitary organization, and induced workers to spend time drilling. They did all this, moreover, at a time when their previous chief source of income, donations from wealthy opponents of tsarism, had dried up.[53] Just as textile manufacturer Engels had made possible the study and writing of Karl Marx, a capitalist government made possible the triumph of Lenin's party.

It is commonly urged, even by critical writers,[54] that although Lenin was unscrupulous regarding the source of his funds, his policies were not influenced thereby. In other words, it is assumed that Lenin in no way acted for the

Germans; their purposes merely coincided at one stage of Lenin's career. It is certainly true that Lenin was not a German agent in the manner of Helphand, receiving detailed instructions, although there was ample opportunity for consultations. But it is hard to imagine that German financing had no effect on his actions. Lenin may have been immune to a sense of gratitude, but he may well have been concerned to keep the golden stream flowing and possibly to see it grow, and the Germans may conceivably have exerted pressures on him. Even a strong-willed politician is likely to be swayed by the source of his income.

If Lenin could count on bountiful assistance from an unconfessable source, this fact at the very least enlarged his choices in some directions and narrowed them in others. The support coming from abroad made it easier, for example, for him to take an antiwar position in April 1917 that was at first politically damaging. In subsequent months, the awareness that he could count on financial help may conceivably have emboldened him to drive for the overthrow of the Provisional Government. This German connection in the background may also have had something to do with the fact that in early 1918 Lenin went contrary to his reportedly stated ideas and to the feelings of most Bolsheviks, not to speak of most Russians, in demanding acceptance of the German terms at Brest Litovsk. Soviet foreign policy up to the defeat of Germany was notably pro-German. Lenin wanted to have German forces enter Russia to help oust the Allied forces rather than vice versa, and in August 1918 he entered into an accord that was very favorable to the tottering Reich.

No less important were the intangible but no doubt weighty psychological effects of the Bolshevik-German connection. The link helped Lenin materially but hurt him morally—and others, too, for a good many must have been aware of the unacknowledgeable reality. Because of this shady background, leading Bolsheviks must have felt more defensive, more inclined to defy the opinions and feelings of others, and more determined to hold onto the governmental power that shielded them from prosecution. If for no other reason, censorship was necessary to keep the stigma covered and to maintain the myth of the proletarian revolution. It is less remarkable that the Bolsheviks were intolerant of rival parties when they could suppose that loss of control of the government might mean hanging for treason. The suspicions also tended to isolate the Leninists from other parties and currents of opinion and to make both sides distrustful and reluctant to compromise and cooperate. Thus, the German connection strengthened the bias of Leninism toward falsification, terror, narrowness, and dictatorship.

THE SUMMER OF DISRUPTION

Because the Provisional Government failed to press its counterattack, and perhaps also because of the party's sound economic base, the Bolsheviks suffered remarkably little damage as a result of the abortive uprising, if it was really that, of July. The party's membership continued to grow steadily and sharply even while its leaders were in hiding or imprisoned; at the Sixth Congress, from July 26 to August 3 (August 8−16), the party claimed to have 240,000 members. The question of the quality of the membership, which had been so important in the controversies of the exile years, was forgotten; all who wished to enter were welcomed.[55] The Bolsheviks held about half the workers' section of the Petrograd Soviet and a fourth of the soldiers' section,[56] and these fractions rose steadily in the constant flux of membership in the soviet.

The Bolsheviks benefitted greatly from the formal adherence to the party, shortly after the July riots, of Trotsky and his band of followers, the "Mezhraiontsy" or "Interborough group," who had been edging into the Bolshevik camp since March. They formed a small party of antiwar internationalist revolutionaries who brought to Lenin's party no mass following, but a number of gifted leaders who made memorable contributions to the Soviet government in its first years. The group included Lunacharsky, Riazanov, Manuilsky, Pokrovsky, Uritsky, Yoffe, and Volodarsky. Trotsky, who had been elected to the Central Committee while he was in jail, became, by his oratorical skill and quick mind, the effective leader of the party in Lenin's absence.[57] Possessing great self-confidence, and characterized as "cool, snobbish, formal" in contrast to Lenin's simple manners,[58] Trotsky was something of a loner. He had long been on the fringes of Menshevism, but he broke with the Mensheviks because of their refusal to accept his theory of immediate, "permanent" revolution. He had many times crossed swords and exchanged bitter accusations with Lenin before 1917—a record that damaged him in the later contest with Stalin—but in 1917 he saw Lenin and the Bolsheviks following his theory and approach, so he aligned himself with them and joined the party. In 1915 Lenin had tried to keep Trotsky out of the Zimmerwald Conference,[59] and it was something of a comedown for Lenin to accept the ambitious young revolutionary (who was nine years his junior) into the party as a near-equal in 1917. He was perhaps led to this acceptance by the need for a driving leader at the party center while he was in hiding across the Finnish border.

After the July Days, however, Lenin seemed practically to give up for the time being his hopes of grasping power. Instead of calling for "all power to the soviets," a real and widely supported program, he agitated for an improbable insurrection of armed workers under Bolshevik leadership. There was considerable opposition in Bolshevik ranks to this change of policy, and it was probably a blunder. But Lenin, who was apparently angered by the unhappy turn of events, called the soviets "the figleaf of counterrevolution" and declined to reinstate the slogan "all power to the soviets" until well after the Bolsheviks had become the largest party in them.

Meanwhile, as the summer ripened, everything was going badly in the land; the days of tsardom were coming to seem the good old days. Production was falling as workers, encouraged by the Bolsheviks, formed factory committees, interfered with management, or chased managers away and tried to run the works. The railroads were collapsing. Taxes were difficult to collect, and the government was near bankruptcy. Inflation roared on ever faster as the government paid its way by printing money. There were increasing food shortages in the cities.

Bread was short partly because the countryside was in a state of growing unrest as the peasants tired of waiting for land distribution. It is not easy to understand why the agrarian question was so acute, since all accounts agree that the peasants already had about four-fifths of the country's arable land (although this represented less than half of the total landholdings), and in most places their holdings were rather large by European standards.[60] But the peasants had wild hopes and violent hatreds, and they increasingly lashed out to satisfy their instincts by land seizures that the government could neither halt nor sanction. Millions thus became radicalized, in the sense that they feared the loss of their land and punishment if conservative authority should ever be restored.

The army, too, fell apart. Since June the Bolsheviks had a military organization to penetrate the armed forces, and their defeatist message found ever more listeners. The failure of the touted July offensive was fatal to the government's authority with the soldiers. The officers and men turned away for opposite reasons, the former because of the government's failure to prosecute the war more vigorously, and the latter because of its insistence on prosecuting the war. The soldiers believed that the continuing futile war was postponing their hopes for social justice and their return to the villages where they wanted to share in the land grabbing. The stream of deserters swelled, and having deserted, these soldiers became enemies of the established power, probably contributing to the disorders in the countryside or, if they went to the cities, becoming potential recruits for the Bolsheviks (who promised an early end to the war) and supporters of the drive to overthrow the government.

The conservatives naturally became alarmed, and tension rose within the Provisional Government. At this juncture, on August 21(September 3), the Germans made a breakthrough on the weakly defended front, taking Riga and posing a threat to Petrograd. General Lev Kornilov, who had been named commander at the front in the wake of the July affair, determined to restore discipline and requested special powers. Partly because of misunderstandings and poor communications, Kornilov undertook to march on the capital and establish a military dictatorship. He accused the Provisional Government of working with the Germans under Bolshevik pressures, and he promised not only to hang the Bolsheviks but also to scatter the soviets.[61]

Kornilov appealed to the rightists since he was, in their eyes, the only man capable of putting the army back into shape, defending Russia, and ending incipient anarchy. But he frightened moderates and socialists of all kinds; he seemed to incorporate precisely the threat of military counterrevolution they had always learned to fear as the gravest danger to the power of the people. The frightened Kerensky sought all possible support, including the Bolsheviks. The soviets and unions mobilized their forces, and Kornilov was defeated by the mass movement; there was no real fighting because no soldiers were willing to fight for the commander.

Lenin rejoiced over the Kornilov affair, correctly foreseeing that it made possible the Bolshevik victory that came eight weeks later.[62] Kornilov's defeat ended the authority of the old officers, who for the most part had favored him. The soldiers viewed their officers as counterrevolutionaries and lynched many of them. Soldiers in the rear refused orders to go to the front, and soldiers at the front became more demoralized when no replacements came. Desertions further increased, as soldiers listened to the Bolshevik siren song of land, freedom, and peace.

The government became increasingly divided. The moderates, liberals, and conservatives were struck by fear and resentment. Many had hoped for Kornilov's success, and they were convinced that the conflict was at least partly the fault of Kerensky, who had at first wanted help against the radicals and had then changed his mind. The moderate socialists, on the other hand, turned away from the middle-class leaders who countenanced a military coup. Although Kerensky was legally something like a dictator, he had no reliable military forces after the Kornilov episode and little solid political backing.

The only beneficiaries were the Bolsheviks. They had received arms for the Red Guard to use in fighting Kornilov, and they kept them. They had recovered from the discredit that had clung to them since the July days, and the imprisoned Bolsheviks had been released. Above all, the Bolsheviks profited morally. It seemed confirmed that the danger to the Russian Revolution, as to the French Revolution, could come only from the right and the military, and it seemed essential to guard against any underhand moves by the conservatives. In particular, it seemed necessary to keep the radically inclined garrison in Petrograd to defend the revolution, and it was ostensibly for this reason that the Bolsheviks moved on October 25 (November 7).

The authority of the self-proclaimed Provisional Government became more provisional and conditional in the weeks after Kornilov's defeat. In its division it seemed increasingly unable to make decisions on the major questions of the day: the distribution of land, the organization of the economy, the rights of minority nationalities, the political constitution, and the conduct of the war. The liberals felt unable to withdraw from the war, yet the government lacked the strength to wage it. Kerensky finally got around to declaring Russia a republic on September 1 (14), but the commission that was to prepare a Constituent Assembly dawdled for months, not scheduling elections until November; waiting for the assembly became a convenient excuse for postponing decisions. In August a big state conference was called, with representatives from the soviets, parties, unions, industry, and so on, but the oratory only increased the divisions. Kerensky tried to build support again in September with a Democratic Conference of 1150 delegates, but it only demonstrated the basic split: the right wanted law and order, the left, democratization and the expected benefits of the revolution.

The Provisional Government had given up the means of rulership used by the tsars (and later by the Bolsheviks). It could only exhort, not discipline. It had no censorship; the most inflammatory writings circulated with total freedom. It had little in the way of police, and the jails had been largely emptied. Hence, it could hardly hope to restore order, and the conservatives consequently began to give up on it. Believing that Kerensky must go, they in effect sided with the Bolsheviks, whom they did not regard as dangerous because they considered them incapable of ruling. On the other hand, Kerensky did not feel able to govern without or against the "bourgeois" or upper-class elements. His last government contained three Socialist Revolutionaries, four Mensheviks, four Cadets, and six non-party members, who were mostly conservatives (four of the ministers were well-known millionaires while Trotsky was promising to give soldiers and workers the fur coats of the rich).[63] The Mensheviks and Socialist Revolutionaries[64] felt frustrated as they bore responsibility for the government that disappointed their followers. They saw the masses swinging to the Bolsheviks, with their radical demagogic slogans, which gained attractiveness as the situation deteriorated. The left wings of both parties tended to split away, forming the Left Socialist Revolutionaries and the Menshevik Internationalists (led by the old Menshevik figures Martov and Dan). Both groups took positions that were close to those of the Bolsheviks, although the first faction was agrarian-oriented and the second was repelled by Bolshevik tactics.

Hiding just across the border in semiautonomous Finland, Lenin watched the sinking of the Provisional Government with eager anticipation. Fretting at his enforced inaction, he wrote repeatedly to the Petrograd organization and, when they did not heed him, to his followers behind the backs of the leadership, urging action, damning Kerensky and his followers in every possible way (even accusing them of selling out to the Germans), and whipping up hopes and fears. Forgetting his old caution and obsession with organization, he took up the ideas that best suited the popular desires, not the Marxist notions of nationalization of the land and the formation of state farms, but the popular demand for land for the peasants, not the need to turn the imperialist war into a civil war, but "peace without annexations or indemnities." Excited by the smell of revolution, he decided that Russia had the most glorious opportunity in history to strike the great blow for the liberation of mankind. To square revolution in Russia with Marxism, he postulated early proletarian revolution in advanced countries, especially Germany—the theory of uninterrupted or permanent revolution, which was ridiculous in the light of Marxist historical materialism, but beautifully suited to Russian Marxists eager to have their revolution.[65]

The most effective plank of the Bolshevik platform was the promise of a quick peace. This issue more than any other aroused passions. It was the problem that divided both Socialist Revolutionaries and Mensheviks and immobilized and weakened the Kerensky cabinet. Loathing for the war brought to the Bolsheviks a multitude of persons who knew little of the Bolshevik political ideas and organization or who even disliked them, not only soldiers who had no desire to see the front, but a host of antiwar activists, many of them basically individualists who were later to fall away from Leninist orthodoxy.[66] To be for peace was almost equivalent at this time to being a Bolshevik.

In this period Lenin completed the writing of one of his longer tracts, *State and Revolution*, an effort to state his long-term aspirations and to explain how the Bolsheviks could hope to govern.[67] It was simple, Lenin said in effect; whatever government would be necessary under socialism could be easily managed by the people through their elected soviets. Unless *State and Revolution* is taken to be mendacious opportunism designed to deceive the masses, it is a remarkable testimony to the duality of Lenin's thinking. He hardly mentioned his lifelong preoccupation, the party, and laid full trust in the masses as potential rulers. It is practically anarchistic, a naive vision of nongovernment by soviets or communes (Lenin related the soviets to the Paris Commune, which Marx regarded as an example of incipient socialism) almost magically transforming Russia. This vision, like much of Lenin's *Imperialism*, was in large part borrowed from Bukharin;[68] in it, the "dictatorship of the proletariat" would be dissolved into the rule of the masses. There would be no state, because the state was regarded as an expression of class interest. There would be no violence, no compulsion, no conscription. In the nonbureaucracy all would take turns at the simple tasks of management.

The hardships of the moment made it easier to dream such dreams, but at this time Lenin seemed to have been converted to elementary Russian radicalism, the authentic Russian traditions of violent thought and action that had become outmoded in a hundred years of Westernization but resurged when Russia was de-Westernized as a result of its troubles and thrust back to a more primitive age. These were wild days, when sailors lynched people on the streets because they were well dressed, and the poor vented their class hatred for the educated and privileged and joined the Bolsheviks.[69] According to Bakunin, the world of the Russian Revolution was a world of robbers.[70] Despite their nonproletarian origins, Lenin and Trotsky were sufficiently imbued with ideology to see themselves as spokesmen for the masses and leaders of this violent world.

The Mensheviks shrank back, as did most of the educated except those who were most impassioned against the war. Society was not so much radicalized as polarized. Not only the Bolsheviks, along with the parties farthest to the left, the Anarchists and Maximalists, but also the Cadets, the most conservative party that could function, gained adherents. The regular Socialist Revolutionaries and the mainstream Mensheviks lost members. The moderates felt that the revolution had gone far enough and wanted to pull back; the masses were disappointed that it had not gone further.[71] There was a "flight of intellectuals" from the Bolshevik party, too,[72] a withdrawal of the theoretical revolutionaries who took fright at dirty workmen and common soldiers; the loss of middle-class support left the Bolsheviks nearer the street radicals.

But there were many more poor than comfortably situated people, and Bolshevik popularity grew rapidly during September and October. In September the Bolsheviks gained control of the soviets in both Moscow and Petrograd. On August 31 (September 13) the Petrograd Soviet passed a Bolshevik resolution against the Provisional Government by a margin of 279 to 115 (with 51 abstaining), and on September 9 (22) Trotsky became its Chairman. In general, the Bolsheviks by late October dominated most of the soviets in industrial areas and the garrison soviets, with special strength in the Petrograd, Moscow, Ural, and Siberian regions and in the northern front and the fleet, while the Socialist Revolutionaries prevailed in front-line and village soviets, and the Mensheviks retained superiority only in Georgia.[73] The Bolsheviks were also gaining control of the trade unions; in June they controlled 36 percent of the delegates to an all-Russian trade-union conference, and in September, 58 percent.[74] Most remarkably, in the Moscow elections for the municipal Duma, the Bolsheviks garnered 51 percent in September against only 12 percent in June.

With the soviets thus Bolshevik-dominated, the incapacity of the Provisional Government was compounded. Since the early days when the Petrograd Soviet had claimed a general right of control and had acted virtually as a cogovernment, the soviets had tended to lose ground. The participation of the Menshevik and Socialist Revolutionary parties in the government made it the political center, people became accustomed to seeing the Provisional Government as indeed a government, and the election of local governments by universal suffrage undercut the soviets' claim to speak for the people. But the inadequacy of the government created such a vacuum that many local soviets, Bolshevik or not, were taking charge—or calling upon the All-Russian Executive Committee of the Congress of Soviets to do so—well before the Bolshevik revolution.[75] To seize power, the Bolsheviks had only to claim for the rather irregularly elected and manipulable soviets a little more authority than these had asserted at the commencement of the revolution.

THE COUP

Lenin, who hid himself like an animal pursued by hunters even though the Provisional Government had released its Bolshevik prisoners, bombarded his comrades with letters demanding instant action. From mid-September he was urging an immediate seizure of power on the basis of Soviet majorities in the principal city soviets. He was probably influenced to his frenzy by the fact that by September Finland was virtually ruled by Bolsheviks in local soviets and the

Baltic fleet was heavily Bolshevik.[76] As a voluntaristic Marxist, Lenin had strikingly little faith in the forces of history. He believed that it was necessary to grasp the opportunity lest it be forever lost. The German revolution was already flickering on Lenin's horizon; therefore Russia must move quickly.[77] Since Trotsky had become Chairman of the Bolshevik-controlled Petrograd Soviet, Lenin had restored the slogan "all power to the soviets"; but, in contradiction to this slogan, he was unwilling to wait for the meeting of the Second Congress of Soviets, which was scheduled for October 25 (November 7). His impatience was extreme; as though infused with Russian messianism, he was urging his colleagues on October 24 (November 6) that "a delay in the uprising is equivalent to death"[78]—a delay of a single day.

Those whom Lenin had trained as fellow professional revolutionaries were much more cautious, shyer in October than in July, when they had been weaker; they were probably chastened by the earlier failure. Lenin's letter (of October 12 [25]) specifically demanding seizure of power right away was burned by the Central Committee. Despite Lenin's insistence on an immediate coup, nearly everyone at the top of the party wanted to wait for the Congress of Soviets, in which the Bolsheviks, with their radical allies (chiefly the Left Socialist Revolutionaries), would have a comfortable majority. It was the general expectation that this congress would pass a resolution transferring the power to itself, and the government would have little choice but to yield.[79] Trotsky, among others, held this view, and he stated it in a speech to the Petrograd Soviet on October 17 (30).[80]

Two of Lenin's most faithful followers, Kamenev and Zinoviev, led the doubters. In a letter to major Bolshevik organizations dated October 11 (24), they realistically urged that an early coup was risky, that the party should build up its strength, and that the forces of history made haste unnecessary.[81] When a Central Committee meeting of October 15 (28) finally acceded to Lenin's demands and put the uprising on the agenda, although without fixing a date, Kamenev and Zinoviev demurred. They were influenced in part by the orthodox Marxist view that the bourgeois revolution needed at least a little time to ripen before socialist revolution was in order, but they were mostly deterred by practical considerations. As they stated, "We are told 1) that the majority of the people of Russia is already with us; and 2) that the majority of the international proletariat is with us. Alas!—neither the one nor the other is true, and this is the crux of the entire situation."[82] They did not see any great yen for uprising among the workers and soldiers; and they wanted both to build up the Bolshevik membership, which may have been about two hundred thousand,* and to wait for the indispensable German revolution, which Lenin would anticipate.

---

*In support of the call for a coup, Sverdlov, on October 17 (30), estimated it at four hundred thousand, but four months later, while emphasizing the rapid growth that was to be expected after the seizure of power, he put it at three hundred thousand. Rigby, *Communist Party Membership*, pp. 61–62.

Kamenev and Zinoviev were sufficiently concerned about the issue to break party discipline by discussing it in a nonparty paper, Gorky's *New Life*. In their article Kamenev and Zinoviev denied that the Central Committee had made plans for an insurrection, although rumors of such a move were floating everywhere. Lenin, however, exploded angrily at the "strikebreakers" and demanded their expulsion from the party. His anger seems to have been caused not so much by any disclosure of secrets—the Kamenev-Zinoviev article might have been considered a cover-up—as by the fact that the miscreants had revealed to the outside world dissension within the party. Kamenev and Zinoviev ruefully expressed their regrets (as they were to do several times for Stalin) and were permitted to return to party councils, even to take places on the newly formed Politburo.

It is not clear why Lenin was so desperate to get power independently of the Bolshevik-dominated soviets at the time when he was trumpeting the need to turn power over to the soviets, unless it was because of nervous anxiety. To move ahead of the soviets was to make a risky gamble of a fairly sure bet; he was depriving himself of the legitimacy of prior sanction by the generally respected soviet organization and narrowing his narrow power base. It may be that he felt violence was necessary to inaugurate a new era, but there is no specific evidence of any such ideological consideration. His general approach had seemed to be concentration on the principal thing, power, without much worry about how it was to be achieved; here the sane and sensible policy would seem to have been to wait a few days so that he could use the handy tool for the transfer of power, the Congress of Soviets.

In fact, the revolution did not come as Lenin planned and it was very nearly left to the Congress of Soviets. Nor was it made, strictly speaking, by the organization Lenin had crafted during many years, but largely outside it, nor by the Bolshevik old-timers but under the leadership of the neophyte Bolshevik Trotsky, who acted more in his capacity of Chairman of the Petrograd Soviet than as a Bolshevik party leader. In the crisis, such old comrades of Lenin as Krassin and Lunacharsky had practically disappeared from the scene; the doubters, Kamenev and Zinoviev, also had little part; and Stalin, while siding with Lenin on the desirability of action, seems to have done nothing more exciting than to edit and write for *Pravda*.[83] The party belatedly set up (October 16–17 [29–30]) a Military Center to work with Trotsky, but it seems never to have functioned.

Leadership of the revolution rested with a formally nonparty organization, the Military Revolutionary Committee of the Petrograd Soviet. This was the successor to the Committee for the Struggle against Counterrevolution, which had been set up to combat Kornilov. It was formed on October 9 (22) on the motion of a youthful Left Socialist Revolutionary ostensibly to look to the defense of Petrograd, but actually to oppose the expected attempts of Kerensky to reshuffle the garrison and remove radical, pro-Bolshevik units from the capital. It was chaired by Trotsky and was largely Bolshevik in composition, since the Mensheviks and rightist Socialist Revolutionaries declined to participate.

The Military Revolutionary Committee set about gaining the adherence of the garrison by playing on the soldiers' fears that they might be sent to the front. The soldiers stationed in Petrograd had a fairly comfortable life and undemanding duties under slack discipline; the last of their desires was to trade this tolerable existence for the uncertainties of the front. There were also many deserters among them, who had no reason to feel loyalty to the government.[84] They had been the recipients of much attention from the Bolsheviks, who had published special newspapers for the soldiers and had had agents circulating among them for months past, and the soldiers were quite prepared to listen to those who told them to look to their own welfare.

The Military Revolutionary Committee step by step secured its acceptance as spokesman for, and defender of, the garrison. The Bolsheviks spread rumors both that Kerensky wanted to send troops to the front and that he proposed to remove the capital to Moscow—a logical move—and surrender Petrograd. By October 17 (30) Trotsky was boasting that the soldiers were loyal not to the Provisional Government, but to the Bolsheviks.[85] On October 21 (November 3) Kerensky and his commanders gave substance to the fears by trying to shift some troops away from Petrograd; the garrison resolved to obey only the orders of the Petrograd Soviet. The control of the Military Revolutionary Committee thereafter spread rapidly. On October 22 (November 4) the committee proclaimed that the garrison should obey only orders countersigned by itself. Kerensky reacted and forced the committee to retreat slightly, but on October 23 it appointed commissars for all units in and around Petrograd.[86] The authority of the government was effectively at an end.

The government, which still thought itself strong, however, launched an ill-conceived counterattack that gave the Soviet state material for many a story and legend of revolutionary heroism.[87] First Kerensky went to the preparliament, to muster support in the crisis. This huge and widely representative body was convened on October 7 (20) as a successor to the Democratic Conference to provide a basis for the government; the Bolsheviks attended, contrary to Lenin's wishes, but immediately walked out with a bitter denunciation. Yet the preparliament failed to give Kerensky a vote of confidence in his hour of need, October 24. The moderate left blamed the government for the failure to meet popular demands and urged Kerensky to take the steam out of the revolutionary movement by announcing immediately plans for land reform and peace negotiations.[88] But Kerensky was only irritated by political advice and proceeded to try to summon loyal forces. Meanwhile the Bolsheviks proclaimed the danger of counterrevolution in the Kornilov manner; on October 24 Trotsky and the

Military Revolutionary Committee were still speaking of using force only to protect the garrison, the Congress of Soviets, and Russian democracy against hostile forces. Kerensky then took the initiative by ordering the closure of the Bolshevik papers. The Bolsheviks thereupon moved to protect their establishments and prevent Kerensky's forces from raising the bridges over rivers and canals to isolate sections of the city, and the battle was engaged.

Neither side had any large forces. The Bolsheviks could count on a handful of soldiers, some sailors (Left Socialist Revolutionaries and Anarchists as much as Bolsheviks) and about two thousand poorly trained Red Guards.[89] But inadequacy of the Red Guard was a minor factor compared to the mood of the Petrograd garrison.[90] No one, including the Bolsheviks, had any idea how little force Kerensky could command. Only a few military cadets, a women's brigade, and the police were ready to fight when the forces under Trotsky's leadership, on October 24 (November 6), began occupying strategic buildings and communications centers. After Lenin arrived on the scene shortly after midnight, the Bolsheviks really went onto the offensive to smash the old government.[91]

Kerensky fled the Winter Palace, leaving his ministers to be arrested, but he still thought he could recover by gathering units from outside Petrograd and from the front to crush the mutiny in the capital. The officers did not know enough about the Bolsheviks to be much afraid of them, however, and they regarded all socialists as sons of the devil. They were inclined to say good riddance to Kerensky and refused to use whatever influence they still retained to save him.[92] Even the Cossacks, who had traditionally been the pillars of authority in Russia, answered repeated pleas with the message that they were saddling their horses, but they never got ready for action.

Lenin had still a long road ahead and many obstacles to overcome before his power was complete, but he was now the commanding figure in Russia. It was something of a historical miracle. Lenin was a complete outsider who had never held any official position. He was the head of a small group of fellow outsiders, many of them non-Russians, who had built up a large following only in the turmoil of preceding months. In many ways he was at odds with the people who had uplifted him: antinationalist among nationalistic Russians, atheistic among a strongly religious folk, antitraditional in a society mostly wedded to tradition, an exponent of the rule of the proletariat where the proletariat, strictly speaking, consisted of less than 2 percent of the population, an authoritarian where prevailing aspirations were democratic or libertarian.

Yet if Lenin's seizure of power was in this sense abnormal, it was almost expectable in the abnormal conditions of 1917. The qualities that had led to Lenin's isolation in prewar years—his uncompromising truculence, dogmatism mixed with opportunistic flexibility, insistence on conformity, and wholehearted drive for power—led to his victory in the confused and trying circumstances of military defeat and economic and political breakdown.[93]

The liberals, who would have been hard pressed to rule Russia under the best of circumstances, came to power under the worst of circumstances. They were cut off by the war from their natural allies in the West and compelled, in the name of their commitment to liberalism, to carry on a war that was beyond their capacity. Lacking the institutions, habits, and consensus necessary for a functional democracy, they had had no time to develop suitable structures and attitudes. The liberals could not govern in the old way with the tools of despotism, and they could not forge new tools capable of transcending the Russian anarchy.[94] To the contrary, the liberal government had to bear the burden of a host of problems that were not of its making, and its failure was the more disillusioning as the illusions of freedom had been at first so euphoric.

In the uncertainty and confusion, in which the guideposts of the old order were gone and the Western-liberal approach came to seem unworkable, the fragmentation of the other parties was one of the Bolsheviks' greatest assets. On the left, the bickering idealists were unable to decide whether they preferred Marxism or the rule of law, and were unable to guide popular emotions; although they realized that Russia could not be governed democratically, they shrank from dictatorial methods. They refused to grasp power when it was almost thrust upon them because they knew they could not rule democratically. Those on the right increasingly feared change and tried to cling to the past; they demanded the maintenance of order without a basis on which that order could rest and preservation of the empire which they had no means of holding together. Even worse, perhaps, they failed to perceive the distinction between the equalitarian leftists and the authoritarian leftists (the Bolsheviks). Kerensky felt that he had to work with both of these groups, but they could not work together. His determination to keep the Cadets in the coalition excluded moves that would have earned the support of the moderate socialists,[95] while to the day of his overthrow he was fearful of the rightists and the generals.[96]

Most of the parties claimed to be socialist, but they had no clear idea what socialism was or how it was to be attained. The Socialist Revolutionaries had only a hazy notion of freedom and equality for the peasants; the Mensheviks were in the confusing condition of believing that socialism was unattainable, at least in the near future. The conservatives and liberals had only the vaguest ideas about how a new Russia should be organized and how it could be held together in freedom and equality. Only Lenin's party had a clear-cut direction, although what it in fact did when it had consolidated power bore little relation to the promises it had made while it was clambering toward power.

The glorious revolution, which was in reality a military coup, was not made in the name of the Bolshevik program or of proletarian power, but for the purpose of protecting Petrograd from counterrevolution and its garrison from being sent to the front. Soviet historiography has had to maintain contrary assertions: that the revolution represented an upsurge of the oppressed proletariat in the "weakest link of world capitalism," and that its success was due to the genius-leadership of Lenin, the master architect of revolution. The outcome was decided, as is usually the case in such uncertain times, by the men with guns.

But Lenin's party had the organization the others lacked. In 1917 it was by no means the disciplined, military-style revolution-making machine he had been trying to construct for many years, and the role Bolshevik discipline played in 1917 has probably been overrated.[97] But it had aspirations to be such a machine. It had a core of persons who were accustomed to working together under Lenin's leadership, and it was at least the most effective apparatus among the sundry chaotic parties, made possible not only by Lenin's theories but by German money.

It is unlikely, withal, that Lenin could have achieved power if the major groups had been strongly opposed. The other parties mostly disliked one another about as much as they disliked the Bolsheviks. The moderate socialists, despite all the venom of old quarrels, regarded Lenin as a fellow socialist, albeit somewhat harsh in his ways. He was opposed to what they opposed, autocracy, capitalism, big industrialists, bankers, landlords, the exploitation of workers and peasants, and oppression of the minorities. He used the egalitarian vocabulary and promised power to the proletariat. His activism and determination seemed admirable, especially when so many were pusillanimous.

Despite some warnings, the non-Bolshevik leftists could hardly imagine a "socialist" autocracy; autocracy was a product of the old regime, a danger that was posed by generals and reactionaries. With recollections of both the French Revolution and their own revolution of 1905, they feared above all a rightist reaction—a Bonaparte, or, as had been threatened a few weeks earlier, a Kornilov. This failure to appreciate the potentialities of Lenin's party was wholly understandable; despite his frequent references to "dictatorship of the proletariat" Lenin himself probably had no idea what would come out of his seizure of power.

The moderates saw less reason to try to block Lenin because they were convinced that the Bolsheviks could not possibly hold power. It was easy to suppose that the immensity of Russia's problems would quickly prove too much for this untried band. Perhaps, they thought, it was as well to let Lenin have a turn at it; he would show his inability to cope with shortages, war, disorders, and popular unrest, and then Russia could return to normal. (The bread ration was already down to about a quarter of a pound daily.)[98] But the many who refused to be alarmed at the idea of Lenin's power failed to realize how a determined minority could impose its will, given the reins of government, even though the economy continued to skid to such an extent that the hardships of the summer of 1917 came to seem like prosperity in retrospect.

Lenin and his followers were prepared to fill the vacuum of leadership. With none of the doubts and scruples of the more moderate parties, the Bolshevik party had a self-confidence or self-righteousness that gave it strength at every critical turn. The party's claims were rationalized or legitimized by Marxism as it was interpreted by Lenin, and its members regarded themselves as an unimpeachable elite, the vanguard of the working classes and hence of history. They could promise more with more conviction than anyone else, and the worse the situation was, the more credible their promises became—even the utopia of a wholly free and equal society of justice and abundance. Above all else, Lenin promised the war-weary people peace—not a peace of defeat but of revolutionary victory—and indefinite happiness thereafter.

Lenin also deserved to win in a way, because he represented realities that were close to Russian tradition at a time when Russia was isolated from the West and had turned back upon itself. To look to a Western political solution, as the moderate democrats and the Mensheviks had done, was to court futility. By rejecting the "bourgeois" revolution Lenin in effect rejected Westernization. The Provisional Government represented a true break with Russian tradition. Leninism, with all its Marxist-Western vocabulary, represented in basic ways a reversion to the old Russia; ultimately, under Stalin, it seemed to revert to the Muscovy of the centuries before modernizing currents had eroded the fullness of authority. This was a Russia of the monarch, and his servants picked for loyalty, ruling in the name of an idea without legal restraint; it was also a world of force and coercion, along with loyalty and discipline, of grand but factually unrealistic pretensions, of theoretical equality but an actual hierarchy of power. In this world qualities of rationality and moderation, Western virtues, ceased to be rewarding; Lenin's party rose by virtues that were more relevant to primitive Russia: self-confidence, group loyalty, and uninhibited determination.

Yet the victory of Bolshevism should not be considered in any way inevitable. It was a piece of fortune that would hardly have been possible had not many circumstances combined to open the way to power for Lenin's group: the incapacity and blindness of the tsar and tsarina and the decadence of the court, the fortunes of the war, the German eagerness to finance subversion, the Allies' lack of understanding of Kerensky's difficulties, the blundering Kornilov affair, the lack of dynamic leadership in other parties, the brilliance of Trotsky, and so forth. Nothing was inevitable.

THE PARTY BECOMES A GOVERNMENT

With Petrograd in Bolshevik hands, Lenin went before the opportunely assembled Second Congress of Soviets and proclaimed the overthrow of the Provisional Government and the transfer of power to the Congress of Soviets. The Mensheviks and majority, or rightist, Socialist Revolutionaries made their exit to protest the Bolsheviks' use of violence. This was an understandable reaction, since the ministers of these parties were under arrest, but it was politically naive. It left the stage and the institution of the soviets in the hands of the Bolsheviks, along with the Left Socialist Revolutionaries, who by staying had in effect allied themselves with the Bolsheviks. Before the walkout these two parties had a fairly slender majority of 370−380 out of 650 delegates. After it, the congress proceeded to approve the power seizure almost unanimously, in a glowing resolution about socialism, peace, and power for workers and peasants.[99] The Bolsheviks, holding about 300 places, were able to set up the permanent organ of the congress, the Central Executive Committee, almost as they pleased and to claim that it represented the working people of Russia.

Lenin allegedly said, "We shall now proceed to construct the socialist order,"[100] and then read a decree on peace without annexations or indemnities, on repudiation of secret treaties and self-determination of peoples. The assembled mass went wild with joy, assuming that the war was thereby ended. Lenin next proposed a decree abolishing private ownership of land without compensation and turning the land over to local organs for distribution to the peasants.[101] He also nominated a new ministry, which he rebaptized the "Council of Peoples' Commissars" (after the commissars of the French Revolution).* The next day the congress was sent home; "all power to the soviets" lasted approximately twenty-four hours. Lenin had no more use for the representative body of the people than the seventeenth-century tsars had had for the Zemsky Sobor. The Council of Commissars gave itself the authority to make laws.

The decrees on peace and land were followed by nationalization of the banks, a move that had long been on Lenin's agenda as a requisite for socialization of the economy, and a few days later by the "Declaration of Rights of the Peoples of Russia," including freedom of secession, and a decree on workers' control in industry. Except for the expropriation of banks, these measures were all incompatible with the long-term goals of Lenin's movement, but they accorded with the sentiment and needs of the moment and gave Lenin's party great popularity and a beginning of legitimacy. After them it seemed that to oppose the Bolsheviks was to propose to deprive the peasants of land, to desire to continue the war, to wish to restrict the minority peoples, and to favor bankers and industrialists.

These popular moves assisted the spread of Bolshevik (now nearly equivalent to Soviet) power across the vastness of the Russian empire. The provinces had in any case long been habituated to taking their directions from the capital, and the former government had disappeared. Bolshevik-dominated local soviets fell into line without delay; where the local soviet was not Bolshevik, an effort

---

*Lenin exulted over the name: "That's splendid; it smells of revolution" (Leon Trotsky, *Lenin: Notes for a Biographer,* p. 119). Stalin reverted to "Ministers" after World War II.

was usually made to change it or perhaps to bypass it with an ad hoc revolutionary committee. In most places there was little resistance. An exception was Moscow, where resistance, centered on the elected city Duma, lasted about a week.

Much, perhaps most of Russia was lifted onto a cloud of euphoria. People really believed what they were told—that it was a magnificent liberation, a lifting of the age-long burden of oppression, that the people would enjoy the estates of the rich, that there would be peace and open diplomacy; visiting Americans were also enveloped by the glow.[102] Alexander Blok enthused:

> *Change everything*. Renew everything; let the falseness, the filth and the weariness of our life disappear and let it become free, just, pure and beautiful. Whenever such desires, which fill the souls of the people, break down the dams and gush out with a force that washes away whole sections of the shores, then we behold the revolution. . . . The ambition of the Russian revolution is to envelop the whole world. . . .[103]

Less edifyingly, the proletariat liberated liquor stores and warehouses, and for some days an epidemic of drunkenness left Petrograd half paralyzed and practically knocked out the garrison.[104]

The agitators-turned-governors, like the drunken sailors, soon awakened to confront problems. One of the first was the composition of the new government. Many people, including some Bolsheviks, thought that the coup, in which non-Bolsheviks had played a part, represented the victory of a leftist coalition. Many or most assumed that it was impossible for the party, which was obviously very much a minority in the country and totally without experience, to rule alone, and that a one-party government, maintained by terror and violence, would surely lead to civil war; few realized that Lenin aimed at sole power. The slogan "all power to the soviets" meant at least that the government should reflect the composition of the Congress of Soviets. Places were even left vacant on the Executive Committee for the parties that had absented themselves. The Left Socialist Revolutionaries at first declined to join the Council of Commissars because they believed that a broader coalition was necessary. Labor unions also pressed for a coalition government, especially the railroad workers, whose cooperation Lenin needed to prevent any counterattack by Kerensky or the army commanders.

Lenin was consequently forced to enter into negotiations with the Mensheviks and the majority Socialist Revolutionaries. To his relief, they rejected a coalition except on the condition that Lenin and Trotsky be excluded. Although they had previously been in coalition with the Cadet party, they were alienated by the Bolshevik violence that had been exercised in part against their own members, and they hoped to force the Bolsheviks to retreat. This hope was not entirely unrealistic, although the moderates failed to grasp the essence of the situation. Almost half the Bolshevik leadership favored acceptance of the humiliating condition of removal of their two top leaders. Lenin had no little difficulty in securing the support of his party; at one time he threatened to split the party and take his case to the sailors. Five of the twenty-two members of the Central Committee (with Kamenev and Zinoviev again leading the doubters) resigned in protest against Lenin's intransigence on this issue and also against his suppression of opposition papers in violation of earlier promises. The Left Socialist Revolutionaries, however, were willing to ally themselves with the Bolsheviks largely because of the Decree on Land; they thereby enabled Lenin to claim peasant support in the basically peasant country. On November 27 (December 10) eight Left Socialist Revolutionaries joined the Council of Commissars. The Bolsheviks never permitted any real sharing of power, but the partial coalition pacified the railroad union and greatly strengthened Lenin's hand. It is unclear why Lenin did not make a stronger attempt, in this transition period, to secure a greater basis of support through a broader coalition. The Bolsheviks could always have expelled their rivals from the government when they were no longer needed, as Communists since proceeded to do when they headed coalition governments in Eastern Europe.

A very different problem was to put together an administration. At first all was chaos, and the Bolsheviks, following old habits, thought more about propaganda than about governing. It had been more or less assumed that the changed class nature of the state would solve problems, or that the imminent revolution in Western Europe would take care of them. One of Lenin's top priorities was to publish Marxist works, and early decrees were intended more as programmatic declarations for psychological effect than as administrative measures.[105] The agitators moved into makeshift offices, however, and began their new trade. Lenin was the chairman of the Council of Commissars, Rykov handled Interior, and Lunacharsky was in charge of Education. Stalin, who was held to be an expert on nationality affairs, took charge of that department. Trotsky declined Interior because of his Jewishness (or so he said), but he took Foreign Affairs on the grounds that it would occupy little of his time. As he stated, "What diplomatic work are we apt to have? It will issue a few revolutionary proclamations to the peoples of the world, and then shut up shop."[106]

When the commanders were set in place, there was still the problem of getting the troops to obey. The overwhelming majority of the big and little bureaucrats regarded the Bolsheviks as illegitimate and refused to follow their orders. Led by the "Committee for the Salvation of the Revolution and the Country," they went on strike.[107] Soviet officials had to bring riflemen along, practically like bank robbers, to get funds out of the state treasury. However, under the pressure of economic necessity supplemented by coercion, the clerks returned gradually to their places and to their habits of obedience to their superiors. They had nowhere to go and nothing else to do, so they served Soviet Russia as they had served tsarist Russia until the new masters eventually supplanted them with a new Soviet officialdom.

The Bolshevik party concurrently turned itself into a new governing apparatus. Although the agitators had suddenly become officials, they could only slowly assume the appropriate new habits of mind. Tough-mindedness was yet to come; many were indignant over the closure of various non-Bolshevik papers in the first days after the seizure of power, and Lunacharsky earned a note in history by resigning (briefly) in grief over the destruction of architectural monuments in the fighting in Moscow. But those who withdrew over the questions of a coalition, freedom of the press, and related issues in the first few days eventually drifted back and accepted party discipline, for which they had no alternative. The opposition was leaderless and incoherent.

The party itself underwent a fundamental change, from an organization of persons desiring to overthrow the established order to a management group. To belong to the party became not an opportunity to struggle for power but a key to enjoying it. Requirements relating to social origins and other qualifications changed. On the one hand, the party badly needed educated persons of tested loyalty to fill a host of positions; on the other hand, party membership became useful, possibly necessary for a multitude of bureaucrats and administrators if they had ambitions to advance their careers, perhaps even to retain their employment and livelihood. Starting very soon after the October Revolution, in consequence, the educated strata became and continued to be overrepresented in party membership. Manual workers, unless they desired to cease being manual workers, usually dropped out after the party got into power, while white-collar workers usually did their best to enter it.[108] The extent to which this occurred cannot be judged from the limited statistics that have been published because of ambiguity about the definition of a "worker" and the desirability for both individuals and local party cells of reporting members to stretch the classification of "worker" as broadly as possible. Official doctrine decreed that members should be drawn first from the industrial proletariat, and second from the poorer peasantry, but it could not be forgotten that Lenin and most of those near him were of nonproletarian background, and the need for competent staff prevailed over the ideology of class.

The party also set about securing and enlarging its own authority and moulding Russian—or Soviet—society to its demands. In the first days of Leninist rule little was outwardly changed. But following the first sensational decrees there came a torrent of laws designed to shatter the old order and irrevocably institute a new one. Revolutionary tribunals that were made up mostly of workers and peasants took over from the old courts, women received legal equality, the church was separated from the state and deprived of most of its holdings, inheritance was abolished, and so forth. Grain requisitioning was begun, to feed the cities without paying the peasants.

The Soviet state, far from rapidly withering as Lenin had proposed in *State and Revolution* a few weeks earlier, evolved with extraordinary rapidity toward dictatorship. Whatever respect Lenin had had for freedom before the revolution vanished as soon as freedom became a claim for non-Bolsheviks. The first to go was freedom of the press. Some papers were shut by the Military Revolutionary Committee on the very night of the takeover.[109] Lenin had great respect for the power of the written word; in the infancy of the new government he closed first "bourgeois" papers, then non-Bolshevik socialist ones. A decree of October 28 (November 10) supported this practice, with an avowal that it was only a temporary measure. Despite the indignation of many Bolsheviks who associated freedom with socialism, including Kamenev, Zinoviev, Rykov, and Nogin, the restrictions grew increasingly stringent. A decree of January 28, 1918, called for shutting down any paper that made "distorted statements about public life."[110] The last non-Bolshevik paper, *New Life,* which was published by Lenin's old and celebrated friend Maxim Gorky, was brought to an end on July 16, 1918. In the same spirit, the Bolsheviks brought back the old tsarist fetish of secrecy; as had been the case under the tsars, meetings were closed to public view and the doings of the party became steadily more obscure—a trend that continued unremittingly until the death of Stalin more than thirty-five years later.

Control of information was the milder side of these early measures. Shortly after the seizure of power, the engineer and expropriator Leonid Krassin said, "The country needs a strong government. The Russian peasant must be cleansed of his age-old mange."[111] Lenin cleansed the former upper classes even more drastically. The day after coming to power, the euphoric Bolsheviks, who failed to appreciate their leader, formally abolished the death penalty. This was an old aim of the Russian radicals and a concession to soldiers who were theoretically subject to the severity of military discipline. Lenin exploded on being informed of the measure that had been taken in his absence. According to Trotsky, "When he learned about this first piece of legislation his anger was unbounded. 'Nonsense,' he kept on repeating. 'How can one make a revolution without firing squads?' "[112] He might have saved his anger, because the decree never had effect and there were abundant executions before the death penalty was officially restored in June 1918.

Shortly before the October Revolution a Bolshevik, V. Volodarsky, predicted, "We . . . shall have to introduce terror . . ." on taking power.[113] As early as November 28 (December 11), it was decreed that all Cadet leaders were "enemies of the people" subject to arrest and trial.[114] Barely six weeks after the coup, on December 7 (20), Lenin resurrected the political police as the All-Russian Extraordinary Commission for Combatting Counterrevolution and

Sabotage, abbreviated as "Cheka." This organization was presented as a temporary expedient, like censorhip, and its first purpose was to whip into line boycotting public employees.[115] At this time, according to Trotsky, "Lenin stressed the inevitability of terror at every suitable opportunity."[116]

Almost immediately after its inauguration, the Cheka assumed a right of trial and punishment, including death, and soon went on to commit excesses. Lenin expressed himself eloquently on the subject:

> Thousands of practical forms and methods of accounting and controlling the rich, the rogues, and the idlers should be devised and put to a practical test by the communes themselves, by small units in town and country. Variety is a guarantee of virility here, a pledge of success in achieving the single common aim—to *purge* the land of Russia of all vermin, of fleas—the rogues, of bugs— the rich, and so on and so forth. In one place half a score of rich, a dozen rogues, half a dozen workers who shirk their work (in the hooligan manner in which many compositors in Petrograd, particularly in the Party printing shops, shirk their work) will be put to prison. In another place they will be put to cleaning latrines. In a third place they will be provided with "yellow tickets" after they have served their time, so that all the people shall have them under surveillance, as *harmful* persons, until they reform. In a fourth place, one out of every ten idlers will be shot on the spot. . . .[117]

By January 1918, following such directives, the Cheka was shooting suspects capriciously, more or less on its own initiative. By February Lenin was demanding terror against all opponents or presumed opponents. The Left Socialist Revolutionary Commissar of Justice, Steinberg, expostulated, "Then why do we bother with a Commissariat of Justice? Let's call it frankly the Commissariat for Social Extermination and be done with it." Lenin brightened and replied, "Well put . . . that's exactly what it should be . . . but we can't say that."[118]

Lenin answered any charge of dictatorship by asserting that his state embodied the will of the proletariat, and that any opposition was ipso facto "bourgeois" or counterrevolutionary. He swung his party behind him. If a large majority of Bolsheviks had scruples about dictatorship in November, they were carried forward by the imperatives of emergency, wartime indifference to violence, the logic of power, and the success of ever harsher methods to the acceptance of ruthlessness in almost any degree that seemed to be useful to the party.

In the aftermath of the October Revolution most of the higher Bolsheviks strongly felt that they should share power with other parties; by January they were ready, with little dissent, unceremoniously to disperse the Constituent Assembly that had been the dream of generations of Russian radicals. On the day after the coup, Lenin himself promised to respect the will of the people as it would be expressed in the election for the Constituent Assembly, and the elections were held (contrary to Lenin's wishes) as scheduled by the former government, about three weeks after the coup. The voting was reasonably free, although the Bolsheviks were able to make some use of their control of the official apparatus; for example, they sent Bolshevik soldiers home to campaign for Lenin's party as the party of peace.[119] The Bolsheviks received slightly less than a quarter of the vote overall, but much more in the sectors in which they were best organized, and these happened to be the most important ones politically—the armed forces and the centers of Petrograd and Moscow. The percentages were as follows:[120]

	Overall	Army and Navy	Petrograd and Moscow
Bolsheviks	23.6	40.4	46.3
Socialist Revolutionaries	40.9	38.1	12.6
Mensheviks	3.0	3.3	3.0
Cadets	4.8	1.6	29.9

Of the 707 elected delegates, 175 were Bolshevik, 40 were Left Socialist Revolutionary, and 370 were majority Socialist Revolutionary.

There was no possibility, however, that the Leninists would surrender power because of votes; thus the Bolsheviks began a campaign to discredit the assembly well in advance of its meeting. In December the Bolsheviks used force to scatter the elected Petrograd Duma and expel the right wing half of a peasant congress. In preparation for the assembly meeting Lenin ordered the arrest of the Cadet leaders, and on December 11 (24) the Central Committee gave its approval to the suppression of the assembly, which was due to convene on January 5 (18).

Lenin had no more difficulty than Cromwell or Napoleon in disposing of an inconvenient elected body. He demanded that it recognize his government and adopt his program. It declined to do so. The guard, which was composed of the faithful Latvian rifles and anarchist sailors, occupied and closed the hall. The Left Socialist Revolutionaries, many of whom were quite willing to see the assembly closed, wanted to keep a rump for appearances, but Lenin was not sufficiently concerned to retain such a shred of a democratic facade.

There was no stir as a result of this slap at the many millions who had aspired to a popularly elected assembly. The deputies who had been locked out did not try to reassemble elsewhere until long afterward, when the Bolshevik flaunting of force over the popular will had become history; there were no angry demonstrations. One reason was the war situation; the government was trying to make peace and finding it difficult, and the outlook was bleak. Another was the timidity of the anti-Bolsheviks. The largest party and the one with most to lose, the Socialist Revolutionaries, wanted to use only legal methods to oppose the Leninists when legal methods hardly existed. On the eve of the assembly, non-Bolshevik troops were prepared to parade in support of it, but the Socialist Revolutionary leaders asked that they do so without arms. Lacking such naive compunctions, the Bolsheviks sent Red Guards with arms to rout the pro-assembly demonstrators.[121]

The closure of the assembly was a landmark. Its success silenced the Bolsheviks who still nourished qualms about legality. The Soviet Executive Committee (new elections, which were by now well managed by the Bolsheviks, had produced a quite conformist Congress of Soviets) and the Council of Commissars were left as the only visible government of Russia; it now dropped the "Provisional" in its official title and declared itself to be legitimate. But all the non-Bolsheviks except the Left Socialist Revolutionaries and a few Anarchists were pushed into opposition by violence, the prevalent means of political action.

BREST LITOVSK

The Bolshevik party asserted itself with exemplary effectiveness in its first months, scattering and undercutting its rivals and enemies, giving Russia a determined and purposeful government, and inaugurating a historically unprecedented program aimed at the remodelling of society. But one problem seemed to defy solution, one that contributed much to the downfall of the Kerensky regime, namely, the continuing unsuccessful and unpopular war.

The decree on peace that had been welcomed so clamorously by the Second Congress of Soviets amounted only to an assertion of the desire to end the war and an invitation to the belligerent governments to enter into negotiations on a basis of no annexations—a move in fulfillment of the moderate socialist policy of peacemaking that Lenin had harshly derided during his years in Switzerland. The Allied Powers, which were bitterly opposed to the Russian effort to pull out of the war and convinced that Lenin was a traitor receiving German pay, left the invitation unanswered, but the Germans accepted. An armistice was agreed on, and in December the Bolsheviks sent a delegation, including symbolic representatives of the people and a few Left Socialist Revolutionaries, to negotiate peace at Brest Litovsk, near the front lines.

The negotiations were the first official dealings of the Bolsheviks with a power that represented the class enemy. The meeting was a picturesque encounter between two worlds—on the one hand, a set of revolutionaries recently off the streets, and on the other, the aristocratic German diplomats and generals. With considerable effrontery, the Russians, claiming to speak on behalf of the peoples of the earth, harangued the German proletariat, who were supposed to make a revolution not only to liberate themselves, but also to come to the assistance of their hard-pressed Russian comrades. The subsidiary purpose of the Bolsheviks was to kill time until the laggard German workers acted. The German negotiators had a more practical aim, to convert their victory over Russia into concessions that would both satisfy their political ambitions and help to win the war on the Western front.

Since there was a difference between a defeated country and one that could still count itself victorious with a powerful army, no German revolution was in the cards, and the generals endured the Soviet rhetoric with remarkable patience. Their time was running out, however, so they finally pressed their terms. They demanded "self-determination" for most of the western borderlands of the Russian empire, which contained about a quarter of the former subjects of the tsar; this territory included the Ukraine, which had already declared its independence, and the Baltic provinces. They asked for no ethnic Russian territory and no indemnity.

The almost unanimous Russian reaction was to reject these terms as unconscionable; although Germany had been victorious in Russia, it was far from winning the war. All the non-Bolshevik parties were totally opposed. Even the Bolsheviks were sufficiently nationalistic to regard them as shameful; self-determination was not acceptable when it operated in favor of the Germans and meant the loss of the Russian gains of centuries. At a Central Committee meeting on January 8 (21), only fifteen of the sixty-three members who were present supported Lenin's motion for acceptance. Trotsky's effort to evade the issue by refusing to sign the peace agreement but ceasing to fight ("neither peace nor war") received sixteen votes; thirty-two members were in favor of revolutionary war against imperial Germany. The majority considered it treasonous to the workers to accept such a dictate from the militarist-capitalists—a retreat that would be damaging to the cause of German revolution, which was deemed essential for the salvation of the Russian Revolution.

Lenin refused to accept this majority decision, and the bitter debate continued. On February 9,* the Germans brought it to a climax by submitting their terms as an ultimatum. Lenin, who a few months earlier had argued for a revolutionary coup on the basis of the imminence of the German revolution, now derided the hopes placed on it. He argued that it was necessary to make any concessions to give the new Soviet state a "breathing space" to gather its strength. Perhaps his most compelling argument was his threat to resign. This move won over Trotsky, whose theory of permanent revolution was cause

---

*Soviet Russia had adopted the Western calendar as of the end of January.

enough to reject the treaty since it would end the spread of revolution; Trotsky simply could not envisage the party carrying on a revolutionary war without Lenin.

Bukharin led the opponents, the leftists who insisted on resistance by any possible means—a holy war of world revolution to inspire the world proletariat by heroic example at whatever cost. They believed that peaceful coexistence with capitalist states was impossible; as they saw it, the revolution had to go forward or decay; to halt was to compromise with evil. They also demanded a more radical social program of control by workers and nonbureaucratic rule by local soviets, in the Leninist spirit of September 1917.[122] The proletarian revolutionary cause also became mingled with feelings of Russian nationalism and enraged Slavic masses rising against the Germanic onslaught.

Revolutionary war was popular in the lower ranks of the party. The Bolshevik organizations in both Moscow and Petrograd demanded a rupture in the negotiations with Germany. The Moscow committee was the most forceful in its stance, defying the central party authorities and urging new elections. It was only after much oratory that Lenin was able to swing the vote to acceptance at the Seventh Party Congress on March 6–8, 1918—the last congress at which the outcome of a debate was in doubt.

Lenin won because everyone believed that his leadership was essential for the party and hardly anyone (except Lenin) was prepared to risk a serious split that would possibly entail the loss of power. Moreover, Lenin had the backing of the party regulars, the apparatus-men who were steadily taking the places of those whose chief qualification had been revolutionary fervor. Bukharin and his followers kept agitating, and for a short time they managed to publish a paper of their own, *Communist*. But passions cooled, and like other groups of dissidents, they drifted back to the organization after a short time. They had nowhere else to go, and the peace was a *fait accompli*.

One reason the Bolshevik left gave up was that the Left Socialist Revolutionaries split with their erstwhile Bolshevik partners over the issue of peace with Germany. The Left Socialist Revolutionaries wanted a peasant guerrilla war. Having voted against the concessions to Germany in the Congress of Soviets, they resigned from the coalition and went actively into opposition to arouse the country. A few Bolshevik leftists were prepared to enter into negotiations with the Left Socialist Revolutionaries, with whom they agreed on most issues, but they were not really prepared to ally themselves with non-Bolsheviks against Lenin, who, as before, was prepared to let his repentant critics resume their places in the party.

Lenin has many times been praised for his vision and practical sense in taking the difficult and unpopular position for acceptance of the German terms.[123] The Bolshevik government was indeed badly in need of time to get on its feet—Lenin's prized "breathing space"—and the Germans could undoubtedly have occupied the main centers and the chief seats of Bolshevik strength, Petrograd and Moscow, with little effort. But it was a dubious gamble. If Germany had won on the Western front, it certainly would not have permitted the continued existence of a Bolshevik neighbor in truncated Russia, treaty or no treaty. On the other hand, if the Allies won and class interests counted for anything, they would presumably either punish the Bolsheviks or give the Germans a free hand to liquidate the state that was not only a class-enemy but also treasonous to the alliance. Only fortunate circumstances and the fact that the Western powers behaved as only halfhearted capitalist-imperialists permitted the survival of the Soviet state.

A major premise cited by those favoring acceptance of the peace was that the Germans would be satisfied and would not proceed further. In fact, they continued to advance regardless of the treaty, especially in the Ukraine and the Caucasus, the areas whose resources interested them; their penetration was limited only by the need to use their forces in the west. The period of recuperation that Lenin gained for his government was in any case only about three months, and by his action he bitterly divided his own party. He alienated the last non-Bolshevik supporters of the regime, the Left Socialist Revolutionaries (who were also unhappy over Bolshevik treatment of the peasantry), convinced most others that he was a German agent or stooge, persuaded the Allies to assist the anti-Bolsheviks, and set the stage for a long and dangerous civil war.

Lenin's excuse for yielding to the German demands was that there was no means of resistance, but he may have been too pessimistic. It is true that the Russian army was in a state of dissolution, but the German forces were also badly weakened and were hardly capable of a major offensive; they probably did not contemplate any extensive penetration of Russia proper.[124] Guerrilla harassment might have created great difficulties for the Germans; sabotage of the railroads, which not long before had proved effective against Kornilov, was not even attempted against them. Lenin also exaggerated the unwillingness of the Russians to fight. A call for volunteers in February brought more than ten thousand volunteers in Petrograd,[125] and a deep German penetration certainly would have provoked an outburst of Russian patriotism. A few months later, in even more difficult circumstances, the Bolsheviks were able to mobilize an army of millions to fight for the Soviet state, not against the traditional German enemy but against other Russians.

In these conditions, it would seem that Lenin might well have placed himself at the head of a movement of national resistance. It is difficult to see how a large majority of the nation could have failed to rally around him and his party. The willingness of the anti-Bolsheviks to flock to the Soviet banner in the 1920 war against Poland is convincing evidence that they would have been willing to follow Lenin in a battle to save the Russian Fatherland from the Germans. His earlier defeatism would have been forgotten since his was the only government; the spirit of nationalism would have combined with that of revolutionism to support him. If he had been willing to fight, Lenin would also have received American and Allied help, although he could not perhaps have felt certain of this. It is true that the Bolshevik strength was concentrated in vulnerable cities, but the government also had strength elsewhere. Lenin might have even retreated to the Urals region, if necessary, to emerge in short order as a national hero. To carry on the struggle in such a manner would have been in the nature of the Communist movement. Post-Leninist leaders such as Mao, Tito, and Ho Chi Minh demonstrated how effectively national liberation could be combined with Communism.

Lenin's own writings and speeches indicated that he would do just that. In adhering to the Brest Litovsk peace he not only dropped the only Marxist excuse for making the October Revolution but also turned his back on his own policy toward the war from 1914 to 1917. In a letter to Shliapnikov on August 23, 1915, he had stated, "If 'we' were to defeat Czarism completely, we should offer peace to all the fighters on democratic conditions and on refusal we should conduct a *revolutionary* war."[126] In his April Theses he had said, "The class-conscious proletariat can give its consent to a revolutionary war, which would really justify revolutionary defensism, only on condition [that power pass fully to the proletariat]."[127] On April 29 (May 12) he had stated, "If need be, we shall not draw the line at revolutionary war. We are not pacifists. . . ."[128] But when almost everyone else felt it necessary to continue the war against the capitalist enemy power, Lenin refused.

This can hardly be attributed to temperament. Lenin had long paid attention to military affairs; he especially admired Clausewitz. It may well be, however, that Lenin's policies were influenced by the fact that he was beholden to the Germans (and feared the revelation of that fact). If the army was totally incapable of offering resistance to the Germans in February–March 1918, this was to a large extent Lenin's doing. After the Bolsheviks gained power, they rather strangely continued to dissolve the Russian army, which they soon controlled from top to bottom. It was surely a service to the Germans that on December 4 (17), during the peace negotiations, Lenin decreed the demobilization of the army. On February 11 the Bolshevik commander, Krylenko, again ordered complete demobilization, and hardly any units survived this move (the Latvian sharp-shooters were the most important exception). This was not mere disintegration in difficult times but purposeful dissolution.

At the same time, German financial help seems to have continued to flow. Shortly after the October Revolution, the Bolsheviks were asking for money from the Germans, with whom they were formally at war. Lenin's agent Vorovski telegraphed on November 16, "Please fulfill your promise immediate-ly. We have committed ourselves on this basis, because great demands are being made on us."[129] German Secretary of State Kühlmann wrote on December 3, 1917, of the Bolsheviks' need for German support once the Allies had abandoned Russia, and proposed a loan,[130] and the German ambassador in Sweden promised the Bolsheviks a substantial loan as soon as peace should be concluded.[131] Futile negotiations were carried on with the Allied powers—perhaps significantly, by Trotsky rather than Lenin—for aid in case the Soviets refused to ratify the peace of Brest Litovsk, but these discussions were paralyzed by distrust on both sides and had very little influence.

Soviet policy after Brest Litovsk was decidedly favorable to Germany, and German support may have continued into the summer of 1918. On July 4, prior to the assassination of the German ambassador by Left Socialist Revolutionaries who wished to reignite the war, the Soviet government threatened death to persons attacking the German forces.[132] In an agreement of August 1918, the impoverished Soviet state agreed to pay the tottering Reich an indemnity of six billion gold marks and promised sundry other concessions, including the delivery of oil. A few days earlier the Soviet Foreign Minister, Chicherin, had requested, and the Germans had refused, German military assistance against British forces in the north of Russia.[133]

Wise or not, the peace of Brest Litovsk marked a turning point in the history of the party. It was an end of dreams. With the defeat of ideological revolutionism, the party ceased to be a movement and came to maturity as the directorate of a state. This shift was symbolized by two measures that were taken at the time of acceptance of the treaty. The name of the party was changed from "Social Democratic" to "Communist," with "Bolsheviks" in parentheses. This change, which had long been desired by Lenin to emphasize the party's separation from the Western socialists and the old international movement, was rejected by the party in April 1917, but accepted unanimously in March 1918. The capital was also shifted from exposed Petrograd—the most European of Russian cities and the window Peter had carved to the West—back to Moscow, from which Grand Prince Ivan Kalita had begun the expansion of Russia five centuries earlier.

CIVIL WAR

At the time the unpopular peace of Brest Litovsk was accepted, Lenin's authority and that of the Soviet state were at a low ebb. There was no army, and Lenin had no more force at his disposal—chiefly the faithful Latvian regiment— than Kerensky had had at the time of his overthrow. The government hardly functioned. Decrees poured forth but had little practical effect. Lenin had only a small staff when he moved his workers' government from Petrograd to the medieval fortress of the Kremlin.

The opposition was moving toward civil war. Arbitrary repression, the dissolution of the elected Constituent Assembly, censorship, attacks on religion and the church, what appeared to many to be an assault on the family, the forcible and often violent requisitioning of grain from the peasants, the ever-increasing shortages, and perhaps most of all the unpopular peace with Germany offended a host of people, especially people of the formerly influential classes. Those who had been injured or frightened began to stir as they came to an appreciation of what Bolshevism meant in practice, and civil war became inevitable.

Rightists had been drifting to south Russia since the time of Kornilov's failure, September 1917; there an army of the discontented, led by tsarist generals, gradually assembled among the Cossacks. In January 1918 a Cossack republic was proclaimed. In March 1918 British forces landed at Murmansk, at first to protect munitions stores from falling into German hands. Their purpose broadened to include helping anti-German, then anti-Bolshevik, forces in Russia; and subsequently French, Japanese, and American detachments entered Russia along with the British at several locations. Without engaging in much fighting, these forces encouraged and supplied sundry groups that offered themselves as alternatives to Communist government.

As 1918 progressed, blows began to rain on the Bolsheviks. The Ukraine had gained its independence. Czech prisoners who were being repatriated via Siberia rebelled against the conditions Trotsky tried to impose on them; forty-five thousand Czechs strung out along the Trans-Siberian railroad removed Communist power from the area between the Volga and Vladivostok. Nearer home, the Left Socialist Revolutionaries resorted to violence. Demanding the abolition of the Cheka terror and renewal of the war against Germany, they assassinated the German ambassador, whom they regarded as the boss of Russia, and attempted a coup in Moscow on July 6, 1918. This uprising was suppressed in a few hours, and the Left Socialist Revolutionaries were removed from the few responsible positions they still held in the government. Days later similar unsuccessful Left Socialist Revolutionary uprisings occurred in many cities.

Since the end of February, the Soviet state had begun rebuilding its fighting forces. Trotsky, who had not a jot of military experience and whom Lenin had picked simply as a trusted and capable colleague, demonstrated great energy and ability in whipping the Red Army into shape within a few months. By the summer of 1918, this army had halted the advance of the anti-Communists or Whites at Kazan, on the Volga east of Moscow. Fronts seesawed rapidly, and several times the Soviet state seemed to be in grave danger. In 1919 the forces on both the Red and White sides were larger and better organized. Admiral Alexander Kolchak, who headed a government in Siberia, threatened Moscow from the east in the spring, with Allied backing. General Anton Denikin, who commanded a separate White force in the south, approached Moscow in the fall.

Simultaneously, General Nikolai Yudenich so threatened Petrograd that Lenin thought of evacuating the city and Trotsky rushed to save it.

A less resolute party would have surrendered. Not only was the area controlled by the Leninists reduced to a tiny fraction of the empire, mostly around the Moscow-Petrograd line, but Bolshevik Russia was almost entirely cut off from the outside world. By 1919, because of war and blockade, foreign trade had been reduced to smuggling. The cities had little food or fuel; the commissars huddled in sheepskins and felt boots in unheated offices throughout the Moscow winter. Transportation and industrial production virtually collapsed, and the cities were half empty.

Yet it was not the Soviet state but its enemies that collapsed. The several White offensives lost momentum, sagged, and broke up. By early 1920, the Soviet government seemed reasonably secure, Allied support for the anti-Bolsheviks had ended, most foreign troops were gone, and trade was reopening with the outside world.

The civil war had a postlude, however—war with Poland. The Polish state had been resurrected by the Allied victory in Europe, but its boundaries were uncertain. When it appeared that the Whites had failed, the Poles proceeded to try to take as much as possible of the once-Polish Ukraine. They advanced rapidly and occupied Kiev; then the Red Army counterattacked and rapidly drove them back to the ethnic borders of Poland. In this war Russian nationalism fused with Bolshevik revolutionism, as the restoration of Russian power coincided with the spread of revolution. Many tsarist officers came to Lenin's support, and Communist patriotism was born. In misguided enthusiasm and over the opposition of a number of leading Bolsheviks, Lenin opted to give world revolution a push by invading ethnic Poland, to link up (he hoped) with the ever-imminent German revolution. But the Polish workers failed to welcome the foreign invaders, the Red Army was pushed back, and peace was made on terms that were favorable to Poland. This defeat marked the end of any realistic prospect of spreading the revolution by force until World War II.

There was a final White offensive in the south late in 1920, but the blockade had been lifted, the last interventionist forces (Japanese) soon withdrew, foreign trade resumed, and the Soviet state prepared to take a place never contemplated by the makers of the October Revolution, that of a radical, supposedly proletarian state surrounded by, and peacefully coexisting with, "bourgeois," class-enemy states. The state had failed to spark a revolution, but it had survived and held nearly the whole empire of the tsars.

Its survival, against long odds, was somewhat miraculous. But the factors that had enabled it to pull through were approximately the same as those that had given victory to the Leninists in 1917. Foremost among these was the division of their opponents. In the breakdown of authority, the anti-Communists could never agree on a single leader or government. In 1918–19 a dozen or more authorities, mostly at odds with one another, with none recognizing any legal superior, claimed sovereignty over more or less of the former empire. The non-Bolshevik radicals hated the moderates, and the conservatives despised both, sometimes even preferring the Bolsheviks as the more disciplined group.[134] As the contest wore on, it became practically a two-sided duel between the Bolsheviks and the monarchists, or supporters of military rule. In this division, the Mensheviks and the Socialist Revolutionaries, who still regarded Lenin's followers as social radicals like themselves, sided with them against the representatives of the old order. Those who liked the general ideas of popular soviets, workers' and peasants' power, socialization of industry, and so forth, fought for and saved the Soviet state which promised these things.

Moreover, the minority nationalities, each of which was concerned only for itself, clashed with the Russian nationalists, who wanted above all to restore the empire; thus the Whites, who were operating from the fringes, usually found themselves based on unfriendly territory. The Czechs, caring nothing about the Russian generals, opted out of the fight. The war-weary Allies gave only desultory and poorly coordinated assistance to the Whites and began disengaging from them in April 1919, although a modest effort a few months later might have tipped the scales against the Moscow government. For example, when Petrograd was near falling, the British navy refused to intervene. The Poles also refrained from helping Lenin's enemies; they feared that a White Russia might be more dangerous to them than a presumably weak Red one, and so held back until 1920.

Likewise, the classes that might have opposed the Bolsheviks failed to join together to do so. Beginning in 1918, Lenin, with his undogmatic flexibility, was recruiting the former educated classes as "specialists" to make the economy work, and they generally set aside their prejudices to cooperate faithfully with those who proclaimed the destruction of most of what they stood for. This policy irritated principled Communists, who believed that a prime virtue of the revolution was its humbling of the privileged and resented the salaries paid to the bourgeois experts. Tsarist officers also served, usually with professional competence, in the Red Army. Their participation was even more disturbing to the comrades, many of whom felt competent to command, but the practicality of using the enemy to destroy the enemy prevailed. The peasants also generally stood by the Soviet power, although they were promised little in the Bolshevik ideology and were badly hurt by the squads that were extracting grain at gunpoint. The word went out, and the peasants believed it, that the Whites would return lands to their former holders; thus the peasants bore with what they considered the lesser evil. The Bolsheviks were also able to divide the peasants, setting up "Committees of the Poor" and rewarding them with power in the villages and a share of the grain that had been extracted from the wealthier segments of the population.

Compared to their confused and squabbling enemies, the party of Lenin was a well-motivated, thoroughly ruthless, and solidly organized apparatus of power. It had a program called socialism, which everyone believed should produce a far happier world than anything known before, and many people were willing to believe that utopia was near. Lenin had expected the arrival of socialism within six months, and in January 1918, when experience had already proved sobering, he said, "for its success, socialism in Russia needs a certain spell of time, *at least a few months.*"[135] There were dreamers everywhere and all manner of great schemes, in the confidence that the Bolsheviks could do anything.[136] Measures of control were regarded as steps toward socialism. Nationalization, which had been advancing since late 1917 and had been decreed for all large enterprises in June 1918, the inflation that led to the valuelessness of money, the distribution of goods by rationing, and the complete control of manufacturing and trade in the latter part of the civil war were not thought to be mere responses to the emergency but the institution of the new order of communism and the sharing of property.[137] At its Eighth Congress, in March 1919, the party adopted a new program to replace that of 1903 and to cover the transition to the utopian communist society. When reality fell short of dreams, this was blamed on the circumstances; as long as the war lasted, the Communists could believe that they, representing the proletarian governing class, were truly and rapidly building socialism by decree.

The Communist cause was also bolstered by the conviction that it was truly the vanguard of a world historical movement that was worthy of any sacrifice, and Communist utopianism was confused with Russian messianism. From November 1918 to February 1919 hopes were bright for the great German revolution, and they flickered from time to time thereafter. The Soviet leaders watched eagerly for signs of the next revolutionary upsurge in the West, and in the aftermath of the war there was no lack of riots and disorders to raise their hopes. In March 1919, at a dark hour, came news of the Communist revolution in Hungary, a beacon that lasted about two months. At this time, to symbolize the Soviet party's identification with the vibrant new workers' movement and its separation from decrepit Social Democracy, the Bolsheviks held what they called the First Congress of the Communist International. In the parlous conditions of the hour and the difficulty of communication and travel, hardly any real foreign delegates could be mustered, but some miscellaneous leftists who happened to be in Russia were brought together to make a simulacrum of internationalism. They heard the president of the new International, Lenin's faithful Zinoviev, make such predictions as, "Within a year we shall be beginning to forget that there was a struggle for Communism in Europe, because within a year all Europe will be Communist."[138]

A little over a year later, in August 1920, during the heat of the war with Poland, a much larger and more successful Second Congress of the Comintern was held. It endeavored to make Lenin's revolution the universal model and to extend his ideas of party organization to the international scene by adopting his "Twenty-One Points" as the condition for affiliation with the glorious Russian Revolution; acceptance of them meant agreeing to the separation of foreign Communist parties from their societies and their subordination to the Russian center. The Bolsheviks thereby introduced a permanent split into the world Marxist movement that was analogous to the division of the Russian Social Democratic Party into the Mensheviks and the Bolsheviks.

But ideology and visions of world victory were supported by solid coercion; it was, above all, the mingling of utopianism and ruthlessness that set the Bolsheviks apart from and over other parties. As dedicated as he was to the written and spoken word, Lenin never relied on popular support and voluntary action and never rejected physical coercion as a means of political action. He regarded the Cheka and terror as prime instruments of the dictatorship of the proletariat.

The chief instrument of violence was the Cheka, an institution that, despite several name changes, remains prominent in the Soviet state (presently as the KGB). Its first chief was an ascetic, dedicated, utterly ruthless Pole, Feliks Dzerzhinsky, who set up shop after the move to Moscow at 22 Lubianka Street, an address that is still well known to Soviet dissenters. Latvians, Poles, and other non-Russians were prominent in the organization, as were Left Socialist Revolutionaries until their attempted coup in July 1918. Wholesale terror began only in the civil war, however, especially after the assassination of Uritsky and the wounding of Lenin on August 30. Lenin's assailant was an unattached female Socialist Revolutionary, but the attack was made the occasion for a hecatomb of hostages and randomly picked "class enemies"; the Bolsheviks in a day took more lives than Stolypin did in all of his repressions.

In the civil war, terror became not only a defense against counterrevolution but a means of government, a "morale-builder" and a weapon against slackness and inefficiency, as well as sabotage. The Cheka went wild, acting almost as an independent entity, in the Red Terror; hardly checked by party protests, it killed thousands and hundreds of thousands* who had no connection with any specific wrongdoing.[139] Lenin paid close attention to the operations of the Cheka, sometimes tempering its asperity, sometimes urging greater severity; he loved to play with children but did not mind placing a horde of innocents before the firing squad. The terror even carried a mystique as a laudable purification of the imperfect society.[140] A Ukrainian Cheka paper wrote on August 18, 1919:

> Our morality is new, our humanity is absolute, for it rests on the bright ideal of destroying all oppression and coercion.

---

*It is impossible to compare this cruelty with the brutalities of the anti-Communists; mercy was not esteemed, and prisoners were usually shot on both sides.

To us all is permitted, for we are first in the world to raise the sword not in the name of enslaving and oppressing anyone, but in the name of freeing all from bondage.[141]

Terror was a response to the narrowness of the support for Lenin's government; since other means of rewarding or punishing were lacking, it became a chief lever of power. During the civil war, Lenin wrote to Stalin, "Threaten to shoot the idiot who is in charge of telecommunications and does not know how to give you a better amplifier and how to have a working telephone connection."[142] Stalin obeyed and shot the engineer and his two sons as well. Lenin was ready to threaten bullets for almost any dereliction; for example, he had a resolution passed to shoot foresters who failed to deliver the required quantities of wood.[143] Trotsky's ordinary remedy for difficulties was to shoot a few people; in a typical order (November 24, 1919), he ordered death for anyone who encouraged retreat or nonfulfillment of an order, sold part of his equipment, or harbored a deserter; a house where a deserter was found was to be burned.[144] Lenin did not much care for civilian lives, whether they were proletarian or not; angry at a delay in taking Kazan, he wrote, "One should not take pity on the city and put off matters any longer, as merciless annihilation is what is vital once it is established that Kazan is in an iron ring."[145] In the war against Poland he offered a bounty of one hundred thousand rubles for each kulak, priest, or landowner hanged.[146] This was, of course, justified by the ideology of class; as Lenin told the Communist Youth League in 1920, "Communist morality is that which serves this struggle," and "to a Communist all morality lies in this united discipline and conscious mass struggle against the exploiters"—an often-repeated sentiment.[147]

CONSOLIDATION OF THE PARTY

The hardening of Bolshevik morality was paralleled by a strengthening and consolidation of the party. In March 1918 it was still a loose-jointed, ineffective organization, with some of the character of the prerevolutionary debating society. The apparatus was lame and feebly staffed, and there was little communication with the provinces and less discipline. Local organizations were left free to oppose the center, as they did notably over the Brest Litovsk question. The Seventh Congress, which was held in March 1918, brought together only sixty-nine delegates, many of them with uncertain mandates. Nearly everything remained to be done. As late as the beginning of 1919, only a small minority of party committees were fulfilling their duty of sending regular reports to the center.[148]

But the Leninists had advantages that more than offset their weaknesses. The leadership, which Lenin called the "Old Guard," had the energy and capacity for dedication and sacrifice of youth. When Lenin came to power he was the oldster at forty-seven; others of the party nucleus were in their thirties and Bukharin was barely twenty-nine. In 1919 half the members of the party were under thirty.[149] Through 1921 the average age of the delegates to party congresses remained about thirty.[150] It was an activist group whose members were impatient to remake the world, cost what it might, eager for change in a world where change was badly needed. For them it was the time to start everything afresh, unencumbered by any outworn "bourgeois" notions. They worked closely together with intense loyalty to the brotherhood of the party, which took the place of family, friendships, and country. Their zeal was multiplied by the stakes: victory meant glory and supposedly secure power; defeat meant probable hanging.

At their head stood Lenin, an exceptional agitator who became an effective wielder of power. His speeches were rather dull and repetitive, and he was hardly what has come to be called charismatic, but he was the acknowledged supreme authority in the party without formally occupying any position above those of his colleagues. He was modest and unpretentious, and he was at least broad-minded enough to allow persons who rebelled against his policies to return to responsible positions after their repentance (this was exemplified in the series of defections during the first months of his new regime). Kamenev, Zinoviev, Bukharin, and their fellows were part of the old crowd, and Lenin valued them even though they might have differed with him. Lenin even liked a bit of controversy, since it gave him the opportunity to down his opponents by his wit, and he was the uncontested authority in the party, the indispensable apex. Lenin had no real or lasting intimates, however; during the civil war Sverdlov was probably closest to him, followed by Dzerzhinsky.

Lenin was exceptional as a dictator in that he did not set himself up as military leader. Although he had taken a great interest in mlitary affairs earlier, he remained rather incomprehensibly remote from the conduct of hostilities. He did not preside over strategy, affect military uniform, or visit the troops in the field; he may have known little of what went on in Trotsky's army.[151]

With habituation to power, however, Lenin became more the autocrat. He grew more skeptical of his subordinates and less tolerant of their weaknesses. However smoothly a person may have worked with Lenin in the past, if he ventured a serious difference of views he was cut off entirely, as were Shliapnikov and Alexandra Kollontai. Lenin became the decider. As Trotsky reported in the Council of Commissars, "At the proper moment, Lenin would announce his resolutions, always with an intentional sharpness; after that the debate would cease or else would give way to practical suggestions."[152] The elevation in the status of the leader was marked between the Seventh Congress, in

March 1918, and the Eighth, a year later. At the first meeting, Lenin had to labor long to secure acceptance of his proposal; at the second, he was the unqualified leader whom the delegates, rising, acclaimed by their cheers.[153]

As the leader was being raised to commander, the party was becoming more the tightly structured political machine that Lenin had envisaged at the outset of his career. In the aftermath of the split over Brest Litovsk, the organization began removing dissidents from positions of influence. At the Eighth Congress, in March 1919, a number of momentous organizational changes were made to improve central direction. A Workers' and Peasants' Inspectorate ("Rabkrin," as it came to be known), was set up; Stalin was nominated by Zinoviev to head it. This body had wide powers of inspection and discipline over the whole party apparatus, and it gave Stalin a basis on which to build a personal following. An Organizational Bureau ("Orgburo") was established to deal with party organizational questions, especially appointments. Stalin was a member of it, too, and used it as another basis for forwarding his position.

The party Secretariat was also strengthened. Before 1917 Lenin's longtime associate, Yelena Stasova, acted as party secretary; she was joined by Yakov Sverdlov in April 1917, and they were given several assistants in August. After the October Revolution, however, Sverdlov continued to act virtually as the Secretariat, carrying a large part of the records in his head (while also functioning as the formal head of state, the president of the Central Executive Committee of the Congress of Soviets). He died in March 1919, however, and the party congress established a regularized Secretariat headed by a now nearly forgotten figure, N. N. Krestinsky, with an adequate staff organized into several departments, including an allocation department to assign party members to posts. Krestinsky was joined at the Ninth Congress, held in March 1920, by Preobrazhensky and Serebiakov (all three were eventually executed by Stalin) and the Secretariat was charged with overseeing party management.[154] With 745 employees, the Secretariat was already a major potential power in the party.

In March 1919 the Politburo was reborn, or perhaps born, since the Politburo of prerevolutionary days had never functioned. Its full members were Lenin (the head of the party and government), Trotsky (the military leader), Stalin (the party manager), Kamenev (Lenin's assistant) and Krestinsky. This group was almost the equivalent of the party's entire leadership. The most important men outside it, Zinoviev and Bukharin, were not demeaned by exclusion, however; they had other duties. The Politburo was not intended to supplant the Central Committee, but to expedite the work of the large body; almost from the first, however, it began taking charge and making decisions on its own, seeking confirmation from the Central Committee only on major questions.[155] A Secret Department was also set up as a secretariat for the Politburo, Orgburo, and Central Committee Secretariat.[156]

Concurrently, the membership of the party was being tightened. The Secretariat began keeping a file on every party member. At the Sixth Congress, in July – August 1917, even before the Bolsheviks' seizure of power, submission to party orders was made a condition of membership, and provisions were laid down for expulsion. From October on, membership became a very desirable commodity for the ambitious, and the party slowly began turning into a privileged corps of rulers and administrators of the Soviet state. Because of the desire for purity and good ideological standing in those who were permitted to become members, or because those in the circle of the elite preferred not to dilute their privileges, the party's membership grew much less rapidly than might have been expected. The official figures indicated that there were 390,000 members in March 1918.

In March 1918 it was resolved to scrutinize applicants more carefully and the party's growth was checked. By March 1919 the membership was back down to 350,000. The Eighth Congress then opened the doors wider to workers and peasants, while decreeing selectivity for other candidates. It also ordered a reregistration of party members—in effect the first cleansing or purge. It might be supposed that those who had stuck with the party through the evil months would have been regarded as adequately tested, but in the summer of 1919 the membership shrank to less than half its size in March—about 150,000.[157] Lenin rejoiced at the reduction, which was in line with his old preference for a narrow party. However, the purge was followed by a mass recruitment of workers and, for the first time, peasants. The membership shot up to 430,000 by January 1920, 612,000 by March of that year, and about 750,000 by March 1921.

Thus, by the end of the civil war, most of those who had made the October Revolution had left the party, although the inner corps remained almost intact. The lower ranks had mostly been renewed, with the revolutionaries replaced by persons of relatively low economic station, workers or peasants, to provide a reliable staff for the growing state apparatus or to watch over bourgeois specialists who were doing jobs for which more education was required. Very few worker recruits remained factory workers, however; most of them went into state or party jobs, and most of the remainder into the army, probably in positions of authority.[158]

The membership was also becoming more hierarchic. In 1918 the party set up a category of ''sympathizer groups''—a sort of submembership or trial membership, but these groups fell out of use because they overlapped various near-party organizations, such as the trade unions and the Communist Youth League (Komsomol). At the end of 1918 the category of candidate member was established to test new members, and to this day candidates have constituted an important percentage of the total party membership. More important was the hierarchy within the party. By the end of the civil war, the party consisted essentially of three categories: full-time party workers; leaders in the army, government, unions, and so on, who belonged to the party and had been put there by the party; and the rank and file who carried out orders. The party officials themselves were divided into five grades corresponding to grades in the government service.[159]

Hierarchy inevitably implied privilege, even in a time of revolutionary enthusiasm. Lenin thought the workers should suffer material privations gladly for the sake of the new social-political order, and that party members should labor out of duty and devotion without special material rewards. The pay of party leaders was to be the same as that of skilled workers. But money meant little in any case, and party people, at least those of higher station, could soon live much better than others by virtue of their perquisites and special stores. Lenin himself justified special rations for Communists on grounds of the need to care for the champions of the workers.[160]

But party people were expected to earn all their privileges and more, to work the hardest, to take on the most difficult assignments, and to risk their lives. To be a communist in the civil war was practically to wager one's neck; party men, who were ready to go into the most threatened sector, held the Red Army together through the civil war. In disorganized, chaotic Russia, where all the old institutions were crumbling or broken, the Communist party stood fast as an organized, purposeful body of several hundred thousand, bound together by a common faith and hope mixed with a sense of power in union with strong leadership.

Consequently the party became the effective government of the Soviet state; under it the official state organization acted as the administrator of party-fixed policy. The party took on the functions of making basic decisions and setting ideological directions, of seeing to the fulfillment of directives, of filling all positions of importance, and of mobilizing and persuading the masses. Although Lenin spent a good deal of time presiding over formal governmental bodies, such as the Council of Commissars and the Council of Labor and Defense, the real power went to the Politburo at the top and to the party secretaries at lower levels. The soviets, both central and local, no longer saw any significant debate if they even troubled to meet, and party-supported resolutions were passed unanimously. By 1920 a commissar might simply order the imprisonment of a local or regional soviet.[161] The councils in whose name Lenin's revolution had been made were merely instruments of the party, like other organizations, and in all of these it was the duty of the party faction (according to a rule of December 1919) to oversee and guide the organization and to check or nominate candidates for all positions of confidence.

This system came into being partly because of the Bolshevik distrust of leftover tsarist bureaucrats, but it was basically a means of exercising the closest possible supervision to prevent any deviation from party policies. It developed into an elaborate hierarchy of control over the administrative apparatus, the most effective way to prevent bureaucratic dilution of the will of the party and its leadership. It was a new state form, a great political invention, which arose in part spontaneously, in part from the consciousness of Lenin. It made the dictatorship that Lenin defined as follows at the end of the civil war: "The scientific term 'dictatorship' means nothing more nor less than authority untrammeled by any laws, absolutely unrestricted by any rules whatever, and based directly on force."[162]

Chapter 4

The Liquidation of Dissent

THE END OF ALLIES

The major contest was over by the end of 1920; it remained only for the Bolsheviks to recover parts of Siberia and Central Asia, to put down peasant disorders, and to suppress large-scale banditry. But having smashed its enemies, the party no longer had a simple, understandable mission, the fight for survival. It found itself in a situation that was totally contrary to Leninist predictions and expectations. The revolution had not spread, and the Soviet state was surrounded by strong class-enemy powers. On the other hand, far from withering away under socialism or even beginning to wither away to inaugurate the freedom of the workers, the state had grown into a big, bureaucratic, highly authoritarian apparatus. Yet it was not clear what purpose Bolshevik rule could have except the installation of socialism.

Moreover, the country was in a state of material misery that was almost unexampled for European populations in modern times. Food production was down to about half the prewar level, transportation was chaotic or nonexistent, industrial production had slumped to a fifth of its prewar level, and the real wages of workers were about half what they had received under the previous regime. With the end of the war emergency, discontent consequently erupted on all sides and within the party itself. The masses that had supported Bolshevism from interest or conviction began to raise their voices. It was no longer possible to demand sacrifices in the name of repelling counterrevolution and the assault of world capitalism (as the intervention of the Allied powers was characterized). Nor was it possible to postpone expectations until the end of the war and to excuse impositions and repressions as measures necessitated by the emergency.

But the Bolshevik party entertained no thought of yielding any fraction of its power or of sharing its political monopoly in the slightest degree. The difficulties and terrible cost of winning the glorious victory over foreign and domestic enemies had strengthened the party's resolve to surrender nothing. The Bolsheviks had gained enormous self-assurance from their triumph against fearful odds, and the sacrifices made it seem the more necessary to fulfill the promise of the revolution. The party was not only more hated than ever but also larger, better organized, and tempered in the conviction of its role. As Trotsky wrote, "The victorious commanders assumed leading posts in the local Soviets, in economy, in education, and they persistently introduced everywhere that regime which had led to success in the civil war."[1] The dictatorship of the proletariat, which in Russia necessarily implied minority rule, was taken to justify any measures necessary to keep power in the hands of the powerful; this rationalization roughly paralleled the earlier claims of the Russian autocrats to a right to total power because they were acting on behalf of the people.

The peasants had perhaps the most reason to rebel when they ceased to fear the return of the former landowners. As Trotsky had predicted long before, once the peasants had gotten what they desired from the revolution, they ceased to be revolutionary. They did not even have the gratification of the flattery that was being lavished on the urban proletariat; no one pretended that the future belonged to them. They were no longer amenable to requisitions, and the Bolsheviks could supply them with almost nothing in return for their crops. Food production for the cities was off in any case because of the breakup of the estates, which had furnished a disproportionate fraction of the marketable surplus. Hence force was more than ever necessary, and at this time Lenin saw not big capital, but small, peasant property as the enemy.[2] For the most part the peasants simply suffered, but there were countless little uprisings and corresponding punitive actions. One revolt, in the Tambov region in 1920−21, was so large that it caused serious worries.[3] It was put down with extreme cruelty; the families of the insurgents were shot unless the miscreants turned themselves in.

Much more dangerous was the mutiny of the Baltic sailors at Kronstadt in March 1921. There had been unrest for some time, but the action was touched off by labor troubles in Petrograd. In the last week of February, rations were cut in the midst of a shortage of food and fuel; strikes followed and grew into something resembling a general strike. In support of the workers, the crew of a battleship passed a resolution calling for the free reelection of soviets, freedom of speech for workers and peasants, freedom for peasants and handworkers to produce with hired labor, and equality of rations.[4] Speakers whom the party sent to calm the sailors were howled down. An emergency was declared in Petrograd, food was rushed in, and the incipient revolt there collapsed for lack of organization and leadership.

Meanwhile the Kronstadters declared their autonomy and appealed for a "third revolution" to uphold the ideals of the October Revolution. According to their manifesto:

> After carrying out the October Revolution, the working class hoped to achieve emancipation. The result has been to create even greater enslavement of the individual man. . . . The Communists have created . . . moral servitude . . . they have bound the workers to their benches, and have made labor not into a joy but into a new slavery. . . . They answer with mass executions and bloodthirstiness. . . . the Russian Communist Party is not the defender of the toilers. . . . having attained power, it is afraid only of losing it, and therefore all means are allowed: slander, violence, deceit, murder. . . .
>
> The present overturn at last makes it possible for the toilers to have their freely elected soviets, working without any violent party pressure, and remake the state trade unions into free associations of workers, peasants and the laboring intelligentsia. At last the policeman's club of the Communist autocracy has been broken.[5]

It can hardly be said that ordinary Russians lacked appreciation for democratic values.

The party blamed the insurgency on the White Guards or foreign agents or Socialist Revolutionaries and hastened to attack the fortress lest the melting of the ice should make it impregnable. Delegates from the Tenth Congress, which was then meeting, were mobilized to join the Communist forces, which included Tatar regiments.[6] The sailors wanted to compromise and failed to move aggressively.[7] The fighting lasted for eleven days, and at the end many or most of the surviving mutineers were executed. Since many party members had been sympathetic to the uprising, it was used as an excuse to silence opposition in the party; criticism, it was claimed, led to revolt.

The Kronstadt insurrection failed to spread because no organizations capable of taking up the cause remained in Russia. During the civil war the Mensheviks, Socialist Revolutionaries, and some minor parties who supported the Bolsheviks were permitted a little freedom of action. After the civil war the party considered it all the more necessary to eliminate them entirely because of their popularity. The Socialist Revolutionaries could speak for the unhappy peasant majority, and most of the few industrial workers who remained went over to the Mensheviks. Lenin permitted some feeble opposition until 1921, presumably for propagandistic reasons and so that he could chide his opponents within the party for speaking like Mensheviks.

In 1920 a Menshevik congress could still legally be held, and some Mensheviks and Socialist Revolutionary deputies were still being elected to the Congress of Soviets. But soviets were elected by a show of hands, and elections could be manipulated as desired; the last independent deputies were eliminated in 1921. The last non-Communist trade unions, which were dominated by Mensheviks and other non-Communists, were broken up and "reorganized" and the leaders arrested in 1920—21.

Some Bolsheviks wanted to bring loyal Mensheviks into the fold in 1921,[8] but Lenin was singularly inhospitable to his old rivals. In September 1921 he wrote, "In my view among the Mensheviks who entered our party after the beginning of 1918 not more than one in a hundred should be reconfirmed as a member and even that one should be checked three or four times."[9] In a gesture of mercy, in 1922 he permitted some Mensheviks, including Martov, to leave jail for exile. But his report to the Eleventh Party Congress, held in March—April 1922, stated, "For the public manifestation of Menshevism our revolutionary courts must pass the death sentence, otherwise they are not our courts but God knows what."[10] The Mensheviks, who always eschewed violence as a means of anti-Bolshevik action, emerged with only moral credits.

The majority Socialist Revolutionaries were frankly regarded as enemies and harassed to extinction. A number of them were put on trial in the summer of 1922, the first open political trial of former revolutionaries; the death sentences were remitted only grudgingly because of the indignation of foreign socialists. Left Socialist Revolutionaries were more leniently treated; in 1920—21 they were even allowed to publish a few issues of a journal. Many of them were permitted to join the Communist party.

THE END OF FACTIONS

As Russia was being finally cleansed of non-Communist parties, differences of opinion within Lenin's party came to the fore. Inner-party factions took the function of expressing some of the discontent of the country until these were also eliminated in 1921—22.

Revolutions never turn out as the makers hope, and at the end of the civil war those who had been brought to Lenin's side by the ideals of peace and socialism had to ask themselves what they were doing there. Lenin himself had no clear idea where to go when the fighting was over and gave no strong lead. Hence the party was in a ferment that ended only when those of an idealistic or independent temper were silenced by the pragmatists of the party apparatus.

Contentions focussed around several issues wherein Marxist doctrine and revolutionary-equalitarian feelings clashed with practical and political imperatives. These issues included those of state versus worker or local control of industry, the use of bourgeois specialists, the relations between central and local authorities, and the role of the trade unions—in sum, the question of centralization and dictatorship versus antonomy and a form of democracy.

In the Leninist style, the answer to all problems was an increase in direction or control, and the party emerged with the utmost faith in its autocratic powers. Its first tendency was to attempt to solve the problems of peace by the methods that had rather miraculously won the civil war. Trotsky, in particular, sought to apply his military methods to the civilian economy; he even set out in his famous armed train to oversee the production fronts. Labor armies, under military command and discipline, were established to run whole regions in 1920; transportation, which was in an especially parlous state, was especially militarized.[11] At the Ninth Congress (1920), Trotsky and Radek spoke of the obligation of every worker to follow the commands of the "workers' state," casting aside the "bourgeois prejudice of freedom of labor,"[12] and this obligation was concretized in a military draft and peremptory command.

It soon proved materially impossible to drive men to work as they had been driven to fight. This unpopular and unsuccessful strategy shook the party, aroused widespread resentment in the lower echelons (especially among trade-union officials), and gravely weakened the authority of the Central Committee. It also injured the standing of Trotsky, who was generally seen as coleader of the party with Lenin. Trotsky's policies on labor armies, the militarization of transport, and reduction of the trade unions were party policies that had been approved by the Central Committee and Lenin, but Trotsky bore responsibility for them. Zinoviev, who had long nourished a grudge against Trotsky for pushing him out of his spot next to Lenin, set himself up, along with Stalin, as the champion of democracy; this move increased the influence of Zinoviev and Stalin in the party apparatus. Their first success against Trotsky—a foretaste of the battle of 1924−25—was his removal as Commissar of Transport at the end of 1920.

The protest movements originating outside the inner core were less opportunistic. Although the freedoms of people outside the party were crushed, it was still believed suitable and necessary for true and trusted party members, who had been properly indoctrinated and tested, to criticize and propose changes. Discussion groups and candid talk persisted through 1920−21. A small group that formed in 1919, more as a tendency than as an organized faction, became known as the Democratic Centralists. They were largely mild intellectuals, many of whom had been Left Communists in 1918, who were troubled by the reduction of party democracy to a mere form as a result of the increasing control by the central apparatus of all party bodies down to local cells. This group called for freedom of discussion and local autonomy. Its chief spokesman, T. V. Sapronov, noted at the Ninth Congress, in March 1920, that local committees were now being appointed by the center and asked Lenin, "Who will appoint the Central Committee? Perhaps things will not reach that stage, but if they did, the Revolution will have been gambled away,"[13] ignoring the fact that the Central Committee had always been largely appointed.

A larger but equally diffuse group, the Workers' Opposition (the name was a label inflicted by its opponents), grew up in 1919 among the proletarian sector of the party. One of its first protests was against the giving of good jobs to "bourgeois specialists," and it went on to deplore the loss of proletarian influence in the party, as well as its growing bureaucratism and centralism. Its ideas were close to those of the Democratic Centralists, but there was not much sympathy between the two groups; the Workers' Opposition had the ordinary workers' distrust for the intellectuals who should have been their natural allies. The Workers' Opposition wanted election instead of appointment to supposedly elective positions and more freedom for trade unions. Somewhat in the Maoist style, its members urged that all Communists do at least three months' manual labor yearly.[14] Taking the party's ideology seriously, they demanded fulfillment of the promise made in the 1919 party program that management of the economy would be turned over to the unions. They contended that since Lenin had argued before the revolution that the workers had to be guided by the party in the bourgeois-dominated society, it was inescapable that after the revolution the workers should be able to speak for themselves—or at least through the Communists who worked among them.

These currents of opposition came to their climax and defeat at the Tenth Congress, in March 1921—a watershed of party history. The principal issue was the role of the trade unions. In December 1920 an official party debate was opened on the subject, partly because Lenin and Trotsky were at odds. Groups were permitted to canvass support on the basis of their different ideas, and various platforms were presented by Trotsky, Lenin and Zinoviev, Bukharin, Shliapnikov, and others. Shliapnikov, the leader of the Workers' Opposition, was one of the very few leading Bolsheviks who was of working class origin; he had been Lenin's chief lieutenant inside Russia for some years prior to the revolution. He was joined early in 1921 by a more eloquent debater, Alexandra Kollontai, who vitalized the Workers' Opposition and led it to a more generalized criticism of party rule and the dictatorship of the Central Committee, heresy-hunting, the stifling of criticism, and the failure to permit workers to occupy important posts.

At the Tenth Congress, the Workers' Opposition urged that the trade unions share in the management of the economy. Trotsky wanted the unions to be simply agencies of the state to cooperate in organizing production. Lenin took what appeared to be a middle position, but it turned out to be not far from Trotsky's: that the unions should have no administrative authority but should protect the workers while forwarding the interests of the state. The defeat of the Workers' Opposition (and Democratic Centralists) was overwhelming; they received only 45−50 votes out of 694 voting delegates.

The Workers' Opposition could not have succeeded in any case, because the consolidation of the central apparatus had gone too far. The Secretariat, whose staff was expanding year by year, had many means of pressure; it could use promotions, good or bad assignments, posting to qualifying training, and members' dossiers. The control of the central levers of power was crucial, of course, but by this time the whole party was essentially a group of officeholders who were inevitably concerned with keeping the favor of those above them. The "workers" in the party had become ex-workers. Official figures gave the number of workers as 225,000 (44.4 percent of total membership) in 1922; yet at this time all of the Communists in factories and workshops, including many white-collar workers, totalled only 90,000.[15]

By 1921 the unions also had been welded into the bureaucracy, which excluded ordinary workers; it is notable that the chief bosses of the union organization, Tomsky and Rudzutak, did not support the Workers' Opposition. The Workers' Opposition had no publications, no membership, and no generally agreed-on policy alternatives; it was only a loose set of "outs," favored by no member of the Central Committee. It could not really bring itself to work against the apparatus in the conviction that opposition meant becoming a second party, and that under Marxism such a move would be nonproletarian and counter-revolutionary.

The Workers' Opposition failed less gloriously because the movement's philosphy was basically inconsistent. It claimed to favor individual rights and it was ultimately based on Western ideals of freedom and democracy, but it offered nothing for the peasants; instead, it seemed to share the animosity of the townsfolk against those who were supposedly at least better fed. Moreover, it did not favor freedom for non-Communist workers. Delegates from the Workers' Opposition and the Democratic Centralists, who occupied their own positions through force and fraud, joined wholeheartedly in the repression of the Kronstadters, who demanded free elections. The movement had no desire to surrender any part of the party's power; it only asked that the power be shared more equitably. Rights for people in general have never figured in the program of any opposition group within the Communist party.

The Workers' Opposition also harbored an ideological delusion regarding the role of the workers. It saw a special virtue in persons who had proletarian affiliations, advocated closing the doors to all nonproletarians, and wanted a purge of the bourgeois elements in the party, apparently without realizing that any purge conducted by the central authorities would simply strengthen the center. Hence it was easy for the Leninists to neutralize much of this opposition sentiment by symbolic concessions, such as promising to admit more workers, to have Communists take turns at manual labor, to struggle against careerism, to hold elections, and the like. Trotsky, for example, advocated "productive democracy," which entailed no limitation on autocratic power but provided opportunities for talented workers to rise in the party's service.

Placated by ostensible concessions, the oppositional elements were repressed politically. Under the impact of the Kronstadt revolt, the party took steps to eliminate the kind of controversy it had just witnessed. The three secretaries (Krestinsky, Preobrazhensky, and Serebriakov) who had been relatively sympathetic to the views of the lower ranks were removed not only from the Secretariat but from all positions of influence. Molotov was made chief secretary with two deputies, and other Stalinists were promoted. The Central Control Commission was established to oversee the party as the Workers' and Peasants' Inspectorate was supposed to oversee the government. In addition, on the last day of the congress, Lenin introduced two resolutions without warning, one forbidding factions, and the other specifically condemning the Workers' Opposition (as "the Syndicalist and Anarchist Deviation").

Lenin's first resolution prohibited factionalism of any kind, no matter how dedicated the representatives of such groups might be to party unity; it ordered the dissolution of all groups within the party, and threatened factionalists, even members of the Central Committee, with expulsion. His second resolution affirmed the absolute necessity of leadership over the proletariat by the party, much as he had stated in 1902.[16] In presenting his resolutions Lenin spoke of the need for unity in a party surrounded by enemies, and the Bolshevik idealists as usual swallowed their qualms for fear of endangering the party and of excluding themselves from it and hence from the building of socialism. Even the deputies who were in opposition voted to outlaw their own movement.

The Workers' Opposition and the Democratic Centralists had done nothing contrary to party rules and practices; they had been invited to promote their platforms for the Tenth Congress. But Lenin, who had been the proud and forthright leader of a faction of the Russian Social Democratic party, thought the time had come to squeeze the party into the uniformity he had always desired and to end any organized promotion of deviant ideas—"to put an end to opposition," as he stated.

Lenin attacked the oppositionists for endangering "the dictatorship of the proletariat," and shortly afterward reprisals began, effectively banning not only the formation of factions but also any criticism from below the top ranks. Dissenters were given undesirable assignments or posted away from Moscow, the center of influence. The power of the Central Committee over the trade unions was sharply asserted; if a union elected officers who were disagreeable to the Central Committee, they were simply set aside and others were appointed.

Most seriously, a new purge was undertaken just two years after the 1919 cleansing of the party rolls. It was ostensibly directed not against deviationists, but against careerists and other unsuitable elements who might have wormed their way into party ranks. The special commissions that were set up to conduct the purge were to be staffed, so far as possible, by prerevolutionary comrades.

Between August and December 1921, between a quarter and a third of the party was expelled—members of peasant origin suffered the most, white collars were next, and "workers" were harmed the least.[17] This purge actually seems not to have been directed against oppositionist opinions—dissenters were subject to removal directly by central organs—but it underlined the insecurity of the members. Exclusion from the party meant exclusion from political life, very likely the end of a career, and membership was contingent on good behavior in the eyes of the authorities.

The prohibition of factions was regarded at the time as a temporary measure that was necessitated by the dangers to party rule, of which Kronstadt was the climax.[18] But it represented only another step toward totalitarianism. For a few years echoes remained of the old controversies about the role of the workers in the party; the members had absorbed too much Marxism to forget quickly that the proletariat was supposed to be the ruling class under socialism. For example, a small "Workers' Group" argued at the Twelfth Congress, in April 1923, for freedom and power for the workers.[19] But after 1921 a critical tendency within the party could hope for a hearing only if it was associated with major figures of the central oligarchy.

LENIN'S RETREAT

The political tightening of 1921, the elimination of the other parties, and the repression of coherent dissent within the party came at the same time as a relaxation in economic and other spheres. On the one hand there was a stiffening of controls, on the other a retreat from ideological claims. The reason for both developments was the same, a desire to preserve the power of the party: the repression permitted the relaxation, while the relaxation necessitated the repression.

By the end of the civil war, the economic chaos—the failure of agricultural and industrial production and distribution—was evident, and hunger had become widespread. The ruble was practically valueless. The standard of living of the workers was much lower than it had been under tsarist exploitation (as Khrushchev acknowledged in 1924).[20] Controls were worthless; most food was sold illegally and state industry was dependent on black-market supplies. Nevertheless, faith in centralization was hardly shaken. Even the fiasco of the labor armies failed to convince most party members that the remedy for the breakdown of controls was not more and better controls. The political-ideological system seemed almost compulsively bound to think in terms of centralization.

Lenin, however, had the good sense or flexibility to recognize, after three years of economic breakdown, that Russia was not ripe for socialism, as nearly all Marxists had maintained before 1917. Before the Tenth Congress he cautiously brought up the desirability of a retreat on the economic front, but his colleagues were strongly opposed to such a move. However, under the pressure of peasant revolts, especially the Kronstadt uprising, Lenin introduced his proposals at the end of the Tenth Congress, and they were passed with very little debate and against slight opposition from Trotsky and some leftists.

The primary element of Lenin's "New Economic Policy" (NEP) was to relieve the peasants of requisitions, and instead to levy a fixed grain tax. It also granted freedom to buy and sell and allowed limited freedom to manufacture for the market. In essence, it legalized the private trade that already existed and encouraged agricultural and industrial production by private enterprise. Under the circumstances it was the only possible course and it probably saved the state. Upon being informed of it, many Kronstadt rebels felt that they did not need to fight any longer because their cause had triumphed.

Yet the opposition was passionate. For Marxists who took seriously the belief that the political order was determined by the economic base, the retreat from controls (which they equated with socialism) seemed to threaten the power of the party. At least, they thought, the mixed economy logically called for a coalition government, although no one in the party suggested sharing power. Before the NEP the party had been held together and inspired by the belief that it was building socialism; this hope compensated for all the material sufferings. To surrender this dream of utopia plunged the party into moral uncertainty about its ultimate purposes and its legitimacy. The Mensheviks had from the outset doubted the possibility of socialism in Russia in the near future, and had advocated measures like those adopted by Lenin; the fact that they had been proved right made it more necessary to crush them. Within the party, the issue was too divisive for open discussion. The Workers' Opposition led the denunciation of the NEP as a bourgeois measure; as a result, they, like the Mensheviks, who also decried the NEP as bourgeois, were branded as counterrevolutionary. Since ideology had failed to uphold the unity of the party, this goal had to be reached by fiat—by organization and compulsion.

Some were disillusioned, especially young Communists, even, in a few cases, to the point of suicide. But the NEP was a great success. The majority of the population greeted it with profound relief and credited Lenin with wisdom and courage in overcoming the dogmatists. Non-Communist Russian intellectuals (and many foreigners) welcomed it on the same grounds that Communists hated it—the conviction that economic liberalization was certain to lead back to political moderation—and they decided that it was again worthwhile to work for the future.

Lenin himself seems to have been impressed by the success of his mixed state, which actually incorporated most of what he had envisaged for Russia in 1905, a capitalist economy under the dictatorship of the proletariat (or party). He expected it to last a long time, presumably decades, and he turned around to favor individual farming, aided by cooperatives. He saw trade as very important, and "learn commerce" became an uncharacteristic slogan of the Communist party.

Lenin presided over a whole series of changes generalizing the retreat. The currency, a few months earlier seemingly slated to disappear, was reformed and stabilized with a backing of gold (a metal Lenin had previously consigned to the making of toilets). The state, which was originally supposed to wither away, was refashioned on a permanent basis. The various minority areas, such as the Ukraine, Armenia, and Azerbaidzhan, which had been theoretically independent republics joined somewhat irregularly by the party, joint military forces, and sundry treaties, were formally brought together in December 1922 (largely under the management of Stalin) to form the Soviet Union. New law codes were promulgated that were essentially bourgeois in content. The political police (the Cheka) was eliminated, but a supposedly less arbitrary substitute, the GPU (State Political Directorate) was put in its place, and terror remained a permanent, although diminished, factor. The party made a peace of sorts with the church. The arts were permitted substantial latitude so long as they did not attack the party and state, and artists became more creative than they were to be ever after in the Soviet Union. There was also some drawing back from the sexual freedom and antifamily attitudes of an earlier day.[21]

The relations of the Communist state to the non-Communist world also evolved in an ideologically unforeseeable direction, accentuating the ambivalence inherent in the friendly dealings of the revolutionary regime with, or its dependence on, those whom it overtly would destroy. In 1921−22 drought brought famine, and Lenin appealed, through Gorky and other respectable figures, for help abroad, Foreign aid, mostly American (later dismissed as espionage), saved millions of Russian lives. Revolutionism was toned down in harmony with the NEP, as the Third Congress of the Comintern, in June 1921, proclaimed a strategy of a "United Front" with non-Communist leftists. Theoretically, the party was still a sector of the international revolutionary movement, and Lenin continued to claim that resumption of the war between capitalism and socialism was inevitable, but foreign commerce grew rapidly after its renewal in 1920. Late in 1921 a Soviet delegate at trade talks in Riga promised abolition of the foreign-trade monopoly, a fundamental of the socialist state. This concession conformed to the spirit of the NEP and to general sentiment in the party and was supported by Stalin; Lenin, who was already sick, had to battle in alliance with Trotsky to secure its reversal.[22] Another signal shift away from revolutionary ideals was the rapprochement with bourgeois Weimar Germany, an economic agreement that was supplemented by the Rapallo entente of April 1922. Military collaboration followed; thus, while the Communist party (through the Comintern) was encouraging and arming German Communists, the Soviet state was providing facilities for the Reichswehr, which was repressing German Communists.

The Communist state even invited foreign capitalists to collaborate, like Russian capitalists, in the building of the Soviet economy. Lenin hoped for a large influx of foreign capital and expertise. He told the assembled world revolution makers in 1922 that "we are trying to found mixed companies, that we are already forming them, i. e. companies in which part of the capital belongs to private capitalists—and foreign capitalists at that—and the other part belongs to the state."[23] There was much talk of concessions, especially for the development of Soviet natural resources by foreign enterprises; Lenin even toyed with a fatuous scheme to rent Kamchatka, in the Soviet Far East, to an American adventurer. Krassin, a skilled engineer, onetime organizer of expropriations, and former recruiter of "bourgeois specialists," became one of the leading promoters of relations with foreign capitalists. Nevertheless, despite Lenin's enthusiasm, Krassin's talents, and much interest on the part of Western entrepreneurs— there were thousands of applications—few contracts were signed, and these mostly fizzled.

The failure of the concessions policy notwithstanding, the "state capitalism" inaugurated by Lenin seemed successful and permanent. Under it the Communist Party held a monopoly of political power and the "commanding heights" of the economy, large enterprises, means of transportation, banks, and so on, while leaving to private ownership and management what it could not competently handle in any case, agriculture, small industrial plants, and most trade. It seemed to be a rational synthesis between Russian autocracy, which was perhaps inescapable at best, and economic imperatives. By about 1928, this policy had brought the standard of living up from the depths of 1920−22 to the level of 1914, with a good deal less inequality.

The NEP seemed permanent. It was excused as a temporary retreat at the outset, but this was simply a gloss to make it less repulsive to the dogmatists. The system expanded for at least five years, and there was no reason to suppose that it would be reversed. The revolution had apparently worn itself out, and Russia was returning, after the freshening and equalizing ordeal, to something like the patterns of tsarist Russia.

But part of the strength of the new economics and the rebirth of some nonpolitical freedom was undoubtedly due to the weakness of the leadership at the center. Lenin was incapacitated most of the time from his first stroke (in May 1922) until his death in January 1924, and leadership was divided for a few years thereafter. During this period the government took no strong initiatives but mostly let the country drift, to its great benefit. No one could guess how much potential for change remained latent in Lenin's party.

LENIN'S LAST YEARS

The party was so dependent on its sole and uncontested founder and leader that it was fortunate to have nearly two years to adjust to his disappearance. In fact his health had not been good since he was wounded in the neck in August 1918. During his last six years he hardly left Moscow and the Kremlin. He had long been subject to neurasthenic or psychosomatic illnesses, marked by insomnia and headache, and these became worse after the latter part of 1921.[24] The death and funeral at that time of Inessa Armand, at which he grieved deeply, may have injured his constitution.[25] In May 1922 he suffered a cerebral stroke, which, according to Trotsky, caused in him a deep inner fear.[26] Lenin recovered sufficiently to return to work in the fall, and he spoke to a Comintern congress in November, but December 12, 1922, was his last day at his desk. He suffered a second, more severe, stroke, after which he probably saw no political leaders but communicated only through his wife Krupskaya and occasionally his secretaries. A third stroke in March 1923 completely incapacitated him. Again he gradually recovered a little, but he finally died on January 21, 1924.

Even before Lenin's serious illness, his grip had been weakening. He took little part in the Eleventh Congress, which was held in March 1922. The congress had enough independence to decline, contrary to Lenin's wishes, to expel from the party the leaders of the former Workers' Opposition, Shliapnikov, Medvedev, and Kollontai; it also disregarded Lenin's proposal that the probationary period be lengthened for peasants to make the party more proletarian. After Lenin was removed from the scene, the remainder of the Politburo (Trotsky, the outsider, was generally not included) took over the reins, assuming much of the authority that rested in the Council of Commissars even though Lenin still chaired it. The chief leaders were Zinoviev, Lenin's longtime second-in-command, Kamenev, who was the Moscow party secretary and presided over the Politburo in Lenin's absence, and Stalin.

Of these Zinoviev was the most celebrated and, after Trotsky, the heir apparent to Lenin's authority. Kamenev was personally the closest to Lenin of the leading Bolsheviks. Stalin was the organization man, not much seen or heard, who occupied several strategic positions in the apparatus. His strongest power base was the position of Secretary General of the party, to which he had been named (with Molotov and Kuibyshev as assistants) in April 1922, on the eve of Lenin's stroke, with at least the concurrence of Lenin, who seems to have wanted Stalin to tighten party discipline.[27] As party manager, Stalin was charged by the Politburo with conducting relations with Lenin and supervising his care during his illness.

Stalin seems to have endeavored to isolate Lenin as much as possible on the grounds that excitement was dangerous for him. Whether or not it was healthier for Lenin to chafe in frustration than to receive visitors, read, and write, the formerly active leader was largely kept in isolation, rationed in the length of time he could dictate, restricted in his reading, and so on. In these last months of enforced idleness, so far as he could function, Lenin seems to have reconsidered his life's work. He saw the Soviet state turning out to be not a vision of freedom, but practically a new autocracy. A short while before his stroke, he had written in a letter to the Central Committee, "It must be recognized that the Party's proletarian policy is determined at present not by its rank and file but by the immense and undivided authority of the tiny sector that might be called the Party's Old Guard."[28] Afterwards he became increasingly weighed down by the feeling that the old Russia lived on—that his revolution had only put a new bureaucracy in place—and he foresaw bureaucratic degeneration. He even stated that the culture of the leading Communists was less advanced than the wretched culture of the old order, and used such phrases as "Com-boasts" and "Com-lies," as though he had turned anti-Communist.[29] He saw the control agency he had created to combat mounting bureaucratism, the Workers' and Peasants' Inspectorate, turning into a bureaucratic monstrosity. He seemed to have surrendered much of his utopian vision of the new society, since he now regarded cooperatives as the basis for what could only be a very gradualist approach to socialism.

But Lenin's analysis of the fundamental problem of politics, the prevention of the abuse of power, was restricted by his Marxist preconceptions. His only recipe for halting the invidious trends was proletarian oversight—a curious reversal of his earlier insistence, both before and after the revolution (indeed up until his incapacity), on the necessity for the party to guide and oversee the workers. He proposed creating a new control commission, or expanding the Central Committee, by adding a large number of true-blue workers and charging this new worker-dominated Central Committee with supervision of the Politburo and Council of Commissars.[30] Naively, he had no suggestions about how these pure workers should be chosen or how a Stalin might be prevented from bringing in unsophisticated supporters of his personal dictatorship. (Most "workers" in the party, it may be noted, had nonmanual positions and were "workers" only by alleged background.)[31]

Lenin also turned away from his predilection for centralization when he was no longer at the center of things. His old hatred of Russian domination came to the fore, and he concluded that the minority peoples of the just-formed Soviet Union should have much more freedom than Stalin and others in the party wanted for them and much more than they presently enjoyed. He wanted true federalism, with all-Union commissariats only for foreign affairs and defense and with other matters returned to the separate republics.[32] He also wanted the various nationalities to furnish in sequence the presiding officer of the Soviet Union.[33] Lenin took such ideas very seriously, and, together with a concern for rights and an abhorrence for violence that were quite out of harmony with his previous career, they led him into serious conflict with Stalin.

Much of Lenin's irritation with Stalin in 1923 may have been caused simply by the fact that Stalin was carrying out the will of the Politburo in restricting and isolating the ailing boss. Lenin's anger came to a head, however, over the

Georgian question. Georgia had come out of the turmoil of the revolution and civil war as an independent socialist (largely Menshevik) state, with its independence formally recognized by Soviet Russia. In February 1921, however, the Red Army invaded and sovietized it, on the initiative of Stalin and Ordzhonikidze, but with the concurrence of Lenin and the Politburo.[34] The Georgian Bolsheviks, who were eager to earn popularity, assumed a nationalistic stance in relation to their state's economic and political integration in the Soviet Union that was being put together in 1922. In particular, the Georgians did not wish to be amalgamated first into a Transcaucasian Federation.

After some controversy over this and related issues, Ordzhonikidze went to Georgia to bring the locals to heel; there he resorted to strong-arm methods, and in the course of an altercation struck a Georgian Communist. Up to November 1922 Lenin had shown full confidence in Stalin, but he turned away from him when he learned of the coercion of the Georgians, despite Stalin's efforts to keep the affair from him. What Stalin, with Ordzhonikidze and Dzerzhinsky (all non-Russians), had done to Georgia was not especially brutal, however, certainly no more brutal than the original invasion, and Stalin could brush aside criticisms by pointing to similar or graver abuses in the Ukraine and Central Asia. Consequently he may have felt greatly injured when Lenin went onto the offensive in the first part of 1923 against the three leaders who had squelched the Georgian Bolsheviks.

Stalin was already angry with Krupskaya for her part in maintaining communications between Lenin and Trotsky, to Stalin's detriment, and at this stage he treated her to an uncharacteristic outburst of bad temper. On March 5 Lenin threatened to break off all personal relations with Stalin because of his rudeness.[35] The next day Lenin telegraphed support to the leaders of the Georgian opposition and expressed his outrage at ''the arrogance of Ordzhonikidze and the connivance of Stalin and Dzerzhinsky.'' Lenin had already bitterly criticized the inspectorate headed by Stalin (without naming Stalin) in an article, ''Better Less but Better,'' whose publication in *Pravda* Stalin had managed to delay by four weeks.

According to Trotsky, Lenin was thinking of establishing a Lenin-Trotsky bloc to oppose Stalin and the apparatus; Lenin had already urged Trotsky by letter to ''undertake the defense of the Georgian affair at the Central Committee.''[36] Stalin seems to have epitomized for Lenin the aspects of the Communist state he had turned away from in his meditations during his grave illness. But the ''bomb'' Lenin was preparing against Stalin for the Twelfth Congress[37] never exploded. On March 10 Lenin lost forever the power of speech, and whatever statement he had prepared may have been destroyed by Stalin. Nevertheless, his attack continued through the odd document known as ''Lenin's Testament.'' This was a set of notes that had been painfully dictated from December 22 through December 31, 1922, with a postscript added on January 4, 1923. It is a rather rambling and confusing document.[38] The main purpose of the Testament was to warn the party against a split between Trotsky and Stalin, but it gave no advice about how to avoid such a rift. It was surprising to most leaders that Lenin should have included Stalin as one of the two most important individuals in the party.

In this document Lenin characterized Stalin as follows: "Comrade Stalin, having become General Secretary, has unlimited authority concentrated in his hands, and I am not sure whether he will always be capable of using that authority with sufficient caution." Trotsky was treated a little more severely: "He is personally perhaps the most capable man in the present Central Committee, but he has displayed excessive self-assurance and shown excessive preoccupation with the purely administrative side of the work." Lenin also slyly mentioned Trotsky's "non-Bolshevism." Somewhat oddly, Lenin referred to the behavior of Kamenev and Zinoviev at the time of the October Revolution and then said that they were not to be blamed. Also rather oddly, Lenin called Bukharin "the most valuable and biggest theoretician of the party," and then went on to doubt that he was really a Marxist, saying that he had never fully understood the dialectic.

The Testament thus seemed designed to damage all of Lenin's potential successors; for reasons that remain unknown, it was especially hurtful to Trotsky. The postscript composed about four days later, however, proposed specific action against Stalin: "Stalin is too rude, and this defect, although quite tolerable in our midst and among Communists, becomes intolerable in a General Secretary. That is why I suggest that the comrades think about a way to remove Stalin from that post. . . ." It did not, however, ask that Stalin be relieved of any of his other posts.

Trotsky read Lenin's Testament with its postscript at a party meeting on May 22, 1924. It did not hurt Stalin as much as it might have; he was already in a very strong position and the Politburo did not desire to publicize the document since it reflected ill on everyone mentioned and Lenin suggested no alternatives. However, it probably delayed the rise to personal dictatorship that seemed foreordained for Stalin in view of the strategic positions he had held since 1922. Lenin's rueful thoughts on the sickbed were thus not without results.

LENIN THE LEADER

Lenin was honored as he neared death. Kamenev and Zinoviev exalted him rhetorically at the Twelfth Congress, the first he was unable to attend. In October 1923 the Institute of V. I. Lenin opened its doors. Immediately after his death, the second city of the Soviet Union and the scene of his special victories was named Leningrad. A mausoleum was built on Red Square to house his body, which became a holy relic of Soviet and world Communism (Krupskaya, who found this paganism tasteless and contrary to Lenin's modest taste, opposed this decision).[39] Countless commemorative services and exercises were held, and an unending series of eulogistic tributes, articles, books, and so on, began that has increased up to the present day. The departed Lenin took on for his party something of the importance of the living Lenin as guide and central figure.

In the Soviet Union Lenin became greatest of the great; he was overshadowed for a time by Stalin but restored and raised to even greater heights when de-Stalinization deprived the country of that idol, and even more when Brezhnev was raising himself over his colleagues. Lenin was held up as the perfect man, utterly wise, completely just, free of error, and absolutely devoted to the noblest of causes. Many non-Communist writers have also given Lenin high marks as a character and political genius, a man of exemplary sagacity and judgment who was ruthless at times but personally unpretentious and driven by deep idealism— a determination to bring about the social forms he believed (perhaps erroneously) would give the greatest happiness to his people.

Some of the respect Lenin elicits even from those who dislike his doctrines derives from the sheer fact of his success. Lenin's name has come to be one of the most celebrated of history, in company with those of Buddha, Mohammed, and Napoleon, and the like; his revolution was one of the great turning points of history. Anyone who had such gigantic impact must be regarded as a giant among men.

But it may be irreverently suggested that if Lenin had fallen from a cliff while mountain climbing during his years in Switzerland, the judgment of posterity would have marked him down as no great genius. At that time in his life he was only one of many voices of international socialism. He had shown no tremendous magnetism and was notably unable to win the allegiance of the recognized lights of Russian Marxism. He was the leader of a small party that was outstanding only for its activism. His publications were not much noted; they have become important only because of his later fame. He was capable of grubbing for facts, but his writings lack the erudition, wit, and subtlety of Marx's. Turgid and repetitive, interesting only where he occasionally makes an important point, Lenin is far less readable than numerous writers of the socialist persuasion, such as Karl Kautsky, Eduard Bernstein, Rosa Luxemburg, or even Bukharin. It is asking too much, however, to expect the man of action to be a polished writer. Lenin did well to combine reasonable expository ability with party leadership. His output kept up even after he became the ruler of Russia; although he no longer took time to produce books, he dashed off a multitude of articles.

Lenin can hardly be rated a major political thinker. He was far less concerned with realities than with what a few Marxists said about them, and his polemics against his rivals—the largest body of his writings—contain far more sarcasm and dogmatic assertions of a sole claim to truth than facts or analysis.[40] The Marxist framework that compressed Lenin's thinking gave him many pseudoanswers, but tended to impede his political understanding. Lenin paid little attention to political institutions except in broad, propagandistic terms; in his Marxist approach only "class" counted.

Lenin had little idea of law or legality, and he gave minimal attention to the problem of controlling power. He seems to have assumed that since his party somewhat mystically represented the virtuous proletarian class, he could have centralization without bureaucratism and careerism. Only at the end of his career did he present a solution, the bringing of workers into the top echelons of the party. This was an incredibly naive answer coming from a man who did not adhere dogmatically to the letter of Marxist doctrine and who had had experience of the foibles of persons of all origins in positions of power—whose primary thesis, in fact, had been the ideological flabbiness of the workers.

If consistency is an essential part of greatness, Lenin fell short of it. He was ready to change his policies according to the political needs of the moment in the areas of land reform, the revolutionary role of the soviets (several times), and the war. After having laid all his emphasis on political-ideological improvement, he turned around after gaining power to stress technological improvement and engineering, the electrification of Russia as the key to the building of the communist order. He was an inconsistent Marxist in that he hated rival socialists more than capitalists, Kautsky more than Churchill.[41] Unlike many socialists, he did not thoroughly despise the old order and desire everything to be changed.

Lenin's chief immodesty was his absolute conviction of the rightness of his own views.[42] His personal life was rather conventional and austere until near the end. His morality was old-fashioned in the eyes of many morally liberated revolutionaries. He was not opposed to symbols of the past. After occupying the seat of the Romanovs, he ate from plates bearing the tsarist double eagle.[43] Near the end of his life, Krupskaya put up a Christmas tree for him.

It is easily said that Lenin was truly consistent in the single thing that really counted, the unqualified drive for power. It is difficult to believe, however, that he seriously envisioned himself as the ruler of Russia before 1917. He certainly did not behave in 1905 as though he expected to play a great role in the big world of Russian politics; instead, he stood on the sidelines as though confused by it all, never plunging in to assert his supposedly indomitable ambition. To the contrary, he was a professional revolutionary and probably, like many professional revolutionaries, enjoyed that life. It demanded no regular discipline, and it was an easy existence as long as finances were manageable. It was also an intriguing life, with its conspiratorial comings and goings, secret messages, and the like. There were endless talkfests about changing the world, gossip about the small community of the exiles, and articles to be written for the party paper— an interesting life buoyed by the conviction that he was performing the highest service to humanity. Lenin seems to have become inspired to reach for real power only when the tsar was overthrown and a vacuum was created that no one was better able to fill.

In his drive to power, Lenin was unhampered by morality in the conventional sense. He had long equated morality with the party, whose will was not that of the membership but of the center, and in case of any difference, his own. In his view, he was the revolution and all who did not go with him were counter-revolutionary. More correctly, Lenin did not deal in morality at all, but in Marxist science (as interpreted by Lenin); thus he was able to lift issues above ordinary human considerations while flexible enough to twist the dialectic to make it politically suitable. Finding his justifications in "class" terms, Lenin could be as deceptive or cruel as he pleased. He was ruthless enough to shoot people for minor offense or merely for having the wrong background, and he could be harsh about trivial matters. For example, he once ordered a sanatorium director imprisoned for cutting down a tree.[44] He stated frankly that morality meant simply the good of the revolution. His 1920 brochure, "Left Wing Communism, An Infantile Disorder," is a long plea for the use of practically Machiavellian tactics of deception for the sake of power.

Lenin did not become a despot, but it may be that circumstances saved him from the corruption of power. He had too little time as ruler, hardly a couple of years of peace before the shadow of death came over him. He behaved rather modestly in power, but that modesty was in part pretense. At a time when millions of Russians were near starvation, he rode in a Rolls-Royce. He insisted on limiting the pay of Communist officials, but permitted them to have privileges and perquisites that were worth much more than money.

Lenin's great strength was precisely his flexibility, his inconsistency if one will, within his consistent purposes. He made errors of political judgment, but he was the great pragmatist even as he spoke in terms of fixed principles. He knew only roughly where he was going and was always ready to change directions; perhaps his greatest stroke was the reversal of the NEP. He especially liked the Napoleonic motto, "On s'engage, et puis . . . on voit." He was arrogant about the essence of power, but not about its details; he claimed to have been many times outvoted in the Central Committee on organizational and personnel matters.[45] His achievement was to have overcome the typical Russian overstress on theory and the indiscipline of the intelligentsia to forge an instrument of power in an incoherent society.

THE ADVENT OF STALIN

It was Lenin's party and it became Stalin's; it was originally shaped by Lenin but later reshaped by Stalin. Indeed, Stalin not only replaced nearly all of the old

Leninist leadership, but he became much more the master of the party than Lenin, with his much shorter tenure of governmental power, had ever been. And if Lenin was responsible for the formation of the party, it was Stalin who made it the mighty instrument of government that has, without major change, endured to this day.

Yet Stalinism was only Leninism written large. Stalin set out in no new directions but, as soon as he was able, pushed Russia farther along the road on which Lenin had embarked in 1917–18, only to turn away in 1921. Stalin completed the transformations that had been implicit in Lenin's revolution. If Lenin had departed from European Marxism and Social Democracy, Stalin deepened the divorce (ultimately turning Marxism-Leninism into Marxism-Leninism-Stalinism). Stalin collectivized agriculture forcibly where Lenin had hoped it might be done voluntarily, incarnated Lenin's dreams of technological change under party leadership as the way to utopia, and made the party totally conformist (as Lenin had indicated but perhaps never really desired). Lenin had taught that the revolution could be started by political action in a country that was not ripe for socialism; Stalin went on to teach, in effect, that socialism could be made by purely political action and gigantic coercion.

Stalin had much less formal education than Lenin and never compensated for that lack by wide reading.[46] He was much less Western, far more Asian than Lenin. He came from a harsher and more violent world. Unlike Lenin, he never looked to the German comrades to lead the way and he took no interest in Lenin's favorite child, the Comintern, rarely attending any of its meetings and never doing so after he reached supremacy. Unlike Lenin, he never referred to Asia as a symbol of backwardness[47] but took a special interest in the development of his Asian territories.

Such cultured persons as Trotsky and Krupskaya regarded Stalin as uncouth. Although Lenin found Stalin very useful for many years, he finally concluded, ''Stalin is too rude.'' But this only makes Stalin's success the more puzzling. He rose to power through persuasion far more than coercion,[48] and his early followers were no mere yes-men or careerist toadies; this is why most of them were eventually purged. Up to 1929 Stalin usually represented common sense and loyalty to Lenin and the party, and he was the more credible because he was simple and unpretentious in manner. He was a poor public speaker,[49] but in the long run this may have served him well because he remained inconspicuous and was not perceived as a threat by his rivals. Stalin certainly had a fine sense of political timing, patience, a feeling for others' weaknesses, and enormous ambition unchecked by scruples.

Stalin had far more reason than Lenin to hate the educated classes of Russia. In addition to belonging to a subject nationality, he arose from poverty that was in marked contrast to the affluence of the Ulianovs. His father was a poor cobbler, born in serfdom (Stalin was unique among Bolshevik leaders in this regard). Some effort has been made[50] to link Stalin's character with the beatings Vissarion Dzhugashvili probably inflicted on his wife and son. Cause and effect are dubious here, but it is certain that young Joseph was early familiarized with violence and evasion. Perhaps equally important psychologically were a complexion disfigured by smallpox, a left arm stiffened in childhood by infection, and a stature that was some inches shorter than Napoleon's—he was about 5'5" and used elevator shoes.

Stalin's formal education consisted of eleven years of religious training, from the ages of nine to nearly twenty (1888–99). His intensely religious mother managed to send him to a church school in Gori. Upon graduation, he passed the entrance examinations for the seminary in Tbilisi, the Georgian capital, with high enough marks to win a scholarship. The seminary, the only higher education open to the Georgian youth, was more successful in producing revolutionaries than priests. Stalin credited its crushing discipline with assisting his conversion to Marxism.[51] A key influence was the monks' effort to keep the students' minds pure; not only radical literature but also modern scientific writing was forbidden. Despite these prohibitions, the seminary became a center of nationalist and socialist talk, and Joseph Dzhugashvili became affiliated with a local Social Democratic group. He was expelled from the seminary, formally for his failure to take examinations.

Put out on the street short of the age of twenty, embittered against the official Russian church (Russian was required in the seminary), a member of the intelligentsia unqualified for any occupation other than the priesthood, the ex-student quickly drifted into revolutionary activities. Within months he was caught up in the exciting but dangerous life of an agitator, which was composed of strikes, demonstrations, secret meetings, subversive leaflets, and conspiratorial maneuvers. He was the active organizer of revolutionary violence that Lenin never was. In 1902 he was arrested for the first of many times; unlike Lenin he spent nearly seventeen years either on the run from the police or in their hands. As a Georgian of no particular standing, he was also treated more roughly than Lenin, an upper-class Russian.*

In another age a discontented Georgian might well have sought romance and self-fulfillment in banditry, but as Stalin came of age Marxism was the prevalent rationale for revolution in Georgia as in central Russia; it was the more appealing to the minority nationality because Russia was identified with the upper classes and serf-holders. Stalin was something of a nationalist early in his career, and he used the nickname Koba (after the hero of a Georgian tale) until he adopted "Stalin" (from the Russian-German word for "steel") in 1912. But where

---

*That Stalin had some affiliation with the tsarist police, as is often asserted, is unproved, but it is circumstantially indicated and not improbable in view of the frequent mingling of Okhrana and revolutionary activities.

national independence was hardly a practical possibility—as was the case for small Georgia, which was squeezed between Russia, Turkey, and Iran—nationalism went easily into Marxism.

Stalin went into the Bolshevik faction of Georgian Social Democracy, although the Mensheviks had an overwhelming majority in the area. This choice reduced his effectiveness in the Caucasus, but Stalin disliked some of the Menshevik leaders, either for personal reasons or because they were more educated or because there were many Jews among them. He claimed to have been attracted by Lenin's militancy; moreover, Lenin's doctrines made full-time revolutionaries like Stalin the heirs of the future.

As a leading Bolshevik in the Caucasus, Stalin was in contact with Krassin and Kamenev. In 1905 he engaged in an activity he pursued with great success in his later career, restating Lenin in bold and simple terms. A brochure in which Stalin summarized the Leninist creed came to Lenin's attention and greatly impressed him. Not long afterwards Stalin was sent to the Bolshevik conference at Tammerfors, Finland, and there he met the leader. He was also at the 1906 Stockholm congress, although with dubious credentials, and was again a nonvoting delegate at the 1907 London congress. In that year he also became a member of the Bolshevik committee in Baku, to which he had transferred after quarrels with Social Democratic circles in Tbilisi and Batum.

Stalin spent nearly seven of the following ten years in Siberian exile, from which he escaped several times. In 1910 he left the Caucasus to work in the Russian arena. He made trips abroad, but left the safety and comfort of Western Europe after a few weeks to return to the hazards of action in Russia. His signal rise in the party came early in 1912, when, after the Prague congress that sealed the separation of the Bolsheviks from the Mensheviks, Lenin co-opted him into the Central Committee as one of eleven full members. Lenin chose him no doubt for his loyalty, since that quality was especially in demand when Lenin was setting up his formally organized party. A little later, the Central Committee created a Russian bureau to direct its activities inside Russia; this consisted of Stalin, Ordzhonikidze, another Caucasian, and a Russian—tributes to the importance Lenin ascribed to the Caucasus and to his trust in Stalin. Late in 1912 Stalin went to visit Lenin in Krakow, and the leader honored him with the assignment of writing an essay on the nationality problem. Despite his ignorance of foreign languages and his scanty education, Stalin went to Vienna, worked in the libraries, and came up with a piece that pleased Lenin and earned his praise for Stalin as "the wonderful Georgian."

By this work Stalin earned his spurs as a Marxist theorist and advanced his party standing.[52] Unlike most Bolsheviks, he was not prone to theoretical controversy and consequently did not make many enemies; most important, he had almost no record of differences with Lenin, although he had taken a non-Leninist position on the agrarian question, the boycott of the Duma, and other issues.[53]

Stalin was arrested on his return to Russia. This was the work of Lenin's favorite, Malinovsky, and it may have burned into Stalin a fear of traitors in high places. He was sent to a dismal location near the Arctic Circle, where he wrote nothing—he had never written during his various periods of exile—and had little to do with his fellow exiles. By 1916 the government was so desperate that it was drafting revolutionaries, but Stalin was exempted because of his bad left arm. After the fall of the tsar, Stalin hastened back to Petrograd to place himself, with Kamenev, in charge of *Pravda* and unofficially at the head of the local Bolsheviks. His general tone then was reasonable and tolerant, but upon the return of Lenin he put himself firmly behind the leader's intransigence. Thereafter Stalin faded from prominence, although the fact that he received the most votes for the editorship of the party paper in July indicated his popularity in the party. He had very little to do with the coup or with the formation of the new government, although his post of Commissar of Nationalities was fairly important. This office put him in charge of dealings with nearly half the population and gave him a basis for recruiting support among the party leaders of minority areas.

In the civil war Stalin had a role that was much inferior to Trotsky's but still honorable. He was the organizational leader of the party (under Lenin) and a roving inspector of the fronts; as such he inevitably came into friction with the truculent Commissar of War, whom Stalin resented as a newcomer to Bolshevism. Stalin also sided with the old-time Bolsheviks who resented Trotsky's employment of tsarist officers. The chief clash between the two future enemies came over the conduct of the defense of Tsaritsyn (later Stalingrad). Stalin and Voroshilov took charge, to Trotsky's chagrin. In the ruckus, Stalin came forward as the one who wanted to talk things over, while Trotsky made peremptory demands for the removal of those who had crossed him.[54]

Stalin's civil-war activities were largely out of view, and he took very little part in the party debates of 1920−21. By 1921, however, Lenin had come to rely heavily on him and to hold him up as an example of the good Communist who was always willing to do the party's bidding. When Lenin was stricken in 1922, Stalin had been a Central Committee member since 1912, a member of the Politburo since its beginning, a member of the Orgburo since 1919, the head of the Workers' and Peasants' Inspectorate since 1919, and the holder of sundry other posts; although he was no toady to Lenin, he was the only major figure never to have stood against the leader publicly. Beginning in April 1922, he was General Secretary of the Central Committee and chief orchestrator of the apparatus—the incarnation of its bureaucratism and mediocrity in Trotsky's eyes.[55] He was also the chief manager in the formation of the structure of the Soviet Union in 1922. In hindsight, he was an obvious candidate to step into Lenin's shoes.

STALIN DEFEATS TROTSKY

The popular figure who was closest in rank to Lenin, however, was Trotsky; and Trotsky, the victor in the civil war and the respected commander of the armed forces, in all probability could have seized power if he had chosen to act. Stalin won for the simple reason that he industriously built up his power while Trotsky rather obtusely, or from inappropriate diffidence, stood back and watched his position crumble.[56]

Stalin always spoke in the name of the party and as its humble servant; he made himself the exponent of the party and its spokesman, so that to attack him was to attack the party, the instrument of progress and history. He held organizational jobs that were grubby and demanding of continuous attention, hence not attractive to most old Bolsheviks. Moreover, he did them well, at least to the satisfaction of most. He was more accessible to underlings than any other leader, listened more than he talked, had no visible vices or extravagances, and was relatively tolerant of different viewpoints—a man of very democratic manners, as Khrushchev remembered.[57] His Secretariat, which gradually took over functions of the Orgburo, had a decisive advantage over the more prestigious Politburo in that the Secretariat was a continuously functioning body that could handle countless details for which the Politburo had no time—not only managing personnel, but deciding what matters were to be presented to the Politburo and how, and controlling the implementation of decisions. Moreover, it kept dossiers on party members that proved to be effective levers when expulsion was a possibility and promotion was a hope. As General Secretary, Stalin could send men to Siberia or abroad, citing only party need; for example, Rakovsky, a prominent Trotskyite, was put out of the way as ambassador to London in July 1923. A little later Trotsky complained that his supporters were being scattered and that it was necessary to be anti-Trotsky to get a good job in the party.[58]

Stalin's colleagues were not unaware of the potential of the secretaryship at the time he was appointed; in 1920 the three Secretaries, headed by Krestinsky, had become powerful over the apparatus, and Zinoviev had intrigued against them, helping to secure their ouster in 1921. But other Politburo members were not afraid of the Georgian and hoped he would manage the apparatus for their benefit. However, the power of the General Secretary was greatly increased in 1922–23 not only by the character of the occupant, but also by virtue of Lenin's incapacity, in addition to the fact that the Politburo was in disarray. Moreover, the Council of Ministers had lost standing in the absence of its chairman. The apparatus capped by the Secretariat developed a life of its own, independent of the brain at the top, the Politburo, which supposedly directed it. The apparatus was central to the unity and strength of the party, and it always prevailed except on the few occasions when Lenin opposed it. The unity of the party has always been more important than any question of principle, and party unity is virtually equivalent to the strength of the apparatus.

To make the party his own, Stalin made it largely new; he had only to follow the wish of the sick leader for the inclusion of more virtuous proletarians. He enlarged the Central Committee from twenty-seven members in 1922 to fifty-three in 1924, a step that made it less capable of managing the regular apparatus and diluted or replaced old-time Leninists with new-style bosses of nonintellectual background who were prepared to work with Stalin.

Stalin also gave the party pyramid a new base. There was a sharp and prolonged contraction of party rolls in 1921−23, probably because of Lenin's obsession with purity,[59] but in 1922, at the Eleventh Congress, Lenin decided that the party was still too big, with about 500,000 members (candidates included). In 1923, however, a recruitment drive was begun among the peasantry, who had hitherto been unrepresented, and in 1924 Stalin began a massive "Lenin enlistment" of industrial workers, few of whom were fervid Trotskyites. At the Thirteenth Congress, in 1924, a goal was stated of bringing in "the whole basic mass of the proletariat" so that "the vast majority of members of the party in the near future should consist of workers directly engaged in production."[60] Some 250,000 were admitted under the relaxed entry requirements. A second "Lenin enroll-ment," which was proclaimed on the anniversary of his death, added another 300,000, more than doubling the total rolls. Subsequently the party kept on growing, although more slowly, until it reached 3.5 million in 1933. Democracy and ideological purity were served by preferentially drawing into the party workers who were supposedly exempt from careerist and bureaucratic vices—an ever-persuasive theme. But recruitment provided endless opportunities for rewarding friends and forwarding potential supporters to new positions in the expanding hierarchy.

The recruitment of new workers was supplemented in 1924−25 by a purge that removed a large fraction of the holdovers, some 100,000 of them—mostly students, teachers, and other intellectuals who were more likely to be favorable to Trotsky than to Stalin.[61] Stalin was the purge coordinator through the Central Control Commission, which was headed after April 1923 by a faithful Stalinist, Kuibyshev. The purge was effective not only with regard to those who were removed but also with regard to those who passed muster, because party membership meant good jobs at a time when unemployment was substantial. In view of the pressures the center could exert, it is remarkable that opposition was still very much alive in 1924.

The possibility that dissenters at the base of the party could make their views felt shrank steadily, however. The installation by the center of nominally elected party officials had been growing ever since 1917; Stalin had only to carry it a little farther to make the hierarchy of secretaries and committeemen as dependent and disciplined as army officers. Party officials were switched around frequently to prevent them from developing local roots and to keep them dependent upon Stalin as sole source of their authority and well-being. Democratic or semi-democratic practices were reduced. For example, provincial party conferences, which were quarterly in 1919, were held only annually after 1923.

To further strengthen his grip, Stalin built up in the party his own faction, to which the antifaction rules could not be applied. Stalin's faction differed from earlier oppositional movements in that it was held together not by a philosophy or program, but by the ambitions of its members and leaders. This practice was in the Leninist tradition that had been building since the Bolshevik group had first formed, and it gained for Stalin's group the same advantage Lenin had had in the power struggle—that of unencumbrance by any theoretical fetters and hence freedom to maneuver regarding issues.

Stalin organized his faction as the "activists" in the party cells. Ambitious members were invited to "activist" meetings, and this special organization became almost a party within the party. Stalin's group came to dominate the party in much the same way the party faction dominated nonparty organizations. Thus Stalin's activists, as "representatives of the party masses," could be turned against elements of the party that were still unaware that their chief duty was loyalty to the central, that is, Stalinist, authorities.[62] Stalin had only to call for votes in party congresses or in the Central Committee to expel from power, legally and democratically, the upper ranks left over from Lenin's day.

Stalin nonetheless felt it necessary, in the still fervent ideological temper of the time, to present himself as a philosophical spokesman, a theoretician of revolution and socialism, and 1923–29 was the prolific period of Stalin the writer. His forte, as long before, was the exposition of Leninism as he understood it and its application to the problems of the day, especially the unity and discipline of the party. Speaking in simple, often forceful terms, he restated Leninism as a set of unambiguous propositions that could easily be understood by the less sophisticated party members. From the day of Lenin's death, Stalin also made himself the chief spokesman of the cult of the departed leader; that cult was to his advantage, since he was reputed to have been Lenin's most loyal follower. Trotsky, on the other hand, tended to oppose the idolization of Lenin,[63] as well he might in view of the bitter words Lenin had directed against him on many occasions before 1917.

Stalin laid claim to being Lenin's successor in his liturgical funeral eulogy. Filled with biblical images and sequences, as well as the repetition of phrases such as, "Departing from us, Comrade Lenin enjoined us to . . ." and "We vow to thee, Comrade Lenin, that we will fulfill this thy behest. . . ," it was exceptionally effective—the best of Stalin's oratory. Stalin went on promoting the semireligious cult in many ways—exhorting the party to keep faith with Lenin; calling for the collection of Leniniana for the Lenin Institute; getting the Congress of Soviets and other bodies to swear allegiance to Lenin; holding memorial meetings; having countless speeches made, articles written, and the like, in Lenin's memory—all in a magnificent demonstration of love for a man whom he seems to have hated intensely. Leninism suited Stalin, however, since it legitimized his own authority, and shortly after Lenin's death the Central Committee decreed that party schools should concentrate on party history and on Lenin's ideas.[64]

However, Stalin had to get over the departing Lenin's embarrassing injunction to remove him from the position of General Secretary as too rude. He was saved by his rivals, who also desired to bury Lenin's Testament even as Lenin was being canonized. Krupskaya released the Testament on the eve of the Thirteenth Congress, in May 1924, but the oligarchs showed it to only a small group, with the explanation that it was a product of Lenin's illness and resentment against those who were trying to spare him excitement. Only ten out of thirty present voted to publicize it. Kamenev and Zinoviev still saw Stalin as an ally, and Trotsky preferred Stalin to have the position of General Secretary instead of Kamenev or Zinoviev or one of their adherents. Not long afterward, the Testament was published abroad by Trotsky's supporters, but he vigorously denounced it as fraudulent, probably because he, too, was injured by it. It was not released in the Soviet Union until the approach of de-Stalinization in 1955.

Stalin was not content merely to build himself up as an exponent of Leninism. In 1924 he hit upon an appealing and useful doctrine, "socialism in one country," that went contrary to Lenin's effort (following in the line of Trotsky's permanent revolution) to square revolution in Russia with Marxism by viewing it as only the opener in the world revolution. Lenin had overtly made the Russian Revolution more or less conditional upon the German upheaval it was supposed to trigger. It was possible to keep up hopes for the spread of revolution to industrialized Europe during the civil war, and these hopes were essential for Soviet morale. But the prospects for it dimmed steadily after 1918, and they were feeble indeed after the Red Army was thrown back from Warsaw in August 1920. Nevertheless, Soviet leaders (excluding Stalin) continued to attach great importance to the envisioned world revolution and the instrument that had been designed to advance it, the Comintern. In February 1922 Lenin was still writing that "the victory of socialism requires the joint effort of the workers in a number of advanced countries."[65] Trotsky similarly stated that the contradiction of a workers' government in a peasant country could be overcome only "in the arena of the world proletarian revolution."[66] At this time, the leaders of the Workers' Opposition, Kollontai, Shliapnikov, and twenty others, applied to the Comintern for relief from the oppressions to which the Soviet party had subjected them, as though the Comintern were the superior body and the world movement were superior to the Russian.

But the dream was increasingly becoming a delusion. Lenin lost interest in it. He devoted his later writings almost entirely to domestic and party affairs, and adopted policies of peaceful relations with "capitalist" governments that clearly implied that no world revolution was to be expected for a long time. In the fall of 1923, the Comintern's big effort to stage a revolution in Germany failed ignominiously, and it seemed increasingly futile for the impoverished Soviet state to be spending many millions of gold rubles on foreign propaganda and subversion. It was also difficult to say how the party was justified in trying to build something called "socialism" if socialism required the support of the German proletariat.

By 1924 the time was ripe to awaken from the daydream, and Stalin was qualified to expound the new deviation from Marxism. Never much impressed either with abstract Marxism or with the importance of the West, he had foreshadowed "socialism in one country" in August 1917 by saying that Russia had a broader base for revolution than Western Europe and so might lead the way.[67] Early in 1924, Stalin was still repeating the accepted Leninist doctrine that revolution abroad was necessary, but later in the year he came around to the theme, partly suggested by Bukharin, that Soviet Russia could indeed proceed to build a socialist economy on its own.

Stalin was only stating what had been the Soviet practice for years and the only politically practical position. Moreover, in the ensuing debate, his position and that of his opponents were really not far apart. Stalin conceded that socialism could not be completed until the revolution was broadened, and he remained theoretically eager to see the revolutionary cause prosper everywhere. On the other hand, Trotsky and the leftist-internationalists were not prepared to sacrifice the Soviet state on the altar of the world cause, and they had no thought of giving up power or retreating from the socialization of the economy at home.

Stalin's theory brought Trotsky's theoretical competence into question, while Trotsky thought that Stalin, in turning his back on the world mission of the proletariat, was betraying socialism and opening the workers' state to bureaucratic degradation.[68] The oratorical battle—the last major public airing of philosophical differences within the party—was briefly furious. It was largely scholastic, with quotations from Lenin hurled back and forth. Stalin had difficulties because he had to misuse the few statements from Lenin that could be found to support his thesis.

Stalin won, however, because most of the solid party leaders were weary of waiting for the Germans or anyone else, and many were fed up with the whole idea of worldwide revolution. Stalin promised stability. It seemed increasingly foolish to keep banking on a world revolution that had faded away in the face of the stabilization, albeit temporary, of capitalism. It was also satisfying to bring Russia from the periphery of the great movement of the age into its center. To doubt the possibility of the Soviet Union's carrying forward its construction of socialism was to lack faith. Stalin was encouraged to press his case by the failure of a coup Zinoviev was trying to engineer in Estonia in November–December

1924, and for him Soviet preeminence became a real and deep issue[69]—and a very successful one.

Trotsky was left ideologically beached, standing on the position that Russia alone could not construct a socialist society, hence that the party had no mission, its rule no theoretical basis, and its "socialism" no true significance. Trotsky could not, in any case, easily divorce himself from world revolution; he was a cosmopolitan intellectual and the universal movement was central to his thinking. Its failure was his failure, and that of those who thought like him at a time when cosmopolitan intellectuals were being displaced by parochial bosses and administrators.

Trotsky's fall was virtually consummated, however, before "socialism in one country," and it was due much more to character than to dogmas. Trotsky was a latecomer to Lenin's party and as such was resented by the veterans who saw themselves pushed aside by him. Moreover, he was vulnerable because of years of conflict with Lenin—in his sketch for a biography of Lenin Trotsky completely passed over the years 1903 to 1917. He might have overcome these handicaps, which were shared to some extent by many leading Bolsheviks, had he been more flexible and a better leader. But he secured a following only by his brilliant writing and speaking, not by gaining personal sympathies. His civil-war victories caused envy in some Bolsheviks who thought they could have done quite as well, and his insistence on the maximum use of tsarist officers generated widespread resentment. After the war his militarization of labor and efforts to harness the trade unions also cost him popularity.

Trotsky made no effort to blend into the Bolshevik Old Guard. He was imbued with feelings of superiority to everyone except Lenin, particularly to Stalin ("Because of his enormous energy and ambition, Stalin could not help feeling at every step his intellectual and moral inferiority").[70] Trotsky had an elitist mentality, regarding people as poor creatures who needed his guidance; his attitude toward the masses in whose name he wanted to destroy the old order is indicated by his calling humans "malicious tailless apes."[71] High Bolsheviks always addressed him formally,[72] and many of his supporters called him "lord" ("*barin*").[73] Trotsky understood something of this; he wrote, "There is no doubt that in routine work it was more convenient for Lenin to depend upon Stalin, Zinoviev, or Kamenev rather than on me. . . . he understood only too well that I was not suited for carrying out commissions."[74]

An outsider at the top of the party, Trotsky was strangely reluctant to fight for his position. He was inhibited from using the army to oppose the party because that would have made him an opponent of the proletariat. He rather inexplicably failed to defend himself when his reputation was at stake, much of the time being paralyzed by chronic illness. His fever would come on at the most critical moments, perhaps psychogenetically—an escape from the unbearable conflicts of a revolutionary idealist with the realities of advancing Stalinism.

In his illness, Lenin had turned to Trotsky for help, probably mostly because Trotsky was not a member of the oligarchy that was isolating him. But Trotsky's behavior during Lenin's illness was by his own account inconsistent and irresolute. When Lenin wanted to make him Deputy Chairman of the Council of Commissars, Trotsky declined the honor, opening himself to censure for dereliction of duty. Trotsky claimed afterwards that he had held back from pressing the attack on Stalin on the Georgian question early in 1923 lest he seem ambitious,[75] a rather strange excuse for an ambitious leader to give. Stalin saved himself by his flexibility. He tried to mollify Trotsky by nominating him as rapporteur for the Twelfth Congress; according to Trotsky, Stalin wanted him as an ally against Lenin and was infuriated by Trotsky's rejection.[76] In the debate at the congress, Stalin praised Lenin and shone for his modesty and reasonableness, while Trotsky stood aside. At the Twelfth Congress, Stalin appeared to be the approximate equal of Kamenev and Zinoviev and the champion of party unity. There was some murmuring against the party bureaucracy, but it lacked program and leadership, and the resolutions proposed by the leaders were passed unanimously.

A triumvirate (Stalin, Kamenev, and Zinoviev) was formed early in 1923 primarily to oppose Trotsky, who reaped only additional hostility because of Lenin's favor for him and who also represented the supposed bonapartist threat to the revolution. The triumvirate constituted a nucleus of strength in the Politburo. Although Zinoviev was a vain and shallow character, he was known as a faithful Leninist, he was a good orator, and he headed the Petrograd party organization. Kamenev, who was instinctively a moderate, was the party strategist and the boss of the Moscow organization. Stalin, the organizer, drew his strength from the outlying regions. All three had been Bolsheviks nearly as long as Bolshevism had existed, and they shared a dislike for Trotsky, who believed that the rest of the Politburo was engaged in a conspiracy against him.[77] In any event, it was easy for the triumvirate, presenting a solid front, to swing the Politburo (whose exact composition was unpublicized at the time) because the others were at odds among themselves.

In the latter part of 1923, Trotsky and others began attacking the party apparatus in the name of democratic rights—a leftover from the Western tradition that sounded a bit strange coming from the hard-line disciplinarian of 1921. The oppositionists did nothing to appeal to the industrial workers or peasants, however, and the Politburo had only to promise some concessions of form to defang its critics, who could then be branded as factionalists.

In 1923 a substantial majority of the party might have welcomed a change of leadership,[78] and Preobrazhensky, Sapronov, Piatakov, and others were sniping at the apparatus while Trotsky stood on the sidelines. Until autumn, the triumvirate was desirous of conciliating Trotsky to prevent his assuming the leadership of the extensive discontented element within the party. In October,

however, he declared war through a letter denouncing the dictatorship of the
Secretariat, and a sharp personal war of words began. A few weeks earlier,
Zinoviev had made a move to clip Stalin's wings as General Secretary, but Stalin
had warded off the blow by offering to resign and inviting others to share in the
Orgburo. Now Stalin again assumed the position of a moderate by letting
Kamenev and Zinoviev take the lead in attacking the hero of the revolution.
Trotsky was bedridden as usual, and he petulantly asked to be relieved of his
duties in Russia to join the revolution the Comintern was trying to ignite in
Germany.[79] While criticizing the abuses of the apparatus, he failed to offer any
alternative leadership.

In November–December 1923 the Politburo permitted an open debate in the
party, with the rule, however, that factions or groupings were banned—a rule no
one felt prepared to challenge in the name of freedom. Hence, the opposition
remained shapeless and incoherent. There was a lively debate, however, the last
of its kind in the Soviet Union. *Pravda* printed discussion articles and reported
contrary views. But in mid-December the Politburo decided that it wanted no
more controversy, and since then *Pravda* and the rest of the party press have
presented only material that has been approved by the central apparatus. After
1923, it was very difficult for Trotsky or anyone in disagreement with the
apparatus to get a hearing in the party.

Trotsky fell further after Lenin died. Trotsky claimed that the Politburo had
misinformed him that the funeral would be a day sooner than it was actually held,
so that he was discouraged from returning from his cure in the Caucasus; he lost
stature by not appearing and speaking. But the fault was largely his. If he had
been prepared to fight, he would have come as soon as possible; there were
plenty of ceremonies for Lenin and opportunities to speak out in the days
following the funeral. Shortly afterward, at a party conference (composed mostly
of appointees of the General Secretary), Trotsky was attacked as an oppositionist. Stalin accused him of causing a division in the party, of inciting the youth
against the party, and of speaking for the "petty-bourgeois intelligentsia."
Trotsky was absent, sick as usual.

For a time, Preobrazhensky, who was no great power in the party, was the
chief spokesman of the opposition; Trotsky kept silence. He did so also when
Lenin's Testament was brought up. He even (he claimed)[80] restrained his
friend Joffe from publishing a conversation with Lenin praising Trotsky. The
Thirteenth Congress, held in May 1924, again condemned the opposition
("petty-bourgeois deviation"). Zinoviev, who was trying to build himself up as
Lenin's disciple and perhaps successor,[81] set a precedent by asking that the
oppositionists not only demonstrate their loyalty, but abjure their own opinions.
Trotsky nearly did so, and thus put himself morally at the mercy of the party:

> Comrades, none of us wishes to be right, or can be right, against his party. The party is in the last resort always right, because the party is the unique historical instrument given to the proletariat for the fulfillment of its fundamental tasks. . . . One can be right only with the party and through the party, since history has created no other paths to the realization of what is right. The English have a historical proverb: "My country, right or wrong." With far greater historical right can we say: "Right or not right in individual particular concrete questions, but it is my party."[82]

The opposition, which was half led by Trotsky, suffered from several weaknesses. It had support among students and teachers and in the army, but little following among industrial workers, who were supposed to be the ruling class; consequently it was open to the accusation that it represented non-proletarian elements. Moreover, those who stood up against the ruling powers attracted various discontented sectors; the opposition could thus be tarred as antiparty even as it declined to rally people against the party's monopoly of power. Much of the opposition suffered also from the fact that it stood for more controls over the economy and for less freedom for the peasants at a time when these policies were unrealistic and unpopular. Trotsky tried to represent ideological purity and dedication to the cause of revolution—including revolution abroad—at a time when most people both inside and outside the party apparatus longed for relaxation and a little of the materially better life for which they had been called to sacrifice these many years past. Trotsky had become a puritanical, humorless individualist who made the less dedicated bosses uncomfortable.[83]

In October 1924 Trotsky committed a blunder that virtually completed his ruin. After the ignominious failure of the Comintern-sponsored uprising in Germany in October 1923, Trotsky composed an article, "Lessons of October," making Zinoviev responsible for the German fiasco, recalling the vacillations of Kamenev and Zinoviev at the time of the October Revolution, and blaming the woes and backslidings on such pusillanimous leadership. Trotsky was desperate enough to publish the article in connection with the 1924 anniversary of the revolution. This stung two members of the triumvirate so that they counterattacked violently, and they as well as Trotsky greatly lost stature as a result. Trotsky was sufficiently weakened to resign without demurral as Commissar of War (his command had already been undermined) when he was asked to do so in January 1925. Shortly afterwards, Trotsky was given some minor jobs to remove him from the political scene, and he cooperated in his self-effacement. A year after Lenin's death Stalin had thus overcome the greatest obstacle to his monarchy. It was remarkable that the solidarity of the top leadership had lasted as long as it had and that it took Stalin nearly three years from the time of his appointment as General Secretary to undo his chief rival.

STALIN CRUSHES LEFT AND RIGHT

The triumvirate existed only to counter Trotsky and it fell apart immediately after he ceased to be a threat. Stalin took the lead in breaking it up simply by ceasing to consult with the partners he no longer needed. It was a sign of Stalin's power that in April 1925 a major city, Tsaritsyn, was named for him—a smaller one had already been named after Zinoviev. Stalin still had the advantage, however, that few discerned in him the potential dictator. One reason was that Lenin had ruled by his authority as maker of the revolution and by his personality and oratorical ability; it was assumed that Lenin's successor should have these qualities, and Stalin plainly lacked them. Stalin's rivals also felt fairly secure because they were members of the top party body, the Politburo, to which no acolyte of Stalin's was admitted before 1926. With somewhat unaccountable patience Stalin refrained from using his control of the Central Committee to change the membership of the Politburo until late in the day; Trotsky was expelled (along with Kamenev) only in October 1926.

In the spring of 1925, Zinoviev (and Kamenev, who followed his lead) drifted toward alliance with the Trotskyites—joined, incidentally, by Krupskaya. A new ideological division developed, the principal issue being the amount of freedom to be permitted to the landholding and individually producing peasantry. Against the left in the Politburo, led by Zinoviev and Kamenev, a rightist group emerged led by Bukharin, who was supported by Rykov and Tomsky. Bukharin led the attack by his faction, stressing the importance of encouraging production even at the cost of permitting some peasants to become (modestly) rich. The leftists favored more pressure and taxes on the wealthier peasants, a (theoretically) voluntary program of collectivization, and a rapid industrialization program—policies that were later plagiarized by Stalin. In 1925 Stalin took the position of judicious moderation, denouncing the kulaks but pronouncing himself in favor of middle peasants and accusing Kamenev and Zinoviev of undercutting the alliance of workers and peasants that had been cherished by Lenin in his last years. The Bukharinites were the closest to Lenin's line at the end of his active life.

The opposition suffered from the fact that its policies were broadly unpopular at a time when the country was just returning to tolerable levels of production under the NEP. They were also handicapped by their association with world revolution. Stalin rightly foresaw a "stabilization of world capitalism," and his "socialism in one country" was declared official doctrine by a party conference in April 1925. Moreover, as Kamenev and Zinoviev became aligned with Trotsky, Stalin, who was skilled in exploiting the weaknesses of his opponents' positions, had only to republish what these three had written about each other. The opposition was wrecked basically on the old rock of party unity. It could hardly be democratic and claim adherence to democratic rights when it accepted Marxist theory and the dictatorship of the proletariat. It could not oppose those who were in charge of the party apparatus without endangering, or being accused of endangering, party unity. By agreeing that there should be no factions the party leaders gagged themselves.

Zinoviev nonetheless tried to organize support for himself in his semiautonomous party fief, the Leningrad organization, which ran its own *Leningrad Pravda*. The showdown came at the Fourteenth Congress, in December 1925. Stalin had the votes; Zinoviev and his supporters were crushed, 495 to 65 (there were 41 abstentions), and hecklers made it difficult for oppositionists to speak. Krupskaya spoke for the opposition, but Stalin put her down as unimportant; he is said to have threatened a little later to provide Lenin with a new widow.[84] Three outright Stalinists, Molotov, Voroshilov, and Kalinin, were added to the Politburo. The membership of the Central Committee was again nearly doubled, to 106, making room for a host of Stalinists that swamped the remnants of Lenin's Central Committee. Stalin still spoke sanctimoniously of the necessity for collective leadership (mentioning among others Tomsky, Rykov, and Bukharin, who were all later to be purged as traitors), but the congress hailed him as the great leader. In a mopping-up operation, Molotov and Sergei Kirov were dispatched to bring the Leningraders into line; within two weeks the Zinoviev apparatus had been smashed and Kirov had become the Leningrad leader until he was murdered in December 1934.

The oppositionists replied with what few means were still available to them. Trotsky absented himself for an extended visit in Germany in the spring, but in July he joined Kamenev and Zinoviev to accuse Stalin of selling out to the kulaks and steering the Soviet Union back to capitalism; they continued to advocate pressure on the wealthier peasants, rapid industrialization, a workers' share in management, and greater promotion of world revolution. The opposition also tried to organize military support through a Trotskyite Deputy Commissar of War, but the exposure of this effort brought serious discredit on them.

In response, Stalin further increased his stature as an ideological authority. In 1926 he published *Questions of Leninism,* which set forth the basic principles of Stalinism; he added little to them in the following twenty-seven years of his power. In this work, Stalin exercised his freedom to adapt Marxism-Leninism in accordance with changing circumstances. As he wrote later, "What would have happened to the Party, to our revolution, to Marxism, if Lenin had been overawed by the letter of Marxism and had not had the courage to replace one of the old propositions of Marxism?"[85] He made an able elementary exposition of Marxism as the rationalization for party rule and leadership, and insisted on a militant stance and complete conformity as indispensable conditions for the party's survival.

Meanwhile, Stalin was using his apparatus to solidify his position, weeding out the supporters of Trotsky and Zinoviev. Freedom of opinion was frankly outlawed; as *Pravda* wrote on October 7, 1926, "Discussion is impermissible . . . because it shakes the very foundation of the dictatorship of the proletariat, the unity of the party, and its dominant position in the country. . . ." By the Fifteenth Congress, in October—November 1926, he celebrated another stage in the march to absolutism. Trotsky and Kamenev were removed from the Politburo, as Zinoviev had been earlier, and replaced by Stalinists; the Politburo now contained no more anti-Stalinists. Bukharin replaced Zinoviev as President of the Comintern. Significantly for the future, Trotsky, Zinoviev, Kamenev, and Piatakov confessed errors (a concession Lenin had never required) and promised to reform.

Whether through idealism and courage, or self-delusion and conspiratorial habits, Stalin's leading opponents kept up their criticism and efforts to undermine his position—or that of the "rightists," Bukharin and his followers, who were widely assumed to be the real victors by those who thought in terms of polemics rather than power.* The apparatus-men broke up meetings of the oppositionists and shouted them down when they tried to speak. The dissidents then resorted to measures such as clandestine work, illegal organizations, and underground printing, as in tsarist times. Reverses in foreign policy gave them some material; Britain broke its relations with the Soviet Union over alleged subversion, and Chiang Kai-shek turned on and massacred the Chinese Communists who had allied themselves with him on Stalin's orders. The latter development caused a little war scare, and Trotsky could say that he had been right on China policy, but Trotsky gave Stalin a stick to flail him with by offering himself as a dictator in case of emergency, and the setback to the Chinese comrades hurt the devotees of world revolution.

Nonetheless, Stalin did not secure the expulsion of Trotsky and Zinoviev from the Central Committee—even the Stalinists were too fearful of a purge in the party—until they broke the unity rule by overt action. For the November 7 anniversary in 1927, Trotsky and Zinoviev organized separate, implicitly although not explicitly anti-Stalinist demonstrations. The unauthorized demonstrations were broken up by force, and the leaders and more than seventy others were expelled from the party, although Kamenev and Zinoviev again recanted. Trotskyism was declared to be incompatible with party membership, and the remaining Trotskyites were told to recant or expect expulsion.

In January 1928 Trotsky was sent away to Alma Ata in Central Asia; Preobrazhensky, Piatakov, Rakovsky, and others were also exiled about the same time. Thoroughly aroused from his lethargy, the beaten Trotsky intensified

---

*Stalin was still so inconspicuous that Samuel Harper could write a chapter on the Communist Party (in *Civic Training in Soviet Russia* [Chicago: University of Chicago Press, 1929]) without mentioning him.

his campaign against the Stalinist leadership, sending hundreds of letters to his sympathizers. Early in 1929 Stalin deported him from the Soviet Union. Trotsky had some trouble finding a place to settle; he complained bitterly and at length in his memoirs at the reluctance of "bourgeois" governments to give shelter to his revolutionary activities.[86] He finally came to rest in Mexico, from which he maintained as much contact as he could with the opposition elements in Stalin's realm until an agent of the dictator cleaved his skull in 1940.

Why Stalin expelled Trotsky instead of imprisoning and eventually killing him remains mysterious. It is a mistake Stalin never repeated. It led, however, to the idea that there was a classic enmity, a lifelong grudge between the two. The battle became celebrated because Trotsky, who was a brilliant writer, could carry it on freely long after Stalin's domestic opponents had been silenced. But in 1918, Stalin had rather generously praised Trotsky for his role in the revolution, calling Lenin the inspirer and Trotsky the organizer, so there is no reason to assume that Stalin's relatively friendly attitude toward Trotsky in 1922 was pure hypocrisy. Nevertheless, Trotsky became Stalin's chief opponent and remained a thorn in his flesh in exile, even organizing an anti-Stalinist international and offering his version of Communism as an alternative to Stalin's, while Soviet propaganda magnified Trotsky as the execrable and infinitely dangerous enemy. Theirs became the burning hatred of giants, to be carried on by their successors of another generation.

As soon as Stalin rid himself of one set of rivals or potential rivals he turned on another, as though preferring a new fight to the enjoyment of victory. By 1928 Stalin was thoroughly the master of the apparatus; the secretaries throughout the hierarchy were virtually all directly or indirectly his appointees. Rising young men owed their careers to him, and others hoped to rise by serving him—the only way to progress in a political career, when almost all careers were more or less political. Yet there were still men in the top bracket who did not owe much to Stalin, men who had been eminent in Lenin's day, chiefly Bukharin, Lenin's onetime favorite, Rykov, Lenin's successor as Chairman of the Council of Commissars, and Tomsky, the worker Bolshevik who headed the trade unions. Moreover, these men saw the victory over the leftists as their victory as much as Stalin's—proof that they had been right all along.

However, these new rivals to Stalin never had such a firm basis of party support as Trotsky and Zinoviev. The Stalinist apparatus had ample votes to swamp them "democratically" in any congress or Central Committee meeting. As soon as Stalin turned on Bukharin and his allies, victory was quick and easy, an anticlimax after the power struggle of the last several years. They were dispensable; Stalin used them and discarded them when he no longer needed them.

The issue was again the treatment of the peasantry, who formed the popular majority in the country. During the party's rightist turn in April 1925, concessions had been made to the peasants with regard to taxes, permission to hire labor, and leasing of land. Bukharin had called upon the peasants to "enrich" themselves. But to the party stalwarts this meant the growth of a class that was inherently hostile to, or at best independent of, party power. The prosperous farmers clamored for more tax relief and for more freedom to produce capitalistically—leasing more land for longer terms and hiring more labor. To encourage production for sale to the cities meant favoring the larger producers who had a greater disposable surplus; these producers in turn acquired a lever, their ability to withhold grain from the market in times of food shortage. Fear of the wealthier peasants as a non-Communist class, the desire to implement socialism, or a managed economy, and urban jealousy of the relatively good life of some peasants all combined to generate pressures against capitalism in the countryside.

Whether from calculation or conviction, Stalin in 1927–28 turned to the left by instituting a policy of squeezing the peasantry and promoting rapid industrialization at its expense—as Stalin conceded in a speech of July 1928. The Bukharinites had to react because their following, especially in the trade unions and among the peasantry, was based not on organizational ties but on general philosophy. Belatedly seeing Stalin as a potential dictator, they turned to Kamenev and Zinoviev for support, but these two had none to give, even if they could have seen the point in helping those who had led the fight against them. Many former leftists were encouraged by Stalin's turn to expect restoration to grace, and they fell into line behind him.

To avoid a direct confrontation with Bukharin, Stalin attacked the "rightist danger" without naming its chiefs, and even denied that any differences existed: "We in the Politburo are united and will remain so till the end," he said in October 1928.[87] Meanwhile Stalin began removing supporters of the moderates from positions of influence and placing his deputies beside the leading Bukharinites. Beginning in November 1928 there was a new campaign that required the "verification" of party cards, with recruitment primarily of workers instead of peasants and the preferential promotion of workers to undercut the propeasant position. When Bukharin, Rykov, and Tomsky realized that their position was becoming untenable, they offered to resign in protest, but Stalin insisted that they should remain.

Stalin preferred his victims to go when he, not they, chose. By April 1929 he was pointing to Bukharin as the leader of the rightist opposition, and in the following twelve months all the major rightist leaders lost their principal positions. They kowtowed to Stalin and were allowed to live on, mostly in the provinces, until the purges swallowed them. In 1929–30 still another party cleansing emphasized the need for everyone to keep in step with the leadership and to avoid contact with anything that could be called an opposition.

By May 1929 Stalin's authority was virtually complete, and the blooming of his personality cult began. The press dwelt on the superlative qualities of the man now called "vozhd" or "leader." It became more important to have read Stalin than Marx or even Lenin. Stalin's fiftieth birthday, on December 21, 1929, was made the occasion for a still greater overflow of adulation, and the party and press fawned upon the new master as they had never glorified Lenin.

Each defeat of an opposition movement meant a constriction of the area of permissible disagreement in the party, the elimination of those on all sides for whom principles were important, and the settling of habits of obedience. Loyalty, discipline, and conformity were increasingly demanded. Trotsky saw Stalin's victory as the result of a drive by the apparatus to augment its own power, forgetting its dedication to the workers. Stalin's victory was indeed that of the apparatus; unlike Hitler, he did not hold sway by charisma, and the cult of his person was utterly synthetic. But the workers were always objects in the power struggle, and Stalin had quite as valid a claim to speak for them as Trotsky. The opposition could never appeal to the will of the people or the workers, because all factions accepted the basic right of the party to rule; the highest principle was the fear of dividing, and so endangering, the party. Where there were no limitations to the power of the party over the country, there could be no limitations to the power of the apparatus over the party.

Joseph V. Stalin   (*World Wide Photo*)

Chapter 5

Stalinism in Power

THE CONQUEST OF THE PEASANTRY

With the defeat of the moderates, who were mislabelled "rightists," Stalin was prepared to reverse the party's reversal of Lenin's post−civil war economic policy and to carry out the transformation and harnessing of the country, in agriculture, industry, and culture. This Stalinist transformation was a veritable second revolution, as it has often been called, a revolution that was not made by "spontaneous" forces, but imposed by the "conscious" powers above. It became possible at the end of the 1920s because dissent and the idea of dissent had been crushed step by step, revolutionary libertarianism had largely faded, and the apparatus of autocratic rulership had been set in place, tempered, and hardened. At the same time, the semifreedom of producers under the NEP had restored the economy to pre−World War I levels, so that Stalin could feel free to proceed with his sledgehammer tactics. Prior to the Stalinist transformation, the Soviet Union had been an authoritarian country, ruled arbitrarily and often brutally by a self-chosen elite, but it was not basically different (except in the period of War Communism) from a multitude of dictatorships. Through the changes of 1929−34 it became a party dictatorship of another order, a Communist state in the sense in which this term is ordinarily used today.

Through collectivization of agriculture and state-managed industrialization Stalin was carrying out the aspirations of the revolutionary party. Before the revolution, Lenin had wanted state or collective farming, although he adopted the Socialist Revolutionary program of land for individual peasants out of political expediency. In 1918 some effort was made to establish state farms and to encourage peasants to set up collectives. Most of the few collective or communal farms that were established during the period of War Communism were dissolved in the NEP, but official policy sponsored collectivization of agriculture even during the years of general retreat.[1] Industrialization under party direction had also been Lenin's dream; at one time he had seemed to hope for a utopia of modern technology and engineering by party direction.

The economic retreat beginning in 1921 was a blow to the party idealists and to those who believed in and/or enjoyed maximal control. If the Soviet Union were to be managed in approximately the same way as Western states, with the major part of the economy in private hands, they could hope for only gradual improvement as productive factors grew and perhaps look forward to the degradation of the system and a return to something like tsarist ways. The long struggle for power, the revolution, and the bitter sacrifices of the civil war would seem to have been for little; the life of the devoted party member was drained of higher meaning. The obvious failure of world revolution was also galling. Hence many were ready to welcome Stalin's compensatory efforts to build "socialism in one country" rapidly, to press the conversion of total political power into total control of the economy, and to acclaim a new vision of economic socialism through political action. Stalin was constructing the new order not as a successor to capitalism but as an immediate alternative to it, a new answer for modern ills and a recipe for happiness.

Hence in 1928−29 Stalin could effectively condemn the gradualist approach of Bukharin, Rykov, and Tomsky as a reversion to capitalism and take over the leftist program that had been promoted by Trotsky in 1925 for putting the peasants into the harness of collectivization and extracting from them the capital for the rapid development of industry—although the radicalism of Stalin's actions far exceeded anyone's program.

The political and economic problem that faced him was the old one of how to fit the peasant majority into the "dictatorship of the proletariat" and how to build industry in a poor, largely agricultural country. For the party, the peasants were an alien class that was always to be distrusted; for Stalin, they were the supporters or potential supporters of an opposition movement, just as Trotsky's theory of revolution had predicted. The Bukharinites not only leaned on the peasantry when they were in power, but also sought support from them after the defeat of their group.[2] The fact that the majority of the population was producing privately for the market made party rule seem a discordant superstructure.

A more obvious reason for proceeding to collectivize was economic. The tsarist state of the 1890s had financed industrialization by squeezing the peasantry through taxation. Stalin was happy to do so also, but it was not easy. The equalization of the revolution had reduced the marketable surplus, and despite the industrial recovery the peasants could not buy much with the products of their sales. Hence the obvious way to get much more out of the countryside was to apply heavy taxes to millions of small producers and forcibly requisition their crops.

After 1927 the grain supplies began to fall short of demand because of taxes, discrimination against the larger producers, the low fixed prices of agricultural commodities, and the high prices demanded for industrial goods. Stalin convinced himself that the more prosperous peasants (who were pejoratively dubbed "kulaks" or "fists" after the village capitalists-money lenders) were maliciously holding back the grain he needed. He had to choose between reducing burdens and discriminations and subjecting the peasantry to party control. With no knowledge of economics or agriculture—he is said never to have visited a village after 1928—but with full faith in force, Stalin proceeded to an attack, which became all-out war, first on the wealthier peasants and then on all who failed to subscribe to his scheme for the socialization of agriculture. Stalin believed the grain was there for the taking; according to Khrushchev, he was ready to think the peasants could pay the state more than their total earnings.[3] But to make it easier to take the grain (and to control politically), the peasants had to be joined in large farms the party could oversee. At the same time, the state could proceed to the mechanization of the large farms in a manner that was impossible for the peasant holders—an attractive prospect that became realizable only long afterward, because when Stalin began the agricultural upheaval the Soviet Union had only seven thousand tractors.

At the Fifteenth Party Congress, in December 1927, Stalin spoke of collectivization as "the main task of the Party in the villages," but the program was conceived as a gradual and voluntary one. The Sixteenth Congress, which took place in July 1929, adopted a plan for the collectivization of 17.5 percent of the country's plowland within five years.

Stalin, bathed in adulation, soon found such a gradual tempo too slow. At the time of his birthday celebration in December, he undertook "the liquidation of the kulaks as a class." There were no real kulaks,[4] because the levelling of 1917–18 had been thorough; there were no large landholdings, and even in the NEP period the Soviet system did not favor capital accumulation. Nevertheless, some peasants had prospered while others had not, it was necessary to have a "class" rationale for the attack on the peasantry, and the land, tools, and livestock of the wealthier peasants were needed for the new collectives.

In January 1930 the Central Committee proposed the complete collectivization of the more important grain regions by the end of the year or the middle of the next. But the campaign ran wildly ahead of even this overly ambitious target, turning into a storm in the first months of 1930. Party workers obediently drove peasants into collectives, or *kolkhozes*, and sent back reports of success that encouraged Stalin and his fellows to demand more. Many of the kolkhozes existed only on paper, but large numbers of peasants were herded into ill-prepared collectives, and deprived not only of their land but also of their tools and stock (even their chickens), so far not destroyed. The peasants resisted violently with whatever means were available; disorders spread; even the Red Army, which was mostly composed of peasant lads, was affected. Stalin was compelled to draw back a little.

In a short *Pravda* article of March 2, 1930, entitled "Dizziness from Success," he blamed the excesses on the enthusiasm of his underlings, decried the use of force ("Collective farms cannot be set up by force. To do so would be stupid and reactionary"), offered to permit peasants to leave the farms into which they had been dragooned, and promised that collective farmers would be permitted to keep a few animals and to cultivate a garden plot for themselves. These household plots were intended only to facilitate collectivization, but they became permanent because their contribution to the food supply was (and has remained) disproportionately important.

Most of the nominally collectivized peasants withdrew in the next few months, and the Central Committee still had enough independence to bridle at Stalin's attempt to transfer the blame to his subordinates. But in the latter part of 1930 the program was resumed more carefully and systematically. It still amounted to a virtual war on the villages, however. Stalin told Churchill during World War II that ten million "kulaks" had been liquidated or removed, as though he were proud of that fact.[5] The violence was supposedly directed at the kulak class enemy, who was defined as a peasant deriving capitalistic profits, and the middle and poor peasants were to be mobilized against such people. But anyone who was opposed to collectivization became a 'kulak," and anyone who had been so characterized was not permitted to enter the collective farm that took his holdings, even if he wished to do so. Toward the kulaks there was little mercy; as a Communist official put it, "Don't think of the kulak's hungry children; in the class struggle, philanthropy is evil."[6]

Since collectivization was made an ideological issue, the campaign was accompanied by a renewal of warfare on the religious front, which had been quiet since the beginning of the 1920s. Priests were driven out, and churches were turned into warehouses. In socialist zeal mixed with "gigantomania," the authorities preferred state farms that were simply giant grain factories to the collective farms, which were theoretically cooperatives and hence represented shared private property. However, the state farms (*sovkhozy*) had to be largely given up as too expensive because it was deemed necessary to pay wages to the peasants employed on them, whereas the kolkhozniks could be made to work outside the framework of state employment for almost nothing. On the other hand, the collectivization campaign also meant giving up the little centers of communist idealism that had been established voluntarily in the countryside, the communal farms or communes.[7] Communes dedicated to the full sharing of property represented a discordant element and "petty bourgeois equalitarianism."

Collectivization was largely achieved by the end of 1932 through the expulsion of its opponents and the compulsion of hunger, as the state took the grain and left individual peasants to starve. A death penalty was enacted as punishment for taking any collective grain for individual use or for refusing to deliver grain to the state collectors. Delivery quotas were set that were beyond the capacity of the peasants. A historically unique famine resulted that was both created by the state and concealed by it. While the Soviet Union was continuing to export grain, although at reduced rates, to pay for the equipment needed to achieve industrialization, millions were left to starve, especially in the Ukraine.

Perhaps Stalin did not intend to exploit the peasants quite so severely. In April 1929 he had conceded that the peasants were subject to a supertax and said that it should be abolished as soon as possible.[8] In November 1932, after the suicide of his wife, Nadezhda Alliluyeva, he offered in a Politburo meeting to resign. It is not clear whether he was serious or was testing his colleagues; in any case, Molotov assured him that the party needed him and urged him to stay, and nothing more was said.[9] The peasantry was driven into submission, the 1933 harvest was relatively good, the mass deportations were ended, and Stalin continued to promise concessions that never came. By the uninhibited use of violence backed by an ideological rationale that disarmed opposition and excused wholesale massacres in the name of a utopian goal, the Stalinist party, which constituted only a tiny minority of the nation, was able to manhandle the immense peasant masses and to eliminate in a brief time their traditional mode of work.

The victory was great. Stalin had demonstrated his ruthlessness and earned the lasting plaudits of the party. Officially, the Soviet Union has always remained proud of its collectivization. At the height of the de-Stalinization campaign Khrushchev held it up as a credit. Only in his more candid memoirs did he admit that it was un-Leninist in manner.[10] The bankruptcy of what remained of the opposition was demonstrated; in the breakdown of 1930 it could not bring itself to oppose the party on behalf of mere peasants. It was mute in 1932 when several millions may have died in the induced famine.[11] In the shared guilt, the ability to protest was crushed, and whatever moral conscience came through the revolution and civil war was crippled. The party was brutalized and ready for the purges that were to follow.

The economic and political gain for the party was substantial. The peasants were placed in a situation in which it was difficult for them to evade working for the state or to claim any more of the harvest than the state saw fit to allow them. The first commandment of the collective farm was to deliver grain; only after the collectors were satisfied—a sometimes impossible task—was grain to be set aside for seed and personal consumption. The peasants were thrust back into a serfdom that was in many ways more severe than the condition from which they had been freed in 1861.

They were also placed in organizations where they could be politically directed, watched, propagandized, and required to support the party and its leader. The better to manage them, farm machinery, as it became available, was held in the hands of state agencies, Machine Tractor Stations, and political sections were established in these agencies to combat any oppositional tendencies. The party base in the countryside was changed from the village to the kolkhoz, and the party named the nominally elected chairman and other officials. The last large independent group existing within the Soviet state became the dependents of the party. Stalin had reason to exult, at the Seventeenth Congress in 1934, that the party had "no more enemies to fight."[12]

For the people as a whole, however, collectivization was a disaster. Agricultural production was diminished by half for a time; in 1941 it still had not recovered to the 1928 per-capita level. The available power on the farms was less in 1938 than in 1928; the tractors that had been added did not make up for the horses that had been lost.[13] About half the livestock of Russia had been destroyed, either by those who preferred a barbecue to surrendering cows or by neglect in unprepared collectives. Almost all the peasants who had demonstrated exceptional competence as farmers had been driven out of farming, and in millions of cases, physically destroyed. The peasants, who were generally passive and docile, were alienated from the party for many years to come; reconciliation came only when a new national unity was forged under the fierce German assault. Through the 1930s, the big problem for the party, the one demanding the most attention from the Central Committee, was to try to make collectivized agriculture productive.*

INDUSTRIALIZATION

Concurrently with the transformation of Soviet agriculture, Stalin undertook the transformation of Soviet industry. Both programs rose to a frenzied climax about the same time, both contributed to a radical reduction in the standard of living for some years, and both enormously increased the party's and Stalin's control of the Soviet state and people.

Stalin's industrialization program was in the old Russian tradition of governmental promotion of militarily useful production; under Stalin as under Peter, despotism imposed modernization. In the West, Communism or socialism was seen as an answer to the problems of industrial society; in Russia it meant a way to apply despotic power to catch up with the West. There was a strong defensive need, as Stalin remarked in 1931:

> To slacken the tempo would mean falling behind. And those who fall behind get beaten. But we do not want to be beaten. No, we refuse to get beaten! One feature of the history of old Russia was the continual beatings she suffered because of her backwardness. She was beaten by the Mongol khans . . . Swedish feudal lords. . . Polish and Lithuanian gentry . . . Japanese barons. All beat her—

---

*By a recent judgment, Stalin's collectivization policy represented utter incompetence and its outcome was sheer disaster. James R. Millar, "What's Wrong with the Standard Story," *Problems of Communism* 25 (July–August 1976): 55.

because of her backwardness, military backwardness, cultu
political backwardness, industrial backwardness, agricultural k

There is no other way. That is why Lenin said on the eve of t'
tion: "Either perish, or overtake and outstrip the advanced capitalist counᴜᵢᵥₛ.

We are fifty or a hundred years behind the advanced countries. We must make good
this distance in ten years. Either we do it, or we shall be crushed.[14]

There was a special need for haste in catching up, because Russia in 1928−29
had barely recovered her prewar level of production. Not only was socialist
abundance a distant dream, but Russia was farther behind the Western world, in
both its standard of living and its defense capability, than it had been in 1914.
The rationale for the drive, however, was strongly ideological and political. Just
as the collectivization of agriculture harnessed the independent producers and
destroyed those whom the relative freedom of the NEP had enabled to improve
their conditions, the industrial mobilization program destroyed the small-scale
manufacturers and traders who had prospered under the NEP. Hence it was welcomed by the party men who deeply resented the capitalistic affluence of some of
the new entrepreneurs. The industrialization program also combined with collectivization to give a conviction of rapid progress toward the socialist utopia. The
one program needed the other; the peasants had to be collectivized to provide the
resources for industrial growth and the food for the cities, while increased
industrialization was needed to provide the agricultural machinery that would
make collective agriculture productive.

The industrialization program, plus socialization of the peasantry was greeted
with enthusiasm as the birth of socialism in the Soviet Union, sanctioned by
Stalin's theory. The political revolution had failed to bring utopia; the social
and economic revolution would turn the trick and make the necessary sacrifices
a small price. The big mechanized communal farms and the smoking factories,
dams, and furnaces were to fulfill the revolution. This doctrine represented a
further deviation from the earlier understanding of Marxism. Just as the peasantry
was not allowed to grow into socialism but was hurtled into it by the party bosses,
industrial development was to be not the cause of proletarian power but its result. The socialist state was to produce the developed economy, instead of vice
versa; indeed, the socialist state was practically to produce the proletariat in
whose name the party ruled. The infrastructure was not to generate the superstructure but the active superstructure was to provide itself with an appropriate
infrastructure.

Such logical reversal did not dampen the enthusiasm of either Stalin and his
fellows or the many, especially young people, who were inspired by the vision.
Stalin cast aside the reasonably calculated estimates of the planners and jacked up
the targets, and soon afterward raised them again and again. In the First Five

ᴄar Plan, which was officially begun late in 1928, the Commissar of Finance wanted to allocate 650 million rubles for capital investment. Stalin wanted 850 million, then suddenly in mid-1929 he raised that sum to 3,400 million; actual investments totalled 1,300 million rubles. The plan was changed from a design for rational management to a political instrument, a means of guiding and pushing production under party leadership, and there was no limit. Production of basic commodities, especially steel, was to be doubled and redoubled. As Stalin said in 1928, before the fury really began, ''There are no fortresses Bolsheviks cannot storm.''[15]

The First Five Year Plan was not to be the mere initiator of an endless series of such plans, as it turned out, but the prelude to utopia. By a much-repeated official statement, ''The fulfillment of the five year plan will enable the Soviet Union to overtake and outstrip the technically and economically most advanced capitalist countries.''[16] In the dream, the peasant would soon ride in an automobile, if not in an airplane.

The campaign approached economic madness, and its cost was high. Expensive machinery imported from abroad rusted in the snow; inexperienced managers wasted untrained labor; bungled designs caused terrible losses. Everything had to be as huge as possible. Investment was poured into the priority targets of heavy industry, which was favored for its grandiosity and power. Small-scale and artisan types of production were destroyed before they could be replaced. The standard of living sank to a low point around 1931−32 and recovered substantially only in 1934−36. Food and the few consumer goods that were available had to be rationed as though in war time. Hardships caused by the exaggerations in industrialization and collectivization troubled even party circles that were normally indifferent to suffering. Stalin reached a low ebb of popularity in 1932, as doubts seeped into the circles closest to the dictator.

Yet the First Five Year Plan was not a failure. Giant plants were built, new cadres were trained, the industrial labor force was expanded, and a basis was laid for the industrialization of Russia, which was carried on at a less feverish tempo and with better blueprints and more experienced organization in the Second Five Year Plan. It was an exaggeration to announce that the First Five Year Plan had been accomplished by 1932 in four years. But overall industrial production probably grew about 50 percent during that period,[17] with the output of basic materials, coal and steel, increasing the most. The green landscape of Russia was dotted with spectacular projects such as the Stalingrad tractor factory, the Magnitogorsk steel plant, and the Dnepr dam.

The successes were possible only because of the selfless dedication and vibrant energy of many, especially young people, who worked and studied with eager enthusiasm and suffered immense hardships in the name of building socialism in Russia,[18] sacrificing today for the vision of a happier tomorrow for all. The world depression that began at the same time as Stalin's transformations was also a morale builder; the Bolsheviks saw the troubles of the West (which they much exaggerated) as their own vindication and as proof of the superiority of the socialism they were painfully building.

These were all achievements of Stalin's party. Stalinists had taken charge throughout the government and other organizations; for example, a large majority of the trade-union officials were replaced by Stalinists from 1929 through 1930. More than a million workers were drawn into the party in 1930–31[19] in an unexampled expansion that brought the party near its goal of having half its membership in the worker category. The new Stalinist Communists were called upon to take command and demonstrate their ability to make the plans work. Generally young people of uneducated background whose prospects of advancement would have been slight under the old regime, they responded with enthusiasm. Fortified and inspired by the new Marxist-Leninist-Stalinist vision of creating the socialist utopia, they sacrificed themselves and others for the cause.

Enthusiasm was coupled with stern discipline, however. In October 1930 a series of decrees were enacted that restricted the movement of labor, penalized absenteeism or lateness, and practically made the worker an industrial serf, albeit much better treated than the collectivized peasant. The internal passport, which had been detested as a means of control in tsarist times, was reintroduced in December 1932. When there were derelictions, workers were subject not only to the ordinary penalties but also to expulsion from their apartments and deprivation of their rations. Peasants were also brought to the cities in a condition of virtual bondage under contracts made by collective farms with industrial enterprises.

On the other hand, there were increasing material rewards for those who fulfilled the wishes of the party. Equality had been probably the strongest ideal of the revolution, and much protest had been raised against the paying of relatively high salaries to "bourgeois specialists" in the civil war; Lenin had excused this practice on grounds of absolute necessity and viewed it as temporary. Inequality grew considerably under the economic freedom provided by the NEP, but the enthusiasm behind the new drive to build socialism in 1928–29 led to a renewal of the equalitarian ideal. There were to be only proletarians, and no Communist was to earn more than a worker's salary; high officials lived like ordinary workers.[20]

This levelling trend was contrary, however, to the hierarchic spirit of Stalinism. In 1931 Stalin announced that equalitarianism was "petty bourgeois," anti-Marxist and un-Leninist, and he called for unequal rewards to spur production. Wages were to be based on output, with higher rates for overfulfillment of the norms, and more and more categories were introduced to reward the skilled and productive (and penalize the less willing or less capable) until the wage differentials became extreme, as much as thirty or forty to one.

This drive to get people to work harder for more pay, with honors thrown in, came to a climax in the Stakhanovite movement, a typically Stalinist campaign.

In August 1935 Alexei Stakhanov allegedly mined 102 tons of coal in one shift, about 15 times the norm. This feat required much preparation and assistance, but it was celebrated and made the model for a general speedup of labor. The campaign to emulate his and similar heroic feats of production became the dominant theme of the press and the main business of local party organizations for years thereafter. Through the Stakhanovite movement the labor aristocrats—the managers and directors who were essentially the elite of the new state, centered on the Communist party—raised themselves further above the masses.

THE GREAT PURGES

By 1934 the Soviet Union was emerging from its time of most traumatic economic and social change; Stalinism rose triumphant as a result of its victory over the peasantry, its socialization of the economy, and its construction of a heavy industrial base. All independent sectors had been destroyed, and the country was ready for the institution of totalitarianism. But the dictator seems only to have been able to continue destroying his rivals or opponents. The stage was set for a time of horrors, of a self-immolation of an elite that was without historical parallel.

The purges were not without antecedents, however. Arbitrary police action for political purposes began a few weeks after Lenin took power and never ceased entirely. The terrorism of the civil war and the reprisals against those who rose against the Soviet state at Kronstadt and in the provinces set precedents for violence. In collectivization the party had become hardened to the exile, imprisonment, enslavement, and murder of millions who could be counted as opponents by the leadership.

The purge trial was also a tradition. In 1922, when the country was at peace, a group of Socialist Revolutionaries were subjected to a political trial and sentenced to death; Lenin became angry when the sentence was commuted under pressure from European leftists. In 1928 Stalin held a show trial of fifty-three mine managers and engineers for alleged sabotage and counterrevolution with foreign involvement. In 1930 an "Industrial Party" of saboteurs was discovered and put on trial, as were sundry other groups in following years, but no protest came from within the party against the obviously false accusations and extracted confessions. The party elite was still secure, although Stalin repressed ordinary folk, including party members, at will. Nadezhda Alliluyeva learned of the horrors of collectivization from fellow students at the Industrial Academy and remonstrated with Stalin, an act that led to her suicide. Stalin arrested those who had ventured to speak the truth to his wife.[21]

The nonviolent cleansing of the party also helped to set the stage for the blood purges. The rolls had been checked, and large numbers expelled in 1919, 1921, 1929, and 1933. The last of these cleansings decreased the membership by a third and dragged on until the next and still more drastic purge occurred in 1935, preparatory to the massacres of 1936−38. Such checks on membership, with the penalty of expulsion, became increasingly severe as the role of the party became ever more overwhelming. The party leaders selected members for their docility, inculcated in them a fear of the authorities, and accustomed them to the idea of arbitrary action in the name of vigilance and virtue.

These purifications had little effect on the upper echelons of the party, who did not have much to fear as long as they stayed clear of factions (such as those led by Trotsky, Kamenev and Zinoviev, and Bukharin). And there was a tendency toward mutual protection within the company; those who cheerfully watched or shared in the killing of outsiders, the "bourgeoisie," peasants, or simply non-Bolsheviks, were still opposed to the murder of party brothers. But under the stress of Stalin's radical program, tensions rose. Many members began to have grave doubts, and a few tried to check what they considered to be a disastrously wrong course. In December 1930 a candidate Politburo member, T. I. Syrtsov, and a Central Committee member, Ivan Lominadze, circulated a memorandum criticizing Stalin and urging curtailment of his power; for the time being they were only expelled from the party. In the summer of the disastrous year of 1932, when it could hardly be denied that Stalin's policies had been lamentable, some second-rank party men headed by M. Riutin passed around a long petition outlining the causes of the disaster and urging the removal of "the evil genius of the Russian Revolution" as General Secretary. The criminals were ousted from the party and imprisoned, but the Politburo refused Stalin's desire—supported only by Kaganovich—to execute them. A year later Stalin wanted to shoot some Old Bolsheviks (A. P. Smirnov and others) who had ventured to agitate for a lessening of the burden on the peasants, the independence of the trade unions, and the removal of Stalin; again, a majority of the Politburo, including Sergei Kirov, Ordzhonikidze, Kuibyshev, and others, opposed him.

Stalin doubtless marked those who balked him and began devising ways to crush them. For the moment, however, the weathervane pointed to moderation. The situation in the country was easing, and by 1934 the economic crisis was past—at the same time that the West began recovering from its depression. In 1933 a number of former oppositionists who had been expelled and exiled in previous years were allowed to return in contrition. The Seventeenth Congress, in January 1934, heard Zinoviev, Kamenev, Bukharin, Rykov, Preobrazhensky, and others recant, praise Stalin, and ask forgiveness, which was apparently granted. The congress was proclaimed to be that "of victors," the leftists, rightists, peasants, and doubters having been vanquished. All the speeches included fulsome tributes to Stalin, the Great Victor, and it seemed that the united party would go forward in brotherly harmony.* A few months later, in July 1934, the party took what seemed to be a major step toward relaxation. The political police was subordinated to and made a branch of the Commissariat of the Interior, under Genrikh Yagoda. A *Pravda* commentary stressed its legality and dependence on the courts.[22]

The lightning struck out of an apparently clear sky. On December 1, 1934, Sergei Mironovich Kirov, boss of Leningrad, Secretary of the Central Committee alongside Stalin, and virtually the second-in-command in the party, was shot and killed in his Leningrad office. It was a turning point of history, a murder mystery that has never been clarified. However, the clues point to Stalin. The assassin, a young Communist named Nikolaev, was provided with a pistol and a building pass by the NKVD (as the political police was now designated) and admitted without inspection while Kirov's bodyguard was detained. Within hours, Stalin and Yagoda, the police chief, were in Leningrad; the same night a decree was issued providing for the immediate execution of death sentences in political cases—a decree that had been prepared in advance according to Khrushchev's Secret Speech. Soon afterwards, Kirov's bodyguard was arrested and killed by the NKVD in a faked automobile accident (again according to Khrushchev). The escorts of the prisoner were later shot, as were the members of the team that investigated the murder.

Khrushchev suggested the complicity of Stalin, the only person who could have authorized the murder, and he promised an investigation both in 1956 and in 1961. If it has been held, its findings remain secret, but the case against Stalin is strong. He was surely impressed with the success of Hitler's blood purge of June 1934 (a trifling affair by Soviet standards, taking only about a thousand lives) in eliminating Hitler's competitors and solidifying the dictator's control. Stalin had some cause for dissatisfaction, because he had not been able to secure the party's authorization for the execution of those who wished to dethrone him and his popularity was low even among those whom he had selected and who obediently sang his praises. According to Medvedev, in fact, Stalin was barely elected to the new Central Committee in 1934.[23] Kirov, to the contrary, received the largest number of votes. Unlike Stalin, Kirov was an effective speaker who was quite popular in party circles. He was elected Secretary of the Central Committee in 1934—at that time Stalin formally ceased to be General Secretary but became the equal in title of Kirov, Kaganovich, and Zhdanov. Kirov had a power base of sorts in Leningrad, where he was Zinoviev's successor. For Stalin,

---

*Ulam has suggested that there was a plot to remove Stalin from active leadership by placing him on a pedestal as a venerated elder statesman. Ulam, *Stalin*, pp. 372–373.

whose dictatorial power was based on no clear authority, Kirov obviously represented a mortal danger.

Perhaps to thwart that danger, Stalin wanted to bring Kirov to Moscow, but Kirov postponed the shift until 1938. There were other differences between the two; in particular, Kirov wanted to bring former oppositionists back into party work, a policy that Stalin must have found threatening. Shortly before Kirov's assassination, Stalin was highly critical of him, according to Khrushchev.[24] Stalin's daughter believed that he was too fond of Kirov to have killed him,[25] but she probably underestimated Stalin's power of dissimulation and his willingness to destroy friends.

The assassination was totally successful. It not only removed Kirov but also enabled Stalin to plead emergency and terrorist dangers and so to secure authorization for the execution of party members, who had previously enjoyed immunity from the police until they were expelled. In line with the terror decree that was issued and approved in the wake of the murder, numerous alleged terrorists unrelated to Nikolaev and the assassination were executed within days. The Central Committee sent a letter to all party committees asking them to ferret out, expel, and arrest all former oppositionists (followers of Zinoviev or Trotsky) remaining in the party. The net was spread wide in Leningrad; anyone who had attended a Komsomol meeting with Nikolaev was pulled in as a coconspirator, and the assassination was linked by confession to Kamenev and Zinoviev. These two were arrested on December 16, along with others, and condemned to prison terms. Within a few months, thirty to forty thousand Leningraders were deported.[26]

Stalin moved politically to immobilize the old party people who would find it hard to accept his dictatorship. He dissolved the Society of Old Bolsheviks, which had some political importance as a center for the old hands and a means of communicating with the country. He also terminated other centers of the Leninists, the Society of Political Prisoners and the Communist Academy, although the older oppositionists seem to have been weary of the long battle and desirous only of tranquility and perhaps an opportunity to serve.

Kirov's murder was taken as adequate proof of the theory, which had been stated by Stalin as early as 1929, that the class struggle was sharpening: "Lenin, on the contrary, teaches us that classes can be abolished only by means of a stubborn class struggle, which under the dictatorship of the proletariat becomes *ever fiercer* than it was before the dictatorship of the proletariat. . . ."[27] The assassination was made the occasion of a campaign for vigilance, with the warning that any deviation was likely to lead to criminal opposition in league with foreign and domestic reactionaries. Indoctrination was stepped up, with the emphasis on party history and Stalin's victories over his rivals. The propaganda apparatus was also reorganized to intensify its supervision of writers and media.

The Central Control Commission was reorganized as the Party Control Commission and headed by a Stalinist of exceptionally low moral qualities, N. I. Yezhov, after whom the worst of the purge was to be named "Yezhovshchina." The purge that had begun in 1933 was still dribbling on when in May 1935 the Central Committee decreed a new "verification" of party documents, which, in an atmosphere of mounting hysteria, meant that any black mark or unseemly association was a likely cause for removal.

A decade after Stalin had become clearly the head of the party, it was still not adequately terrorized, however. There were still mutterings against Stalin, especially among the youth, and the apparatus had managed largely to exempt itself from the purges, which struck mostly the lower ranks and persons in governmental and economic posts.[28] But the earlier, less murderous purges prepared the way for the mass killings of 1936−38, which struck former leftists, the army, "bourgeois nationalists," and Stalinists—high and low alike, party and nonparty—no longer in the thousands but in the millions. The story, which has been often and well told,[29] is a vast complex of sadism, hypocrisy, and fiendish brutality, with many villains, countless victims, and few heroes. The spectacular show trials, with the weird confessions of lifelong party stalwarts to collaboration with foreign enemies and plans to restore capitalism, were a trifling fraction of the mass terror; they were significant mostly as propaganda. The Red Terror of civil-war times was comparable to the terror of the French Revolution, although on a much grander scale; the Stalinist purges were madness of another order of magnitude.

Just as it remains unknowable how much of his seemingly cunning rise to dictatorship Stalin planned in advance, it is unclear to what extent he planned the massacres in advance,[30] and to what extent they simply grew and snowballed. In any case, there is no evidence that the purges were carried on by the police independently of Stalin's desires. By mid-1935 Stalin had a total grip on the party's central apparatus, the Secretariat, the Party Control Commission, and the NKVD. He used the police and placed them above the party to some extent,[31] but he allowed them no real power of their own. In the purges he changed command as he desired, and he personally sanctioned countless executions. In 1937−38 he approved 383 execution lists that included many thousand names.[32] As Khrushchev put it in 1956:

> Stalin originated the concept "enemy of the people." This term automatically rendered it unnecessary that the ideological errors of a man or men engaged in a controversy be proven; this term made possible the usage of the most cruel repression, violating all norms of revolutionary legality, against anyone who in any way disagreed with Stalin, against those who were only suspected of hostile intent, against those who had bad reputations. This concept, "enemy of the people," actually eliminated the possibility of any kind of ideological fight or the

making of one's views known on this or that issue, even those of a practical character. In the main, and in actuality, the only proof of guilt used, against all norms of current legal science, was the "confession" of the accused himself; and, as subsequent probing proved, "confessions" were acquired through physical pressures against the accused.[33]

The opener of the spectacular terror was the sensational trial, on August 19–24, 1936, of Kamenev and Zinoviev and fourteen others (eleven of the sixteen were Jewish). They were accused of plotting, in league with Trotsky, the murder of practically the entire Soviet leadership. Andrei Vishinsky, an ex-Menshevik who gained celebrity as the chief prosecutor during the purges and ultimately became Foreign Minister, made a concerted effort to convince the world of their guilt—an effort that was by no means fruitless. The evidence was partly the testimony of provocateurs, but mostly the confessions of the accused. For some reason, no fake documents were presented, but there was apparently a compulsion to have duly acknowledged confessions, no matter how unrealistic, perhaps as a result of the desire to accomplish the moral as well as physical undoing of the defendants. All varieties of pressure, ranging from deprivation of sleep to the infliction of pain, were employed, along with appeals to party loyalty—a chance to serve the party's need—and promises of mercy. Before the trial, the defendants were several times assured that their lives would be spared in return for their cooperation.[34]

The purge then went rolling on, but Stalin found it too slow. By a telegram of September 25, 1936, he directed the Politburo to replace Yagoda as police chief by Yezhov, stating enigmatically that Yagoda had fallen "four years behind" in unmasking traitors (although he had been in charge for only two years). Yezhov put party men in place of the old professionals of Cheka days and proceeded energetically to slaughter as his boss desired. Consequently, he seemed to enjoy Stalin's esteem. In October 1937 he was made a candidate member of the Politburo and early in 1938 he was treated as second only to Stalin by the press. Khrushchev, in retirement, recalled him as a pretty fine fellow,[35] but he seems to have been singularly lacking in human qualities.

A new show trial of less celebrated defendants (Radek, Piatakov, and fifteen others) was held on January 23–30, 1937, to keep up the momentum. It was very similar to the Kamenev-Zinoviev trial, although credibility declined with repetition. Since Piatakov had been Deputy Commissar for Heavy Industry, his condemnation began a hunt everywhere for industrial saboteurs. In the first part of 1937, however, some members of the Central Committee seem to have become sufficiently worried about their own safety to make a feeble effort to check the terror. The last fairly high leader who dared to contradict Stalin was P. P. Postyshev, who at the February-March Central Committee plenum permitted himself to doubt the guilt of some purge victims. Such indocility may have infuriated Stalin and persuaded him to wipe out the last vestiges of resistance. In 1937 he turned still more furiously on various classes, including faithful Stalinists. According to Khrushchev, arrests of "counterrevolutionaries" increased tenfold during the period 1936–37.

One of the harshest terroristic rampages was directed against the armed forces. In May 1937, Stalin began shifting commanders around to separate them from their supporters; party commissars, whose offices had been abolished in 1925 since it was no longer necessary to watch ex-tsarist officers, were reintroduced into the larger units. In June a number of the highest officers, headed by Tukhachevsky (of civil war fame), were arrested and executed. Faked documents, which were provided by the Gestapo via the French and Czechs in a bit of picturesque intrigue, were used to incriminate them. However, there is reason to suspect that Soviet agents may have planted the incriminating evidence in the first place, and Stalin had a number of reasons for bringing trumped-up charges: he had a personal grudge against Tukhachevsky dating from friction in the Polish campaign; high officers had protested the excesses of collectivization and perhaps other Stalinist follies; there may have been murmurings about the effects of the purges on munitions production; and some officers may conceivably have thought it justifiable to try to unseat Stalin, although no evidence of such a plot has appeared. In any case, the military represented a power center that was potentially capable, at least in a time of stress, of providing alternative leadership; therefore it had to be crushed.

The deadlines of the purge refutes the idea, which has been widely accepted in the West, that Stalin was preparing for war by removing possible traitors. The terror spread to the point where it was enough merely to have served under an "enemy of the people" to become one.[36] Those who acted as judges of the first set of victims in courts-martial became victims in their turn, and many who were not shot were driven to suicide. The purge killed many more senior officers than the four years of World War II, eliminating three out of five marshals, fourteen out of sixteen army commanders, eight out of eight admirals, sixty out of sixty-seven corps commanders, eleven out of eleven Vice Commissars of War, and seventy-five out of eighty members of the Supreme Military Council—altogether about thirty-five thousand officers or half the corps.[37]

After the purge of the army, the police that had carried it out came up for attention. In late 1937 and early 1938, a large number of NKVD officials were arrested and mostly shot, including nearly all the provincial directors and section directors and probably thousands of others.[38] When former chief Yagoda was put on trial, he confessed to having arranged the murder of Kirov, allegedly on the orders of Yenukidze; however, if Yenukidze had had anything to do with the affair, he could not have acted without Stalin's direction.

Yagoda was a defendant in the last grand show trial, of Bukharin, Rykov, and nineteen others—the "bloc of Rights and Trotskyites." Tomsky missed this trial because, when immediately after the Kamenev-Zinoviev trial the Soviet press began calling for an investigation of their relations with the "rightists," he took the hint and killed himself. He must have had a guilty conscience; the only remaining high Bolshevik of proletarian origins, he had opposed excessive demands on the workers he supposedly represented as the head of the trade unions. Although it had been announced in September 1936 that Bukharin and Rykov had been cleared after an investigation, and in February 1937 they were allowed to speak in their defense at the Central Committee plenary meeting, they were arrested shortly afterward. At the trial they were accused, in the usual style, of treason and working for the Nazis. Vishinsky was eloquent in the finale of his harangue:

> Our whole country, from young to old, is awaiting and demanding one thing: the traitors and spies who were selling our country to the enemy must be shot like dirty dogs!
>
> Our people are demanding one thing: crush the accursed reptiles!
>
> Time will pass. The graves of the hateful traitors will grow over with weeds and thistle, they will be covered with eternal contempt of honest Soviet citizens, of the entire Soviet people. But over us, over our happy country, our sun will shine with its luminous rays as bright and as joyous as before. Over the road cleared of the last scum and filth of the past, we, our people, with our beloved leader and teacher, the great Stalin, at our head, will march as before onwards and onwards, towards communism![39]

Few except eminent suspects were sentenced to death; most ended their days in labor camps. Sentences ranged from ten to twenty-five years, but the term mattered little, since prisoners were not released at the expiry of their terms, even if they managed to survive the hard work, cold, malnutrition, and general neglect. In March 1937 Stalin explicity approved physical torture, encouraging methods that were already amply in use, and he greatly increased the severity of treatment of political prisoners. In a marked departure from the older tradition, political prisoners were treated much worse than ordinary criminals and were often placed under their orders. The enlightened Soviet idea of rehabilitation through useful work, which was widely touted in the 1920s, was perverted into a ghastly system of slavery. This became important for the economy, especially for construction projects in inclement regions to which it was difficult to draw voluntary workers. The NKVD thus had an economic interest in making the maximum number of arrests. This did not prevent the police, however, from sometimes simply slaughtering prisoners en masse to be rid of them.[40]

Those who were the most likely to be exempt from the purges were the most obvious opponents of the Soviet regime: ex-priests, former tsarist officials, ex-members of other parties, and the like. Those who were most afflicted were

Bolsheviks of prerevolutionary vintage. Anyone with a foreign connection of any kind was peculiarly vulnerable to denunciation as a spy or agent. The purges of foreign Communist parties were especially extreme, so far as their leaders were in Soviet power or obeyed orders to come to Moscow. Nearly all the Polish leaders died and the Polish party (which was needed for the invasion of Poland only a year later) was abolished. Various other foreign parties, such as the Yugoslav one, suffered only slightly less. A large majority of the Soviet officials who had been in Spain to help the anti-Franco forces were liquidated, presumably because of possible contamination by Trotskyism. The Latvians, who had been so prominent in helping Lenin in his hour of need (1917 – 18), suffered severely. Other minorities also suffered disproportionately; indeed, it was more realistic to accuse Central Asians or Ukrainians than Russians of conspiring with Germany or Japan. The Ukrainian party, which had enjoyed some feelings of national autonomy, was purged (the top leadership was almost totally destroyed) and purged again. When the Central Committee demurred in Kiev, it was invited to Moscow and murdered.[41] In sum, the purges conducted by the Georgian despot did much to Russify the leadership of the Soviet party, except for the trusted Georgians Stalin brought in as special assistants.

Georgians were not necessarily favored, however. Anyone familiar with Stalin's early life was lucky to remain alive. Stalin also decimated his in-laws. As a chivalrous Caucasian, he spared a number of female Old Bolsheviks, even outright opponents, such as Kollontai, the onetime star of the Workers' Opposition, Yelena Stasova, and Lydia Fotieva, secretaries of Lenin who knew things inconvenient to him, and Krupskaya, who heeded his warning. Chivalry did not go far, however. The wives and children of alleged traitors were commonly imprisoned, and the death penalty was extended in 1935 to twelve-year-olds.

That Stalin did away with nearly all the surviving old followers of Lenin, including all of Lenin's 1920 Politburo except himself and Lenin, is less surprising than the fact that he dispatched countless persons whom he had raised up and who were to all appearances loyal to him. Of the 1,966 delegates to the Seventeenth Congress, 1,108 were arrested and probably perished; of the 138 members including candidates of the Central Committee, 98 were shot. This was presumably in reaction to their lack of enthusiasm for purging the high party leadership, but nearly all the provincial and republic party leaders were annihilated without such cause, as were all the leaders of the NKVD up to 1938. Not only the Leninist Politburo of 1920 but the Stalinist Politburo of 1932 was largely annihilated. Kirov was murdered; Kuibyshev died allegedly of heart disease early in 1935, a demise that was later charged to Yagoda as medical murder; Kossior and Rudzutak were executed; Ordzhonikidze was driven to suicide, apparently because he tried to defend managers in his Commissariat of

Heavy Industry. Other onetime Stalin intimates who lost their lives were Yenukidze and Chubar. The survivors included Voroshilov, Stalin's old drinking companion; Kaganovich, who hesitated at no bloodshed (and who lost two brothers to the purges); the unimportant Andreyev; and Molotov. Molotov (who was apparently in disfavor in 1936), Kaganovich, and Voroshilov were the only prerevolutionary Bolsheviks remaining in the top leadership.

The party was recleansed three times between 1935 and 1938, and each time a new set of hidden enemies was uncovered. Its membership, which had been 3.5 million in 1933, shrank to less than 2 million at the beginning of 1938. But a Central Committee resolution of January 1938 condemned careerists who made false accusations and required due process in the consideration of expulsions. Arrests continued but on a reduced scale. There were some rehabilitations, and a recruitment campaign began to fill the gaps in the rolls. In July 1938 Stalin's deputy in the Caucasus, Lavrenti Beria, was brought to Moscow with a corps of Georgian aides to work with Yezhov in the NKVD. Stalin seems to have become suspicious of Yezhov or to have found him too powerful. He was gradually reduced in rank, perhaps lest he react. Beria became the commander, and in December Yezhov was demoted to Commissar of Water Transport—an ironic appointment in view of the role of slave labor in digging canals—and he subsequently disappeared. Beria made nearly a clean sweep of the upper ranks of the NKVD, sending many to join the prisoners they had recently been interrogating. Some prisoners were released, and the great purges were finished, although arrests continued at a rate of about a million per year.

In 1939 Stalin convened the Eighteenth Congress. He then blamed the "excesses" on subordinates and promised that there would be no more mass purges. The depth of renovation of the party was shown by the fact that less than 2 percent of the delegates who had acclaimed Stalin at the Seventeenth Congress returned, and of the top elite that had been represented by the Central Committee, only 14 out of 139 were still on the scene.[42] In another aspect, 81 percent of the 1934 delegates had been members of prerevolutionary standing, but in 1939, only 19 percent had that dangerous distinction.

Stalin may have called a halt to the wild slaughter through weariness and fear that the madness might overtake him also, but it seems probable that the state of the world recalled him to moderation. Nazi power was rising, and its theme, which was welcomed by many conservatives in Europe, was the destruction of Bolshevism (along with anti-Semitism.) In October 1938 the threat became acute with the signing of the Munich agreement that practically delivered Czechoslovakia to the Hitlerites. The Soviet Union, like Western observers, interpreted this as an invitation to Hitler to turn east. It was imperative to rearm, but industrial production had already suffered from the removal of countless managers and engineers as well as less obviously useful persons. Stalin had repeatedly found a new opponent each time he had vanquished one. He had exhausted the domestic opposition, real or potential, by 1938, but he perceived a looming menace and opportunities for glory abroad.

The purges were madness, even from Stalin's own crudely self-centered viewpoint; although they consolidated his power, their exaggeration was certainly unnecessary, they gravely weakened the Soviet Union and exposed it to possible defeat, and they put Stalin in danger of a coup or assassination. As madness, they are not susceptible to rational explanation.

Madness implies a madman, and there is justice in the latter-day Soviet attribution of the terror to Stalin's personality. There has never been a comparable purge in any other independent Communist country; the nearest equivalents have been small-scale bloodbaths in East European countries that were under Stalinist domination near the end of Stalin's life. Elsewhere, as in China, Yugoslavia, Cuba, and Vietnam, the brotherhood that made the revolution has usually held together fairly well and ruled the country with little or no murder of old comrades. The governing hierarchy has lasted basically intact to a ripe age. Stalin's actions in killing sixteen out of Lenin's Central Committee of twenty-four and in making practically a new party from top to bottom were thus grossly abnormal. In fact, in the world's history of despots, from Nero through Genghis Khan to Hitler, Stalin stands out uniquely for his irrational destruction of his own supporters.

A consideration of Stalin's personality[43] furnishes only limited enlightenment. The available knowledge about Stalin's background and youth is too sketchy to permit psychoanalysis. However, Stalin grew up in the violent tradition of the Caucasus, where banditry and blood feuds were the order of nature; he received an education in hypocrisy in the seminary; and he became a professional purveyor of violence during his life in the revolutionary underground. At one time he was something of a Georgian nationalist, and the purges might possibly be construed as the fulfillment of youthful dreams of vengeance on the Russian oppressors. As a follower of Lenin, he had no moral standards except the success of the cause, which he equated, not unnaturally, with his personal security. It is quite possible that his relations with the tsarist police, if not actual service as a police agent, weighed upon him, made him neurotically fearful, and increased his suspiciousness. As a Georgian trying to pass for Russian[44] and ruling the Russian empire, he could realistically imagine that many people would regard him as a usurper and like to replace him. His own ability to dissimulate and wait until the time to strike, which he demonstrated in 1923, probably made him suppose that others would do likewise and convinced him to eliminate those who were conceivably capable of someday turning on him. He was not swayed by apparent repentance, but only pushed to eliminate those who had reason to hate or envy him—either in reality or in his imagination. Any suggestion that his power was to be curtailed was equivalent in his eyes to a plot to murder him.

It has been often speculated that Stalin had bitter feelings against the revolutionaries who had passed years in the cafes of Paris and Geneva while he struggled with the tsarist police. He got along well enough with the emigrés for some years, however, and he might well have been grateful to Kamenev and Zinoviev for their action in covering up Lenin's Testament. Many others suffered as severely as the intellectuals who had been in exile abroad.

The murder of Kirov may have been decisive in raising the Stalinist repressions from barbarity to insanity. Having perceived a perhaps genuine threat to his position from a much more popular person—one who had the advantage of being Russian—Stalin may have succumbed to the temptation to remove the menace by an easily arranged murder.

But once the murder had been committed, all those involved had to be eliminated to keep the secret. This could be done only in a climate of hysteria. The tide of terrorism was running, and Stalin observed what he could not have known before—that slaughtering people high and low in the party caused not indignation and protest but awestruck submission. Hence he felt free to do what he had doubtless always desired to do, namely, suffocate whatever aspirations for freedom remained from the revolutionary days and eliminate all potential alternative leadership. In Stalin's view, the success of the purge justified more purges, leaving him increasingly alone in absolute power.

Still, it is difficult to account for the insane purges on the basis of Stalin's personality. Prior to them, he had always seemed to be a moderate, reasonable man. He was neither a fanatic doctrinaire nor an arrogant and conceited bully. He was characteristically cautious, but in the purges he threw caution away. He was above all a party man, the builder of a political machine, and it seems unnatural that in his late maturity (he was fifty-seven in 1936) he should do so much to destroy the party. He was a maneuverer and organizer, a supremely successful one, and people are usually prone to continue with methods that have brought them success. Nevertheless, late in life he turned around to murder his lieutenants. This turn can hardly be explained as a developing psychosis, because not long afterwards Allied war leaders perceived him as a very sane and rational negotiator. Perhaps, however, he was the supreme example of the corruption of power. It was only in relation to his inferiors that he was paranoid. As his daughter related, if he once took a notion that someone was against him, no evidence or pleas by intimates of many years' standing could sway his opinion.[45] He was, moreover, extremely capricious. He shot many who strove only to please him, but sometimes spared stiff-necked persons such as Pasternak and even a few ex-Trotskyites and oppositionists.

It must be granted that conditions were favorable to the terror. The precedent of the Leninist Red Terror, when hostages and innocent or slightly guilty persons were shot by the thousands, made the executions of the 1930s seem less shocking. Russian history has long been bloody; Stalin admired Ivan IV's massacres of the boyars and blamed Ivan only for his failure to be more thorough. There were plenty of persons who were prepared to act as butchers at Stalin's orders; the NKVD was even capable of shooting homeless children to be rid of them.[46]

There was phenomenally little resistance to the purges. They were largely secret; most people simply vanished, and it was learned only afterwards, often many years later, that they had been killed or had succumbed. Neither Russians nor the outside world had any idea at the time of the magnitude of the disaster. Ordinary life was not much changed, and the most attention was given to the economy and the Stakhanovite movement. When Tukhachevsky was being shot, the Soviet Union was celebrating the flight of a Soviet aviator, Chkalov, over the Arctic to San Francisco. And the new Soviet constitution, which had largely been drafted by Bukharin but credited to Stalin, was adopted just as the tempest was rising to its full fury in 1936; it opportunely diverted attention from the purges both in the Soviet Union and abroad. The constitution was celebrated as "the most democratic in the world" (although it in fact formalized the leading position of the Communist party, the "vanguard of the toilers," and severely qualified the rights it proclaimed), and even Bukharin thought its specious promises and democratic principles might be realized.

So far as people were aware of the slaughter that was going on, they had little inclination to become enraged. The more conspicuous party victims aroused little sympathy because they had for the most part practiced or countenanced repression of nonparty people; hardly any had shown any concern for human rights. There were always candidates to step into the positions of those who were removed; the tough young Stalinists, who had been politically educated by collectivization, were neither compassionate nor fearful. Their pressure for promotion, in Rigby's opinion, helped the purges along.[47] The new class gave little thought to the loss of the old. The purges also placated the people to some extent. The victims were accused of sabotage and made scapegoats for all manner of failures, from the diseases of livestock to the bungling of plans. This interpretation conflicts, however, with the fact that 1934–36 saw a marked improvement in the economy.

Opposition was also muted by the fact that Stalin was very successful in shifting the blame for his misdeeds to his underlings. It was as it had been with the tsar: evil counsellors must be to blame. "If Stalin only knew," people would say, when Stalin was actually pulling the strings. Tortured ex-comrades of Stalin who were about to be executed would shout, "Long live Stalin!"

It seemed more necessary to believe that Stalin was not responsible for the mistakes because the idea grew that no one could take his place, that a change of leadership would be dangerous. In the traditional Russian fear of disorder, the opposition was hesitant to try to set Stalin aside. Even Trotsky had written, in 1932, "At present, the upsetting of the bureaucratic equilibrium [Stalin's rule] in the USSR would almost certainly benefit the forces of counterrevolution." In

1933 Trotsky commented further, "They all speak about Stalin's isolation and the general hatred of him. . . . But they often add: If it were not for that (we omit their strong epithet for him) . . . everything would have fallen into pieces by now. It is he who keeps everything together. . . ."[48] Stalin disarmed the opposition by making himself the incarnation of the sacred unity of the party, in whose name he spoke.

In the last analysis, the terror was rational from Stalin's point of view, if we assume that he had a compulsion to be flattered if not revered. The lesson of the purges was that one was safe only in loving Stalin heart and soul, so people acted as though they loved him and in so acting actually came to love him, so far as they knew. Millions wept when the grim secluded monster died. Unpleasant as it is for the members of an individualistic culture to admit it, fear generates affection. When a terrorist holds a gun over people, they are grateful to him for refraining from killing them. The free use of the powerful argument of force in 1935–38, and its steady application thereafter left the Russian people obedient and submissive, in awe of Stalin and his party.

THE STALINIST SYSTEM

From the beginning of the Stalinist transformation in 1928–29, what had been a fairly loose and open Soviet society was steadily tightened and closed. Statistical information about the party and state, which reached a maximum in 1927, decreased year by year, as a blanket of secrecy was drawn over the brutalities and failures of collectivization and industrialization. Bombast and falsification took the place of information. From the early 1930s until after Stalin's death, not even membership figures for the party were revealed, and it became the policy totally to conceal political life. Among the people, a fair amount of semifree speech was permitted until the purge years, but then ordinary folk, like the party bosses, learned that a careless word might mean a denunciation, and silence or pretense became the rule everywhere outside the most trusted circles.

The intellectual scene darkened. Foreign travel and the importation of foreign publications were closed down; flight abroad became a capital offense, subjecting the relatives of the criminal, even if they had been unaware of his intentions, to exile. Writers in the 1920s were invited to create as they would, within limits of respect for the party and its ideology. But with the inauguration of the Five Year Plan, they, too, were mobilized to assist in the building of the new society. Proletarianism in the arts was ended with the dissolution of a fairly free leftist writers' association in 1932.[49] In 1934 the Soviet Writers' Congress established the Union of Soviet Writers, under party sponsorship and control. Andrei Zhdanov, who again emerged as the purifier of Soviet letters after World War II, urged writers to turn away from the West, to follow the canons of the newly defined "socialist realism," and to glorify the party and Stalin. There was no more room for art for art's sake or for mere entertainment, but thousands of plays and novels told the virtues of the leader and the heroic feats of Soviet workers who had been inspired by Stalin and the party. Stalin himself became the chief critic of art, music, and literature. Philosophy and the social sciences were made the servants of the party so far as they survived.

Fervid concentration on the building of socialism in the Soviet Union meant the neglect of world revolution and the growth of a new nationalism. Speeches included obeisance to the struggle of the workers abroad, and the world cause was an important morale builder into the 1930s (it is still used to some extent today), but Stalin paid attention to the Comintern only when it served his own purposes. The Seventh (and last) Congress of the Comintern was held in Moscow in July 1935, and it was devoted not to the making of the delayed revolution but to the defense of Stalin's Soviet state against fascism by alliance with Social Democrats (who had been execrated as "Social Fascists" not long before) and other antifascists in "popular fronts." Stalin thus broadened and liberalized his policies abroad at the same time he was narrowing them at home.

Marxism-Leninism was converted in practice into a variety of nationalism, as Stalin made a great power the spokesman for a class and equated loyalty to the "Socialist Fatherland of the Workers" with loyalty to the world revolutionary cause. Stalin strongly appealed to nationalistic instincts from 1931 on: Russia should be the leading force in the great movement of liberation of humanity, and it was necessary to build up its industry to protect Russia. The term "Rodina," or "Fatherland," came back into currency. *Pravda* editorialized: "For our Fatherland! This call fans the flame of heroism, the flame of creative initiative in all pursuits and all fields of our rich life. For our Fatherland! This call arouses millions of workers and alerts them in the defense of their great country."[50] The new railroads, combines, power lines, and smoking chimneys represented the new greatness of old Russia, the ruler of one-sixth of the earth's land and the most progressive of nations technologically, socially, and politically. Stalin thus set a pattern of socialist nationalism, or national socialism, that other Communist leaders, such as Mao, Tito, Ho Chi Minh, and Castro, were to follow.

It was necessary to revise the writing of history. In 1931 Stalin called for the proper approach to historical writing—in effect, for subordinating history to politics. By 1934 Pokrovsky and the Marxist-determinist interpretation were rejected in favor first of acceptance, then of glorification of the past, with homage to tsars and generals; Alexander Nevsky, Ivan the Terrible, and Peter the Great became symbols of Russian greatness and virtual precursors of Bolshevism. Stalin reversed Lenin, adopting the "lesser evil" theory, that incorporation into the Russian empire was a blessing for minority peoples, who were thus saved from worse oppressors. Russian nationalism, which Lenin had detested, was no longer seen as a problem; only the "bourgeois nationalism" of minority republics was to be repressed. Stalin was always a centralizer, and in the 1930s he increasingly used Russian nationalism to support his central rule and dictatorship. Russification became the tacit policy of the party in the 1930s, with stress on the use of Russian as the language of the great socialist state. Only the Georgians were spared some of the Russifying pressures.

As a corollary, by the mid-1930s the revolution was ended. Equalization, the breaking of bonds, and attacks on old privilege were replaced by the creation of differences, the stabilization of new bonds, and the segregation of new governing and privileged strata. Legal discriminations against members of the former ruling classes were abolished both in the party and the state, and the Stalinist constitution hailed the end of class conflict with the full victory of socialism. During the worst of the purges, the policy toward the church was eased. In all walks, from the factories to the army, from successful writers and actors to party bosses, those who pleased the ruler gained material and social preferences and distinctions. The "party maximum," an effort to restrict the pay of Communists to that of a skilled worker (at least outwardly), was abolished in 1932, and salaries of officials grew rapidly thereafter.[51] Beginning in 1931 the authority of schoolteachers was restored, grades and examinations were emphasized, educational experimentation was halted, and students were supposed to study hard to make themselves technical specialists and productive citizens. Stalin found that the family stabilized society and that good family men and women made the best workers; the Soviet family, which was infinitely superior to the bourgeois family, was exalted as the basis of socialist society, in complete antithesis to traditional radical ideas of the dissolution of the family in the larger collective. Divorce was restricted, abortion was outlawed except for medical necessity, and women were rewarded for childbearing, as in the fascist states at the same time. Ideology was revised to decree that the role of the state was not to disappear under socialism but to rise until some distant future universal victory of that order; in any case, little was said of the utopian future. True communism, it seemed, was equivalent not to Marx's freedom and abundance but to discipline and obedience.

To manage his state, a task of governance that was far beyond that ordinarily assumed by any traditional elite, Stalin needed a corps of dedicated managers, who had to be rewarded with goods and status for their loyalty, hard work and risk taking. It was an armylike hierarchy, as Stalin outlined in 1937. There were, he said, 3000 to 4000 first-rank leaders in the generals' corps; the middle-rank leaders, or officers' corps, numbered 30,000 to 40,000; the lower-level leaders or noncommissioned officers were 100,000 to 150,000 strong.[52] Below them were the ordinary members, at that time less than 2 million, and below the party were what Stalin called "transmission belts" for carrying the will of the leadership to the masses, organizations such as trade unions, cooperatives, women's groups, and the youth organization, which were officered and guided by party members. The last group, the Komsomol (the young people's auxiliary of the party), had special importance for Stalin. It grew while the party shrank, increasing from 2 million members in 1928 to 9 million in 1939, and provided a reserve for the party and a corps of helpers for almost any task.

Party membership was burdensome and at times dangerous, but it was the way to elite status, the road to advancement for the new intelligentsia. Up to the time of the purges, the growth of the party rolls had been proportionate to the growth in the number of educated citizens and in the urban population.[53] During the purges, admissions were halted for a time, and they resumed on a considerable scale only in 1938; by that time the expulsions were nearly ended, and party membership rose during 1938 by 400,000. The next year the party began to rebuild in earnest, growing by 1.1 million to a total of 3.4 million (a little smaller than it had been in 1933), and to 3.9 million at the beginning of the war in 1941.

It was hardly a representative party. In 1937 two-thirds of the Soviet population was still rural, but only about one-fifth of the party members were classified as peasants, and after the purges membership was rebuilt more gradually in the countryside than in the cities. In the 1920s there had been a strong preference for recruitment within the favored class, the factory workers, and in 1929 some four-fifths of the entrants belonged to that category. But a party of proletarians was practically impossible because party people were needed for and pushed into administrative jobs, and managers and engineers had to be included in the party. After 1930 the party began looking favorably upon recruitment of the new class of Soviet intelligentsia that was coming out of the technical institutes. The proportion of entrants described as "workers" declined until by March 1939–June 1941 it was less than 20 percent.[54] On the eve of the war the party had been almost completely renewed, since the prepurge members were then only a minor fraction of the total.

The ordinary members were consulted less and less, however. Ironically, at the time of the purges, Stalin introduced the secret ballot for party elections, but authority was concentrated at the top and in the Secretariat. The party congresses, at which the membership could hope to make itself heard before the revolution and during the first years after it, were totally controlled after 1927. Nevertheless, they were held with decreasing frequency. They were convened yearly until 1926 was skipped, but after 1927 the party congress was called only in 1930, then in 1934 and 1939, and not again until Stalin's senility set in in 1952, party statutes to the contrary. The Central Committee was at first the most important body, and members were allowed to attend Politburo meetings (without speaking) into the early 1930s.[55] The committee was still sufficiently authoritative early in 1937 to force Stalin to secure its consent for the intensification of the terror, but in 1938 it had been thinned too much for formal meeting and thereafter it almost lapsed. The Politburo likewise receded, becoming only a sort of cabinet, which the leader consulted as he chose. The Secretariat itself was a sort of government, with functional sections for managing the party and the state. It was a sign of its direct dominance that in 1934 it acquired branches that corresponded to the sectors of the economy over which it watched.

Stalin, who was the acme and focus of power, modestly enjoyed no supreme title, only acknowledged omnipotence. He had his lieutenants and followers, but no real second-in-command or heir apparent. Molotov was usually by his side, and Lazar Kaganovich was next to Stalin in prominence for some years, but he lost stature during the purges and was shunted to economic work. Yezhov seemed briefly favored. It was not always safe to stand near Stalin; of the seven who were closest to him in 1934, three, Kirov, Kuibyshev, and Ordzhonikidze, were soon to die. After the fall of Yezhov, Beria probably enjoyed Stalin's greatest confidence, but he was soon joined by Malenkov, a newcomer. One of the most influential persons in the Soviet Union for many years was totally unknown to the public; he was A. N. Poskrebyshev, Stalin's personal secretary from 1930 to 1953.

Stalin managed power craftily, using the agencies that were directly under himself, the state commissariats, the police, and the (purged) military, to offset the primary power of the party. He endeavored to assure his authority by making himself the capstone of the whole structure and permitting no one else to get a foothold from which to challenge him. He was also the fountainhead of truth. Unlike Lenin, he did not take naturally to writing, and his works published after 1934 are few. But he authored, or partly authored and supervised, the official party history, which was published in 1938–39 and is ordinarily known as the *Short Course*. This account gave the obligatory postpurge version of the party history, practically eliminating the Old Bolsheviks and leaving room only for Lenin and Stalin. It became and remained until after Stalin's death the ideological nourishment for generations of Soviet citizens; through it Marxism-Leninism became Marxism-Leninism-Stalinism.

In his absolutism, Stalin took on the ways that have been associated with grand despotism since ancient times. His need for adulation apparently grew steadily, and the Stalin cult became more and more exaggerated, through praise in the papers, the quotation of Stalin at every turn, paintings, statues, the naming after him of mountains, farms, and factories, and the kowtowing of all around him. Already in the early 1930s high party figures were afraid not merely to contradict Stalin, but also to take up distasteful matters with him.[56] He secluded himself from public view and ceased to appear in public except on infrequent ceremonial occasions. Stalin was a distant, awesome figure, especially to the younger generations that knew no other god. After his wife's suicide in 1932, Stalin's household was run by the police and became itself a bureaucratized establishment with a swollen staff, and a center of intrigue.

Yet Stalin made a curious effort to maintain the appearances of a democratic state, speaking always for the party and the workers. He promised civil rights, elections, and modern constitutional procedures in the 1936 "Stalinist" constitution. With his taste for irony, in 1936 Stalin stated his opposition to having a single president of the powerless Supreme Soviet (instead of the plural Presidium) on the grounds that this might be conducive to dictatorship.[57]

THE EVE OF THE WAR

The heroic age of the party ended with the recession of the Great Terror which was heroic in its proportions, however macabre. Since then preservation has been the rule rather than change. There have been few important new ideas, little idealism, and much obscure politicking, but not much struggle for principles, in the predictable running down of the revolution. No real sense of social change has been evident; much more attention has been paid to great power politics. Foreign affairs captured Stalin's interest after 1938, in terms not of world revolution, but of diplomacy, force, and territorial gains.

The Eighteenth Congress, which occurred in March 1939, was dedicated to consolidation. Stalin denounced the excesses and falsifications of the purges, but found the results to have been good. There were no more ideological groupings, only loose personal followings of such rising Stalin lieutenants as Malenkov, Zhdanov, Beria, and Khrushchev. Of these, Malenkov seemed the most promising; the epitome of the organization man, he was the head of the Cadres Administration of the Central Committee, with considerable control over records and assignments. The supervisory role of his branch was extended by the Nineteenth Congress to cover the commissariats, in addition to party organizations, the Komsomol, the press, and so on.[58]

Turning to foreign affairs at the congress, Stalin hinted of his willingness to deal with Nazi Germany. Stalin had been certainly piqued by his exclusion from the international dealings in 1938 that had culminated in the Munich pact. After the Nazis occupied the rump of Czechoslovakia during the Eighteenth Congress, Stalin found himself newly desired as an ally by Britain and France. However, he negotiated concurrently with both sides. Hitler could offer the Soviet Union a free hand with the territories on its western borders, mostly lands that Russia had lost in 1917—18. Moreover, Hitler offered the Soviet Union a chance to remain neutral while opening the way for a war that could be as advantageous for it as it was disastrous for the West.

On August 19, 1939, the Soviet Union signed a trade treaty with Germany, and on August 23, Nazi Foreign Minister Joachim von Ribbentrop arrived in Moscow to sign a nonaggression pact with overtones of alliance, including a secret protocol providing for Soviet annexation of eastern Poland, the Baltic states, and Bessarabia. It represented a diplomatic triumph for Stalin thus to set at each other the capitalist states that by Marxist logic should have joined together against the workers' state. It was also a demonstration of contempt for Western "bourgeois" society; Stalin had more trust and understanding for his fellow dictator than for the British and French governments. It showed scorn for the international Communist movement, which had been fervently denouncing the "fascist bandits," as the Soviet masters desired, and which was not consulted. The fact that the reviled enemies suddenly became respectable semifriends was confusing for the Soviet people, however. The lack of any breath of overt opposition evidenced the effectiveness of the purges.

Stalin thereby plunged into realpolitik. The Nazi-Soviet pact was followed in a week by the German invasion of Poland; while the German forces were breaking Polish resistance, the Red Army took the eastern half of that country as had been agreed. Stalin thereby acquired nearly thirteen million new subjects, mostly Ukrainians and White Russians. Their "liberation" was justified on ethnic, not class, grounds. The organizational and coercive powers of the Soviet system were demonstrated by the fact that in a little over a month Soviet-style elections could be carried out in the occupied areas, leading to a unanimous petition for admission to the USSR.

Stalin also used armed forces as bearers of the proletarian revolution where-ever he felt free to do so. Lithuania, Latvia, and Estonia were required to admit Soviet forces, establish Communist governments, socialize their economies, ban non-Communist organizations, and request the final liberation (as it is celebrated in the lands concerned) of entering the Soviet Union. The Finns balked, and the Soviet Union, probably on the initiative of the Leningrad party organization headed by Zhdanov,[59] attacked. The self-delusion of the Stalinist dictatorship was shown by its belief that the Finnish masses would rise to welcome the Red Army. Fighting fiercely, the Finns prevented the Soviet forces from advancing for several months, and in March 1940 Stalin settled for limited territorial gains.

Meanwhile the friendship with Nazi Germany was prospering. By mid-September 1939 the Communist parties in the Western democratic powers were taking a defeatist, antiwar line similar to Lenin's in 1917—opposing the "imperialist war" of Britain and France. The official Soviet line was that the contest between capitalist states was of no concern to the workers, but in fact Soviet propaganda was directed only against the Western Allies, who were blamed for carrying on the war after the knockout of Poland. Communists in the West sabotaged their governments, while the Soviet Union made a great point of fulfilling its economic commitments and furnishing raw materials to Germany. Indeed, Stalin wanted much more military collaboration than Hitler would countenance. In reply to Hitler's exuberant congratulations on his sixtieth birthday, Stalin replied, "The friendship between the peoples of the Soviet Union and Germany, cemented by blood, has every reason to be solid and lasting."[60]

There was some tendency to view the Nazis more critically after they demonstrated their potential through their victories in the spring of 1940 in Scandinavia, the Low Countries, and France. But in this period of crudest nationalistic foreign policy, hardly shaded by Marxist-Leninist language, Stalin cherished expansionist goals in the old tradition—the Balkans, the Straits, and Persia—that might be achieved in cooperation with the Nazis, in the same way that much had already been gained. In October 1940 Molotov, who had become Foreign Minister when the German agreement was just being negotiated in May 1939, went to Berlin, and Stalin seems to have been prepared to discuss joining the German-Italian-Japanese Axis.[61] But Molotov and Hitler were singularly incompatible characters; Hitler lost patience when Molotov presented his shopping list, negotiations were adjourned, and orders went to the German staff to prepare for an attack.

The Soviet Union, meanwhile, was also polishing its armor, although probably more from a desire to play a strong part in world affairs than from fear of Germany, since Stalin evinced enormous confidence in the huge fighting forces he had built up. Important military officers were still being purged in June 1941, and by the inertia of the machine, executions continued for months after the country was invaded. But the Soviet armed forces, which numbered less than a million in 1934, were doubled by 1938 and redoubled by 1940, to four million. The authority of the officers was increased, the political commissars were downgraded, discipline was tightened, the separation of the ranks was increased, and indoctrination was made more nationalistic. Defense spending, which had accounted for about 12 percent of the budget in the early 1930s, was raised to 43 percent in 1941. It was probably also in the expectation of an active role in world affairs that Stalin assumed in May 1941 the place of head of the government, a title he retained until his death. To some extent this implied a further move from party-ideological to personal-dictatorial government, a trend that was also evinced during the war.

THE WAR

Even after the humiliating setbacks of the Finnish ("Winter") war, the Stalinist planners assumed that a war with Germany would be easily successful and fought on German soil. With supreme incompetence, they even failed to fortify the new line that had been acquired in the West.[62] Because of self-confidence and isolation among yes-men, Stalin refused to believe that his policy of dealing with Hitler was a failure; thus he neglected to take defensive precautions in the spring of 1941, and ordered reports of impending Nazi attack to be treated as provocations.

The reality of the attack threw Stalin into a state of shock. He disappeared from view for eleven days; and, in the words of one of his generals, in the first days of the war "he was depressed, nervous, and of an uneven disposition," hoping to be saved by a miracle.[63] According to Medvedev, when the Politburo came to see Stalin after the attack, he apparently thought they were going to arrest him[64]—he had executed thousands for far less egregious errors. When Stalin reappeared, on July 3, it was to address himself rather humbly to his "brothers and sisters" concerning national defense, although he spoke of uniting around "the party of Lenin and Stalin."

Although the Soviet forces enjoyed a large numerical superiority in manpower, planes, and tanks at the outset, the Nazi onslaught sent them staggering backward with terrible losses. Within a few weeks an area many times larger than France had been occupied, and both Moscow and Leningrad were endangered. For a few days in October, Soviet power disappeared from Moscow, as the government evacuated most of its offices to the city of Kuibyshev on the Volga. But the German advance halted or was halted just short of Moscow, order was restored, and Stalin and the Politburo were back at Lenin's mausoleum for the November 7 parade, from which soldiers marched to the front. The party was back in charge and remained so throughout the war.

From the first days, Stalin was reassured as the leading capitalist powers came to his assistance instead of aiding the Nazis to destroy the workers' state. Churchill made an immediate statement of support, and in a few days a Soviet-British alliance was signed. President Roosevelt sent Harry Hopkins to Moscow in July, and a stream of munitions and other supplies was soon on its way from America, at first small, but growing steadily until the last days of the war. Lenin's party found itself in league with Lenin's enemies.

This ideological reverse contributed to the marked turn, between 1941 and 1945, away from the vestiges of internationalism to an entirely Russian-nationalistic approach, whereby the party was still further Russified and fused with Russian nationalism. It was a fight for Russian soil and the Russian people, especially as peripheral and mostly non-Russian areas were lost in the west and south. The Comintern was dissolved in May 1943. Although the Comintern bureaucrats working for Stalin continued at their work, many of them eventually to assist in the administration of Sovietized countries, it was a repudiation of Lenin's favorite creature and of the entire idea of revolution making. Leninism was treated as an achievement, the highest achievement, of Russian culture, not of the general Marxist movement. In 1941 Stalin rebutted an attack made by Engels in 1890 on tsarist Russia. Stalin came to an amicable agreement with the Russian Orthodox Church; the Patriarchate was restored, and the church loyally supported the Soviet war effort. Much was made of the Russian past; the great heroes were the tsarist conquerors, not the champions of the workers. Pan-Slavism, the old tsarist ideology of racial nationalism, was revived, and several Pan-Slav conferences were held during the war. The army command was almost entirely Slavic. Stalin's victory toast was not to the workers of the world but to the Russian people, "the directing force of the Soviet Union . . . a ruling people. . . ."[65]

In the fight for national survival, ideology in the old sense was largely forgotten. There was occasional praise for the democratic allies and a sense of disillusion in the workers' movement, which, despite more than twenty years of cultivation, did next to nothing to help the Soviet state to which it supposedly owed supreme loyalty. Under the pressures of reality, even veteran party officals seemed to shed a lifetime of indoctrination.[66] There was no longer any need for deceit.[67] Censorship was relaxed; it was enough that writers supported the war. Indoctrination became superfluous beyond intensifying hatred for the Germans, who well knew how to make themselves hated.

The dictatorship was not relaxed, however. On July 19, 1941, Stalin assumed the supreme command. In a reaction to the first colossal defeats, the commissars were restored to watch over possibly disloyal officers, and several unsuccessful generals were shot. The NKVD moved in as disciplinarian, mowing down troops that tried to retreat without orders. Stalin made his old cronies of civil-war experience, Voroshilov and Budenny, commanders of the northern and southern fronts, until they (especially the latter) demonstrated total incompetence. Abler generals were released from labor camps, however, and Stalin learned to judge his commanders by results and to allow them reasonable freedom of action. In October 1942, as the tide was nearing its turn, the commissars were subordinated to regular officers.

Stalin kept the supreme command very much to himself, and the cult of his personality grew steadily as the war went better. After the battle of Stalingrad he raised himself to marshal, and in 1945 to the unique title of "Generalissimo of the Soviet Union." General Zhukov gave him high marks for knowledge and comprehension of military questions,[68] but he was obviously not an easy chief to work for. It was difficult, although not impossible, for leading generals to argue with him regarding tactics; the generals were more afraid of him than of the Germans,[69] and seldom protested impractical orders. According to Khrushchev, in a bit of frivolity, he elevated a Georgian chef and another helper in his kitchen to the positions of major general and lieutenant general and covered them with decorations.[70]

In his war leadership, Stalin looked mostly to his oldest comrades. On June 30, 1941, party and state governing organs were superseded by the omnipotent State Defense Committee, which was not clearly either a party or a state body. It was composed of Stalin, Molotov, Malenkov, Voroshilov, and Beria. Mikoyan and Voznesensky were added in 1942 and Kaganovich and Bulganin in 1944. To some extent, each member took charge of a particular critical area, for example, Malenkov of Stalingrad and Beria of the Caucasus. The various members also seem to have been entrusted with the supreme management of various branches of the war economy, such as aircraft and munitions production. Malenkov, a man of exceptional administrative ability who was thirty-nine years old in 1941, seems to have been the most prominent next to Stalin, although he was not formally placed on the Politburo until 1946. The Central Committee apparently never met during the war.

The inferior structure of the party remained intact, however, and it was mobilized to win the war. Major leaders such as Zhdanov and Khrushchev (and Brezhnev at a lower level) went to the fronts, became generals, worked closely with the military command, and, after recovering from the first setbacks, helped to maintain strong party control. During the first six months, more than 1.1 million party members were mobilized, and before the end of the war more than half the party was in the armed forces. As in the civil war, party members were supposed to be the bravest and most dedicated fighters; perhaps they were, since about half the 3.9 million members at the beginning of the war were killed in action. Membership decreased in the first year because of war losses, to a little over 3 million; but between 1942 and 1945 it climbed steadily to 5.7 million. The doors of the Komsomol and the party were thrown open to good fighters for Stalin and the fatherland, with no questions asked about their Marxist ideology.

The battle was hard, and the Stalinist regime might well have lost if Hitler had been a little wiser, or even shrewder in restraining his brutality and sacrificing some immediate gains. Stalinism proved itself to be a ghastly failure. Every non-Russian area and some Russian areas the Nazis invaded greeted them as liberators. According to Khrushchev, Stalin would have liked to deport all the Ukrainians after the war but found nowhere to send them. He did deport in their entirety six out of nine minority nationalities, old and young alike, of the German-occupied lands in the south, sparing only persons who were actively fighting in the armed forces.[71] Many hundreds of thousands of prisoners, of Russian as well as other nationality, were quite willing to take arms against Stalin and his state under the banner of Andrei Vlasov, an outstanding Soviet general in the first part of the war who turned against the regime after he was captured. The Vlasovites failed to play a major part in the war only because of Hitler's stubborn scorn for the Russians.

However, the German atrocities convinced the Russians that Hitler was indeed worse than Stalin, and the party-ordered military machine rode on to the greatest victory in Russian history. Mobilizing the economy with singular thoroughness, shifting industries eastward, multiplying the production of munitions, and directing all the energies of the people to the common goal, the party proved its basic strength. It applied all available force and required any sacrifice, and demonstrated, as Communist parties have demonstrated in China, Korea,

and elsewhere, the potency of the Leninist model in the service not of
ɹ̷ian revolution but of fervent nationalism.

HIGH STALINISM

The five years between victory in the war and about 1950, when the system was
wearing down and the dictator was entering senility, were the golden age of the
Stalinist dictatorship. The regime was strong and effective. Stalin was highly
respected at home and abroad as the architect of victory, and his and his party's
authority were legitimated as never before. Materially, the country was fearfully
weakened. The loss of life had reached about twenty million, a total that was
approximately equal to all the purge and purge-related fatalities of the previous
fifteen years. The material damage from battle and from the scorched-earth
policies of both sides was incalculable, and there was a famine in 1946–47
because of drought, together with the rundown condition of the farms. But in
August 1945 the Fourth Five Year Plan was decreed, promising more sacrifices
for the sake of heavy industry. The rebuilding was rapid, and by 1948 the Soviet
Union claimed basically to have made good the wartime destruction. The nation
had become the world's second economic as well as military power. The
recuperation in the standard of living was slow; of this period Barrington Moore
wrote, "The Soviet industrial system is an elaborate mechanism to prevent
industry from serving any immediate aims of mass welfare."[72]

The reconstruction was expected to be inspirational, with monumental
projects such as the 1948 plan to change the climate of the steppes by planting
shelter belts, and the Don-Volga canal, which was completed in 1952 and graced
with an enormous statue of Stalin. More important, the rebuilding provided the
basis for a military strength that corresponded to the newly acquired status of
superpower, a strength that matured to include hydrogen bombs and intercontinental missiles under Khrushchev but began in Stalinist austerity. The system
showed its resilience even in its weakest sector, agriculture. Collective farming
had largely broken down and some fourteen million acres had been taken by the
peasants for private plots, but within a few years discipline was restored.

The period was glorious in foreign affairs. Stalin garnered an East European
empire that surpassed the dreams of the tsars. It amounted to an extension of his
Soviet domain over peoples who were mostly of higher cultural levels than those
of the Soviet Union, and Stalin proceeded brutally and indiscriminately to
impose his model of personal-party dictatorship on them. Hardly less glorious
but much less satisfying for Stalin was the victory of Communism in China.
Malenkov hailed this event in 1949 as the fulfillment of Lenin's 1923 prophecy
that Communism would come by victory in China and India after Russia. But the
enlargement of the Soviet to the Sino-Soviet bloc, however much it raised the

world prestige of Communism, marked the end of the fully controllable movement; and Stalin seems not to have desired it.

Efforts at additional expansion in Greece, Turkey, and Iran were frustrated by the United States, and after 1946 frictions over Eastern Europe led to tension with the United States and the formation of the NATO alliance directed against Communism and Soviet aggrandizement. In September 1947 Stalin evoked a shade of the deceased Comintern in the Cominform, which joined together the Soviet, six East European, and the French and Italian Communist parties. Its chief activity was the publication of a weekly paper, and it should have advanced the Communist cause in Western Europe, but it never prospered and became inactive after 1949. Meanwhile Stalin tested the Western temper with his 1948 blockade of the Western-occupied part of Berlin, only to retreat ingloriously. Worse still, Tito and the Yugoslav party, who had come to power largely by their own efforts, resisted Stalinist pressures and broke away from the bloc in 1948.

Thus frustrated, Stalin seemed to turn inward, regarding the world as divided into the Soviet bloc (building "socialism in one bloc") and the hostile external world (lumping Third World nationalists with the "imperialists"). A token of this attitude was a 1947 decree forbidding marriage between Soviet citizens and foreigners. The limited liberalization of Soviet thinking in the war, when the Russians had not only mostly forgotten their Marxism-Leninism but also hoped that victory in alliance with the Western democratic powers would bring relaxation, had to be undone; millions of persons who had seen Western Europe had to be decontaminated. The return to a stress on ideology as the basis for rulership and unity began as early as 1944—a time when victory was beginning to loom and also when Soviet forces were occupying non-Russian Soviet territories and East European countries. A purification process was begun, including renewed strictures on literature. Indoctrination was strengthened, both inside and outside the armed forces; propagandist-lecturers were put to work, and party schools were upgraded and expanded, with curricula centered on the *Short Course*. The tone became shriller as cooperation with the Western Allies lessened until it was replaced by cold war; much of the blame for the Nazi attack was even shifted to the Allies.

The return to ideology and anti-Westernism reached a climax in the campaign led by Andrei Zhdanov (hence called the Zhdanovshchina) from 1946 to 1948. It opened with an attack on two Leningrad literary journals for their failure to present a sufficiently idealized picture of the Soviet scene and continued into a demand that all writers be active propagandists of Stalinist verities. All branches of literature and art were criticized, as party leaders damned "formalism" and "kowtowing to the West." Artists who were less than totally conformist were forced to recant, expelled from their professions, or (in the case of some Jews) shot as representatives of the enemy. Philosophy, historiography, and the sciences came in for attention, too. Genetics was replaced by the quackery of Lysenko, who in 1948 ended a discussion of genetic theory by announcing that the Central Committee (that is, Stalin) agreed with him. Physiology and psychology were also straightened out according to party dictates; even physics was divorced from the contaminations of relativity and quantum mechanics.

In the effort to de-Westernize and de-Europeanize, Western culture was denigrated, some words of Western origin were expunged from the language, and scholars were told not to refer to Western studies. Russians were found to be the inventors of almost everything useful, from the steam engine to penicillin. Even Russian scenery had to be judged the best in the world.[73] The formerly internationalist party bitterly attacked "cosmopolitanism" as a vice of capitalism that was in contrast with healthy proletarian patriotism.

With the death of Zhdanov in August 1948, the stridency of the campaign abated. However, the anticosmopolitan campaign took on an anti-Zionist and anti-Jewish color. While Britain held control of Palestine, the Soviet Union supported the insurgent Jews and rushed to recognize Israel when it was formed in May 1948. But Stalin soon observed that Soviet Jews were looking to Israel rather than to himself, and he turned away, giving vent to his latent anti-Semitism. Late in 1948 Jewish organizations were dissolved, Yiddish culture was suppressed, and major Jewish intellectuals were repressed. One of the few Jews in high places, Solomon Mikhoels of the NKVD, was murdered—according to Khrushchev, because of his suggestion that the Crimea, which had been emptied of its native Tatars, might be made a Jewish homeland.[74]

Soviet minorities, which had been given some leeway during the war, also felt the pressure of restored centralism. The minority peoples were expected to be loyal to "socialism" above all and to be grateful for the aid and protection of the senior Russians. Minority cultures were purged of "bourgeois nationalism." The most critical area was the Ukraine, the largest and most dangerous of the minority areas; a faithful Stalinist, Nikita Khrushchev, was charged with the re-Sovietization of the Ukraine after the war and the purification of the new territories in the western Ukraine. Stalin seems to have been dissatisfied with Khrushchev, because Kaganovich superseded him in 1947, but Khrushchev was restored to favor in less than a year.

The justification and framework for repression was, as always, something called "ideology," but it contained few ideas and little idealism. It was whatever Stalin said it was, and his pronouncements from time to time on history, economics, military strategy, or whatever immediately became canonical. The crudest expedients were presented not as necessary deviations from the ideal but as the ideal.[75] In the Stalinist picture, the Soviet state and army took the place of the proletariat, and the major constant factor was an insistence on the inevitability of conflict (not necessarily war) with hostile "class" forces.

A more concrete constant was the guiding light of Stalin himself. In the new pseudo-Marxist historiography, great men stood out as makers of history, and Stalin assumed that position for his time. A necessary step was the transfer of credit from the generals to Stalin, insofar as he did not already enjoy all the honors. The outstanding Soviet marshal, G. K. Zhukov, was demoted, removed from the Central Committee, and given a minor post, lest he dim the glory of the chief. The cult went on to describe Stalin in ever more superlatives. He became the cofounder of the Bolshevik party, comaker of the October Revolution, and leader of the Red Army in the civil war. Hardly anything could be written without a tribute to Stalin; it was necessary to include his name to get even lyrics into print.[76] The acme of this campaign came with his virtual deification, Oriental style, upon his seventieth birthday, December 21, 1949. So successful was Stalin in his despotism that people seemed to have no awareness that they were not free.[77]

Stalin did not rely on words to make sure that people loved him and his system of rule. The prison-camp population reached its maximum after the war and remained an important part of the labor force. Almost all those who survived imprisonment by the Nazis were put to prison labor,[78] probably more than five million people. The millions who had lived under Nazi occupation were suspect and subject to discrimination. Purging continued on a moderate scale (by Stalinist standards) through these years, taking few high officials but an assortment of ''bourgeois nationalists,'' Jews, intellectuals, unsuccessful economic managers, and the like. There were few executions, although many died in the camps. The death penalty was officially abolished in 1947, but the executions continued.

The worst late Stalin purge occurred in Leningrad in 1949. The chief victim was the economist, planner, and Politburo member Nikolai Voznesensky. His small book, *The War Economy of the USSR*, won a Stalin prize in 1948 but cost him his life in 1949. Stalin reread it and apparently decided that it revealed too much about the weakness of the Soviet Union.[79] Along with Voznesensky, a crowd of other eminent Leningraders received their dose of lead; all five secretaries of the Leningrad city committee, all five secretaries of the provincial committee, the chairman of the Russian republic council of ministers, and many others.[80] That they were mostly followers of Zhdanov, who had died the previous year, may have had something to do with their end; Malenkov certainly gained by their departure and may have helped to arrange it. It was all accomplished very quietly. Stalin must have been in a grim mood at this time, since he carried out lesser purges in the Crimea and Georgia also.

The party underwent a purification from 1945 to 1950, although it was hardly comparable to the classic purges. Entry was made difficult, and new recruits were roughly balanced by expellees, so that membership declined slightly, from

5.8 million in 1945 to 5.5 million in 1946, and then rose only slowly to 6.5 million in 1951. Some special effort was made to strengthen the party in the villages, where it was still very thin. The Komsomol was much more severely cut down, from 15 million in October 1945 to 9 million by March 1949.[81]

The party that came out of the war was again largely new in membership; less than a third of the members were of prewar vintage and probably a majority of these had joined since recruiting had resumed in 1938.[82] The tasks of the postwar years were indoctrination, training, and consolidation. The number of party professionals was increased to about a quarter of a million; this may have been a maximum, since an effort was made to narrow this elite after Stalin's death.

The party mass was relatively young and vigorous, but the rulership at the summit can only be described as decadent. Although Khrushchev, in his memoirs, gave Stalin high marks for ability,[83] Stalin governed casually and lived dissolutely. He set sycophants in motion with offhand instructions and went off to watch endless low-grade movies, especially American westerns, which he would curse as ideologically bad while ordering more of them. He was a misanthrope who hated to be alone, so he summoned his coterie to debauched dinners that were for men only. Even during the war he regularly indulged in these drunken Lucullan feasts, which resembled Hitler's.[84] All of Stalin's household were NKVD personnel, the dacha was surrounded by minefields, and Stalin took many precautions against poisoning.

Stalin seems to have governed mostly from his dacha, largely between midnight and dawn; his servants had to be ready to take his call at any early-morning hour. He rarely appeared in public, but travelled between the Kremlin, his dacha, and his vacation homes in the south. He gave the appearance of a sage devoting his attention to profound ideological matters.[85] His private views, however, were far from his public image: he cursed the Jews while outwardly condemning anti-Semitism, and he privately sneered at Lenin, while boasting publicly of his partnership with him.[86]

A curious episode that reveals Stalin's mentality was the anti-Marr outburst of the summer of 1950. N. Ya. Marr, a Georgian and onetime protégé of Stalin, was a little Stalin of Marxian linguistics who postulated that languages, being part of the superstructure, would eventually merge in international Communism. Marr died in 1934. In 1950, just as the Korean War was beginning, Stalin concluded that Marr's theory was absurd; the superstructure, he said, is the active power, and, casting aside internationalist nonsense, he proclaimed that Russian would be the language of the future. Stalin's linguistic theory was more sensible than Marr's, and Stalin accompanied his analysis with a sensible and un-Stalinist statement, "Everyone acknowledges that no science can develop or progress without a struggle of opinions and freedom of criticism."[87] Nevertheless it is baffling why the question was so blown up, lasting for weeks, when the world was aroused by the first major conflict since World War II, the Korean

War, begun at least with Stalin's acquiescence. The Soviet press was filled with endless articles reflecting not a struggle of opinion, but commentaries and repetitions of Stalin's opinion on the language that would prevail in some indeterminate future. Stalin's judgment was clearly fuzzy.

Stalin's regime in his last years was disorganized and without a direction except fear. There were no clearly defined spheres of competence,[88] a situation that is characteristic of dictatorships; and there was no evidence of loyalty to the party as such.[89] Possibly the second most influential person was Poskrebyshev, Stalin's confidant and secretary for many years, a person of little education and coarse manners. He was made a major general in 1946 when Stalin was removing real generals. Khrushchev regarded Stalin as so arbitrary at this time that he called the system before 1939 "democracy."[90]

Secrecy descended on the inner workings of the leadership as never before, except so far as Khrushchev's unreliable recollections shed a dim light. But it seems to have been a thoroughly personal government. The Central Committee, which in the infancy of the Soviet state was scheduled to meet at least every two weeks, held a plenary session in March 1946, the first in five years. Another meeting was held in 1947, but it seems to have been the last until 1952. The Politburo was largely dissolved, usually meeting, so far as it functioned, in smaller ad hoc committees that were named by Stalin.[91] Stalin had some sense of propriety. Andreiev was kept formally on the Politburo but excluded in practice. There was no regular deliberative body, even in the sense that a monarch has an appointed council to advise him. The Secretariat was the only effective party organ. Apparently, as Stalin found it harder to keep on top of affairs because of the decay of his faculties, he became reluctant to bring more capable men together.

A photograph published at the end of the war showed that Stalin, who was approaching sixty-six, had turned gray. As it became increasingly evident that the regime could not last much longer, the jostling for position became more intense; at the same time, the weakening leader encouraged factionalism below himself to secure his own supremacy.[92] Malenkov seems to have been Stalin's first lieutenant during the war, and his principal rival, A. S. Shcherbakov, died in the spring of 1945. Malenkov was left as Secretary of the Central Committee along with Stalin, and Deputy Chairman of the Council of Ministers; in March 1946 he became a member of the Politburo. But perhaps because Stalin thought he had grown too big, Malenkov's star declined in 1946, and Andrei Zhdanov seemed clearly to be Stalin's favorite.[93] Zhdanov was the stage manager for the formation of the Cominform in September 1947 and for the cleanup on the literary and artistic fronts then and afterwards.

Zhdanov's glory was brief; in the summer of 1948 he was seemingly losing power, and death took him on August 31. The cause of death was stated to have been heart failure, but it may have been unnatural.[94] His death was followed by the purge of Leningraders wherein all the high victims were associates of Zhdanov's—the first executions of top party men since 1938. Both the decease of Zhdanov and the purge were very beneficial to Malenkov, who returned to the Secretariat from which he had been absent for two years. Malenkov was then the only person besides Stalin to have a place on both the Politburo and the Secretariat.

Next to Malenkov, and perhaps allied with him, was Stalin's most enduring police boss, Lavrenty Beria. Like Malenkov, he entered the Politburo in 1946, and the Minister of State Security, V. S. Abakumov, was his protégé. Other old Stalinists had slipped in rank; Molotov lost the Foreign Ministry in 1949 to the old chief prosecutor Vishinsky, and Mikoyan lost the Ministry of Trade. Stalin brought Khrushchev back from the Ukraine to the Secretariat in Moscow as a counterweight to Malenkov and Beria in December 1949. Khrushchev thus also became a member of the two top bodies, as well as chief of the Moscow regional party organization.

Freshly planted in the capital, Khrushchev perhaps intended to secure the leading lieutenancy by proposing a major reorganization of the countryside, which still held more than half the Soviet population. First he wanted to amalgamate and thus enlarge the kolkhozes. This plan was adopted, and within ten months the number of kolkhozes was halved, from 250,000 to 125,000. More radically, Khrushchev wanted to complete the socialization of the peasants by gathering them into agricultural towns, "agrogorods." The peasants would live in apartments, have only tiny garden plots or none, and go to work in the fields by bus. They would thereby gain greater benefits from Soviet culture, have less opportunity to avoid working on the collective fields, and become more subject to propaganda and pressure. Khrushchev got together a model agrogorod as a "gift" for Stalin's seventieth birthday. Beria and then Malenkov opposed the idea, however; oddly, Malenkov criticized it not as too leftist-radical, but as too consumer-oriented, presumably implying that it would have cost too much money—although Khrushchev wanted the peasants to provide the labor and materials for their relocation. The scheme was dropped; Khrushchev was not castigated, but whatever he had hoped to gain from it was lost.

THE FINALE

In his last months Stalin was evidently decrepit. Still the great symbol of Soviet power, the teacher and inspirer of the people, Stalin suffered fade-outs and memory losses[95] and was apparently unable to keep atop his servants—incapable of directing everything but unwilling to delegate authority. He no longer even moved people around frequently, but lived in complete isolation, with eccentric habits.[96] Beria's adherent, Abakumov, was removed from the Ministry of State

Security, however, and replaced in February 1952 by S. D. Ignatiev, an adherent of Malenkov's. This switch may have been contrary to Stalin's desires.[97] Politics were confused; it was often unclear who was in or out of favor, and those below the summit could only seek safety by attaching themselves to a major figure of the inner circle.

Apparently Stalin's direction was weakening, since the Soviet Union edged away from his policies. After 1950 controls in literature were eased or were less effective, as somewhat more varied views were ventured.[98] The Stalinist "two camps" doctrine was qualified by occasional talk of peaceful coexistence and respect for neutrals. Foreign trade was opening up slightly, and economic controls were relaxed to give managers a shade more autonomy.

A more significant omen of change was the first meeting, in August 1952, of the Central Committee in over five years. This body convoked the Nineteenth Congress for October 1952, possibly against Stalin's wishes. Although the party rules as amended in 1939 called for a congress at least every three years and a party conference yearly, no congress had been held since 1939 and no conference since 1941—indeed, there has never been another. At the inauguration of the Cominform in 1947, Malenkov mentioned preparations for a new congress, but no more was heard of it for five years.

Shortly before the congress, Stalin published his last work, *Economic Problems of Socialism*. A rather confused tract indicative of mental decline, this little book answered queries by Soviet economists by reasserting basic ideas of strict control, especially of agriculture. Its most striking idea was that the collective farms should exchange their products directly with the factories that were producing goods they needed. Stalin was sufficiently pleased with his theorizing to order the arrest of a man who had had the temerity to publish similar ideas earlier.[99] The work was endlessly celebrated in the Soviet media and made the text for discussions at the congress.

Malenkov's priority was indicated at the Nineteenth Congress by the fact that he delivered the general report of the Central Committee. Khrushchev had the second honor, that of presenting the report on party statutes. Saburov spoke of the Five Year Plan, and the directives for 1951–55 were announced nearly two years late. Beria talked of nationality policy, and a little-known regional secretary, Leonid Brezhnev, said a few words on behalf of the Moldavian republic. Stalin himself took the floor for only six or seven minutes.

The tone of the congress was hard; calls were made for vigilance and discipline, and speakers stressed the perennial priority for heavy industry. The congress also underlined its distance from Lenin by shortening the title of the party from "All-Union Communist Party (Bolshevik)" to simply "Communist Party of the Soviet Union." The description of the party as the "vanguard of the working class" was broadened to include the "toiling peasants and working intelligentsia" as equals.[100]

The organizational changes announced by Khrushchev were more striking, and they began a period of fluidity that ended only with Khrushchev's overthrow. The inactive Orgburo was dropped. The Central Committee was nearly doubled in size, from 77 to 126 full members; nearly half of them were territorial prefects, who have ever since constituted the dominant sector of the committee. The Secretariat was enlarged from four members (Stalin, Malenkov, Khrushchev, and Suslov) to ten, and Malenkov was made Stalin's official deputy. Most striking, the Politburo was renamed the Presidium and enlarged from twelve full members and one candidate to twenty-five full and eleven candidate members. All ten Secretaries were included in the new Presidium. The new body could hardly have been intended to be very important, because it took in some secondary figures. It was also too large to function easily as a policy deciding cabinet, and it may never have met as a body. But it seems to have been intended to weaken the position of the old hands, whom Stalin had come to distrust, by bringing new and less prestigious men alongside them. Stalin kept, it seems, an inner section of the Presidium, with additional persons who could be added as he saw fit.

Whether or not Stalin had desired to convene the congress, he probably used it to pack both the Central Committee and the Politburo-Presidium with new men who would feel even more dependent on him than those who had been many years by his side, particularly Molotov, Voroshilov, Kaganovich, and Mikoyan. There is no doubt that Stalin was scheming toward a renewal of the glory of the purges. Possibly, like Mao at the time of the Cultural Revolution, he felt frustrated by those who were supposed to be his servants. He had become decidedly paranoid; according to Khrushchev, Stalin would terrorize a person by saying, ''Why don't you look me in the eye today? Why are you averting your eyes from mine?'' Bulganin allegedly said, ''You come to Stalin's table as a friend, but you never know if you will go home by yourself or if you'll be given a ride—to prison!''[101] In his last months Stalin called Molotov, Voroshilov, and Mikoyan foreign spies, and Voroshilov (again according to Khrushchev's Secret Speech) was excluded from Politburo meetings. Stalin said the same of such leading Soviet literary figures as Alexis Tolstoy and Ilya Ehrenburg; yet they were all left in place.[102] The slavish Poskrebyshev spent these months excluded from the Kremlin, awaiting arrest, and Beria and Mikoyan were out of favor. Stalin's anti-Semitism came to the fore. Kaganovich was under a shadow, and Molotov's Jewish wife was twice arrested and sent to concentration camp, as was Poskrebyshev's. Jewish wives probably brought disfavor on Andreev and Voroshilov. Khrushchev, it may be noted, was clearly not marked for destruction.

There had been purges in Eastern Europe; Titoists and alleged American and Zionist agents had been struck in 1949−51 in several countries, especially Hungary and Czechoslovakia. However, Stalin apparently did not feel free to repress the old Politburo as he had the Leningraders three years earlier without fuss or scandal, or perhaps he simply preferred to do things in the grand style, orchestrating accusations, press campaigns, and presumably trials.

The campaign began very soon after the congress, when the press exposed many cases of alleged "wrecking" in the economy. In December a group of leading Jewish intellectuals was shot. Economists came under attack for allegedly holding the views of the unfortunate Voznesensky. Early in January the press was attacking Zionists and warning lest Soviet successes lead to complacency about spies and enemies within the gates.

The sensational opener came on January 13, 1953, when *Pravda* announced the discovery that nine Kremlin doctors, five or six of whom were Jewish, had consummated numerous medical murders (including those of Zhdanov and Shcherbakov) and were plotting, in league with a foreign Jewish organization and the United States intelligence service, the murders of various marshals and generals. They had been arrested earlier, probably in November, on the denunciation of a Dr. Lydia Timashuk, who was perhaps only a provocateur under the direction of the Minister of State Security, Ignatiev.

A press campaign followed that was reminiscent of those of the 1930s, although less intense, with quotations from the Stalin of that day. There were attacks on security forces, party and Komsomol organizations, and economic ministries for slackness and lack of vigilance, on "cosmopolitanism" and Zionism, and on intellectuals for their foreign ideas.[103] The tone differed from that of the 1930s mostly in the anti-Semitic cast; in many cases Jewish names were given and descriptions included supposedly Jewish traits. This reflected not only Stalin's prejudice, but also a continuing tradition; there was little sympathy for Jews even during the world war; moreover, the support of American Jews for Soviet coreligionists made it possible to link Zionism with "bourgeois nationalism" and "American imperialism."

The campaign was not entirely verbal. Two of the arrested Jewish doctors died as a result of tortures. And the second most prominent Jew in the hierarchy, L. Mekhlis, head of the Military Political Directorate, died under suspicious circumstances. But there was a strange lack of action. The revelations of January 13 called for a spectacular trial of the guilty monsters, and accusing fingers pointed to numerous culprits, but they, like various persons Stalin called spies, were not arrested. The denouncer of the doctors, Dr. Timashuk, was given a medal, but only one fairly prominent Soviet leader joined the outcry—Suslov, a fairly junior Secretary and member of the enlarged Politburo-Presidium. Even more remarkably, the campaign came suddenly to silence on February 23.

Stalin was last seen by outsiders, foreign diplomats, on February 7 and 17, when he appeared to be normally healthy. On the morning of March 4, Radio Moscow told the world that Comrade Stalin had suffered a paralyzing stroke (the same illness that had taken Lenin) during the night of March 1–2. There were a number of odd circumstances about the announcement; one was the fact that it had been delayed without explanation for sixty hours. Another was that it falsely stated that he was stricken in Moscow, although he was really at his dacha at Kuntsevo. Doctors had been brought in, but he had simply been left lying there. To judge from the accounts of Khrushchev and his daughter Svetlana,[104] people just stood around watching him die without thinking of taking him to a hospital. He was obviously suffering from a lack of oxygen, but manual artificial respiration was attempted instead of placing him in an oxygen tent. He was bled with leeches to relieve high blood pressure.[105] He died on March 5.

Svetlana Alliluyeva was convinced that her father's death had been natural, but she had not been living with him and was in no position to know. It came very conveniently for many powerful persons at a time when Stalin did not have very effective control of events around him. Killings presented as natural deaths must have been accepted as common practice in police circles; many accusations of medical murder were made, in the purge years as in the Doctors' Plot. By 1953 the top men in the party were more anxious for security and less prepared to accept the need for purge than in the more vibrant days of the 1930s. Molotov, Malenkov, Kaganovich, Beria, and others of their generation had all been through it and knew well what might be involved for themselves.

A possible agent of Stalin's demise was Beria. The preceding November he had been demoted from the third to the sixth place in the hierarchy, and his career, if not his life, was clearly in danger during Stalin's last days. No one has suggested that Beria would hesitate to annihilate anyone, and he was unable to conceal his satisfaction at Stalin's death.[106] Beria still had strong connections with the top ranks of the secret police, although he had lost formal authority with the dismissal of Abakumov a year before, and the police managed Stalin's household and had him at their mercy. It is difficult to account for the lapse in the purge campaign late in February unless there were some expectation that Stalin would not be able to carry it through. The speed and effectiveness with which Beria quite illegally took charge of the police and of security in Moscow on Stalin's death also seem to imply previous preparation. Moreover, the full-scale reorganizations of the top levels of the party and state announced by the press on the morning following Stalin's departure must have been prearranged.

Chapter 6

The Khrushchev Era

THE NEW RULERS

Stalin's death was accompanied by an unacknowledged coup d'etat. Beria, who had been out of power for two years, assumed charge of the consolidated Ministry of Interior and Ministry of State Security, by procedures that remain mysterious but must have been prepared well in advance. He became commander of a force of about half a million, and took physical control of Moscow and the Kremlin even before Stalin expired. The day after Stalin died he scattered Stalin's staff and private secretariat.[1] Minister of Health Tretiakov, who had been in charge of Stalin's treatment, disappeared without a trace, as did the military commanders of the Moscow district, the city of Moscow, and the Kremlin.[2] About a hundred persons were jailed or shot.[3]

Even more remarkable was the fact that a full reorganization of the top levels of government and party was published on March 6, the day after Stalin died. This shake-up included thirty-four appointments, all of which were new except for some carry-overs in the Presidium and the Secretariat. The appointments were announced in the form of a joint decree of all the authoritative bodies of the Soviet system, the Presidium of the Supreme Soviet, the Council of Ministers, and the Central Committee (the same bodies that had been called upon to lend authority to the State Defense Committee that was established in 1941), but they could not possibly have met to discuss anything.

The most important change was the establishment of a new small Presidium of the Central Committee, which in effect reversed the expansion of the previous October and restored the old Politburo. The demotions of Molotov, Mikoyan, Beria, and Kaganovich were thus undone. Two men who had been brought into

Stalin's enlarged Presidium (Saburov and Pervukhin, both associates of Molotov) were retained in the new one. Khrushchev was given the fifth place in the listing of March 6, after Malenkov, Beria, Molotov, and Voroshilov, but he suffered an apparent setback, losing command of the Moscow regional party. His auxiliary, Leonid Brezhnev, was demoted from Secretary to chief of the political department of the navy. Marshal Zhukov, whom Stalin had semiretired and made almost a nonperson, became Deputy Minister of Defense under Minister Bulganin.

The proclamation of Stalin's death indicated no profound sorrow, although it paid tribute to his greatness. It indicated a considerable degree of nervousness by speaking of "the struggle against the inner and outer foes" and warning against "disorder and panic." Khrushchev afterwards stated that he was very worried about how they would carry on in the absence of the leader they had served through their entire careers.[4] "We were scared—really scared. We were afraid the thaw might unleash a flood which we wouldn't be able to control and which might drown us."[5] According to Stalin's daughter, Malenkov, Kaganovich, Bulganin, Voroshilov, and Khrushchev all shed tears.[6] Yevtushenko saw the people mourning, not so much from love of Stalin as from fear of what might happen with the guiding hand removed, and from anxiety at the loss of someone to think for them.[7]

Stalin lay in state for only three days, four less than Lenin, but the crush of people pressing around to pay their respects was such that hundreds, possibly thousands were compressed or trampled to death.[8] Eight longtime aides of Stalin had the honor of being pallbearers: Malenkov, Beria, Molotov, Voroshilov, Kaganovich, Mikoyan, Khrushchev, and Bulganin. Of these, only Mikoyan was to see honorable retirement (in 1965). Khrushchev was in charge of the arrangements; Malenkov, Beria, and Molotov delivered orations. Only Molotov spoke with personal feeling, and was observed to weep a bit; he alone spoke in the spirit of Stalinism, for struggle and vigilance.

Beria undoubtedly felt unable to try to seize power for himself, and Malenkov emerged as Stalin's clear successor. Most Russians thought Molotov should be the heir, because of his long and faithful association—at one time he had chaired Stalin's Politburo—but he took third place. Malenkov, who was twelve years younger, held a stronger position, having been more or less in charge of personnel since 1934. For a few days he was built up in the press as the supreme leader. On March 10 a fake picture was published of Malenkov next to Mao and Stalin; to put them together it was necessary to snip out Molotov, Voroshilov, Beria, and others.[9] Possibly those who had been so cavalierly treated did not appreciate the implication that Malenkov could excise them. On March 14 it was announced that Malenkov was relieved of his position in the Secretariat at his request to concentrate on his work as Chairman of the Council of Ministers.

Nikita S. Khrushchev   (*World Wide Photo*)

It is not known whether Malenkov, whose entire career had been in the party apparatus, really chose the governmental position when it appeared that he could not be top man in both. It may be that he was influenced by the precedent of Lenin, who was preeminent as Chairman of the Council of Commissars but was only a Politburo member in the party. Late in his life Stalin also seemed to have emphasized his position as Chairman of the Council of Ministers, using this title ahead of his title as Secretary. In the announcement of the new rulers who were to govern after Stalin's death, the priority of place went to the governmental, rather than the party, nominations. Possibly Malenkov calculated that in the post-Stalin era the official state would continue to rise in importance and gain supremacy over the party, in the manner of traditional states. If the Soviet system were to be liberalized, he could better speak for the whole Soviet people as head of the government. However the choice may have been made, Malenkov's departure left Khrushchev the senior individual in the Secretariat, followed by Suslov, Pospelov, and Shatalin—the last of these a representative of Malenkov's. However, practically a duumvirate of Malenkov and Beria emerged, while *Pravda* editorialized[10] that "collectivity is the highest principle of party leadership."

If that collectivity was real, it meant a very different spirit of government. Immediately upon Stalin's death there was talk of a grander mausoleum than Lenin's for the genius-leader, but this was soon forgotten. Not a single Soviet leader published a commemorative article or tribute beyond the funeral speeches, although a few foreign Communist leaders thought it incumbent to do so. In three weeks there was a partial amnesty of nonpolitical prisoners; to release political prisoners was apparently thought to be still too dangerous. Within days of Stalin's death, Malenkov was speaking of the needs of the consumers, and a broad price reduction was decreed on April 1. On April 4 it was announced that investigation had shown the Doctors' Plot to have been a falsification by Mikhail Riumin, who had been named Deputy Minister of State Security in 1952, presumably to manage the proposed purge. The doctors involved were rehabilitated. Anti-Yugoslav propaganda ceased. Beria began a purge of Stalinist purgers in his native Georgia, even while proclaiming his faith in Stalin. Everyone seemed to want some relaxation of the suffocating Stalinist system, although those who were on top had no desire for fundamental change.

It was unlikely, however, that the immediate heirs of a Stalin could readily settle down to harmonious joint enjoyment of the legacy. It is not easy to believe that Beria's colleagues were very happy to see him in charge of the united police ministries. They might have had reason to be nervous, since the police were a major political force in the aftermath of Stalin, with omnipresent informers, a virtual army with military equipment, control of the Kremlin guard, and a network in the armed forces. Before World War II Beria himself had been a power in the party as Molotov and Kaganovich had never been. After Stalin's death the Presidium members found themselves under the surveillance of Beria's agents.[11]

Moreover, in the wake of Stalin's disappearance, Beria appeared to be building up his backing and popularity, advocating measures the others may have recognized as necessary but dangerous to them, especially if they were carried out under Beria's leadership. He promised that "socialist legality" would be observed in the future and proposed that leading positions in minority republics should be given to natives of those republics—an effort, as *Pravda* later put it, "to sow enmity and discord among the peoples of the Soviet Union." He also seems to have advocated relaxation of the collective farm system.

The fact that Beria had shown himself so capable of taking charge of the situation at the time of Stalin's death may have been reason enough to get rid of him. There was certainly no reason to trust the new humanitarianism of the veteran executioner, whose amusements included taking teenage girls off the streets and drugging and raping them. He was not given time to consolidate his base; the riots of June 16 in East Germany, which occurred under Beria's responsibility, may have provided the impetus to move against him. On June 27 the Presidium went to watch the ballet at the Bolshoi Theater; Beria and his aide, Presidium candidate member Bagirov, were missing.

Beria's arrest, which probably occurred on June 26, was not reported until July 10. Several versions of his liquidation have circulated, but it seems clear that the Presidium conspirators had to call on the assistance of high military men. By one of Khrushchev's accounts, the Presidium questioned Beria, decided that there was insufficient evidence to try him but that he was too dangerous to release, and shot him on the spot.[12] Other stories indicate that he was executed months later, in December.

A book of charges was hurled at Beria after his fall, in the style of the classic purge trials. He was accused of illegal repressions, bourgeois nationalism, working for the restoration of capitalism, causing discord among Soviet nations, and even of having been a British spy—a charge that went back to obscure dealings in the Caucasus in 1919.[13] He later became a convenient villain for Khrushchev, who cast blame on him for a host of wrongs, ranging from Stalin's last planned purge (in which Beria was transformed by Khrushchev from prospective victim to chief planner) to the quarrel with Tito's Yugoslavia.

About six accomplices were executed at the same time as Beria, plus approximately eighteen Stalinist police officials during the next three years. Bagirov and a few others were killed in April 1956 under the notorious Kirov decree. Since Stalin's time, however, the only political executions that have been reported have been of police officials, and none of these are known since 1956. Moreover, after Beria, the political police was again separated from the Ministry of Interior to become the Committee of State Security (KGB); at least during the

Khrushchev years, it lost most of its political standing under chiefs who carried no major political weight.

KHRUSHCHEV, THE CHALLENGER

With his most dangerous contender dispatched, Khrushchev, who was the senior Secretary and the only member of the Secretariat who was also on the Presidium, could well take as his model Stalin's rise to General Secretary. Malenkov was busy with administration, and other celebrated Presidium members, particularly Molotov, Kaganovich, and Voroshilov, had less ambition and no real power base. Khrushchev had only to assert the priority of the party and make himself its spokesman to emerge on top.

No one was better qualified for the leadership. Nikita Sergeievich Khrushchev had pushed his way to the top by hard work, loyalty, and political ability; his career was entirely typical of the rise of the tough apparatchik in the service of Stalin.

Khrushchev was born in a small town (Kalinovka) in the eastern Ukraine on April 17, 1894; he was twenty-four years younger than Lenin and fifteen years younger than Stalin.[14] Unlike them, he had only a few years of elementary education, used his ancestral name, played no part in the prerevolutionary struggle, engaged in no agitations as a young man, and took no interest in Marxist theory. Also unlike them, he engaged in manual labor as a youth. He was a cowherd as a boy (he claimed) and later worked in a mine as a mechanic for foreign capitalists. His political education may have begun when he was fired for minor activity in a strike.[15] He must have had some leadership qualities, for in 1917, before the Bolshevik revolution, he was a member of the local soviet and then of the military revolutionary committee, a local organization that was not necessarily Bolshevik but corresponded to the Military Revolutionary Committee that Trotsky headed. After the Bolsheviks took power, Khrushchev became involved in the fighting and, probably in the summer of 1918, he joined Lenin's party. He went into the Red Army and served as a political commissar in what the Bolsheviks viewed as a contest against world capitalism.

In 1920 Khrushchev returned to his home ground in the Don Basin, where his first wife died, perhaps of disease, in the famine. In 1922, at the age of twenty-eight, he stepped onto the political ladder by gaining admission to a "Rabfak" or "Workers' School," one of the crude institutions that had been set up to give rudimentary training to uneducated but willing proletarians. There he became a party secretary and learned something of Marxism-Leninism. After 1925 he was a full-time party man, and already his standing was good enough to make him a nonvoting delegate at the Fourteenth (1925) Congress under the sponsorship of Kaganovich. Apparently a complete Stalinist from the outset, he got into the fight against Stalin's rivals in the Ukraine. His first recorded speech, at a Ukrainian conference in 1926, was even harsher on the opposition than Stalin's line; at the 1927 Ukrainian party congress be again called for stricter discipline and central control.[16] In 1928 Kaganovich made him deputy chief of organizational work with the Ukrainian central committee.

The next big step was a move in 1929 from Kiev to Moscow, where he was nominated to attend the Industrial Academy, a training school for the new Soviet managers. He was much more activist than intellectual, however, and although he rose rapidly at the academy, it was less by mastery of his lessons than by politics. The academy was infested (as the Stalinists would have said) with Old Bolsheviks, especially Bukharinists, and Khrushchev leaped into the fight against them on Stalin's behalf. He was rewarded with the secretaryship of the party organization. He also came to Stalin's attention at this time because Alliluyeva, who was a fellow student at the academy, recommended him.

Khrushchev completed only one year of the academy's three-year course and went rapidly upward. It took only ten years from his arrival in Moscow for him to become full member of the Politburo, as a result of his toughness, loyalty, and industry. He was aided by the sponsorship of Kaganovich, one of the hardest of all Stalinists, who also promoted his future rivals Malenkov and Bulganin. Khrushchev became secretary of the Bauman district party in Moscow in January 1931; six months later he moved up to the Red Presnaya district secretaryship, and in another six months he was made second secretary (under Kaganovich) for all of Moscow. This was a time of much movement and increasing mortality; of nine Moscow district secretaries who were appointed in 1931, Khrushchev was the only one who was still politically alive in 1940.

In 1934 Khrushchev became a member of the Central Committee that was formed at the Seventeenth Congress, the same committee which caused Stalin some concern and most of whose members were subsequently killed. Khrushchev had already proved himself a capable organizer on the basis of Stalinist principles, and in 1934 he gained national prominence as the supervisor of the construction of the celebrated Moscow subway. He excelled both as an active overseer, looking into details and dealing personally with the workers, and as an implacable driver, pushing everyone as hard as himself.

Khrushchev had some part in the purges. In December 1934 he was a member of the Kirov funeral commission, and in this capacity he must have learned something of the strange deaths of people who knew too much. In 1935, when Stalin was promoting only his most reliable followers, Khrushchev became the first secretary of the Moscow regional party. Around this time Khrushchev regularly shared Stalin's family dinners.[17] In return, he was one of Stalin's most forceful followers, calling for vigilance and the unmasking of traitors who were pretending to be loyal citizens; no one was more violent in vituperation against "Trotskyite scum" and other "enemies of the people."

In January 1938 Khrushchev took another leap forward, becoming first secretary of the second most important Soviet subdivision, the Ukraine, and correspondingly a candidate member of the Politburo. He was sent to Kiev to combat nationalism and to purge non-Stalinists. Khrushchev took with him a new team, made up almost entirely of non-Ukrainians, and had a new Central Committee of the Ukrainian party elected to replace the one that had innocently accepted Stalin's invitation to visit him in Moscow. He proceeded to a thorough purge of nearly everyone in responsible positions. In the process, he seems to have earned the title sometimes given him, "Butcher of the Ukraine," and by his own account he was aware of the injustices being perpetrated.[18] He appears to have been fairly close to Beria at this time. However, he was apparently a capable territorial boss, accessible, jovial, and popular—unlike Stalin he was able to be one of the boys. He mixed more than most Soviet leaders, getting out and meeting people of all kinds, learning about their problems, building support, and giving suggestions—he loved to tell peasants how to plant tomatoes. Although his first task was that of purging, he seems to have helped to build up agriculture in the Ukraine.[19]

The war brought new tasks. First, Khrushchev had the assignment of supervising the Sovietization of the Ukrainian-populated territories that had been acquired from Poland. Then invasion swept across the southern part of the Soviet Union, and Khrushchev became an important military-political deputy of Stalin, a lieutenant general and, in due course, the recipient of many medals. One of the few top leaders never included in the State Defense Committee, he spent the war at or near the front. According to his account (in his Secret Speech), he came into some conflict with Stalin and he may have begun to doubt the leader at this time. In any case, it seems probable that the realities of the war substantially changed his character and turned him away from the falsifications that had been an integral part of his career.

It is at least certain that many years away from the imperial presence of Stalin enabled Khrushchev to develop his own character in a way that Stalin's acolytes in the Kremlin could not. He was kept in the Ukraine until 1949 to manage reconstruction, especially of agriculture and the collective farms, but his existence was hardly easy and secure. In 1946 he had to engage in implied self-criticism for insufficient attention to ideology, that is, excessive concern with practical affairs.[20] He came under a cloud in 1947, possibly because of suspicions that he was in sympathy with Ukrainian nationalism, and he was displaced from his position as first secretary of the Ukrainian party by Kaganovich. But he came back rapidly, perhaps thanks to the good reports of his old patron. His open, folksy style was very different from that of Stalin at this time, and whereas Stalin neglected the party apparatus at the top, Khrushchev kept it active in his territory. He enjoyed a local personality cult; verses were composed in his honor, and his busts accompanied those of Stalin across the Ukraine.

In December 1949 Khrushchev was summoned to Moscow to balance Malenkov. There had already been friction between the two men, and in 1950 they again came into conflict, most visibly over Khrushchev's agrogorod proposal. As a result of this dud, Khrushchev gave up his agricultural responsibilities to Malenkov and concentrated on party organizational work, a shift that was perhaps ultimately very helpful to Khrushchev and harmful to Malenkov. Despite his rivalry with Malenkov, Khrushchev was in a strong position when Stalin died. His career had been almost entirely in the territorial organization, which was coming to dominate the Central Committee. He was the only member of the ruling group to be entirely identified with the party; he never held a governmental position until he became Chairman of the Council of Ministers in 1958. If the party was to dominate the Soviet state, Khrushchev was better placed than anyone else to make himself the new leader.

THE FIRST SECRETARY VERSUS THE PRIME MINISTER

The thaw that set in immediately after Stalin's demise continued through 1953 and into 1954. There was little praise of Stalin and some indirect criticism. In July 1953 *Kommunist*, the party journal, strongly attacked the "cult of personality" long before Khrushchev popularized the phrase. The press downgraded the leadership role and stressed party committees and bureaus rather than individual bosses. Stalin's birthday was ignored in 1953. The "special tribunals" of the Ministry of the Interior, which had been a key part of the terror system, were abolished in September. In March 1954 the scope of the KGB was supposedly restricted under its new director, Ivan Serov, a Khrushchev man, and it became outwardly bound to "socialist legality." In December 1954 came the first important rehabilitations, those of Voznesensky and his fellow Leningraders. In foreign affairs the Soviet Union moved farther away from Stalin's rigid stance. Demands on Turkey were renounced. In January-February 1954 the Foreign Ministers of the Big Four powers met (in Berlin) for the first time in five years. A "New Course" of liberalization was inaugurated in Eastern Europe, and several Stalinist bosses were set aside. Malenkov adopted the position that nuclear war could mean the end of civilization and must be avoided at all costs, and military expenditures were slightly reduced.

Among the educated, there was strong pressure for more freedom. Censorship slackened, whether by the design of the supreme authorities or not. Ilya Ehrenburg published a novel that gave its name, *The Thaw,* to the liberalizing tendency, and there was a rash of critical writing in journals. Artists sensed an air of creative freedom, and scientists wanted to cast off the Stalinist shackles.[21] There was some reactionary counterattack, and party spokesmen tried to reassert socialist realism and the duty of the artist to the party. In the latter part of 1953, however, some works of the 1920s that had been banned by Stalin were reissued, and several critical novels were published. In December 1954 a writers' congress was assembled, the first in twenty years; it accepted the obligation of the writer to educate the people to Communist morality but implied that he had considerable freedom in choosing ways of doing this.

Much more important for most people, the government headed by Malenkov called forthrightly for a better deal for consumers. From August 1953 to the summer of 1954 the slogan was much in evidence, "to achieve in two or three years a sudden increase in the production of supplies for the population."[22] In reality, the Malenkov program was very modest, promising only that the production of consumer goods should grow at the same rate as that of producer goods, and it would have had a trivial negative effect on heavy industry. By the budget proposed for 1955, investment in the production of consumer goods would be only 8.8 percent, compared with 7.3 percent under Stalin.[23] Nevertheless, the heretical tendency, and the implication that the party was basing its legitimacy on the satisfaction of material wants rather than on its historic mission, sufficed to alarm party stalwarts.

Another aspect of the loosening of the Soviet system was the shift of authority from the party to the state—a development on which Malenkov seems to have counted and which he, an old party pro, forwarded. A few days after Stalin's departure, the ministries were strengthened by a reduction in their numbers from fifty-five to twenty-five, and the rights and importance of ministers were emphasized. Until the summer of 1954 the Council of Ministers was mentioned ahead of the Central Committee of the party, and the majority of the members of the Presidium came from the governmental apparatus. Malenkov was able to signal this improvement of the status of the administrators by bringing his deputies to the reviewing stand for the May Day parade in 1954.[24]

Feeble as they were, these tendencies pointed toward a more conventional, more pluralistic, and less party-ruled system, a prospect that was alarming to many well-placed persons. Khrushchev was able to make himself the spokesman of this discontented faction within the party.[25] He formed an alliance of sorts with Molotov, Kaganovich, and Voroshilov, all of whom had reasons to be displeased at the Malenkov innovations. Khrushchev built up his forces by placing his own followers in strategic positions: Serov as head of the KGB and A. I. Kirichenko as first secretary in the Ukraine (the first Ukrainian to head that province since its incorporation into the Soviet Union). Adrianov, a Malenkov follower, was replaced as Leningrad boss by Frol Kozlov, who was then a Khrushchevite. Another Khrushchev adherent, Mzhvanadze, took charge in Georgia. In other ways, too, Khrushchev strengthened the party. The authority of the Central Committee was improved by calling it into session regularly. The number of provincial and district secretaries was increased, although party membership grew very gradually. Khrushchev himself was recognized as party leader with the title of First Secretary (avoiding the "General Secretary" of invidious memory) on September 13, 1953; on this occasion *Pravda* gave his speech six pages.

Advancing himself not as an aspirant for power but as an advocate of the party view, Khrushchev nonetheless needed a program to counter Malenkov's policies and set himself up as a leader. He picked an obvious weakness, the miserable state of agriculture. Malenkov had rashly claimed in 1952 that the grain problem had been "solved definitely and finally."[26] In view of the obvious falsity of this declaration, Khrushchev could undercut Malenkov both by attacking numerous persons in the government who were responsible for agriculture and by proposing positive measures. These included lowering taxes on peasants' private plots, reducing compulsory deliveries to the state, raising prices for crops, and giving more party assistance to collective farms. He favored local party authorities by abolishing the political-affairs director attached to the Machine Tractor Stations and passing political controls to local secretaries. Khrushchev also began what was to become a passion, pushing the planting of corn as a more productive crop.

Khrushchev's big play, however, was the Virgin Lands program, which was designed to effect the plowing of an enormous amount of unused acreage, mostly in Kazakhstan, and thus definitely and finally to solve the perennial grain problem. The project was first publicized in March 1954 as a party decision, and soon swarms of people, including a host of enthusiastic volunteers, were undertaking the formidable assignment of settling the almost empty Virgin Lands, constructing huge grain farms where there was only waste and scrub. Khrushchev had to accept a Malenkov associate, Ponomarenko, as the nominal director of the program, but next to him was placed a longtime Khrushchev follower, Leonid Brezhnev. There were many hardships and troubles, and the project proved to be very costly, but it carried some of the heroic overtones and inspiration of the First Five Year Plan, and it was fairly successful for a few years. Thanks partly to the abilities of Brezhnev, and perhaps even more to good weather in the first years, crops were abundant, and the initiative added to Khrushchev's prestige.

Khrushchev had, however, a more direct weapon with which to join battle with Malenkov. The party bosses disliked anything that sounded like an orientation toward consumer goods not only on broad ideological grounds but also because it implied less planning and controls and more reaction to the market. The consumer society is not so fully governable as the militant spartan society. The military saw any turn toward light industry as a threat to its priorities; to the doctrinaires it constituted dangerous revisionism that threatened to undermine the whole role of the party as the guiding force in Soviet society.

The issue was a fake, since Malenkov never proposed to turn the rudder more than a degree or two, but it was the best rallying point for the conservatives who were frightened by the entire drift of Soviet society since Stalin's demise.

Beginning in the spring of 1954, Khrushchev played this theme. In November and December it surfaced in the form of a controversy (very subdued by Western standards) between *Pravda*, the party organ, which stressed heavy industry, and *Izvestia*, the government organ, which defended the attention to light industry. The party view won out; in January the advocates of consumer goods were put to flight by a heavy bombardment. Khrushchev called the consumer-goods approach "a belching up of the rightist deviation, a regurgitation of views hostile to Leninism, views which Rykov, Bukharin, and their like once preached."[27] A *Pravda* article by D. Shepilov stated, "If views of this kind were to become widespread, it would create great damage to the entire cause of communist construction. It would lead to complete disorientation of our cadres as to the basic question of the Party's economic orientation."[28]

The conservative, anti-Malenkov tide had been rising. After the summer of 1954 the consumer-goods slogan disappeared. Assertions of party responsibility for the economy, which were implicitly a slap at Malenkov, were stepped up in the fall. The Central Committee again took precedence in formal announcements. By November 1954 Khrushchev alone was able to sign a Central Committee decree (on atheistic propaganda, dated November 11). In the latter part of 1954, Stalin was again praised, and his birthday was marked in December; he was occasionally cited as having been in support of an emphasis on heavy industry. Another indication of the weakening of Malenkov was the fact that by the end of 1954 the number of ministries was back up to fifty-nine, more than before the post-Stalin reduction. In December 1954, police boss V. S. Abakumov, a former collaborator with Malenkov as well as Beria, was tried and executed for his part in the 1948 Leningrad purge from which Malenkov had profited.

Under Khrushchev's leadership, the party apparatus thus seemed to be turning away from Malenkov, the chief who had left it to lead the governmental bureaucracy. Army leaders also found Khrushchev more to their liking. Malenkov, who not only depreciated heavy industry but bore more obvious responsibility for the great purges (especially the massacre of officers in 1937), was tainted by his association with Yezhov and his close relationship with the despised Beria.

Malenkov seems to have been criticized at a Central Committee meeting on January 25–31, 1955. At a meeting of the Supreme Soviet, on February 8, he presented his resignation, but it was read not by himself but by the presiding officer. In it he admitted no ideological or political error, only lack of experience, especially in agriculture. (This was somewhat incongruous, because supposedly he had not been recently in charge of agriculture. However, Khrushchev had

attacked him on this flank, and he had held such responsibilities under Stalin.*)
No explanation of any kind was ever given in the Soviet press beyond
Malenkov's brief *mea culpa*.

Despite his sins, Malenkov was gently treated—presumably because he still
enjoyed much support. He remained in the party Presidium and in the Council of
Ministers as one of eight Deputy Chairmen and Minister of Power Stations.
Khrushchev was not able to shake up the Presidium. Although Shatalin,
Malenkov's representative in the Secretariat, was removed, apparently Khrushchev could not take the premiership himself; it was given to Nikolai Bulganin,
who had worked with Khrushchev in Moscow in the 1930s and had formerly
been a member of the State Defense Committee and Minister of Defense under
and after Stalin.

Malenkov may have believed that the popularity of his program assured his
survival, but he could not mobilize popular support against the party apparatus
without calling into question the entire Soviet system and the political order that
had raised him to the top. He apparently overestimated the capacity of the state,
in contrast to that of the party, to govern, perhaps because he had seen Stalin
governing largely independently of the party. If this was the case, then he
misjudged his own ability to manage as Stalin had managed. In some ways,
however, his defeat was the defeat of the newer generation—he was eight years
younger than Khrushchev—and it was mitigated by the fact that after his victory,
Khrushchev adopted the policies Malenkov had inaugurated.

DE-STALINIZATION: FIRST ROUND

Up to February 1955 Nikita Khrushchev's career is fairly understandable. He was
raised by Stalin from the formerly deprived and scorned classes, a man of
non-Western background, a power-hungry activist who presumably believed the
slogans of Marxism-Leninism-Stalinism but acted pragmatically within the
framework of the harsh Stalinist politics. Like Stalin, he drove for power, and his
method of attacking the "rightists" was comparable—Khrushchev himself made
the comparison—to Stalin's attack on Bukharin and his followers from the same
vantage point in the Secretariat.

But having risen as a product of the Stalinist machine and played on the
Stalinist priorities of heavy industry, vigilance, and party control, Khrushchev
reversed these priorities and promoted a degree of relaxation at home and abroad.
Worse, he turned savagely against the former demigod, shattered his idol, and

---

*Although according to Khrushchev, Stalin said that Malenkov knew nothing about agriculture.
Khrushchev, *Khrushchev Remembers*, p. 236.

thereby endangered not only the sacred value of the Soviet system, party supremacy, but his own position as well. To be sure, he was not consistent in this course; several times he turned around to praise Stalin, tighten controls on the arts, and so on. Yet on the whole, Khrushchev did much more than any other person to lead the Soviet Union away from Stalinism.

There have been as many attempts to clarify this policy as there are treatments of the period, but none is entirely convincing. One of the two basic contradictory interpretations is that Khrushchev was a liberal at heart who was checked by the dogmatists in the party and had to attack from political necessity.[29] The opposite view is that Khrushchev had basically a dictatorial temperament, as his previous career indicated, and that his concessions to liberalism were simply a political tactic that was necessitated by the mood of the country.[30] After all, Stalin was a moderate in 1925. It may well be said that Khrushchev was a bully, but also a revolutionary idealist, perceptive but ignorant, a humanitarian gangster.

Once he had his hands on the helm, Khrushchev steered in the same general direction as Malenkov—toward liberalization, the loosening and humanizing of the regime—a program the party accepted more cheerfully when it was carried out under party auspices. There was a new emphasis on collective leadership as the Leninist way. Khrushchev and Bulganin seemed to form a well-functioning tandem, with one leader primarily responsible for agriculture and the other for industry, although Khrushchev was plainly in the driver's seat—the press occasionally referred to him realistically but without legal basis as the "head" of the Presidium. It was a token of the more cheerful era that the annual Lenin celebration was shifted from the anniversary of his death, January 21, to his birthday, April 22. Lenin's Testament, with its damaging remarks on Stalin, was published in *Kommunist* in March 1955. The industrial bureaucracy was scolded for its rigidity, overcentralization, and ministerial autarky, presaging Khrushchev's decentralization scheme of 1957. Shackles on science, such as the banishment of relativity, were largely dropped. Literary standards were relaxed, and Dostoyevsky and other blacklisted authors reappeared. The book that had ruined Voznesensky was praised publicly. Restrictions on abortions were relaxed. In September, a large number of prisoners were amnestied from camps.

The new direction was most striking in foreign affairs; 1955 was truly the annus mirabilis of Soviet foreign policy. The first of the un-Stalinist moves was a step toward reconciliation with Tito. In May Khrushchev and Bulganin—the first Soviet rulers ever to travel outside territory controlled by themselves—descended on Belgrade with a high-level delegation excluding Foreign Minister Molotov. The purpose was to present excuses to Tito and urge him to forget the seven years of calumny and return to the Soviet side. In Stalin's day, Khrushchev had used violent language against Tito, calling him a "fascist" and a "chained dog of imperialism," as was expected of him, but in his apologetics he laid the blame on

Beria. He recognized the principle of noninterference and implicitly acknowledged the validity of variant roads to socialism, despite the obvious danger that countries such as Poland and Hungary might interpret this as license to go their own ways also. Khrushchev seems to have felt that a personal talk would set things right. But despite this display of humility by the Soviet leadership, Tito was not ready so quickly to forget and forgive; he declined for the time being to enter into party-party relations.

The Soviet leadership devoted much attention to the issue of relations with the errant Yugoslavs. The Presidium was unable to resolve the differences between Molotov, who saw the backdown as dangerous, and Khrushchev, who believed that flexibility would increase Soviet influence. The issue was passed over to the Central Committee in June, the first foreign-policy question that had been discussed there in fifteen years, and it was also taken up by several republican central committees.[31] Improved relations with Tito were important because of his influence in the Third World, which Khrushchev was beginning to court, and because Khrushchev hoped to reunite the Communist world by persuasion where Stalin had divided it by bluster and pressure.

Khrushchev had the necessary backing in the Central Committee, of course, and Molotov, the hard-liner, was defeated. By a whimsical twist, Molotov was penalized (although he was allowed to remain formally Foreign Minister for another year) by having publicly to admit an ideological error. Months earlier, in February, he had written that the Soviet Union had constructed the "bases of socialist society," whereas the official position had been that socialism had been built "in the main." Molotov's implication must have been that it was necessary to maintain controls; in any case, he publicly confessed his ideological backwardness in September.

Other remarkable modifications of Soviet foreign policy came in the following months. After a decade of stubborn haggling, the Soviet Union agreed (against Molotov's wishes) to a treaty with Austria and withdrawal from the Soviet-held zone of that country. The Porkalla naval base was also handed back to Finland in another of the rare occasions in which the Russian eagle has abandoned land it once held. The Soviet leaders got together with Western heads of state at Geneva, the first such summit meeting since Potsdam a decade earlier. Little that was concrete came of the "spirit of Geneva," but it seemed a potential retreat from the cold war. The Soviet Union began taking the United Nations more seriously. Disarmament talks became more businesslike, and the Soviets made various concessions, although mutual suspicions were too great for concrete results.

Khrushchev moved away from the Stalin-Zhdanov idea of a two-camp world, the Soviet Union and its sovietized allies against everyone else. Gandhi, Nasser, and other anticolonial leaders, who in Stalin's eyes had been stooges of imperialism, now became heroic fighters for independence or potential allies in the "zone of peace." Underlining the new Soviet interest in the nonaligned world, Khrushchev and Bulganin set out on an unprecedented tour of India, Burma, and Afghanistan. On this barnstorming trip they made some outrageous statements about the former colonial power, but showed a new, flexible, extroverted approach to world affairs. At about the same time, the Soviet Union embarked on a policy that was highly disturbing to the West but antithetical to Stalinist rigidity, namely, the diplomatic-military penetration of the Near East, beginning with the sale of arms to Egypt.

Setting aside Stalinist paranoia, Khrushchev slightly opened the border gates. Western science was welcomed as it had never been in the Stalinist era, and in September 1955 Soviet savants attended an international conference (of historians in Rome) for the first time in a generation. The Soviet Union also began to welcome foreign tourists (as distinct from delegations and semiofficial visitors) practically for the first time since the inception of the Soviet state, while a few Soviet tourists were permitted to go abroad. Foreign trade, which Stalin had wanted to abolish, increased sharply.

Khrushchev had an opportunity to put a seal of official approval on his policies and affirm his position of leadership when the Twentieth Congress of the party convened, six months ahead of the statutory time, in February 1956. He had by no means been as free in moving people about as Stalin had been in the 1920s, but in 1955 there had been many middle-level personnel changes. By 1956 about two-fifths of the senior provincial secretaries owed their positions to Khrushchev,[32] and over a third of the 1,355 voting delegates were new to the upper ranks since Stalin's death.[33] Over half the members of the 1952 Central Committee were still in office, but it had been enlarged, as at previous congresses, to make room for new appointees (increasing from 125 to 133 regular members and from 111 to 122 candidate members). The Khrushchev following was very strong because territorial secretaries comprised more than half the committee's membership.

It was much more difficult to change the oligarchy at the top. Stalin took four years to rid himself of Trotsky, and only in the time of the great purges did he acquire the power to remove colleagues at will. Khrushchev was never able fully to do so. By the beginning of 1956, no member of the post-Stalin self-appointed Presidium had been ejected, and only two had been added. Aleksei Kirichenko, the Ukrainian viceroy in the Ukraine, a strong Khrushchevite, had become a candidate member in 1953 and a full member in July 1955. He was balanced by a non-Khrushchevite, Mikhail Suslov, a onetime Zhdanov protégé and a favorite of Stalin's in his last years, a participant in the purges as well as an intellectual specialist in ideology, and eventually an éminence grise under Brezhnev. But at the Twentieth Congress Khrushchev was at least able to add a number of candidate members who were favorable to himself: Zhukov, Brezhnev, Mukhiti-dinov, Shepilov, and Furtseva. Brezhnev, who was freshly back from Kazakhstan, recovered the post in the Secretariat that he had lost at Stalin's death, and Furtseva also became a Secretary.

Khrushchev scored another victory in establishing a Russian Buro, although the significance of this move remains unweighable in the obscurity surrounding such party questions. It was logical to do so; all the Soviet national subdivisions, the "Soviet republics," except the biggest, the Russian republic, had their own party organizations. The purpose of setting up the new buro was probably essentially political, however. As its head, Khrushchev held a new and potentially potent position, through which he could have closer access to party organizations in half the country. Moreover, while it was difficult for Khrushchev to expel current officeholders, he could staff the new buro and the departments emanating from it with faithful followers.

Through these changes, Khrushchev showed himself to be the new leader without a peer. Suslov, at the congress, hailed the Central Committee as the repository of collective leadership and called it the decision-making body, but the congress was Khrushchev's show. He alone received ovations, as *Pravda* recorded, and he made the major reports and delivered the sensational pronouncements.

In this regard, Khrushchev made his mark. Since 1927, the party congresses had heard little of interest to anyone except the Kremlinologists, who appreciated political clues the more as they were concealed in a mass of repetitious bombast; and since Khrushchev, the congresses have reverted to exemplary aridity. Khrushchev wanted to stir things up, however, and he made the Twentieth Congress a landmark.

Oddly, there was no discussion of the big issue of the year before and of many subsequent years, the relative priority of consumer versus producer goods, of light versus heavy (and munitions) industry, except insofar as it was implied by promises of a shorter work week and higher pay. Instead, Khrushchev embarked on a major revision of Leninism and Stalinism. He observed that in the nuclear age, war between major powers must no longer be considered inevitable, as Lenin had insisted, but that it was to be avoided, and that the power of antiwar forces, the Soviet bloc plus the Third World "zone of peace," could prevent it. Stalin had begun to go in this direction, denying the inevitability of war between the Soviet Union and the capitalist powers, but insisting (in his last work, *Economic Problems of Socialism*) that the capitalist powers must come into conflict among themselves, as Lenin's theory of imperialism had indicated.

There were important deductions to be derived from this theory of the non-inevitability of war. Peaceful coexistence had to be the mode of interaction between the Soviet Union and other, especially Western, powers. There could be no peaceful coexistence in ideology, and the class struggle had to go on, as Khrushchev stated and reiterated; but it was proper and desirable to cultivate friendly and businesslike relations with capitalist countries for maximum benefits. The idea of peaceful coexistence went back to Lenin and Brest Litovsk, and Stalin had brought it forward in the Popular Front days of 1935–36. But for them it had been, at least in theory, only a temporary expedient; for Khrushchev it was to be the keynote of an indefinite epoch, and, despite his assiduous denials of ideological relaxation, it represented the consecration in doctrine of the more open attitudes shown in the previous year.

Peaceful coexistence had further implications. The inevitable ultimate victory of the Soviet system would come not through violence or a great war, as the Russian Revolution had come, but by a non-Leninist process of peaceful evolution. The Soviet Union would advance economically and culturally much more rapidly than the decadent capitalist states, with their inferior political-social order. In ways that were not spelled out in detail, the example and the might of the progressive Soviet Union would cause other states to join its "camp," until Lenin's world revolution would finally be consummated.

Furthermore, if war were not to be the midwife of revolution, socialism would come by peaceful process, parliamentary or otherwise; violent overthrow and civil war were no longer to be counted necessary (Marx had postulated this idea long ago for democratic countries, but it was contrary to the Stalinist dictum of the intensification of the class struggle). Khrushchev seemed to have become a gradualist, if not a reformer. Ironically, the examples he cited of peaceful transition to socialism were amazingly inappropriate, including the Baltic states, which had been Sovietized by the Red Army; Albania, Bulgaria, and Yugoslavia, in all of which Communist parties had triumphed thanks to the world war; and China, which had suffered not only a Japanese invasion but also twenty years of civil war.

This broad idea had still another implication, however. If Communist power was not to result from a Leninist revolution but from evolutionary circumstances in individual countries, the resulting socialism would necessarily be variable. There were different admissible roads to socialism and the "dictatorship of the proletariat" would have different aspects. This idea was not new; Lenin had used such terms in Switzerland in 1916.[34] Nevertheless, it was abhorrent to the spirit of Stalinism, which demanded conformity above all, and it was a rather dubious idea to introduce into the Soviet order; if socialism could be variably expressed outside the Soviet Union, it was hard to explain why there should not be much more latitude within it.

As a practical matter, this doctrine invited Yugoslavia, with its aberrant institutions, to rejoin the Soviet bloc. It also promised that the Soviet Union should be the leader more than the commander of its bloc, thereby easing relations. Another possibility opened up by the new policy was that Western Communist parties, especially the French and Italian ones, might gain power and lead their nations to the Soviet side. There was also the hope that Third World nations, observing the superiority of the Soviet way, would follow it without having to copy it closely.

Thus the great dream of the Khrushchev era was sketched—a dream of a new world order led by Lenin's party. For a few years it appeared to be fairly realistic; the Soviet Union was growing in power, production, and the application of science more rapidly than its competitors, and might hope to continue doing so indefinitely. Apparently it would surpass America to become a world leader in a historically short time, and the era of capitalism would be at an end, with the Soviets standing over its burial (as Khrushchev expressed it a little later). Khrushchev himself seems really to have believed this, at least for a few glorious years, and it was an essential part of his political psychology.

Khrushchev offered the congress a much more explosive bomb, however, a fierce attack on the departed deity of them all, including the triumphant First Secretary. There had already been some de facto de-Stalinization. After the neglect of Stalin in 1953, he had received more attention in 1954 and 1955, being cited occasionally in support of foreign and domestic policies. In September 1955 the notorious *Short Course* was reprinted by Khrushchev's order, and Stalin's birthday in December was hailed in the Soviet press. But many actions, from the debunking of the Doctors' Plot on, were in effect slaps at Stalin. None of them was as strongly anti-Stalinist as Khrushchev's attempt at reconciliation with Tito, whom Stalin had sworn to destroy. This overture made a mockery of the infallibility of the old dictator. On the way home, Khrushchev and Bulganin stopped in Bulgaria; there in a speech to the Central Committee and government leaders in June 1955, they anticipated many of the charges that were later to be made against Stalin.[35]

In his opening speech at the Twentieth Congress, Khrushchev gave Stalin only a slighting reference, linking Stalin's name with those of minor leaders deceased since the previous congress. But numerous other speakers criticized Stalin obliquely by references to the "cult of personality" and other deviations. Anastas Mikoyan, who appeared to be third in the hierarchy, made the first direct attack on Stalin's name to be published in the Soviet Union for thirty years, charging him with abuse of power, unrealistic economic views (in *Economic Problems of Socialism*), and distortion of party history (in the *Short Course*).

The stage was thus set when the delegates were called into a closed night session with no note taking permitted, at the end of the congress (February 24-25); there they heard Khrushchev's most important and most famous speech, the only one that has never been published in the Soviet Union.[36] The burden of the speech was a recital of Stalin's misdeeds; although these have become familiar to the world, they were much less well known then and were utterly shocking to the Soviet people. Khrushchev gave Stalin credit for his classic achievements of collectivization and industrialization, but stated that in 1934 Stalin had deviated from the principles of Leninism and gone about murdering good party people wholesale; he cited the familiar figures for the liquidation of the delegates to the Seventeenth (1934) Congress and its Central Committee. Khrushchev was not concerned because Stalin had murdered, however, but because he had turned on his own apparatus and murdered "honest Communists." Subsequently Khrushchev claimed in his memoirs[37] that he postponed the rehabilitation of Zinoviev, Bukharin, Rykov, and so on, because fraternal parties had been committed to denouncing them. He also told of tortures (to which alone he attributed confessions) and instances involving sadism. Special attention was paid to Stanislav Kossior, who had preceded Khrushchev in the Ukraine and in whose undoing Khrushchev may have had a hand. Toward the end, Khrushchev implied, the old Politburo had been in danger of annihilation. Much of the blame was shifted to Beria, but Stalin received credit for the fabrication of the Doctors' Plot. Another accusation, which was perhaps equally shocking for those who had been taught to revere the genius-leader, was that Stalin was a totally incompetent commander who had first refused to believe warnings of imminent German attack and had then turned a deaf ear to his generals and planned strategy from a globe. Stalin was also attacked for his arbitrary rule, which had ignored party organizations and violated party statutes. Moreover, he had treated Lenin, both alive and dead, with contempt. He had cut himself off from the people; after 1928, Khrushchev said, Stalin knew peasant life only from glorifying movies. Finally, with inordinate conceit, Stalin had built up a monstrous cult of his own personality, even adding touches of self-glorification with his own hand. In sum, as Khrushchev put it in retirement, "Unfortunately, Lenin's ideas were put into practice by a barbarian, Stalin."[38]

Not only outsiders but foreign Communist delegates were barred from this damnation of the recently revered leader. But afterwards it was reportedly read in abridged version at party meetings throughout the Soviet Union. Khrushchev wanted the East European parties to know about it,[39] and it was leaked to the West through an East European party, probably the Polish. Published by the U.S. State Department, it was tacitly acknowledged by Soviet authorities and confirmed by Khrushchev in his memoirs.[40] The speech immediately created a storm in Communist circles, which were asked so abruptly to revise their view of the leading figure in the movement for nearly thirty years—the greatest uproar in the less disciplined parties in the West and the least in the Soviet Union itself, a fact that testified to the effectiveness of Stalin's despotism. It was obviously damaging to the movement; assuming that Stalin was a criminal, the natural course for his heirs and former collaborators would seem to have been to disguise the fact and hope that time would bury his crimes. The question arose, why was it done?

The question has never received a real answer, although many partial answers have been suggested. One very partial answer is that Khrushchev and his aides may have naively believed that they could keep the speech secret, hence that it would have no very drastic effect on the nonparty population. Otherwise there would seem to be no reason to snub the foreign delegations by excluding them—an action that was certain to heighten their curiosity and was utterly futile when more than a thousand persons shared the secret. Yet Khrushchev himself said the matter was to be kept under wraps. "We cannot let this matter get out of the party, especially not to the press. . . . We should not wash our dirty linen before their eyes."[41]

But even if those who had been responsible for the speech were so ingenuous as to suppose that such a sensational matter could be concealed, it was bound to be shocking; it even seems intended to be so, particularly in the exaggerated denigration of Stalin as a war chief. It must have been calculated, because it was no last-minute improvisation. According to Khrushchev (in the speech), a party commission had been set up, apparently in 1955, to investigate Stalin's crimes. The speech could not have been put together in less than several weeks; it was long (about twenty thousand words) and abundantly documented, with quotes pulled from Marxist classics that were not familiar in Stalin's time and with many references to materials buried in party archives. Nonetheless, in December Stalin was still in high esteem, as the celebration of his birthday and the reissue of his book indicated. The February issue of *Voprosy Istorii*, on the other hand, which was printed well before Khrushchev's February 25 delivery, began the rehabilitation of the purge victims. The decision seems to have come around mid-January, although there may have been extensive last-minute changes. Moreover, the speech is not in the usual earthy, rambling Khrushchev style but is carefully contrived. Secretary Pospelov probably had at least a hand in drafting it.

The question whether Khrushchev acted voluntarily or under political pressure hangs over his denunciation of Stalin as over many of Khrushchev's policies. Its message is the danger of personal dictatorship, hardly a likely theme for a disciple of Stalin's who was apparently aiming toward supreme power. It may be that Khrushchev's fellows wanted to bring out the evils of Stalinism as a guarantee against a new purge; it is also possible that Khrushchev felt pressure from below for criticism of Stalin and decided that it was safer to take the lead than possibly become a target. If there was such pressure, it could not have come from many of the fellow oligarchs, who were more tarred by Stalinism than was Khrushchev. Khrushchev later (1961) blamed Molotov, Kaganovich, Malenkov, Voroshilov, and "others" for opposing de-Stalinization; in his memoirs he claimed that he had insisted, over their objections, on bringing the subject before the congress.[42]

It is likely that the Secret Speech was a slashing weapon in Khrushchev's battle to get rid of potentially dangerous rivals. Not only did Molotov, Malenkov, and Kaganovich suffer by implication because of their closer association with Stalin, Molotov and Kaganovich were also mentioned specifically as Stalin's helpers in the purge, and Malenkov was depicted as a dull desk-bound general.

Khrushchev may have thought that a dramatic assault on the foundations of their prestige was necessary to clip their wings, possibly to oust them—although they were not removed until they took the initiative for a showdown more than a year later. On the other hand, Mikoyan, a Khrushchev ally, and Khrushchev himself are credited in the speech with standing up to Stalin. Marshal Zhukov, who entered the Presidium as a candidate member at the Twentieth Congress, also came out well. The downgrading of Stalin's wartime role, as well as the rehabilitation of the officers slain in 1937, appealed to the military commanders who resented the accusations of treason and chafed under the exaltation of Stalin as the winner of all the battles and the theoretician with the answers to all questions of strategy. Khrushchev also attacked Stalin for faults that would most trouble leaders who were just below the top: repression of loyal servants, grotesque self-glorification, violation of party rules and procedures, and scorn for advice.

De-Stalinization was, withal, a dubious exercise for a person so vulnerable to quotations from old speeches praising the dictator. It may have been a bold effort to grasp the nettle when he saw the country was ripe and receptive. By doing so, Khrushchev set himself up as no mere follower, but as a leader in his own right; de-Stalinization became his historical claim to greatness.

It is difficult, however, to account for Khrushchev's great policy departure without considering idealism. He seems to have genuinely believed in the great message of Leninism, but the promises had been in large part defaulted; instead of freedom, the revolution had brought a grinding tyranny. The only obvious way to redeem the promise and the system, which should have been the hope of the world, was to attribute the failures to one deviant evil personality. Catharsis requiring grappling with and exposing the reality, to cleanse the system morally and prevent a recurrence, and to open the way for new approaches and new policies. The Soviet Union, Khrushchev declared in his memoirs, was morally subservient to Stalin until it was released in February 1956.[43]

Conscience may also have entered into Khrushchev's decision to undertake de-Stalinization.[44] That his share in the purges may have weighed upon him is suggested by the disproportionate attention in his speech to Ukrainian victims, especially Kossior. The speech was no confession or expiation, but delivering it could have served (in Khrushchev's mind) to separate himself from Stalin's crimes just as it associated others with them. Conceivably some ethical sense was behind Khrushchev's urge, if it existed, to use the previously misused power of the party to help people live better.

After the Twentieth Congress some effort was made to temper de-Stalinization. Although the speech was widely distributed in party circles and beyond, public pronouncements stressed the positive aspects of Stalin and the continuity of policies. Pervukhin, for example, promised a permanent priority for heavy industry.[45] Lenin was built up as a substitute authority and father figure.

The Georgians, seeing de-Stalinization as an attack on their own man who had ruled all the Russias and given Georgia a privileged position, resisted and rioted. For the most part, however, the country seemed to be on the way to a new dispensation, as symbols, portraits, statues, exhibitions, and so on, of Stalin began to disappear.

Relaxation was the leitmotif. Communists began reexamining theory and practice and asking whether there might not be freedom and democracy in socialism.[46] A number of persons had already been released from labor camps; the rehabilitation of persons living and dead now began in earnest, three years after Stalin's death, although it usually consisted only of favorable mention (the injustice itself was generally ignored), and it did not extend to Stalin's opponents before 1934. The security forces lost power, and the 1940 law prohibiting workers from changing jobs without permission was repealed. Economic controls were also slackened a bit, and there was some devolution of management to the republics.

In literary and intellectual circles, new hopes arose that creativity might be deshackled to enjoy at least relative freedom, as in the 1920s. More critical works appeared, such as Vladimir Dudintsev's *Not by Bread Alone*, and numerous writers ignored the demand that they serve the party. Historians were eager to reexamine the past; Suslov warned them against taking the liberality of the party for license to dig deep. There was a substantial relaxation of Soviet control of Eastern Europe, and the Cominform was dissolved (in April 1956). Kaganovich was removed from the Council of Ministers, and Molotov lost his position as Foreign Minister in time for a festive visit to Moscow in June by Marshal Tito, the incarnation of separate roads to socialism and anti-Stalinism. This month saw the zenith of liberalization for a long time; *Pravda* printed long articles critical of Stalin and much of Soviet society by the foreign Communists Palmiro Togliatti and Eugene Dennis. They asked the forbidden question—why the Soviet system, which was supposedly virtuously socialist, should have given rise to Stalinism.

THE DEFEAT OF THE OLD GUARD

The easy projection that the loosening of the Soviet system, which had been given impetus by the dethronement of Stalin, would continue until it was fundamentally changed, failed to take account of the strength of party rule and its resilience. When it became apparent that the weakening of controls threatened party supremacy, the forces of order, in the Communist sense, reacted. Specifically, de-Stalinization was checked because it led to serious dangers to Soviet rule of Eastern Europe, and an anti-Khrushchev sector of the oligarchy was encouraged to try to expel Khrushchev himself. It narrowly failed, but the promise of systemic change was gone.

The storm broke out in Eastern Europe, where Soviet and Communist rule was recent, dating only from 1944−45, and relatively weak, since it represented foreign domination of historically independent nations. Much more than in Russia, de-Stalinization in the East European countries called into question the legitimacy of party domination that had been imposed not by native revolution but by Stalinist force. This was especially true in Poland and Hungary, for which Russia was historically an antagonistic and unloved power.

Strikes and riots occurred in Poznan, Poland, beginning June 28, 1956. The Soviet leadership, by reflex, attributed the disorders to foreign subversion, but Polish leaders, shedding some of their Stalinist indoctrination and supported by Tito, refused to accept this obvious falsification; they simply blamed bad conditions and failed to punish the rioters. Ferment spread inside and outside the party, encouraged by the respect the Soviet Union had just shown to the independent Tito. In July *Pravda* was suggesting that Stalin's terrorism had been necessary, but the Poles were sensing a new freedom. Numerous victims of repressions were freed or rehabilitated.

In the middle of October the Polish Central Committee was convened to elect a new Politburo, which would return to power Wladyslaw Gomulka, who had been imprisoned for his independent views; it was also to exclude Soviet Marshal K. Rokossovsky, who had been foisted upon Poland, with the excuse of his Polish birth, as Minister of Defense. The Soviet leadership was alarmed, and when the Poles declined to go to Moscow, a large fraction of the Presidium (Khrushchev, Molotov, Kaganovich, Mikoyan, and others) hastened to Warsaw to recall the Poles to obedience. There was a tempestuous confrontation, and Soviet troops began marching toward the Polish capital, but the Poles stood their ground, threatened to fight, and had their way. At least, the Russians conceded them a good deal of autonomy in running their own country, while the Poles promised to remain within the bounds of the Communist system and adhere to Soviet foreign and defense policy.

Soviet authorities tried to block out news of this "Polish October," but it served to spark still more serious disturbances in Hungary, a far more anti-Russian and anti-Soviet nation than Poland. The country had been seething since June. Late in October the pot boiled over, liberals began to gain control of the press and radio, police went over to the demonstrators, and liberal Communist Imre Nagy formed a government that included nonparty men. By the end of the month, Hungary had undergone a thoroughly popular revolution to form a liberal regime that was backed by the workers' councils. The Hungarians went farther than the Poles and farther than the Soviets would tolerate, however. They proposed free elections and a multiparty system, and they sought to withdraw from the Soviet alliance. Moreover, unlike the Poles, they had no substantial military force, and the possibility of their receiving help from the West was minimized by the simultaneous occurrence of the Suez crisis. Hence it is not surprising that Khrushchev moved rapidly to crush their insurgency by force.

The killing of many thousand Hungarians because they wanted to be independent of the Soviet Union brought the standing of Communism in the West to its lowest level since 1941. Nevertheless, it ended the movement in Eastern Europe to loosen ties with the Soviet masters, just as forceful intervention in Czechoslovakia did a dozen years later. In the Soviet Union, alarm for the security of party rule led to a widespread clampdown. Khrushchev, perhaps helped by the effectiveness of his reaction—and by an excellent harvest—did not appear to be immediately threatened. But de-Stalinization was called to a halt. Stalin was presented again as a great fighter for the proletariat, whom the Soviet people should emulate in vigilance and dedication to the class struggle. As Khrushchev put it at a reception for Chinese Foreign Minister Chou En-lai on January 18, 1957: "For us Marxist-Leninists . . . Stalin is inseparable from Marxism-Leninism. That is why everyone among us . . . wishes to be faithful to the cause of Marxism-Leninism . . . as Stalin was faithful."[47]

The intellectuals who had ventured to question the need for the party monopoly were set straight. Whatever hopes there had been for freedom of literature after the shattering of the Stalin image vanished. The old controls were not restored in their full intensity, but writers were expected to serve the party and portray things as the party decreed they should be; only limited experimentation was allowed. This period saw the beginning of *Samizdat*, the circulation of uncensored, privately copied materials, and the divorce of a small sector of the educated elite from the party-state. Although intellectuals who had been given hopes saw them snatched away, they were not sufficiently cowed to accept controls with the old passivity.

In foreign policy Molotov again became prominent. Dmitry Shepilov, a Khrushchev protégé, was dismissed from his post as the Foreign Minister, but Molotov was not strong enough to take his place. Instead he became Minister of State Control. A younger professional diplomat, Andrei Gromyko, who had long been Deputy Foreign Minister, moved to the top. The effects of Khrushchev's wooing of Tito were lost. Tito both criticized and supported the Soviet intervention in Hungary, but it never again seemed likely that he would lead Yugoslavia back into the Soviet bloc. A by-product of the Soviet actions in Eastern Europe was growing Chinese skepticism of the value of the Soviet alliance. The Chinese had been faithful to Stalin, although he had treated them poorly, but they were estranged by de-Stalinization, the need for which they did not appreciate. Sino-Soviet relations gradually deteriorated (from early 1956 to the withdrawal by Khrushchev of Soviet experts in China in 1960) into covert polemics; they turned into bitter open polemics in 1964, and into a state that was close to war in 1969.

By early 1957, however, Khrushchev felt sufficiently recovered to resume a reform program and counterattack. In February the Caucasian peoples who had been deported by Stalin for alleged wartime treason were rehabilitated and permitted to return to their homelands. About the same time, a Central Committee meeting struck at Molotov, who was apparently the most determined of Khrushchev's opponents, by calling for the reorganization of his Ministry of State Control.

This Central Committee plenary meeting also set the course for Khrushchev's most ambitious reform, a basic reorganization and decentralization of the Soviet economy. The proposal was to dissolve nearly all the central economic ministries and turn the management of the economy over to one hundred-odd newly formed economic councils in the provinces, under the general supervision of Moscow planning authorities. The stated economic justification was sensible—to get management controls closer to the enterprise, to reduce distant interference, to cut down cross-haulage, and to encourage better use of resources. The political utility may have been equally persuasive. It transferred power over the economy from governmental bureaucrats, who were more or less outside the purview of the party's First Secretary, to the oblast secretaries, whom he promoted and upon whom he could count in the Central Committee.

The plan elicited no enthusiasm in the Presidium, however. After it was laid before the Central Committee, it was put up for public discussion, but of the eleven members of the Presidium, only Kirichenko spoke in its favor. Very many less important people did so, however. From March 31 to May 4 there were hundreds of thousands of meetings that were designed to involve the people, in Khrushchev's populist style, in deciding the shape of the economy. In meetings and in articles, a considerable range of opinion was permitted within the Soviet framework, that is, stopping short of advocacy of workers' control; and the sentiments reflected were taken into account to some degree.[48]

As a result, Khrushchev could go back to the Central Committee claiming, as could no Soviet leader ever before, the backing of the people for his reform. The plan was adopted with some concessions to the governmental apparatus, particularly the retention of six defense-related economic ministries. Khrushchev rejoiced in his victory and went around making ebullient speeches and predicting marvellous progress. He also nourished great expectations from his agricultural reforms and at this time rashly promised to overtake the United States in per-capita production of meat and milk by 1961—an optimistic projection that eventually contributed to his discrediting.

While Khrushchev was gloating, however, his opponents were sharpening their knives. The economic reform may have been sensible and popular, but it cut down the authority of many influential bureaucrats. Perhaps quite as important, it required thousands of men who were comfortably ensconced in Moscow (and

Leningrad), where nearly all Russians preferred to live, to make new homes in the provinces.

The opposition to Khrushchev was greatly encouraged by the troubles in Eastern Europe, but it acquired a solid backing from the sector that had been injured by decentralization. This group included Malenkov, who had been ousted two and a half years earlier by Khrushchev on an issue Malenkov could well regard as unreal. It was powered by Molotov, who came into conflict with Khrushchev from the day their common antagonist, Malenkov, was toppled from his position as Prime Minister. Their differences were mostly over foreign policy; peaceful coexistence did not appeal to the old Stalinist. But Molotov and Malenkov joined in the skepticism regarding the Virgin Lands and the opposition to the economic reform. Kaganovich, who was by temperament a hard-liner, sided with them. Pervukhin and Saburov, who were economic administrators on the Presidium, joined the anti-Khrushchev group because of their unhappiness at what had been done to the ministries they oversaw. Bulganin joined also, probably mostly because he resented being overshadowed, as Prime Minister, by the more dynamic First Secretary. The coalition was based not only on policy questions but also, and perhaps even more, on a balance-of-power principle. The oligarchs believed that Khrushchev was acquiring power so that he could pack the Central Committee from below, as Stalin had done, and perhaps ultimately dispose of them.

The conspirators hid their plans from an unsuspecting Khrushchev. Four days before their attempted coup, Molotov, Malenkov, and the rest welcomed Khrushchev back from a trip to Finland, outwardly with effusive warmth. When the Presidium met on June 18, however, they sprang their proposal for reorganization of the leadership.[49] Molotov was to become First Secretary, Malenkov would resume his position as Prime Minister, and Khrushchev would be Minister of Agriculture. Of the members of the full Presidium, only Mikoyan and Kirichenko stood firmly by Khrushchev from the first; Suslov was out of town. Molotov, Malenkov, Kaganovich, Voroshilov, Pervukhin, Saburov, and Bulganin, seven out of eleven, were against him, although with some differences of intensity. Shepilov, a candidate member who was seemingly close to Khrushchev, also defected, probably because he misjudged the relative strengths of the two sides. But several candidate members, who had been placed on the Presidium in the period of Khrushchev's leadership (including Marshal Zhukov), came to his assistance. The majority was unable or unwilling to arrest Khrushchev, his supporters held the floor, and the wrangling dragged on for three days. Khrushchev, in another innovation, pointed out that he had been named First Secretary not by the Presidium but by the Central Committee (although this was only formally the case), and that hence only the Central Committee could depose him.

Khrushchev mustered support from outside the Presidium—from the security police headed by Serov, and from the military, including Zhukov and the other marshals promoted by Khrushchev (a month after defeating Malenkov, Khrushchev had appointed six marshals). The opposition group was obliged to turn the question over to the Central Committee, which the air force helped to assemble quickly. Their case was thereby lost, because Khrushchev had filled the committee with his supporters at the 1956 congress. Moreover, Khrushchev was generally well liked in the party, the country was doing well under his leadership, the Virgin Lands program still looked successful because of favorable weather, and the territorial bosses who dominated the Central Committee had reason to approve the economic reform.

Yet the forces of the "Anti-Party Group," as Khrushchev dubbed it, were strong enough to force the Central Committee to battle it out for eight days. Khrushchev seems to have been unable to secure the two-thirds vote that was required for the expulsion from the party of a member of the Central Committee; he may have partially succeeded only by separating the prime movers of the conspiracy, Molotov, Malenkov, and Kaganovich, from the others.

The verdict was announced as unanimous, however, with only Molotov abstaining. That is to say, Malenkov, Kaganovich, Saburov, and Shepilov voted for their own removal from the Presidium and (except Saburov) from the Central Committee. They were the first to be ejected from the Presidium since July 1953. They also lost their governmental positions a few days later. Bulganin and Voroshilov remained for the time being, either because Khrushchev lacked the power to deal with them, or because he wanted to divide his foes, or because he did not wish to admit how many in the top leadership wanted him out.

The sin of the "Anti-Party Group" was that of trying to dethrone Khrushchev, but some issues were also involved. The members of the group were accused of having opposed peaceful coexistence and the easing of international tensions, de-Stalinization, economic decentralization, and the relaxation of controls over collective farms; their part in the great purges was also held against them.[50] Khrushchev and his opponents accused each other of failure to give sufficient attention to heavy industry. Khrushchev basically accused the opposition of conservatism; although this charge was valid against some, especially Molotov and Kaganovich, it was irrelevant to others, especially Malenkov. Khrushchev was alleged to be the leader of change and renovation; they, it appeared, wanted only to hold back.

KHRUSHCHEV VICTORIOUS

The hard-won victory over the Anti-Party Group enabled Khrushchev largely to reconstruct the ruling bodies, the Presidium and Secretariat. If he could not eject all those who were inconvenient to him from the Presidium, he could expand it.

No less than nine full members were added, including Zhukov and Brezhnev, both of whom were promoted from candidate members. Zhukov was the first professional military man (as distinguished from such political soldiers as Voroshilov and Bulganin) to reach this power summit. There were also two aged Bolsheviks, Shvernik and the Finn Otto Kuusinen, who were apparently placed there as symbols of continuity with Lenin's revolution. The others were of the territorial apparatus or were Secretaries alongside Khrushchev. No less than eight candidate members also entered the Presidium, including some who were to achieve importance in the post Khrushchev era; these included Kirilenko, Kosygin, and Mazurov. By these changes, the Presidium and the Secretariat were brought close together; the previously state-dominated Presidium became party-dominated. If Khrushchev could only control his fellow Secretaries, he would also control the Presidium.

There were some loose political ends still to be tidied up, however. First was the status of Marshal Zhukov, who more than any other individual had saved Khrushchev in June. Zhukov had shown his potency earlier, in connection with the purge of Beria, and in June he had demonstrated power that was unacceptably independent of the party, reportedly affirming that troops would move only at his command, not at that of the Council of Ministers or the Presidium.[51] He threatened exposure of Molotov and his followers for crimes of the Stalin era, a threat to which Khrushchev was sensitive. Zhukov also seems to have spearheaded a military reaction to de-Stalinization. If the writers, when the idol was smashed, thought themselves entitled to manage their affairs with less party interference, it is not surprising that the military professionals should feel the same. They regretted time spent on party-political indoctrination and wanted political officers, if they had to be around, to be subordinated to regulars. They also wanted protection against Khrushchev's schemes involving cutting forces and budgets.

The dismissal of Zhukov was cunningly planned. The cooperation of other marshals, who were vexed by the preeminence if not the arrogance of their most illustrious colleague, was secured. Then Zhukov was sent away, on October 4, 1957, on a gala state visit to Yugoslavia and Albania; he was demonstratively seen off by a large contingent of generals and ministers. While he was in Albania he was dismissed from the Presidium and the Ministry of Defense; on his return, he was welcomed by his replacement as Minister of Defense, Marshal Malinovsky, a much less forceful and ambitious man and a Khrushchev associate. Zhukov was required to engage in self-criticism for alleged bonapartism, the prerogatives of political officers were increased, and the party regained full influence in the armed forces.

In the next few months Khrushchev completed his reorganization of the leadership. Three local leaders of his following, Ignatov from Gorky, Kirichenko from Kiev, and Mukhitdinov from Tashkent, were brought into the Secretariat. Saburov and Pervukhin, who had been demoted earlier, were denounced as members of the Anti-Party Group in January 1958. Bulganin was removed as Prime Minister in March and as a member of the Presidium in September; he was finally condemned for having belonged to the Anti-Party Group, and was forced to engage in self-criticism in November-December.

Khrushchev assumed Bulganin's place, thereby becoming chief of the state as well as of the party.[52] His rise was now complete and the five-year-long succession crisis was ended. To some extent he must have seen himself as Stalin's successor; the period since the June crisis had seen much less of the liberal and more of the dictatorial in his style. He had upbraided the writers, blaming them for the unrest that had led to troubles such as those in Hungary. He had, in fact, been engaging in partial re-Stalinization, defending Stalin, stressing his positive contributions, and shifting the guilt for the purges to the police bosses, Yagoda, Yezhov, and Beria, and also to the now-helpless Malenkov.

The Khrushchev cult properly flowered after March 1958. Commonly referred to as leader of the Presidium, although no such position existed, he was described as a disciple of Lenin, whom he had never met. He identified himself with the Soviet state and its successes both at home and abroad. His old war record was glorified, and his new travels were celebrated. He accepted credit for the remarkable series of Soviet spectaculars in space, from the first artificial satellite (in October 1957) to the first manned orbital flight and photographing of the back side of the moon—feats that greatly raised the pride and confidence of the Soviet leaders and people.

In his new freedom of power, Khrushchev dictated policy in diplomacy, decided industrial priorities, criticized electric projects, and gave instructions abundantly in agriculture, art, and literature. Like Stalin, he was the authority on whatever he took under consideration, from building methods to cotton growing. Like Stalin but to a lesser extent, he relied on his personal secretariat, which provided him with information and generated publicity.[53] He desired to be, or to appear to be, democratic, but for Khrushchev democracy amounted to the leader's consultation with his appointees according to forms. Thus in 1958 the Central Committee met more often than at any time since 1928. Late in 1958 he began the practice of bringing many outsiders, sometimes hundreds of them, into "enlarged" Central Committee sessions, a practice that tended both to broaden the base of authority and to affirm the authority of the leader. This practice, however, contributed to the alienation of the insiders who eventually turned on him.

Age sixty-four when he became Prime Minister, Khrushchev was in a hurry to move rapidly, and he set about pushing programs for change on many fronts. He proposed modernizing Soviet industry not by shifting priorities toward the satisfaction of consumer needs, but by stressing chemicals more than steel (Stalin's favorite), while getting more technology and credits from the West. But he was never able to achieve anything like the massive expansion he wanted. The economic decentralization plan, which was completed only after the June upheaval, did not work very well; the government was continually tinkering with it and, almost from the start, beginning to recentralize. The chief question, however, was the state of agriculture, for which Khrushchev had various panaceas. It was his basic policy to make the theoretically cooperative farms more and more like state farms, both by enlarging them and by making their members practically hired workers.

A step in this direction was the abolition of the Machine Tractor Stations Stalin had established at the beginning of collectivization to control not only the limited inventory of farm machinery but also the politics of the collectives. In February 1958 Khrushchev enunciated a policy of turning the assets of the MTSs over to the enlarged collective farms, although Stalin had warned against this move in his last writing. The practical advantages of giving the collective farms control of the equipment they used were evident, but so were the ideological—that is, political—disadvantages. The shift lowered the MTSs from the "higher" form of state property to the "lower" form of cooperative property. Thus, it reduced the party's levers of power in the countryside. Consequently it aroused opposition in the party even when Khrushchev was riding highest.[54]

Khrushchev also tried to hurry along the victory of socialism in the world by an active foreign policy that mixed peaceful coexistence with the advancement of Soviet power. He continued to probe areas of Western weakness in the Third World, cultivating relations with leftist-nationalists or almost any anti-Western movement. In November 1958 he tried to bluster the United States with the first of several ultimatums demanding control of West Berlin. He reiterated and strengthened the thesis of the noninevitability of war, yet he also contended that a new world war would be the death not of civilization, but of capitalism. Since relaxation in Eastern Europe had proved to be dangerous, he insisted on Soviet preeminence and the importance of "proletarian internationalism," which was to become a euphemism for Soviet domination a decade later. Favor was withdrawn from Tito, who had been welcomed enthusiastically little more than a year before; the Soviet press even found his condemnation in 1948 to have been basically correct. Polemics were also beginning against the "dogmatists" (by which the cognoscenti could understand "Chinese Communists").

Khrushchev badly wanted to knit together as much of the Communist movement as he could, however. He activated the Council for Mutual Economic Assistance (Comecon or CMEA), which Stalin had erected in 1949 to isolate Yugoslavia but had not used. Khrushchev revived the multilateral Communist gatherings that Stalin had halted; there was a conclave of thirteen ruling parties in 1957. A joint journal was established in Prague in March 1958 that was faintly reminiscent of the extinct Cominform and its journal. For the sake of harmony,

Khrushchev developed another little amendment to Marxism-Leninism: all the socialist countries would enter the utopian condition of communism at about the same time, thanks to the selfless help of the Soviet Union.[55]

For January 1959 Khrushchev summoned the first and only ''extraordinary'' congress of Soviet party history, the Twenty-first Congress. The single item on its agenda was the Seven Year Plan, which was to run from the beginning of 1959 through 1965 and replace the plan for 1956–60. The failure to reach the goals of the Five Year Plan was covered over by the grand promises of the Seven Year Plan for unprecedented expansion of production of both consumer and producer goods, to lift Soviet per-capita production above that of the United States by 1970. There was no more talk of collective leadership, only paeans of almost Stalinist hyperbole to the magnificent achievements of Nikita S. Khrushchev.

Yet even then, the First Secretary was not truly master of the great machine. An unannounced purpose of the meeting—which was hardly needed to talk over the economic plan—was evidently to punish Khrushchev's adversaries. A claque duly called for severe measures, but the confessions of error by Bulganin, Pervukhin, Saburov, and Shepilov fell short of surrender, while Voroshilov was still unexposed. They must have had considerable support in the party; Mikoyan held out against further reprisals, and Suslov hinted that he had reservations about Khrushchev's policies in general. In any case, no personnel actions were taken; none of Khrushchev's enemies were degraded and none of his friends were promoted. The power of the First Secretary to decide who was to be next to him had become very limited. The party was reestablishing the principle of the irremovability of the leading cadres; Stalin had set this rule aside, but it was to become a central principle of the Brezhnev era.

THE TROUBLED VISION

Despite the fact that he registered no progress at the 1959 congress, Khrushchev had reason throughout that year to be satisfied. Perhaps the high point of his career came in September with his sensational visit to America and his conversations at Camp David with President Eisenhower—a supposedly Leninist-revolutionary leader reached his zenith as the honored guest of the citadel of world capitalism and reaction. This was the climax of the policy of peaceful coexistence, which, it was hoped, would be crowned by Eisenhower's return visit to the Soviet Union in 1960 and would lead to broader reforms.

It was also a personal vindication for the First Secretary. As he wrote in retirement, ''Even if we didn't reap material benefits right away, my talks with Eisenhower represented a colossal moral victory. I still remember how delighted I was the first time my interpreter told me that Eisenhower had called me, in English, 'my friend.' ''[56] After the trip, Khrushchev gave it enormous publicity. It was not easy for a Soviet citizen to avoid exposure to a full-length documentary exalting the tour, and an adulatory seven-hundred-page account, *Face to Face with America*, appeared in an edition of millions and was translated into various foreign languages. Soon thereafter, in December 1959, in violation of a law (of 1957) against giving towns, institutions, and so on, the name of a living person, a famous kolkhoz was named after Khrushchev.[57]

Difficulties began to appear, however. It was part of Khrushchev's scheme largely to replace the navy, air force, and partially the army, with a rocket deterrent—the USSR had pioneered in the construction of intercontinental missiles in 1956—and in January 1960 he announced a decision to cut military manpower by a third, or 1.2 million men, in 1960–61. A reduction in the number of men drafted could only have been popular, but the Khrushchev plan called for releasing 250,000 officers, and they did not like it. There were complaints and some passive resistance. A related idea of Khrushchev's, the conversion of the army to a territorial militia system, never moved from the starting post.[58]

There had earlier been some sniping at détente; for example, shortly after the triumphal return of his leader, Brezhnev proposed the neo-Stalinist thesis that "the ideological struggle sharpens in proportion to the achievements of socialism."[59] Doctrinaire Communists implied that peaceful coexistence, if it were to lead to cooperation with capitalist states, was anti-Leninist. In the early months of 1960, the general policy came under some fire; Suslov and Kozlov in particular indicated their reservations in the unobtrusive fashion that is usually mandatory in the Soviet system for those who do not go along with the top leadership. In April Molotov sent to the Central Committee's journal, *Kommunist*, an article strongly attacking peaceful coexistence; he must have been confident of substantial support for his views within the upper hierarchy.

But it was the U-2 incident that blew up the Khrushchev policy, or that was used to blow it up. On May 1 an American high-altitude reconnaissance plane was brought down deep in Soviet territory and the pilot was captured. Khrushchev tricked the State Department into a false cover story, and Eisenhower, instead of disavowing responsibility as Khrushchev invited him to do, accepted it and justified the espionage flights over the Soviet Union.

This was a major blow to Khrushchev, who had just made so much of the friendly reception he had received in the United States. He was also irked by the demonstration of American technological superiority at a time when he was trying to persuade the world of Soviet leadership—the Soviet military had been aware of such flights for several years, but it had been unable to do anything to halt them. Khrushchev used intemperate language and promised nuclear retaliation against countries that were harboring U.S. spy planes. On May 14 Khrushchev went to Paris for the scheduled summit with Eisenhower and the leaders of France and Britain, but he demanded a humble apology from Eisenhower. Not getting it, he aborted the conference he had labored long to set up; in the hardening of policy on both sides, it probably would have produced little that was positive. Khrushchev went away spouting rage that could not hide the failure of his program.

In other respects, also, the Khrushchev plans showed a lack of success. Particularly after May 1960, there was a marked drive for economic recentralization that was headed by two men who did not favor Khrushchev's positions, Kozlov and Kosygin (Kosygin had become the chairman of the chief planning board, Gosplan, in March 1959 and Deputy Chairman of the Council of Ministers in May 1960). The local economic councils were not abolished, but sundry authorities were placed over them and their limited autonomy was sliced away. It was claimed that the local management was inefficient, but a stronger argument was certainly that they were disposed to localism (and potentially to nationalistic deviations), and the central authorities wanted to hold the reins.

Agriculture was also a millstone, as usual, on the leadership of the First Secretary. The Virgin Lands program petered out after 1959 as a result of dry weather, soil erosion, prospering weeds, and possibly mismanagement; eventually it was to be almost abandoned. Nothing came of the grand program for surpassing America in livestock products by 1961. To the contrary, Khrushchev had the embarrassment of waxing enthusiastic over the fulfillment of the triple plan for meat deliveries by the secretary of the Riazan oblast, only to learn that the achievement had been faked. Minor proconsumer measures, including a tax reduction, a shortening of the work week, and a little more investment in agriculture and light industry, encountered opposition. In the view of many in the party, he was giving too little attention to ideology, that is, to party control. According to the critics, the revolutionary struggle, or the unconditional power of the party, had to have priority, and the critics were influential. At the British trade fair in Moscow on May 20, 1961, Khrushchev stated that the primacy of heavy industry would be replaced by equal rates of growth for heavy and light industry, but the words of the First Secretary were not published.[60] Shortly afterwards, an increase of the defense budget by one-third was announced, military manpower cuts were ended, and nuclear testing was resumed. In January 1961 Khrushchev failed to secure the adoption of much of his program to make agriculture better serve the consumer. At the Twenty-Second Congress, in October 1961, Khrushchev made no headway against those whom he called the "metal-eaters."*

Another insoluble problem for the Soviet leader was the growing conflict between the old and new Communisms, the Sino-Soviet split. In June 1959 the Soviet Union informed Peking of the abrogation of their 1957 nuclear-aid agreement, which had been a promise to help China become a nuclear power.

---

*The kolkhoz named after Khrushchev was quietly renamed, probably in 1960, and in the same year a biography of Khrushchev was produced without publicity in only fifty thousand copies. Michel Tatu, *Power in the Kremlin*, pp. 177–78.

Early in 1960 angry words began going back and forth privately, partly as a by-product of the border conflict between China and India, in which the Soviet Union had been courting India. The Chinese made the interesting suggestion that the Soviet Union should formally become the head of the international Communist movement, a suggestion that was subtly devised to require an organization in which China could play a major, ultimately dominant, role. The quarrel came into the open to some extent in April, when the Chinese set forth their revolutionary position in a series of articles outwardly damning Yugoslavia and indirectly jabbing at Khrushchev. In July, either from pique or in misguided hopes of coercing the Chinese (much as Stalin had tried to coerce the Yugoslavs), Khrushchev withdrew Soviet technicians who were helping the reconstruction of the Chinese economy; they departed posthaste, taking their blueprints with them and leaving the Chinese infuriated.

Khrushchev was apparently responsible for much of the fury of the split and the rapidity with which it deepened, because the Chinese outlook of revolutionary dedication, spartanism, and ideological rigor was contrary to his general directions; he seems to have gone beyond the wishes of many in the party. Suslov, for example, expressed worry over the rift.[61] Nevertheless, charges and countercharges flew as though both sides preferred war, until at the Twenty-Second Congress the quarrel was made public for the assembled delegates of the Communist world. Khrushchev attacked China in attacking Albania, and Chou En-lai, in response, rebuked the Soviet leader—practically the first such event in history in a Communist conclave. If Khrushchev fostered the split, it was nonetheless a grave defeat for him. Instead of presiding over a ''socialist camp'' that was swelling as more and more states adhered to it, he saw the large majority of the population of the Soviet bloc abandoning Moscow.

As Khrushchev's policies were suffering, he was also losing or surrendering some control of high-level appointments. He either could not or would not stand by his supporters. In 1959 A. A. Kuzmin, a staunch backer of Khrushchev against the Anti-Party Group, was replaced as Chairman of Gosplan by Kosygin, who was at best lukewarm; various others who had been especially eager in denouncing Molotov and his colleagues lost their positions in 1960–61.[62] It became increasingly evident, in any case, that many of those around him were less than fully committed to him.

A blow was the loss in January 1960 of Kirichenko, who was, at least outwardly, the most zealous of Khrushchev's men, the Secretary ranking next to Khrushchev, and had evidently been the heir apparent. He was demoted to a minor position, afterwards falling out of sight, for reasons that remain mysterious. Expulsions from places near the top have normally been accompanied by some sort of accusation throughout Soviet history, but in this case it can only be conjectured that Kirichenko may have been suspected of minority nationalism (he was Ukrainian) or may have come into conflict with some others on the Presidium, possibly for personal reasons.

In May 1960, at the time of the U-2 incident, there was a major shakeup, the outcome of which was decidedly unfavorable to the First Secretary. Brezhnev, one of the most valuable of Khrushchev's friends, was named to the formal presidency of the Soviet state (following Voroshilov), a post carrying little power; three months later he was released from the Secretariat. Three men, Kosygin, Poliansky, and Podgorny, became full members of the Presidium; none of these could be called a Khrushchev client, although the latter two were allies. Two Khrushchevites, Beliaev and Kirichenko, were ousted. The chief beneficiary of the changes, however, was the former Leningrad boss who had at one time been associated with the Doctors' Plot, Frol Kozlov; he had been raised up by Khrushchev, but had shown quite independent ways and become a spokesman for the party's hard-liners. He entered the Secretariat at the same time that it lost five of its ten members, all of them faithful Khrushchevites, with Brezhnev following not long after.

In the result, Khrushchev had no unconditional partisan on the five-man Secretariat, which included two powerful figures who were basically unfriendly to his policies, Suslov and Kozlov (Kozlov was apparently second to the chief and the heir apparent). With reduced control of the smaller Secretariat, it was more difficult for Khrushchev to dominate the Presidium, on which Suslov, Kozlov, and Kosygin formed a strong opposing nucleus and in which party representatives no longer overbalanced governmental leaders.[63]

Khrushchev must have been chagrined to find himself so powerless as supreme leader, and he undertook a broad new attack against his enemies. The means was de-Stalinization, rather remarkably, since it had proved dangerous for him in 1956. The scene was the Twenty-Second Congress, in October 1961, at which Khrushchev's influence with the provincial party leaders should have been maximally effective. Presumably in preparation, he had effected an extensive shakeup of the middle party ranks, in particular removing a third of the provincial secretaries.[64] The fact that the congress was very large—4,393 voting delegates, or one per 2,000 members instead of one per 5,000 as at preceding congresses—should also have worked in his favor.

There was no advance indication that the Twenty-Second Congress would be the scene for a massive public attack on Stalin's image. In 1959 a new *History of the Communist Party of the Soviet Union* had been published to replace Stalin's *Short Course,* and it contained two pages (out of 763) criticizing the dictator, but de-Stalinization had generally been quiescent. The announced purpose of the congress provided it with quite enough to do, the approval of new party rules and a new party program. Still, attention soon turned to the livelier topic of Stalinism.

In 1961 de-Stalinization was much more closely tied than it had been in 1956 to the attack on Khrushchev's present rivals. Khrushchev denounced Voroshilov even as he was sitting by the podium—the last member of the 1957 Anti-Party Group to be unmasked. Not long before, Khrushchev had roundly praised Voroshilov, and the delegates had innocently elected him to the Presidium of the Congress, although he had been dropped from the party Presidium the previous year. Now Khrushchev repeated for the public record the principal accusations of the Secret Speech, adding and strengthening them in spots. He went on to blacken Molotov, Malenkov, Kaganovich, Voroshilov, and others for their association with Stalin's crimes and with subsequent misdeeds, including following the Maoist line. Khrushchev contended that the culprits opposed him not because of his policies, but because of fear of disclosure of their share in Stalin's evil.

Khrushchev's political motive, the attempt to get rid of some troublesome people, again must have been mixed with broader aims; for example, he believed that more open de-Stalinization might help to vanquish opposition to his policies and that clearing the air was necessary for the further advancement of Soviet society, to break with the past and inaugurate the new era. The speech was too emotional in tone to have been merely the product of a calculation of advantage.

Many others, mostly territorial secretaries but none of the senior oligarchs, took up the charge, recounting the misdeeds of the Stalin era and attacking the "Anti-Party" leaders. But results did not follow. By the second week of the congress, speakers were complaining about the failure to take action against the accused. Mikoyan and Suslov treated the case as closed, and many speakers ignored the matter. Out of seventy-seven speakers, only twenty-three clearly advocated further punishment for the "Anti-Party" villains.[65] If Khrushchev had hoped to widen the attack to bring in others who stood in his way, he had failed completely. In his final report Khrushchev charged the three leaders, Molotov, Malenkov, and Kaganovich, of criminal actions; yet he failed to demand punishment. The final resolution was a clear defeat; those whom Khrushchev and his followers had called criminals were not expelled from the party but only mildly condemned, and the case was referred to the Party Control Commission, where it was buried.

The apparatus was evidently stronger than the leader, and it wanted security. Stalin could destroy people under the assumption that the leadership was surrounded by deadly enemies and that it was necessary to act ruthlessly in defense of the party's very existence. But in 1953 this rationale seemed to be largely worn out; by 1961, it did not avail at all. It is imaginable that Khrushchev might have crushed his enemies by turning them into agents of capitalism, but although the accusation of association with Stalin's purges was helpful in removing the most important of them from high places, it was not enough cause to punish them further. Khrushchev credited himself with mercy, citing Kaganovich's alleged plea to him, "Comrade Khrushchev, I have known you for many years. I ask you not to let them treat me in the vindictive way people were treated under Stalin.''[66] More impressive is the fact that all four of the persons who were dropped from the Presidium at this time were more or less aligned with Khrushchev, while no one who disagreed with him went out. The best Khrushchev could do was to bring several friends into the Secretariat.

De-Stalinization was likewise ineffective. The only anti-Stalinist resolution of the congress that was carried out was the removal of Stalin's body from where it had been lying alongside Lenin's to a burial site by the Kremlin wall among lesser dignitaries. The promised further revelations and the investigation into the death of Kirov never came. The proposed monument to Stalin's victims was never begun. Literary de-Stalinization went forward, however; the revelations inspired many authors, including Solzhenitsyn, to write exposés of the previously shrouded past.

Despite the controversy Khrushchev precipitated at the Twenty-Second Congress, its ostensible purpose was to modernize the party and its outlook by redrafting its rules and official program or statement of aims. The new party rules, which were to replace the rules reported by Khrushchev himself in 1952, actually represented no great change. The chief ideological innovation was a recognition that classes had supposedly long since been abolished in the Soviet Union, hence that the party represented the "militant vanguard of the Soviet people" instead of the "working class, working peasants and working intellectuals." It was likewise stated that the Soviet Union had become the "state of the whole people," instead of the "dictatorship of the proletariat." This claim was surely not premature forty-four years after the advent of Soviet power, but it represented a theoretical loosening of the party's claim to unlimited authority over society; it was consequently disturbing to many of the party faithful.

A change that had more direct practical implications was an attempt to cause the elite to circulate more within the party. It provided that elected party officials should not be eligible for more than three successive terms of office, and that a certain fraction of the party committees (half at the lower levels and one-quarter at the upper ones) had to be renewed at each new election, that is, every two or four years. There was no reason officials could not satisfy the requirement by a little trading of positions, and "highly respected" leaders (doubtless including the First Secretary) were specifically exempt. Still, it was enough to trouble many apparatus-men and the rule was promptly abrogated after Khrushchev's downfall—before it could have any effect.

More publicized was the new party program. The rules were amended at every congress, but the program that was on the books dated from 1919 (it had been authored by Lenin, Bukharin, Zinoviev, Trotsky, Smirnov, and Sokolnikov, all of whom, except Lenin, had been executed by Stalin). The Eighteenth Congress, in March 1939, set up a commission to draft a new program, but nothing came of it. For Khrushchev to replace the old program was to set himself level with Lenin and Stalin. The new party program was verbose, over a hundred printed pages, and it covered everything from the history of the party and the state of international affairs to the future society. It epitomized Khrushchev's views, crediting Lenin, erasing Stalin, expounding peaceful coexistence with ideological struggle, looking to Soviet leadership in the world, and promising a happy social order of harmony and abundance.[67]

Khrushchev saw the party drained of utopian vision. Stalin long before had lost interest in social transformation, not to speak of the necessarily equalitarian aspects of an idealized future, but Khrushchev hoped to rekindle party spirit by the restatement of goals. It is also probable that he was stimulated by Chinese competition; the Maoists claimed in 1958 to be leaping ahead to true communism through their "People's Communes."[68] The program was decidedly less radical-inspirational than that of 1919, however, promising no early withering away of the state or brotherly sharing of all material goods. Instead, it envisioned a fairly advanced welfare society, with an increasing volume of free services, child-care centers, boarding schools for the making of the New Soviet Man, and increasing self-management of the people through party-led public organizations.

The new program was coupled with, and based upon, an ambitious twenty-year plan of economic growth that proposed maintaining a 10 percent annual increase in industrial production over that period, bringing total production in the target year of 1980 to nearly seven times the 1960 level.[69] Although this plan maintained the traditional priority for heavy industry, it was to provide the material abundance that should, in the Marxist view of history, make possible the utopian society. It was more a dream than a calculation, and it never had operative significance. The Seven Year Plan had replaced a languishing Five Year Plan; the Seven Year Plan was overtaken after two years by the Twenty Year Plan; the Twenty Year Plan was in turn forgotten even before Khrushchev left office three years later.

The program stated boldly in its conclusion, which was capitalized, "THE PARTY SOLEMNLY PROCLAIMS: THE PRESENT GENERATION OF SOVIET PEOPLE SHALL LIVE UNDER COMMUNISM!"[70] The condition of "communism" was not defined, but the key question was the role of the state, which by all Marxist theory and logic should cease with the end of private ownership of the means of production and hence of class exploitation. Khrushchev's answer was that the state should wither, but that the party should grow and lead the people to the promised land. The party, then, would practically take the place of the state. There was a difference, however. Khrushchev revived some of the ideas Lenin favored in his semianarchistic moods. More and more of the work of the state should be done by ordinary citizens on a volunteer basis under party tutelage.

The general idea seems weirdly unrealistic, but Khrushchev made some moves toward putting it into effect, at least in the area in which people are readiest to volunteer, the management of others' affairs. An important part of the plan for the improvement of Soviet society was the establishment of a network of semiofficial volunteer organizations to enforce law and morality,[71] ranging from the "druzhinniki" or part-time volunteers, to the irregular "comrade courts" that were established to punish minor offenses, to antiparasite meetings, apartment committees, and a host of control organs to check on everything from cheating store clerks to swindling bureaucrats. Khrushchev also proposed to replace paid party workers with volunteers, and by 1963 it was reported that 10 percent or less of the party workers were professionals—a situation that was doubtless displeasing to the true apparatchiks.[72]

In a letter to the Central Committee, Molotov denounced the party program as "anti-revolutionary, pacifist, and revisionist,"[73] and it was certainly distasteful to many bureaucrats, since according to Khrushchev, bureaucracy should "cease to be a special vocation." Here as elsewhere, Khrushchev's motives were an indeterminate mixture of the urge to advance Soviet society along the lines laid down by Lenin and the desire to raise himself politically by becoming an ideological authority and the leader in a sublime cause. Nevertheless the vision was a fraud in its inception. Khrushchev knew how far behind his country was economically and how it was falling short of expectations. Sundry panaceas in agriculture had failed. Foreign affairs were likewise going badly; if it had seemed plausible in 1958 or 1959 that the Soviet Union would lead the world to "socialism," by 1961, with the failure to advance in the Third World, the split with China (and Albania), and friction with the Western powers, especially the United States, such hopes were plainly unrealistic. There was no apparent thought about how the utopian society should operate; the moneyless economy was hard to reconcile with the emphasis on material rewards for achieving the required productivity. The only answer Khrushchev had was for the party to manage things. Yet the party had continually demonstrated its inability to make the transition from its supervisory, political-ideological role to the administration of society, and Khrushchev knew well its rottenness, which he was continually attacking. The utopian vision was thus not an expression of confidence in the bright future, but an attempt to reaffirm authority that was slipping away.

THE SLIPPAGE OF POWER

After the Twenty-Second Congress brought Khrushchev public triumph as the author of the new party program and political frustration in the pursuit of his enemies, the political scene was confused and changeable. Demands for punishment of the Anti-Party Group tapered off and ceased in the first part of 1962. A few months after the anti-Stalinist outburst of October 1961, Khrushchev was again praising his old master. In March 1962 Khrushchev was unable to get approval for increased investment in agriculture. In consequence, he had to raise the prices of meat and butter. This provoked riots in several cities, most seriously in Novocherkassk, that were an unaccustomed shock to the oligarchy.

In September 1962, however, Khrushchev seems to have felt stronger. Four new men from the apparat were added to the Secretariat, which had already been enlarged at the Twenty-Second Congress. He also had published an allegedly rediscovered writing by Lenin that gave economic questions priority over political ones and urged that economic organizers be placed in charge of the economy—theses that were fortuitously appropriate for Khrushchev's policies. He also brought de-Stalinization to its high point by personally authorizing the publication of Solzhenitsyn's novella of concentration camp life, *One Day in the Life of Ivan Denisovich* (a printing of 750,000 copies), and the publication in *Pravda* of Yevgeny Yevtushenko's "Stalin's Heirs." This poem, which had long been waiting in manuscript, blamed those who denounced Stalin but longed for Stalinist ways; its appearance hinted a general offensive against Stalinists who were still on the stage.

This interesting development was placed in the shade, however, by the Cuban missile crisis. What concrete aims Khrushchev sought to achieve by this venture is not entirely clear,[74] beyond the obvious desire to compensate for Soviet nuclear inferiority by an easy coup. The unexpectedly vigorous American reaction and the Soviet backdown caused Khrushchev humiliation and loss of face that could only partially be disguised by propaganda. Instead of shoring up his position vis-à-vis the Soviet military, especially those in it representing other than rocket forces, Khrushchev lost their respect and regard, or what remained of it after the recent failures in Berlin and his attempts to reduce military manpower and budgets. After the crisis, defense spending was increased, while a press campaign reaffirmed party superiority over the military.

The Cuban crisis represented the end of Khrushchev's forward foreign policy. There were no more spectacular foreign travels or demarches, and the idea of Soviet leadership of a growing community was laid to rest. Soviet policy toward Yugoslavia hardened somewhat, and the Soviet press seemed uncertain whether dogmatism or revisionism represented the main danger. The Chinese took advantage of the Soviet discomfiture to attack Khrushchev bitterly as being at once adventurist, for placing rockets in Cuba without proper calculation, and capitulationist, for bowing to American pressure and removing them. Soviet relations with China and Albania descended further into personal animosity and vulgar name-calling. By February, however, Soviet policy toward China had softened considerably, probably under the influence of Suslov and Kozlov.

The attacks on Stalin ceased with the Cuban crisis, giving way to a counterattack on liberal writers and modern artists, perhaps sponsored by Suslov. On December 1, 1962, while visiting an art exhibition with other Presidium members, Khrushchev reviled a group of modern paintings, although these were not being publicly shown. Antiliberal pressures on literature continued through March. On March 8, 1963, Khrushchev seemingly sought to undo the effects of de-Stalinization by stating that the other leaders at the time had been unaware of Stalin's crimes, Beria being the chief accomplice, and blaming imperialist agencies for misleading Stalin into the purges by fabricated documents. On the other hand, Khrushchev emphasized Stalin's positive contributions. From mid-February to mid-March, Soviet policy turned markedly conciliatory toward Peking.

After Cuba, Khrushchev still complained of the metal-eaters (in effect, proponents of the defense industry), but whatever consumer orientation there had been was definitely shelved. The bureaucracy played on defense needs, and recentralization progressed. Major steps were the establishment in March of a Supreme Council of the National Economy and a major reorganization emphasizing military production and deemphasizing Khrushchev's favorite, the chemical industry. The reform on which Khrushchev had staked his career in 1957 had been by this time mostly reversed in practice. It is understandable that speeches by Kozlov around this time were confident and optimistic, while Khrushchev was gloomy, at least for Khrushchev. In this mood, on April 24, 1963, Khrushchev spoke of his eventual withdrawal: ''I am already sixty-nine years old. Anyone can see I cannot occupy the post I hold in the Party and state forever.''[75]

The tide thus seems to have been markedly contrary to Khrushchev's basic policies in the five months subsequent to the Cuban fiasco. He apparently felt it necessary to bend with the political wind. He did not, however, relinquish any control of the party, but rather tried to make it a more effective and presumably more manipulable tool. In November 1962 he undertook a major reorganization of the Secretariat, placing the departments of the Central Committee under sections of the Secretariat, and he erected a new control apparatus with exceptional powers under Shelepin. A much more important reform, in fact the biggest structural change in the party since the revolution, was the splitting of the party into industrial and agricultural sections; this move was proposed by Khrushchev late in 1962 and approved in January 1963. To make the party more effective in the administration of the economy, Khrushchev set up parallel industrial and agricultural hierarchies up to the provincial level; soviet, Komsomol, and trade-union organizations were also divided.[76]

This was a desperate scheme to activate the party management; although Khrushchev thought it would accelerate lagging growth, it was an administrative absurdity. The plan was never really implemented and it was reversed by Khrushchev's successors, but it was sufficiently threatening to distrub many party hierarchs, especially the territorial bosses who had been Khrushchev's best supporters. It made questionable the membership in the Central Committee of some fifty regional secretaries, probably reduced the pay of many,[77] and threatened many more with dislocation.

Khrushchev's position seems to have been very shaky in the first months of 1963. Six months later, however, he had rebounded. Some credit goes to the Chinese, who intensified their attacks and in March raised the sensitive border issue, thereby driving patriotic Russians to rally around their leader. More important, evidently, was the incapacitation of Kozlov, whose behind-the-scenes importance became most evident in the effects of his disappearance. Kozlov, who was fourteen years younger than Khrushchev and was the acknowledged heir apparent and spearhead of the opposition, had been receiving a publicity buildup that was comparable to Khrushchev's.[78] But he was last seen in public on April 10. His illness was announced on May 4, and he was inactive thereafter, although he lived, like Lenin, for nearly two years after his disabling stroke.

The turnaround was rapid. By June, Brezhnev, who had apparently been put on the shelf by Kozlov, returned to the Secretariat as a reliable Khrushchev follower; Podgorny, who was also fairly close to Khrushchev, accompanied him. Podgorny also inherited Kozlov's base in Kazakhstan. Brezhnev was now plainly the second-in-command. Various other Khrushchev men who had been demoted in 1960 were subsequently reinstated, including Kirilenko, Shchelokov, and Kunaev. In the summer there were sundry liberal measures: the signing of the Test Ban Treaty, another visit by Tito, some proconsumer measures, and harsher attacks on "dogmatism" and the Chinese Communists. Although he failed to get much support in the party, Khrushchev was pressing the ideological line that dogmatism, not revisionism, was the main danger. In a speech of July 19, he damned Stalin violently and apparently extemporaneously,[79] and called for socialism to prove itself by welfare—a speech that was toned down in the *Pravda* version. In the latter part of 1963 Khrushchev was mounting a new offensive for chemicals and consumer goods and again condemning Stalin and the Anti-Party Group. The crop that year was very bad, especially in the Virgin Lands, and the Soviet Union for the first time bought a large quantity of grain from the United States, but these events do not seem to have hurt Khrushchev very much.

Early in 1964, Khrushchev finally had the satisfaction of seeing the enemy trio, Molotov, Malenkov, and Kaganovich, expelled from the party.* The expulsion probably hurt him, however; the younger party cadres no longer had reason to fear the old Stalinists, while they might well be a little apprehensive of Khrushchev. On Khrushchev's seventieth birthday, an enormous quantity of ink was spent in extolling him, although fervor was lacking. Khrushchev seems to have believed the eulogies and withdrew previous remarks about possible retirement. There were still differences in the Presidium; Khrushchev repeatedly argued for economic programs that had supposedly already been decided, as though important people still had to be persuaded. In August Khrushchev even

---

*It was announced only that "Molotov and others" had been expelled.

referred publicly to the division in the leadership, speaking of "some comrades" who differed with him.

In the summer of 1964, Khrushchev was the exalted leader who was credited by the press and public speakers with leadership in Marxism-Leninism, space achievements, military strategy, biology, music, and so on.[80] Beneath the surface, however, discontent was building up. The economy was doing poorly. Not only was agriculture suffering from the effects of the bad harvest of 1963, but none of Khrushchev's many measures, from planting corn to plowing up pastures, seemed to help. The annual increase in industrial production fell (by the always optimistic Soviet figures) from 11 percent in 1959 to 7.5 percent in 1964—a rate that no longer promised early world leadership. The Soviet share of world industrial output was rising little or not at all. Whereas Stalin had gone far toward making the Soviet Union self-sufficient, imports of foreign technology were now becoming more necessary. Foreign policy was going nowhere, and Khrushchev wanted to make things worse by pursuing his vendetta against the Chinese to their excommunication at a world Communist conference.

Probably more important politically than these clouds in the background was the fact that Khrushchev had antagonized many of those upon whom he depended to execute his will. He had affronted the oligarchs by repeatedly bringing swarms of outsiders into Central Committee sessions and also by going outside it to seek support. For example, in September 1964 he unveiled his economic program before a joint meeting of the party Presidium, the Council of Ministers, and the heads of planning organizations. It was especially irritating that he brought his son-in-law Adzhubei into high-level politics, showing more confidence in him than in anyone else. Adzhubei was an outsider to the party oligarchy, a free-wheeling, high-living, modernist outsider and a Tatar at that; yet the Central Committee had to listen to him. At the same time, the aging Khrushchev had lost much of the geniality that had helped him rise to the top. He had become harsh and petulant, less willing to try persuasion and more determined to give detailed commands. Stalin grew paranoid in absolute power; Khrushchev, with less power than he believed he had, grew careless.

KHRUSHCHEVISM

The period dominated by the stocky, ebullient, peasanty Russian, Nikita S. Khrushchev, is more difficult to assess than the one dominated by the saturnine Joseph V. Stalin. Contradiction was its hallmark. Khrushchev was the admiring follower of Stalin and the demolisher of his image, the proponent of peaceful coexistence who blustered and generated crises, the advocate of free creativity who cursed modern artists and repressed deviant poets. It is not necessary to decide whether his liberalism, which consisted more of words than of deeds, was a concession to political forces[81]—Malenkov and Beria also presented them-selves as liberals—or to what extent he was deeply idealistic.[82] One may rather say that he represented the fundamental contradiction between the vocation of the Leninist party to carry through a program of freedom and abundance, and the determination of the party to maintain and maximize its power.

The Khrushchev years saw a revival of the long effort, which had been repressed during most of Stalin's tenure, to find a suitable post-revolutionary role for the revolutionary organization so that it could keep its grip and hence its responsiblity. Khrushchevism represented a late flaring up of the emotions of 1917−20. Khrushchev was the last leader who seemed to believe intensely that the October Revolution should have amounted to a new dispensation for the Soviet peoples and mankind—that it had to amount to something supremely great in the progress of civilization. He acquired a stake in the Leninist movement during the civil war, and his moral commitment seems to have been renewed and elevated by his front-line experience in the Second World War, so that he felt it necessary to see the experiment prosper and produce a social transformation according to its ideals. Latter-day leaders have invested their lives and spirits not in the making and defense of the revolution, but in the making of their careers; their interest, consequently, has not been in giving meaning to the revolution, but in maintaining the order that had served them well.

Khrushchev wanted to keep on making revolution at a time when revolution was no longer in order, to get the benefits of revolutionary dynamism and renewal while holding to the stable order that was desired by nearly everyone below him. This was most obvious in foreign policy, where he coupled peaceful coexistence with wars of liberation; it was also evident in economic affairs, where he wanted to combine a "storming" approach—achievement by enthusiasm—with rational management. But in his progressively relaxing post-revolutionary society he had no means of overcoming inertia and restoring dedication without attacking the holders of calcified power, the party apparatus, as Mao was to do in his Cultural Revolution of 1966−70. Mao was strong enough, as the Lenin-plus-Stalin of the Chinese revolution, to win a qualified victory; Khrushchev could not master the apparatus. Khrushchev sought a way of governing better within the canons of Marxism-Leninism and the axiom of total power to the party; it is not surprising that he could not find it.

Khrushchev's answer, and his chief merit in the history of Leninism, was to restore the vitality and importance of the party after Stalin had suffocated and downgraded it. He revived party institutions and regularized procedures. He seems to have believed that the party that had made the revolution could be shaped into the best instrument for the government of an industrial socialist economy. By means of the party, revolutionary dynamism should be applied to efficient management. Party men should guide the economy on the spot just as the party should give general directions at the top. Khrushchev put the party in charge of the police and gave it more authority in and over the army;[83] the party, the exponent of ideology, should be the moral, political, and especially economic supervisor of the land.

Khrushchev was able to resurrect some of the heroics of bygone years by inspiring volunteers to undergo hardships for grandiose projects, such as the taming of the Virgin Lands or the building of the Bratsk hydroelectric project, although these sacrifices were stimulated by only a faint echo of the enthusiasm of the First Five Year Plan. He was less successful in reinvigorating the party. He increased its membership by no such radical proportions as Stalin did in the 1920s, but he did raise it by many millions. The membership, which had been nearly static for five years after the war, began to grow in 1951, reaching 6,707,000 at the beginning of 1952. At the beginning of 1955, it was up slightly, to 6,957,000, but thereafter, especially after 1957, when Khrushchev became unchallenged leader, it grew rapidly—to 11,758,000 at the end of the Khrushchev era; after that the expansion slowed. Under Khrushchev the party thus swelled far beyond the bounds of the true elite. Moreover, Khrushchev tried to recruit those who, in the Marxist view, belonged in the party—not officials and white-collar workers, but genuine proletarians and collective farmers. In the last Stalin years only about 25 percent of the recruits were classified as "workers" and 15 percent as "kolkhozniki"; during the Khrushchev period the figures were about 42 percent and 18 percent.[84] This accorded with Khrushchev's idea that the simple people, under party leadership, should check the bureaucrats and managers.

The Khrushchev era saw much fluidity on the middle and upper levels,[85] although Khrushchev was unable to halt, but only retard, the aging of the cadres. The Central Committee, which was situated near the top, was subject to rapid turnover. About half its members who were chosen in 1956 were new, and more than half were new in 1961. Of 1,962 oblast first secretaries, only one-eighth had been in office since 1957.[86] The Presidium and the Secretariat were more fluid under Khrushchev than before or since. The reasons for changes were often obscure, but they could not have been merely the volition of the First Secretary, because he never ended up with a Presidium (or Central Committee) that was prepared simply to follow his orders. Under Khrushchev the Presidium became a relatively representative body, as it has remained, in which a number of persons are apparently entitled to a seat by virtue of their positions—the Prime Minister, the first secretary in the Ukraine or Kazakhstan, the head of the trade unions, and so on.

Khrushchev stood atop the party as a sort of semidictator. He was the follower of Lenin and Stalin in the sense that the leader incorporates the idea of the party and represents an unimpeachable authority, spokesman, and judge. There was a quite respectable cult of the Khrushchev personality; he stood up as the leader of world Communism, the maker of new rules, and the initiator of economic programs, and he often spoke to his underlings like an irate schoolmaster. Yet the

Khrushchev cult, unlike that of Stalin, never seems to have carried much conviction, and there were no signs of weeping or even shock when he was deposed. Moreover, his advocacy of a program and its execution were very different matters. He felt it necessary to argue at length for his proposals, to secure the clearance of the Central Committee (which he largely named, it seems, but which had no little independence) or of others outside it. Nobody publicly criticized him or his ideas, but many persons differed from him rather subtly, emphasizing things Khrushchev neglected or ignoring what he emphasized. Underlings quietly polemicized; for example, Leonid Ilichev, Khrushchev's ideological specialist, carried on a running feud with Mikhail Suslov for many years, propounding the Khrushchevian and the conservative ideological views respectively.

The limitations of Khrushchev's power were related to his inability to wield Stalin's sharp weapon of terror. Without it, the ability of the boss to secure obedience is definitely limited. Possibly Khrushchev would have liked to teach people to jump at his command by executing a few, but there was no longer enough passion or revolutionism in the system for top leaders to authorize one of their number to kill others; and even Stalin had had to secure the authorization of the Central Committee to unleash the police on his victims. Stalin could purge, as *Kommunist* commented after the Secret Speech, because opposition "would have been regarded . . . as an undermining of the unity of the Party and the entire state, which would have been extremely dangerous in view of the capitalist encirclement."[87] By Khrushchev's day, the party longed for stability and could only with greatest difficulty be convinced of the need to expel—in no case to punish further—a handful of Khrushchev's special enemies. They got minor jobs and quietly retired.

Khrushchev was also an uncharacteristic dictator in that he was basically a populist who disliked the elitism of his apparat.[88] He was personally typical of the Russian masses, a peasant at heart, scornful of bureaucrats and intellectuals and given to coarse speech and manners—quite different from the members of the new Soviet upper class. He was a sufficient believer in Marxism-Leninism to see special virtues in the workers and peasants. He reasoned that the agricultural machinery should be turned over to the collective farms because the peasants (always led by the party) could be trusted. He hoped that popular initiative would solve the problems of the economy, and like Lenin he postulated that popular control would keep the government pure. Disinterested activists from the people should both stimulate and check officials—an idea the officials did not greatly appreciate. In retirement, he philosophized that "only if a leadership is under public control will it be protected from actions which are incompatible with our Socialist doctrine and harmful to our Socialist way of life."[89]

He wanted to inspire and politically qualify the masses; for this purpose he increased the number of persons attending party schools from 6.2 million in 1957−58 to 36 million in 1964, the large majority of them not party members.[90]

He does not seem to have asked how public control could exist under party supremacy, but he did try to expand the sphere of decision making. In December 1959 he gave increased authority to the trade unions to protect workers from arbitrary actions, and production committees, which were nominally elected by the workers, were promised a voice in management—a promise that was soon neglected. The expanded Central Committee meetings have been mentioned; in 1959 Khrushchev also began to have many of the Central Committee debates published (after an unknown amount of editing). Khrushchev himself, as a genial, homey leader who was tough but earthy, kept in the public view, quite unlike Stalin. He delighted in talking to countless persons of all conditions all over the country; indeed, he probably travelled too much and troubled regional rulers by too frequent criticism.

Khrushchev was also sensitive to the privileges of the elite, and he tried to reduce inequalities in pay. He struck at the gilded youth, who were increasingly scornful of manual labor and presumably of manual laborers, by requiring (according to the 1958−59 educational reform) two to three years' work experience for nearly everyone who desired to enter higher education, the prime avenue for elite status (this was largely aborted in practice, of course, well before it was revoked after Khrushchev's fall).

As a populist, Khrushchev saw communism more as progress toward the abundant life than as a never-ending struggle justifying party supremacy. "I bring you goulash, that is the true revolution," he told the Hungarians in April 1964. In his philosophy, the new society was to come primarily through material abundance, not organization and thought reform as in the style of more ideologically oriented Communists, the hard-liners in the Soviet party, and the Maoists in China. He wished basically to rely on material incentives, and he respected specialists and men of action. Yet here again contradictions arose. Khrushchev wanted to negate the automotive age that was looming on the horizon for Russia as well as other industrialized societies, partly because of the material costs, but also evidently because the private automobile represented potential individualism and the erosion of party rule. Although Khrushchev repeatedly asked for more for the consumer, he never made, or never was able to make, a genuine shift in priorities. He either shared, or yielded to, the deep party fear that consumerism represented backsliding, revisionism, and a danger to the entire moral framework sustaining party supremacy. In the Soviet spectrum, Khrushchev was not consistently either "rightist" or "leftist," and his stress on rationalistic economic policies clashed fundamentally with his reliance on the ideological party rather than the legal state.

The same ambiguity clouded what has often been seen as Khrushchev's "liberalism." He realized the need for more freedom, yet feared any loss of party control; he wanted usefully controlled spontaneity and voluntary action, but only in the correct direction. He believed that there should be freedom and criticism under unquestioned party rule. Society should be loosened and liberalized, yet moralized and organized. As he put it in his recollections, "We wanted to guide the progress of the thaw so that it would stimulate only those creative forces which would contribute to the strengthening of socialism."[91] To state it otherwise, he wanted initiative and innovation without conceding freedom.

Khrushchev was no liberal. He made economic crimes punishable by death. There were anti-Semitic overtones in his policies; more than half the announced death sentences were given to Jews, although only one percent of the population was Jewish.[92] He tried to cut down the little private plots that were still left to the peasants, he closed most of the churches spared by Stalin, and he established irregular organs of justice that were to be guided less by law than by the party. From time to time he lashed out against writers, such as Boris Pasternak, or artists whose work flouted party canons. Like Stalin, Khrushchev gave the quack Lysenko the highest authority in the field of genetics.

Yet as "liberalizer," he deserves credit. His claim that there were no political prisoners in the Soviet Union was false, but he largely emptied the Stalinist labor camps (Brezhnev later partially refilled them). He was sometimes hostile to the writers' demands for freedom, but he placed the liberal poet Tvardovsky on the Central Committee, and in May 1959 he advised writers and artists to make their own decisions without party interference. He held occasional discussions with intellectuals in 1962 and 1963, in which he listened as well as talked, and he invited nonconformist artists to meet with the Central Committee—modest concessions that would have been unthinkable under Stalin and surprising under Brezhnev. He at least permitted a modernization of Soviet society, with interest groups steadily increasing their self-assertion vis-à-vis the party.[93] In the Khrushchev years groups grew up of reformist economists, jurists, philosophers, and sociologists, all with hopes of independence. Moreover, if de-Stalinization as it was managed by Khrushchev was always equivocal, it must be recognized that he at least grappled with a difficult and dangerous issue.

Near the end of his reign, in 1964, Khrushchev was much impressed by Danish society, its prosperity, productivity, and democratic equality; apparently he returned from Denmark with heretical new thoughts.[94] Politicians removed from power easily turn philosophical, but Khrushchev at least indicated a capacity for rethinking. For example, he stated that the readers, not the party, should criticize books, and he regretted having barred the publication of Pasternak's *Doctor Zhivago*.[95] He argued at length for disarmament, even if it was unilateral, and he may have had second thoughts about the entire Leninist adventure: "Sometimes we jokingly say that capitalism is rotten to the core. Yet these 'rotten' capitalists keep coming up with things which make our jaws drop in surprise. I would dearly love to surprise *them* with our achievements as often."[96] It must finally be held to his credit that he was accused, after his fall, of neglecting the class character of the state, that is, the absolutism of party rule.

THE FALL

Khrushchev was a man in a hurry, a seventy-year-old (by 1964) who wanted to remake society. Consequently he tried to do more (and do it faster) than he could, and made himself seem more of a failure than he was. In foreign policy, for example, he wanted to make spectacular advances toward Soviet world leadership, but his habit of mixing reasonableness with ultimatums obscured the fact that he presided over a real broadening of Soviet influence. At home he tried to change radically an inherently conservative system, but he failed to reckon with the interests of the people upon whom he had to rely, the apparatus on which his power rested.

There was some contradiction between moving the state and the economy and keeping his political basis solid. Khrushchev troubled the regional bosses by criticism that was often brutal. No real machine politician, he humiliated and irritated men while, unlike Stalin, leaving them in positions of power. He pressed subordinates into undertaking to achieve unrealistic goals and blamed them for failure. He moved people around indiscriminately, hoping to solve insoluble problems by new approaches or new personnel. Since agriculture was his bugaboo, he had five Ministers of Agriculture in six years; no one ever had a chance to do anything. He apparently caused excessive strain and high mortality among Soviet managers who were in later middle age.[97]

Khrushchev took ideology seriously enough to believe that the Soviet system should perform much better than it did. Seeing inadequacies, he tried to solve them by personal interference and reaped expectable disappointment. In another sense, Khrushchev did not understand the Communist system as a less engaged observer might—and as his successors seem to have done—but believed that there was a genuine relationship between the party and the progressive working class. Hence he was ultimately rejected by the apparatus of which he demanded more than it was prepared to deliver.

This raises the question how a leader who was not in a position to punish his subordinates freely, whose policies were uncongenial to many of them, and who irritated and annoyed them, could maintain himself on top. After all, he had no constitutional position and no definite tenure, and his policies were generally failures, at least in terms of expectations. The answer seems to lie in the Soviet system, which needs a definite leader, a strong and driving personality, if there is to be major change and a symbolic head even if the state is only to drift. Party unity demands a single directing figure at the summit, and party unity is sacred. The party always needs to present a united front to the world; hence whoever is at the apex must be supported. Stain used this feeling to destroy his rivals; it was always necessary to accept his version lest the party be endangered. Likewise, it seemed necessary to tolerate Khrushchev as leader so long as he was tolerable, because he was there as the spokesman of the party, and change was difficult and hazardous. His colleagues moved to oust him only under great pressure and many provocations from the overconfident old man.

In 1964, Khrushchev finally became intolerable to the oligarchs. At the same time an acceptable candidate was available to replace him as chief of the party. Brezhnev on July 15 was relieved of the duties of the ceremonial head of state and permitted to concentrate his attention on his position as second-in-command after the First Secretary. Beyond the causes already indicated—such as failures in agriculture and foreign affairs, disadvantages of economic decentralization, the intensification of the Sino-Soviet split, the division of the party, the insecurity of the cadres, the erratic style of leadership, the boastfulness and dilettantism— various other factors hurt Khrushchev's standing. De-Stalinization became injurious to him when those who had been more closely associated with Stalin were removed; then the anti-Stalin policy seemed damaging to the authority of the party while it undermined respect for the leader. After all, nearly everyone owed advancement to Stalin and the blood purges. The military men recovered from their gratitude for his program of de-Stalinization to resent Khrushchev's squeezing of their budget and prerogatives. At the same time, the mildness of his reprisals against the Anti-Party Group reassured conspirators that failure need not be fatal.

Nepotism played a part. Khrushchev placed his son-in-law Adzhubei in the Central Committee in 1961 and thereafter relied increasingly on his advice. He seems slated to have been made a Secretary in November 1964, a promotion that would have been an injury and insult to those who had worked their way up through long party careers. In the summer of 1964 Khrushchev sent Adzhubei to West Germany to prepare for a Khrushchev visit. The idea of reconciliation with the Germans had caused trouble for Beria and Malenkov in earlier years and was still suspect in the party because of emotional reflexes; that Adzhubei should be managing it over the heads of the regular authorities was one of the last straws.

Khrushchev was becoming increasingly accustomed to pushing personal schemes without consulting his near-peers, and demanding that his ideas be accepted in the name of party unity. Moreover, in October, he overdrew his resources by preparing several radical schemes. One was a major agricultural reorganization under the supervision of the trusted Adzhubei.[98] Another was a scheme finally to give definite priority to consumer goods that went well beyond Malenkov's modest shift in priorities. There were indications that Khrushchev envisioned a major (bloodless) purge at the top, or at least that he wanted to render the Presidium impotent by dividing it (as Stalin had done in his last years) into small commissions.[99]

There was no sign of an impending coup in the first days of October, however, and the ever-confident Khrushchev was certainly unaware that he was in trouble. But his opponents wanted to move before the Central Committee meeting scheduled for November could make changes they wished to avoid. Just how the conspiracy was put together has never been revealed, but Suslov, Khrushchev's longtime conservative antagonist, seems to have taken the lead. The conspirators gained the support of Shelepin, the head of the Party-State Control Commission, and of Semichastny, the head of the security forces. From the military, they needed only an assurance that it would not move.

Their opportunity came when Khrushchev, who had been travelling a large part of the summer, went on a vacation to Pitsunda on the Black Sea, leaving his lieutenants to mind the store. On October 3 Mikoyan, who had been a Politburo member since 1930, flew down to plead with him to compromise with the Presidium majority on economic policy, but Khrushchev refused to bend. On October 12 Mikoyan again tried to get Khrushchev to modify his position and again failed.[100] Khrushchev was summoned back to Moscow, met at the airport by Shelepin and Semichastny, and prevented from contacting potential supporters by the police.

The rest was practically a formality. On meeting with the Presidium, which was united against him, Khrushchev was offered an opportunity to retire honorably. He refused and insisted on appealing, as in 1957, to the Central Committee. However, his opponents were ready this time, having summoned a selected quorum of the committee. In a five-hour indictment, Suslov charged Khrushchev with disorganizing the party, undermining the Central Committee, creating a cult of his personality, failing to devise workable agricultural programs, neglecting heavy industry, pursuing irrational policies, and using nepotism to fill positions.[101] Khrushchev defended himself angrily and ineptly for several hours and was rejected, although not unanimously, early on October 14.

The change of leadership was announced in the papers on October 16 with the statement that Khrushchev had resigned because of age and health. An editorial in *Pravda* the following day offered (without naming the deposed chief) practically the only explanation that was ever officially given. The sins mentioned included subjectivism, bombast, neglect of facts, and hasty action. From that time on, no mention of Khrushchev appeared in the Soviet press, except for a semidenial of the authenticity of his memoirs, which were published in the West, until a tiny notice of his death on September 11, 1971. He was at most referred to obliquely, as when a *Pravda* writer[102] ridiculed the notion that communism was a full belly. Although Stalin is occasionally mentioned, the leader of the party for eleven years has been virtually erased, as though the oligarchs hated the man who tried to shake them up much more than the man who killed hundreds of thousands or millions of innocent and dedicated party members.

Chapter 7

Brezhnev and Conservative Communism

THE NEW REGIME

The Khrushchev succession was quite unlike that of Stalin. Khrushchev's fall was met with indifference by most and was welcomed by many who had come to find him wearisome, including intellectuals who were later to rue his passing. Contrary to the usual Soviet practice of blackening the fallen, he was simply erased. There were no public questions, practically no explanations, and life flowed on for the most part as though nothing had happened— "Khrushchevism without Khrushchev," as the Chinese put it.

Upon the death of Stalin, a new government had been set in place, but Khrushchev's passing brought only minor changes. No member of the Presidium was expelled because he was pro-Khrushchev. The only casualties were a few members of his immediate entourage, the familiar Adzhubei (who was ousted from the Central Committee and given a minor journalistic post), and Leonid Ilichev, whose misfortune was to have been raised up as a counter to the powerful Suslov.

The word was "collective leadership," as had been the case after Lenin and Stalin. The top man in the new government and Khrushchev's successor as First Secretary was Leonid Brezhnev. He was the inevitable choice. Of the other Presidium members, Shvernik was old and insignificant; Voronov, Podgorny, and Poliansky were definitely junior to Brezhnev; Suslov, the ideologue, evidently was not desirous of the top position; and Kosygin was a manager rather than a party apparatus-man. Although Brezhnev had never done anything very striking, he had generally been accepted as number two, he had broad experience in organizational work, industry, agriculture, and military affairs, and he had solid backing both in the party and in the armed forces. He may have been helped by the fact that he was a mediocre orator and no flamboyant personality; the impression of modesty and a lack of excessive ambition doubtless stood him in good stead, as it did Stalin.[1] He does not seem to have been a leader in the plot to unseat Khrushchev because he had returned from a tour of East Germany only two days earlier, but he was the generally accepted choice of his peers and hence started out with a legitimacy Khrushchev had long had to fight for.

The other major Khrushchev post, that of Chairman of the Council of Ministers, fell to Alexei Kosygin, a very different kind of leader. Kosygin was identified with economic administration through his entire career. At age twenty-five he entered the Leningrad Textile Institute. He rose rapidly under the aegis of Zhdanov; at thirty-three (1937) he became the director of a large factory and in 1939, only four years after receiving his diploma, he was the Commissar for the Textile Industry and a member of the Central Committee. In another four years he was chairman of the council of commissars of the Russian Republic, and in 1948 he was a full member of the Politburo. Shortly afterwards, misfortune struck. Zhdanov died, and his associates were mostly shot in 1949–50. Kosygin survived, perhaps because his daughter Liudmila was married to the son of a high KGB general, M. M. Gvishiani.[2] He was under a shadow, however. He was demoted to the status of candidate in the enlarged Politburo-Presidium of 1952, and was left out on the death of Stalin, presumably as a result of Malenkov's influence. Only in 1957 was he readmitted to the Presidium as a candidate member. In 1959 he became the chairman of Gosplan, and in 1960 a full member again, after eight years, of the top party body, and First Vice Chairman, after Khrushchev, of the Council of Ministers. He was obviously the ranking administrator in the party and the natural candidate to head the Council of Ministers.

Behind these two, who at first seemed semiequal in what was called the "Brezhnev-Kosygin regime," stood Mikhail Suslov. Four years older than Brezhnev, he was the senior member, after the departure of Mikoyan in 1965, of both the Presidium (since 1955) and the Secretariat (since 1947). He was the ideologist, which meant, in effect, neither a Leninist idealist nor an author of analyses of Marxism-Leninism, but a self-appointed defender of party orthodoxy. He was offended by Khrushchev's innovations and probably even more by Khrushchev's habit of going outside regular party channels and procedures; harshly authoritarian toward nonparty forces, he was a champion of democracy within the Presidium.

Since policy had had little to do with the dismissal of Khrushchev, the new leaders brought forward no particular new policy line, but promised only a change of style. However, there were immediate shifts of emphasis, and many steps were taken to undo objectionable actions. It was agreed, to avoid a threatening concentration of power, that the positions of First Secretary and

Leonid Ilich Brezhnev   *(World Wide Photo)*

Prime Minister should not be held by one person and that no Presidium member should be removed without general assent.[3] Informally, the Presidium asserted its definite superiority over the Secretariat, a superiority that had sometimes seemed questionable in Khrushchev's day. The superior standing of the Presidium, in which there has been more security of tenure than in the Secretariat, has been maintained and has provided some guarantee of collectivity of leadership.

After Khrushchev, the apparat, especially but not only in the upper levels, gained security and prestige; the new motto was "stability of cadres."[4] A number of persons who had been ousted by Khrushchev (or Kozlov) in preceding years were restored; for example, Kunaev regained the post of first secretary in Kazakhstan within a few weeks. The 1962−63 splitting of the party was rapidly undone, and the old committees and secretaries were put back in place. The 1961 rules for turnover in party organs lapsed. The policy of bringing in outsiders was dropped, and the idea of volunteers staffing or checking on the party was forgotten. Reports of discussions in the Central Committee ceased to appear; a thicker blanket of secrecy was drawn over party affairs in general, as though it was feared that publicity might increase disagreements. Whereas Khrushchev and his aides had mixed rather freely with Russians and foreigners, his successors retreated behind their walls except for occasional formal appearances. Other changes were quietly made. The post-Khrushchev leaders approved de-Stalinization so far as it was necessary to protect them from a new purge, but they wanted no sapping of party authority and no implied criticism of those who had risen under Stalin and by his grace, as all of them had. De-Stalinization gradually faded away, and a hesitant rehabilitation of Stalin began early in 1965, including a more favorable assessment of him as a war leader. A new edition of the history of the party, appearing in mid-1965, omitted most of the scanty criticism contained in the 1963 edition. The new line was that Stalin really didn't matter much, that the party had done great deeds through the 1930s and after, Stalin notwithstanding, and that the so-called "cult of personality" had nothing to do with socialism. The Ministry of the Interior, which had been notorious since Stalin's day and had been dissolved under Khrushchev in 1960, was restored. Voroshilov, Stalin's former pal, who had been blamed in 1961 as a member of the Anti-Party Group, was honored in May 1965. In 1967 a party decree in effect provided for the destruction of any or all documents referring to the Stalin era, 1924−53.[5]

In foreign and military affairs, Khrushchev's departure brought no major change.[6] As in the years since the Cuban crisis, there were no more adventures, but the Soviet Union continued its gradual buildup of strategic power toward parity with the United States. Rapprochement with West Germany was postponed. The Chinese, like many others, thought that since Khrushchev had made their quarrel a personal affair, his removal should open the way to reconciliation, and polemics were halted on both sides. Chou En-lai came to Moscow for the November 7 celebration of Lenin's revolution, but his talks with Soviet leaders produced no agreement. The clash of policies and philosophies was too strong, the Russians were unwilling to give up their claim to leadership, and the Chinese were even less willing to bow to the new men than to Khrushchev. After a few months, polemics were resumed, despite a Soviet commitment to help North Vietnam in the escalating war. In 1965 detente was placed on the back burner.

The initial impression made by the new government was one of businesslike rationality; only gradually, beginning about a year later, did the primacy of ideology, that is, party control, become apparent. Possibly because of uncertainty of direction and lack of assurance in power, perhaps partly to undercut any regrets about Khrushchev's fall, the new leaders permitted a renewed thaw in the arts; Soviet writers briefly enjoyed as much freedom as they had at any time since the late 1920s. The charlatan Lysenko's authority over Soviet genetics was finally overthrown; science was now to rule. The editor of *Pravda*, A. M. Rumiantsev, encouraging the new dispensation for nonorthodoxy, advocated tolerance and experimentation, including "free expression and the clash of opinions,"[7] with a degree of liberalism that had hardly been seen on the Soviet scene since the first days of the Soviet order.

Rumiantsev was rebutted and chided for lack of party spirit ("partiinost"), but for the time being he was left in place. In February and March, *Pravda* and *Izvestiia* were taking different views of cultural freedom, with the party paper paradoxically taking the liberal view. Through the summer, the controllers were winning the battle. In July Brezhnev took a stand by lauding Zhdanov, the hatchet man of the Stalinist controls on the arts in the later 1940s, and in September he placed in charge of the Central Committee's Department of Science and Education Sergei Trapeznikov, an apologist for Stalinism. On September 9 Rumiantsev wrote in favor of literary freedom, but with much more qualification than half a year before, and on September 22 his dismissal was announced.

A much more emphatic signal to the intellectuals to observe proper limits was the arrest in mid-September of two writers, Andrei Siniavsky and Yuli Daniel. They were accused of having published anti-Soviet writings abroad. This practice was not prohibited by any specific Soviet law and it had been tolerated during the Khrushchev era; in addition, the writings in questions were only symbolic, not specific attacks on the party-state. Nevertheless, the two authors were brought to trial early in 1966, the first public "exposure" of a dissident writer and the first trial explicitly for writings in Soviet history. It was also a landmark in another way. At the trial, the accused protested their innocence, despite processing by the police, and brought witnesses in their defense.[8] The old submissiveness was gone; this marked the beginning of a long-term standoff between the party and a sector of the creative intelligentsia that was to become reminiscent of the running battle between the tsarist state and leading journalists and writers.

In the control of the economy, there was a similar tendency toward conservatism after an initial period of uncertainty. Khrushchev's proposed reorganizations were immediately buried, of course, and the attack on the peasants' private plots ceased. In March Brezhnev announced a new deal for agriculture—an end to reorganizations and campaigning, fixed delivery quotas, more freedom of production on the private plots, better procurement prices, better pay, and more investment in agriculture.[9] The collective farms were to be allowed to plan their own production without official interference. Results were meager, however, and it soon appeared that the party was to secure "voluntary" compliance with central directives.

Early moves to reform the administration of industry likewise pointed toward a degree of liberalization and more freedom for producers. Under the sponsorship of Kosygin, it was announced in January 1965 that the Liberman reform proposals would be applied to 336 enterprises in light industry. The proposals of Professor Ye. Liberman, a Kharkov economist, centered on production for sale rather than to fill quotas, and the judging of performance primarily by the profit an enterprise could turn in. These ideas, which were not entirely new, had first appeared in *Pravda*, on September 2, 1962; after much discussion Khrushchev, in 1964, had decreed a trial in two clothing factories. The result was a large increase in both the amount and the quality of their output, and the new government seemed disposed to extend the new policy as far as might be feasible in the interest of rationalizing and stimulating production.

The debate went forward through the spring and summer of 1965, with Kosygin and his followers trying to reevaluate economic administration in terms of getting the maximum output, while party men were increasingly viewing "goulash communism" as a perversion and a danger. Suslov in particular was wary of economic reform so far as it implied a profit motive or stress on economic as opposed to political calculation, while Podgorny sided with Kosygin.

In September an anemic compromise emerged that was touted as a great reform. The economic councils invented by Khrushchev, which had already been whittled down to an extra link in the chain of command, were finally abolished. The old economic ministries, which had largely been brought back already, were restored to their old positions. Many of the party men who had been left adrift by the abolition of the councils were compensated by places in the revived ministries. A number of ministers from Stalin's time were reinstated, for example, V. P. Sotov, Minister of Food Industry since 1939, and A. A. Ishkov, Minister of Fisheries since 1940 (and to the present). N. K. Baibakov, who had been removed from the chairmanship of Gosplan in 1957, was put back in charge of that State Planning Commission (and he was still there in 1977).

The other side of the reform was more freedom for managers of enterprises to manage rationally, with fewer directives from above and with rewards for sales and profits rather than the traditional "val," the quantitative fulfillment of goals. However, mandatory planning was retained for basic production schedules, investments, innovation, and other indicators; thus the liberalizing reform was slowly and hesitantly introduced, and it was enfeebled and qualified as it spread. The controllers at all levels resisted the loss of any part of their powers, while the managers themselves seemed to have no great yen for the responsibilities brought by greater freedom. In the outcome, bureaucratic and party control emerged undiminished.

In the light of these tendencies, it would have been surprising if the leader of the party had not been able to lift himself above his colleagues. In October 1964 Brezhnev was very much dependent on the support of the Presidium and the Central Committee. In November he had to welcome into the Presidium two entrants who were more or less disagreeable to him, Shelest and Shelepin. The latter, who was the more important because of his help in the expulsion of Khrushchev, could not be denied, but he was an obvious threat. Party Secretary, head of the Control Commission, and Deputy Chairman of the Council of Ministers, twelve years younger than Brezhnev, he seemed clearly the man of the future. Moreover, Brezhnev and Kosygin were apparently virtual equals, each dominant in his separate sphere; correspondingly, Brezhnev handled relations with foreign Communist countries and Kosygin dealt with non-Communist states. There was some contest between the two, faintly like the contest between Khrushchev and Malenkov in 1953—55, with Kosygin pulling for autonomy of the state apparatus from the oversight of Brezhnev's party. In the summer of 1965, it briefly seemed that Kosygin might have the upper hand over a weakened Brezhnev.

Brezhnev was able gradually to assert the leading role of the party in various spheres, however, and consequently his own preeminence. There was more talk of discipline; this word, which had disappeared from the holiday slogans from October 1961 through April 1965, was again put forward in October 1965.[10] A significant and symptomatic reaffirmation of party supremacy was the withdrawal of the state committees on radio-television, cinema, publishing, and foreign cultural relations from the Council of Ministers and hence from governmental supervision, to be placed directly under the Central Committee.[11] From April to December 1975, more than half the Central Committee department heads were replaced, mostly by old-time Brezhnev associates.[12]

The marked tightening in cultural policy in the last months of 1965 and the economic compromise represented victories for the party apparatus and Brezhnev. In December, the superior position of the First Secretary was made patent by his victory over two rivals within the Secretariat. Mikoyan retired, with honors but under pressure, from the position of ceremonial head of state, which he had held only since July 1964. Podgorny, who was remarkable in that his political life had begun only fifteen years earlier, at age forty-seven, and who had been Brezhnev's rival in the Secretariat since 1963, was elevated to that dignified but relatively impotent position, losing his power base in the Secretariat. He remained influential, and at times in subsequent years he was accounted second only to Brezhnev, but he could not be a threat. An even greater victory for Brezhnev was the dismantling of Shelepin's Party-State Control Commission—a slightly indirect way of cutting down a dangerous personage—and Shelepin also lost his post as Deputy Chairman of the Council of Ministers. He remained dangerous, or at least disliked, and his standing was whittled away until he was removed from the Politburo (as it became again) in April 1975. The result, in any event, was that a little over a year after Khrushchev disappeared, the succession was settled on Leonid Brezhnev.

LEONID ILICH BREZHNEV

The man who has headed the party longer than anyone else except Lenin and Stalin was the first top leader of the generation that reached maturity after the revolution (he was born on December 19, 1906). Like Khrushchev, he came from Russian stock in the Ukraine. Also like Khrushchev, he can point to an authentic proletarian (metalworker) background. He got a fairly good education and graduated from a Kursk institute for land utilization in 1927. His introduction to party work occurred in the collectivization campaign in Belorussia and the Urals region. In 1930, however, he left this activity when it was becoming hot. He may have been sent briefly to an agricultural institute in Moscow.[13] In a turn that is left unexplained in his official biography, he began a second professional training as a metallurgical engineer in Dneprodzerzhinsk in 1931. Like Khrushchev, he became party organizer for his institute, although he joined the party only in 1931. Unlike Khrushchev, he graduted with a technical diploma in 1935. Sometime in this period he married. In 1935–36 he belatedly did military service and then, in the middle of the purges, began a rapid rise on the party-apparatus ladder.

Brezhnev's first consequential political position was that of vice chairman of the executive committee (administration) of the Dneprodzerzhinsk city soviet; he was a beneficiary of the fact that most of the upper strata in the Ukraine was wiped out in 1937–38. In 1938 he became a full-time party organizer; moving to the regional center of Dnepropetrovsk, he became first a section chief, then one of the secretaries of the regional party committee. This advancement was owed to Khrushchev, who was then Stalin's delegate in the Ukraine, and to Khrushchev's aide, Korotchenko. Brezhnev was charged at first with propaganda, and subsequently with munitions production, a field that was more in line with his training. He was busy at this job when the Germans invaded on June 22, 1941. Although the purges created vacancies for him, he is not known to have participated in them.

The years in Dnepropetrovsk, to which Brezhnev returned briefly after the war, laid the basis for his subsequent ascent. There he worked with many persons, such as Kirilenko, who was later to become a Politburo member and Secretary, and the eventual Minister of the Interior Nikolai A. Shchelokov, an apartment neighbor of Brezhnev's, who later occupied important posts in the Central Committee apparatus and the security forces. This Dnieper clan held together and followed Brezhnev in his subsequent career.

The war years saw Brezhnev rising in the party and adding to his circle of associates. He entered service as a colonel and political officer, at the age of thirty-four, with duties involving indoctrination, morale, party management, and reporting. Marshal Zhukov gave witness to his bravery and dedication, and he earned four medals and was promoted to major-general. He was the only member of the post-Khrushchev Politburo to spend the entire war at the front. While he was in the Caucasus, he owed his advancement to Mekhlis, Stalin's hated assistant and party controller in the military.[14] He worked at one time with Mikhail Suslov, who was then party leader in Stavropol, and made friends or allies of many military men who were subsequently to achieve distinction, including Grechko, who was later Minister of Defense, Sergei Gorshkov, later naval chief, Air Force General Moskalenko, and Yepishev, later chief of political controls in the armed forces.

After marching in the victory parade in Moscow, Brezhnev remained in the army a year. As the leader of political administration in the newly acquired Carpatho-Ukraine, his task was to help Sovietize the unruly population. In August 1946 he went back to his old Dnieper territory and, rising steadily, in November 1947 became first secretary of the Dnepropetrovsk region. One of the twenty-six Ukrainian territorial bosses under Khrushchev and Kaganovich, he worked on the reconstruction of industry and the recollectivization of agriculture. When Khrushchev was transferred back to Moscow as Secretary in December 1949, Brezhnev went with him and, attached to the Central Committee, got his first taste of power at the center. He was moved again before he could really dig into his new job, however; the following July he took a big step upward in prestige to the first secretaryship of the Moldavian SSR (formerly Bessarabia). He must have been very successful in the re-Sovietization of this province, which had been acquired in 1939 and temporarily lost during the war, because after twenty-seven months he was recalled to Moscow with a spectacular promotion over the heads of many persons who were senior to him. At the Eighteenth Congress he was made a member of the Central Committee, a candidate member of the enlarged Presidium, and a member of the also expanded Secretariat. What particular responsibilities he had is not known.

Not surprisingly, after Stalin's death, Brezhnev was demoted. He had risen too fast for the oligarchs, and he was a protege of Khrushchev, who lost his leadership of the Moscow region in the reassortment of March 6, 1953. Brezhnev was excluded from the Presidium and Secretariat to become vice chief of the political directorate of the armed forces with responsibility for the navy. However, he was made a lieutenant general, and he had an opportunity to strengthen his relations with the military. Very soon, in any case, Brezhnev's career was again swinging upward. In February 1954 Khrushchev sent him to Kazakstan as second secretary (under P. K. Ponomarenko); there he was put in charge, practically speaking, of the Virgin Lands program. Brezhnev was successful, because good weather came to the aid of his hard work. In August 1955, after Khrushchev's victory over Malenkov, Ponomarenko, who was a Malenkov adherent, was removed to permit Brezhnev to become the boss of that important republic. His chief associate was a half-Russian engineer, Dinmukhamed Kunaev, who was to be a member of the Politburo during the Brezhnev era.

Kazakstan, with its treacherous weather, was a wrecker of careers, but Brezhnev left in good time. In February 1956 he headed the Kazakstan delegation to the Twentieth Congress and was rewarded with candidate membership in the Presidium. He also regained his membership in the Secretariat, in which he worked on heavy industry and armaments. In the June 1957 crisis, Brezhnev cautiously sided with Khrushchev, and he was made a full member in the reformed Presidium. He was now near the top, with a circle of powerful friends, including candidate Presidium members Kirilenko and Korotchenko, Admiral Gorshkov, and Marshals Malinovsky, Moskalenko, Yeremenko, and Grechko, the last of whom had recently become Deputy Minister of Defense.

There was not much left for Brezhnev to achieve, short of the displacement of his patron. In 1958 he became deputy chairman of the Russian Republic's Buro. He was a principal speaker at the Twenty-First Congress, and he was the keynoter at the Lenin birthday commemoration in April 1959. But in May 1960, when Khrushchev was in trouble, Brezhnev was elevated, but in the process weakened by being named the head of state, with the loss of his position on the Secretariat. This move may be ascribed to his dangerous rival, Frol Kozlov. As usual, however, Brezhnev made the best of his position. As formal President, he received new exposure, travelled widely, met many people, and added to his prestige. However, he was doubtless happy that Kozlov's disability enabled him to return to the Secretariat in June 1963 as the ranking leader next to Khrushchev.

As a Secretary, Brezhnev seems to have dealt with military affairs and the armaments industry, but before his accession to primacy no one ever associated him with any particular ideas or policies. He appears to have been the model apparatchik, the good executor of the will of his superiors, who at the same time built a circle of his own and was a devoted servant of the party and/or an industrious careerist. His personality emerged from behind his career far less than did those of Lenin, Stalin, or Khrushchev. Brezhnev was the son of the new gray day.

THE BREZHNEV ERA: CONSOLIDATION

It is difficult to stabilize the distribution of political power in an oligarchy.[15] In a fluid situation, power gives the means of increasing itself up to limits that are set by personalities and the political system. The leading Secretary has some authority to promote persons who are favorable to himself and demote others, and the exercise of this power naturally increases it. Moreover, the party feels a continual need for a strong leader to sustain its rule over the bureaucracy, military, and security forces.[16] A supreme leader seems indispensable to fix the powers of various persons and agencies and to adjudicate among them, and any attack on the leader may be equated with an attack on the party.

Like all previous party leaders, Brezhnev strengthened his position fairly steadily for a number of years before reaching a sort of plateau; its consolidation was manifest at the Twenty-Third Congress, in March 1966. By the rules, the congress should have met by October 1965, but it was postponed to March. Brezhnev was thus returning to the Leninist practice of holding congresses in March, although he did not propose to follow Lenin in having yearly congresses or in encouraging discussion of issues.

The 4,942 delegates must have found Moscow's nightlife more entertaining than the speeches. Brezhnev was the chief reporter and plainly the man in charge. His dry report, which came to eighty-two pages, pointed out no new directions. The most striking changes he made were conservative or literally reactionary in returning to the ways of Stalinist days. Brezhnev's title was upgraded from "First Secretary" to "General Secretary," a designation that had previously been used only by Stalin; although the title carried connotations of authority, the office carried no insignia and no specific powers. The Presidium also resumed its earlier name of Politburo. Nostalgia for days of greater conviction and clarity may have motivated this restoration.[17] The Russian Buro, which Khrushchev had established to give himself additional channels of influence, was abolished. The Russian Republic was thus no longer to be formally on a level with the Ukraine and other smaller republics, but was made roughly equivalent to the Soviet Union; this move represented both centralization and an assertion of Russian superiority. Other essentially authoritarian changes included rescinding Khrushchev's rules about the renewal of party bodies and the limits on re-election, a stiffening of the conditions for entry into the party (it required sponsors of the recruit to be members of five years' instead of three years' standing), and the restriction of entry by young members to those who had passed through the Komsomol. A rule change provided for the calling of conferences between congresses, as Lenin had done, but this option has never been used.

Personnel changes considerably solidified the position of the General Secretary. Mikoyan and Shvernik left the Politburo. Kirilenko, who was close to Brezhnev, became the Secretary in charge of cadres. Pelshe, a Latvian who had joined the party in 1916, was brought into the Politburo, presumably as a last link to the prerevolutionary struggle after the departure of Mikoyan and Shvernik. Kunaev, Brezhnev's aide in Kazakstan, became a candidate member. The 1961 Central Committee, the group that had checked Khrushchev and approved his ouster, was retained nearly intact; one of the twenty-three survivors who was excluded was the liberal writer Tvardovsky. As usual, the Central Committee was enlarged, to 195 full and 165 alternate members, to make room for new claimants without expelling people.

Of the members of the Politburo, only Brezhnev, Kosygin, and Podgorny took the floor, while much time was given to harmless orations by leaders of the eighty-six foreign parties that were represented by delegations. The 1959 and 1961 congresses at least heard controversial talk and some new ideas, but there was no novelty in 1966. The big issues—Stalin, Khrushchev, the goals of the party, literature, Sino-Soviet relations, agriculture, and the like—were sidestepped or at most given a little bombast. There was hardly a word about Stalin. Khrushchev was flayed by indirection as a traitor to the party because he permitted subversive forces to arise. Khrushchev's party program, his thesis of the noninevitability of war, and the "state of the whole people" were neglected. There were some promises of material benefits, but Khrushchev's ambitious economic goals were scaled down. Consumers were to get more not because of any changes of priorities, but because of better use of resources, and the "metal-eaters" (who were no longer so called) were reassured. There was no name-calling against Peking, but regret over the difficulties, and "revisionism" was regarded as more dangerous than "dogmatism." The world outside was viewed as tense and dangerous (with the justification of the mounting war in Indochina), and speakers urged closer control of contacts with the West. Mikhail Sholokhov regretted that the dissident writers Siniavsky and Daniel, who had recently been tried and sentenced to labor camps, had not been shot.[18] Altogether it was a basically conservative conclave that indicated the settling down of the party after the post-Stalin transitional flux.

After the congress, not everything went strongly in the conservative direction. Some resistance to creeping re-Stalinization was evident. The liberal writers stirred a little. The journals that nurtured them, *Novy Mir* and *Yunost*, were under fire and rather subdued in late 1965 and the first part of 1966, but in the summer of 1966 they were able to revert to their semiliberal style. Party publications emphasized collegiality of leadership in a manner that suggested resistance to the supremacy of the General Secretary.

If there was a hiatus in the strengthening of the leader's position, it was brief. Brezhnev's sixtieth birthday in December 1966 was made the occasion for effusive praise and fulsome cultivation of the personality of the "Hero of the Soviet Union." The following April, Brezhnev's longtime friend Marshal Grechko became Minister of Defense, making the removal of the General Secretary a remote possibility. Soon afterwards, Shelepin was further weakened by his appointment as head of the trade unions, and a few months later he left the Secretariat. Shelepin's associate and successor as chief of police forces, Semichastny, was replaced by a Brezhnev man, Yuri Andropov. Brezhnev was hence assured on all flanks.

In 1968 the party position hardened, as it had in 1956–57, in response to events in Eastern Europe. In December 1967 the Czechoslovak boss, Anton Novotny, was in deep trouble. Brezhnev went to Prague, but refused to help him, and somewhat carelessly told the Czech comrades that it was their affair. There followed the election of Alexander Dubček to lead the party, the breakdown of controls, talk of "Communism with a human face," and the "Prague Spring." The Soviet party and the more conservative Eastern European satellites, which saw their power structures menaced, rumbled ominously. In April the Central Committee decreed general mobilization against "creeping counterrevolution." In an attempt to reach agreement, Czech leaders met on July 23, at a border town, with almost the entire Soviet Politburo. Brezhnev evidently felt unable to negotiate himself, or preferred to spread the responsibility. After three days of wrangling, an agreement of sorts was reached, but the Czechs continued on their course and the Soviets marched in during the night of August 20–21 to "normalize" the wayward satellite.

The invasion of Czechoslovakia was the first such gross violation of international norms since Stalin attacked Finland in November 1939. The repression of the Hungarians in 1956 had been less flagrant because Soviet troops had been stationed in the country since the world war. The decision to intervene militarily was not easy, and it seems to have been taken by a vote in the Politburo. Brezhnev wavered, it is said, until the end. When the decision was made, on August 16–17, Brezhnev, Voronov, Kirilenko, Shelepin, and Shelest were in favor; Kosygin, Mazurov, Podgorny, and Suslov were reportedly opposed,[19] mostly because of their fear of repercussions on the world Communist movement.

The successful, nearly bloodless, disciplining of Czechoslovakia restored or increased the authority of Brezhnev and the party. The awareness that Russians were ready and willing to move quieted the voices of dissent in Eastern Europe. The movement for freedom in art and literature was cut short, especially in Eastern

Europe, where it had progressed the most, but also in the Soviet Union. Economic reformism, a strong point of the Czechoslovak liberals, became economic revisionism. The party called for orthodoxy and discipline, with the implication to East Europeans that there was no choice, and to the Soviet people that slackness was dangerous and unpatriotic. The General Secretary achieved his strongest claim to immortality through the ''Brezhnev Doctrine,'' the claim that by the dictates of ''proletarian internationalism'' it was the right and duty of one socialist country (if it was large and strong enough) to come to the aid of socialism in another socialist country, by invasion if need be.

The compression wave rose through 1969–70. However, the Soviet economy was not advancing very well, or not nearly so well as the leadership thought it should. After some post-Khrushchev recovery, the rate of growth of industrial production had tended to ease; in 1969 an increase of only 7 percent was claimed, the lowest since the beginning of the Five Year Plans. Still more serious was the fact that the return from new input of capital was steadily decreasing, while it was becoming increasingly difficult to raise production simply by bringing new masses of labor into the mines and factories. Moreover, the technological gap, which in the golden age of Soviet space exploits had seemed to be narrowing, was now manifestly widening. Hence it seemed to be unavoidable either to permit more initiative and innovation in the economy by releasing producers from party controls or to expand the importation of Western technology and perhaps capital.

The second alternative was chosen, and it became more feasible as international tensions decreased in 1969 and afterward. The indignation caused by the occupation of Czechoslovakia dissipated perhaps more rapidly than the Soviet leaders expected. And in 1969 the United States turned from escalation to deescalation in Vietnam. Negotiations were begun with the United States regarding the limitation of nuclear arms, and with West Germany on the normalization of relations. In July 1971 President Nixon announced a forthcoming visit of reconciliation to Communist China. Sino-Soviet relations had deteriorated sharply after 1966, reaching their nadir with veritable battles on the border in 1969, and it was necessary for the Soviet Union to forestall a possible Sino-American combination. Hence Nixon was invited to Moscow in May 1972.

The policy of détente with the West, especially West Germany and the United States, seems to have been Brezhnev's own—perhaps the only policy clearly identifiable with him. Brezhnev took the lead in negotiations with Chancellor Willy Brandt in the summer of 1970. Kosygin, who had once been the chief negotiator with the non-Communist countries and the sponsor of such a diplomatic success as the Indo-Pakistan settlement of 1965, was hardly to be seen. In 1971 Brezhnev received Brandt quite on his own, with the assistance of his personal secretaries, especially Alexandrov-Agentov. In 1972 Brezhnev signed agreements with Nixon as though he were head of state, although his only formal governmental position was that of one of fifteen members of the Presidium of the Supreme Soviet.

Brezhnev laid great stress on the meeting with Nixon and the numerous cooperative agreements that resulted from it; it also contributed a Cadillac to the General Secretary's stable of aristocratic vehicles, which already included Rolls-Royce, Mercedes-Benz, and Citroen-Maserati. In 1971 Brezhnev began extensive foreign travels to Paris, Bonn, Washington, and other major capitals, which he acomplished with obvious pleasure and self-confidence. Brezhnev showed a new sensitivity to foreign opinion; the most striking Soviet contribution to détente was the permission, for the first time since the 1920s, for considerable numbers of Soviet citizens to emigrate; some tens of thousands of Jews were released yearly beginning in 1971.

The Brezhnev personality cult had meanwhile been thriving. After the overthrow of Khrushchev, Brezhnev proceeded to exalt Lenin, riding, so to speak, on his coattails somewhat as Stalin had done when he was first climbing to supremacy. The founder of the party was built up as an exalted father-figure; the climax came on his hundredth birthday in April 1970, which became the occasion of countless movies, poems, articles, feats of emulative production, and a general apotheosis. The worship of the departed party leader implied at least enormous respect for his successor, and it gradually became customary to cite banalities from the speeches of Brezhnev, just as Lenin was almost obligatorily cited in serious writing. There were indications of resistance in the summer of 1970. Brezhnev had stated in April and repeated in June that a party congress would be held that year, but he either changed his mind or was overruled, since it was announced in July that the next congress would meet in April 1971. He did not appear to have been weakened, however. It was probably more important that he apparently acted in June 1970 as de facto Chairman of the Council of Ministers.[20] Brezhnev alone signed the published draft of the new Five Year Plan.[21] Two volumes of his speeches were published—for some reason they had come out earlier in Bulgaria—since the leader still had to lay claim to being a theoretician. At the end of the year Brezhnev set a new precedent by giving the Soviet people a New Year's message in the name of the party.

The Twenty-Fourth Congress, which met from March 30 through April 9, 1971, further sealed the Brezhnev ascendancy.[22] His report this time ran to 107 pages. For the first time, Brezhnev was able to add his own men to the Politburo; Kunaev, Shcherbitsky, Kulakov, and Grishin, the new full members, were all party apparatchiks who were apparently linked to Brezhnev. Old Politburo members were kept, and the Secretariat remained unchanged. Suslov was announced as the second-ranking Secretary. In the pronouncements at the congress, the accent was on the authority of the Central Committee and the maximum utilization of the "old cadres"[23] (between 1968 and 1971 only two regional first secretaries had been removed because of unsatisfactory work).

The party rules were changed to assert more clearly the superiority of the party over the state apparatus by giving party organizations in ministries the right of control in fulfilling political directives. Scientists and others were chided for their failure to combat "bourgeois ideology," and party organizations in scientific institutes, cultural organs, and the like acquired rights of administrative control. With respect to the minorities, the congress stressed the "rapprochement" of the Soviet peoples.[24] Another favor for the apparatus-men was an extension of the intervals between the conferences and congresses that conceivably might fire them. Congresses at the all-Union and republic levels were to meet only every five years (confirming a practice that had applied since 1961), and at lower levels every two to three years, instead of every two years at the district and yearly at the local level. Only primary organizations without paid staff were to have yearly election meetings. Brezhnev also announced a screening of the membership through the renewal of party cards. This was potentially a Stalinesque purge, but times had changed. It did not get under way until two years later and affected only 2.4 percent of membership, many of them doubtless already dropouts.[25]

With the ruling apparatus thus fixed, there was naturally no move to change anything of importance. There was even less discussion of real problems than in 1966; their existence was hardly admitted aside from the need to work more efficiently in agriculture and in industry. Instead, it was implied that change was superfluous since socialism was victorious and the transformation of society had been completed. Brezhnev spoke of the Soviet Union as a "developed socialist society," without mentioning when this condition, which was new to Marxist terminology, had been achieved or how it was defined.[26] This phrase became standard, and it carried vague implications of utopia nearly achieved.

A logical conclusion would be that the all-out drive for increased production that had characterized the first Five Year Plans was no longer necessary, and that the time had come to fulfill the old promise of material abundance. The Ninth Five Year Plan was, indeed, rather more modest than its predecessors, proposing an increase of from 37 to 40 percent in the national income, and the draft plan, for the first time in Soviet history, promised a slightly larger (2 to 3 percent) rate of increase for consumer goods than for producer goods. This concession probably resulted, however, less from an increased willingness to sacrifice power to welfare than from the lesson of the Polish riots of December 1970, wherein workers enraged by price increases had toppled the government of Gomulka. Within a year, in any case, the slight priority of the production of consumer goods had been reversed.[27] Regarding the economic reform of 1965, whereby managers were to have a little more autonomy, there was some difference in emphasis between Kosygin, who favored strictly economic incentives, and Brezhnev, who emphasized party control and moral incentives. Kosygin now followed Podgorny in precedence, however, and the Brezhnev approach prevailed. The planning reform continued to fade in the face of a new campaign for raising production by "socialist competition" and qualified recentralization through "production associations."

By the latter part of 1971, adulation for the General Secretary was virtually unqualified. Typically, a worker was quoted as saying, "It is difficult to convey the emotion and joy with which my friends received the words of Comrade L. I. Brezhnev."[28] His power was by no means total, however. It was often rumored in 1969–71 that Brezhnev wished to become the head of the state apparatus, as Lenin, Stalin, and Khrushchev had been, either as Chairman of the Council of Ministers or as President of a new state council, but these hopes, if they existed, were not yet realized. He was likewise unable to remove persons who were displeasing to him from the Politburo. His first victory in this connection was to bring down Shelest in May 1972. Shelest was replaced by Shcherbitsky as first secretary of the Ukraine, and a general purge of the Ukrainian party followed.[29] The obvious reason for the fall of Shelest was his opposition to the Nixon visit (for which Brezhnev had advance sanction from the Central Committee). Perhaps a more operative reason was that in building up his Ukrainian satrapy, he had offered some opposition to Russification and had sought a little more autonomy than Moscow wanted to yield.[30] In September Vasily Mshavanadze, the Georgian first secretary, was replaced by Eduard Shevarnadze, a Brezhnevite and former KGB man. Here, too, localism must have played a part, although the accusations of corruption launched against Mzhavanadze were doubtless well founded.

BREZHNEV IN COMMAND

Brezhnev made none of Khrushchev's mistakes—no personally sponsored panaceas or grand schemes whose failure would discredit him; no flamboyant declarations; no attempt to be the universal expert; and above all, no big reorganizations to make the apparatus groan. But little by little he built up his position, advancing friends and easing rivals or potential opponents out of power, usually by slow degrees. In April 1973 Shelest, who had previously been removed from his Ukrainian base, was excluded from the Politburo and became insignificant. Voronov, the agricultural specialist on the Politburo, was also dislodged, probably because he advocated fundamental reform in agriculture. At the same time, the Politburo and the Brezhnev party within it were strengthened by the addition of Foreign Minister Andrei Gromyko, Defense Minister Grechko, and KGB Chief Andropov. In April 1975 the formerly dangerous Shelepin was finally pushed out; perhaps the fiasco of his trip to England, where he was berated as a police assassin, provided the impetus for his overdue removal. The last potential challenger, youthful (fifty-nine years old) Dmitry Poliansky, was dropped from the Politburo two years later, at the Twenty-Fifth Congress. Thus, without any major Khrushchev-style shakeup, Brezhnev achieved a Politburo that was favorable to himself, consisting of friends and allies plus a few old holdovers, chiefly Kosygin and Podgorny. Shelepin and Poliansky, it may be noted, had been two of the youngest members of the Politburo.

The Brezhnev personality cult continued to spiral a little higher. On the thirtieth anniversary of victory in World War II, May 8, 1975, he presented himself with the titles of marshal and general of the army, ranks never achieved by Khrushchev. It was later revealed that he was Chairman of the Defense Council, that is, commander-in-chief. It had been discovered that one of the decisive battlegrounds of the war was the North Caucasus, where then Lieutenant-Colonel Brezhnev had played a heroic role. At parades, his portraits were the largest of all, sometimes as large as Lenin's. His insipid speeches were printed in huge editions in handsomely bound volumes and pamphlets (they were revised both to make Brezhnev seem wiser and to improve the standing of the Russians in relation to other nationalities of the Soviet Union) and were made available on records for those who preferred to listen. At the Twenty-Fifth Congress, March-April 1976, Young Pioneers recited verses of gratitude to him; he received a thunderous ovation;* and speakers again and again dwelt on his exemplary and noble qualities, his leadership and sublime achievements, his spiritual beauty, modesty, and untiring activity on behalf of the people. The accolades exceeded anything Khrushchev had ever harvested.

New entrants to the Politburo included Dmitri Ustinov, Central Committee Secretary in charge of the defense industry, who became Minister of Defense shortly afterwards, on the death of Marshal Grechko. He was made a marshal a few months later. He was aligned with Suslov rather than with Brezhnev, but the other two entrants, Leningrad party chief Grigory Romanov and Azerbaidzhan chief and professional KGB leader Geidar Aliev (a candidate member) were close Brezhnev supporters, as were two new Secretaries. In the Politburo, Brezhnev had no clear second-in-command; perhaps he was reluctant to tap an heir apparent (he became seventy at the end of 1976). Suslov was sometimes treated as the second figure in the party, but since he was three years older than Brezhnev, he was no potential successor. Kirilenko, who was a few months older than Brezhnev, was reported to occupy the chair as the leader's most trusted colleague when Brezhnev was away, but his standing in the party hardly seemed to qualify him to succeed Brezhnev. Kulakov, twelve years younger, was mentioned as a likely replacement, but in the prestige order fixed by the nominations to the Supreme Soviet in 1975 he ranked only seventh. There was

---

*Brezhnev received 42 seconds of applause, compared to 25 in 1966 and 28 in 1971; the average for the other Politburo members was 2.7 seconds in 1976, compared to 4.6 in 1966 and 3.6 in 1971. *Radio Liberty Bulletin* 128/76 (March 6, 1976): 16.

no indication in 1976 that Brezhnev had any idea of stepping down. He seemed to be stepping up a little to the role of elder statesman, however, leaving details to subordinates. Possibly he could better afford to do this than Khrushchev, because he had no great changes to push through and because he seemed to be genuinely well liked by other leaders to whom he delegated responsibility and whom he left in place and treated with restraint.[31] The byword "trust in cadres" may have been his, and the cadres, grateful for his trust, reciprocated with praise and perhaps affection.

Brezhnev was, of course, the opening and chief speaker at the Twenty-Fifth Congress; his keynote, like that of the congress in general and of most Soviet pronouncements of recent years, was satisfaction in achievements. His attention went mostly to foreign affairs, to which he seemed to have given a large part of his time since 1970. He pointed to numerous victories: closer relations with East European countries, Communist triumphs in various areas, better relations with Western nations, and the "acute crisis of capitalism"—in short, to the successes of peaceful coexistence with ideological struggle—but he gave no new directions and raised no new ideas.

The economic report delivered by Kosygin pointed even more clearly to the end of struggle. The 1976–80 Tenth Five Year Plan was much less ambitious than its predecessor, with targets for industrial growth that were no higher than the levels the world has achieved in recent decades. Although immense improvement in agriculture was needed and feasible, the plan contemplated a growth in output of only about 3 percent yearly. Yet agriculture was to receive a share of investment (34 percent) that was much larger than its proportional contribution to the national product (it was officially 20 percent in 1973). Investments were to rise 25 percent over the five years, compared to 41 percent in 1971–75. Per-capita income growth was projected to be 20 to 22 percent by 1980, compared with 33 percent in the period 1966—70.

The Soviet standard of living rose markedly through the 1960s, somewhat less in 1970–75, especially in the availability of appliances and improved supplies of consumer goods, many of which were imported. By 1975 the Soviet Union claimed to have exceeded the output of the United States in coal, petroleum, steel, cement, and some less basic commodities. But the old promise of abundance was dimming. Not only was no substantial improvement in the food supply expected, the Soviet Union also was not rushing into the automotive age and was not about to make the one-family apartment standard. Contemplated increases in automobile production and housing construction were trivial—less than the projected population growth. Priorities that in 1971 had been slightly shifted in favor of consumers were turned back toward producer goods. To realize its unambitious goals, the plan looked frankly to foreign economic relations, in effect, the importation of Western technology. There was no mention of the old 1965 economic reform or of any new measures of consequence to revitalize the laggard economy. There was not even much mention of the "producer associations" that had been started in 1973 to group enterprises for efficiency and easier planning.[32] At best, it was hoped that scientific management and mathematical analysis could obviate the need for decentralization.

The minimization of change was demonstrated even more clearly in the composition of the new Central Committee. In 1971, 61 percent of the living members of the old Central Committee were reelected; in 1976, 89 percent were.[33] The number of full members was raised from 241 to 287, but the number of candidate members declined from 155 to 139, and in all, newcomers constituted only 12 percent of the new committee. Similarly, this was the first congress in party history to make no changes in the rules. In fact, there were no pronouncements on organizational matters, and no resolutions except acceptance of the main reports and the guidelines of the plan.

The spirit of the congress was one of exemplary harmony. Speakers did not openly, or generally even by faint implication, differ from either the official line or other speakers, and the conclave was suffused with congratulations and self-congratulations. The only exceptions were a few foreign delegates, representatives of European Communist parties (such as the Italian, French, and British) who were striving to show democratic colors in opposition to Soviet authoritarianism. This heretical manifestation of pluralism was tacitly accepted, while the congress went on talking about unity under "proletarian internationalism."

In the mood of harmony and general satisfaction, there were not only no fireworks, but also no discussion of any real problems. No admission was made that anything could be seriously wrong, and there were no references to rising minority nationalism, criminality, alcoholism, corruption, black marketeering, the general slowdown of the economy or the apparently ever-growing technological lag. Nothing was said of ideological questions, of problems of intellectual dissidence, nor of the succession question, which cannot be very far away. It would almost seem that time had come to a halt in the "developed socialist society," under the benign command of the General Secretary.

Politics especially seemed to have come to a standstill, as no visible movement disturbed the Soviet scene except the steady enlargement of the image of the supreme figure. In May 1976 a statue of Brezhnev was unveiled in Dneprodzerzhinsk, where he began his political career. A biography published late in 1976 revealed that Brezhnev had been the foremost economic planner of the 1960s, when most people thought that Kosygin was in charge of that department. Late in 1976 Brezhnev began to be referred to as "vozhd," or "leader," a title previously used only for Lenin and Stalin. Brezhnev's 70th birthday, December 19, 1976, was regally celebrated, with the highest honors that could be invented, including a ceremonial sword and a full length movie of his career, which seemed to make him almost direct successor of Lenin, eliding forty-odd years of Stalin and Khrushchev. In the spring of 1977 he finally achieved what was apparently a long-term ambition. Podgorny, the last person on the Politburo with anything of an independent power base, was unceremoniously removed, probably because he declined gracefully to yield the presidency of the state. A few days later, June 17, Brezhnev permitted himself to be chosen President of the Presidium of the Supreme Soviet, official head of state. Concurrently, the new draft constitution, which had been under consideration for sixteen years, was unveiled. It changed little concretely except that it increased the powers of the president and provided an assistant for him. The new constitution seemed intended primarily as a statement of policies of the Brezhnev era and probably as a monument to the man who stood over it.

Never before had the leading figure in the Soviet system held the formal office of head of state. It was appropriate, however, that he should do so in the postrevolutionary era, finally to regularize the power structure of Lenin's faction grown into a solid and conservative state.

THE BREZHNEV PARTY

"The Communist Party incorporates the collective intelligence, will, and wisdom of the Soviet people. The destiny and aspirations of the Soviet people are fused forever with their beloved party, and their great deeds in the making of the communist society."[34] Whether or not the Soviet peoples are married forever to their beloved party, it is clear that the organization founded by Lenin has become an extraordinarily powerful and effective instrument for the guidance and governance of an immense domain. As it has taken shape under Lenin and Stalin and matured to the settled times of Brezhnev, the party has become perhaps the most complex social structure in history, with interlocking lines of responsibility and control along and between many layers of authority, all designed, expertly and cunningly, to mobilize the will of many under the leadership of few, just as Lenin proposed in *What is to Be Done?*

The party that began as a collection of a few odd radicals united by their dedication to activism and their willingness to accept the chieftainship of Lenin, has become a well-trained, harmonious, skilled group of administrators. As of the Twenty-Fifth Congress, in February 1976, it counted 15,694,187 members. These were grouped into 390,387 primary organizations, many of them subdivided into "shop" organizations and "party groups." Over them stood 4,253 local, village, city, and district party organizations. These in turn were directed by 154 regional organizations, the party organizations of 14 republics, and the central Communist Party of the Soviet Union, with its Central Committee, Secretariat, and Politburo. At each level there were elections, supervised and directed by higher authorities to prevent "spontaneity" and surprises, to form conferences or congresses leading up to the big gatherings of nearly 5,000 delegates in Moscow.

At each level there was a reduced replica, so far as it was feasible, of the structure at the top: a party committee, a secretariat (or secretary at lower levels), an executive section or buro corresponding to the Politburo, and administrative sections corresponding to the departments of the Central Committee. The hierarchy of secretaries formed the backbone of the party, much as the line officers form the backbone of an army; the secretaries at each level are largely responsible for the appointment of those below them and for the staffing, under the "nomenklatura" system, of positions (which are mostly elective in theory) under their jurisdiction.

Party control of the government and of all other major organizations was doubly and triply assured, through control at each level of administration by means of the local party committee, through the power of the leadership to make all appointments of any significance, and through the organization of the party members within any organization (the "party fraction") into a group that was responsible to party authorities and charged with directing the policies of the organization—from a sports club to a ministerial office to the Academy of Sciences or a military unit.

Through such controls, reinforced by the monopoly of public communications and the political police and security forces, the party should be able to manage virtually everything below it. There are still religious groups, some of which are tamed and tolerated, others of which are disapproved and persecuted, but everything that bespeaks power and prestige is under the rulership of the party. Practically speaking, only through the party or with its blessing can anyone make a career.

This means that the Communist party has become to a degree that is novel in history an organized and purposefully directed political elite or ruling class. It forms a self-conscious in-group, offering power and privileges and demanding in return total loyalty—the loyalty and dedication that are necessary to make the system work. Its cohesion is, and has always had to be, strong enough to prevent any sector of the party from linking its discontents with the discontents of the nonparty masses; it has always been treasonous to appeal to workers or peasants (or the party membership) for support against any party policy, no matter how misguided. The party élite has thus become the modern equivalent of a feudal nobility, enjoying a monopoly of power far beyond that of any historic nobility.

The party has become more markedly a corporation of the privileged under Brezhnev. Recruitment decreased from 2,938,111 in 1962−65 to 2,473,576 in 1971−75, despite population growth. Under Khrushchev party membership grew 6.6 percent yearly; recently, the rate has been under 2 percent.[35] In a time of stability, the party has less desire to share the blessings of membership.

Moreover, the new recruits come predominantly from the ranks of specialists and the educated; about two-thirds of the new members who joined in 1970—75 had received higher education. The new recruits are also mostly young people growing up to the party. In 1962—65, 48 percent of party entrants were graduates of the Komsomol; in 1971—75, Komsomol graduates made up 65 percent. In a mere five years, 1971 to 1976, the percentage of party members who had a higher education grew from 19.6 percent to 24.3 percent.[36] Virtually all party secretaries at the city level and above had a higher education in the 1970s. ''Higher education'' here means, however, years of indoctrination, probably in special party schools, a training that is not mentally broadening in the humane tradition and that is open only to the politically correct.

The party tries to recruit people who distinguish themselves in any approved way, from scientists to athletes. It wants in its ranks those who are in any manner leaders of society, so that it can bring them under party discipline and guidance and make them sharers in the rulership. But it cannot be doubted that entry into the party, which is governed by the party group and the secretaries, is easier for the offspring of party members, although data to support (or refute) this theory have not been published. In the tightly knit elite group, the children of the faithful old hands are certain to have the inside track, partly because no one wants to offend longtime comrades, and partly because they are known and reliable.

There is little to prevent the members of the party elite from regarding themselves as a special breed selected for their high caliber, from looking down on the inferior persons who are not so selected, from enjoying the privileges pertaining to their status, and from desiring their meritorious children to inherit their condition.[37] There are more-privileged circles within less-privileged circles, down to the ordinary members who are only a notch above the common people. But the upper elite of a few hundred thousand members form a true aristocracy, living in cocooned luxury apart from ordinary folks and with little knowledge of their lives.[38] With special stores, secluded dachas, private resorts, chauffeured limousines for the very important, and special entertainments with films censored from the people, the elite reward themselves for their dedication to socialism and the masses. On the one hand, there is growing snobbery toward uncultured workers.[39] On the other, the elite itself is riddled with distinctions, which are sometimes indicated by the color of one's pass,[40] and obsequiousness to superiors is balanced by overlordship of inferiors. It opens many doors to be even a distant relative of an exalted personage.[41]

The perquisites are part of the solidarity system, the reward for devotion to the party and to those who stand above; deviance means loss of status, career, and ease of living. Since those who enjoy high status also hope that their children can maintain it, intermarriage is common among prestigious families of the party, military, and scientific communities,[42] the military elite being certainly, and the scientific elite probably, party members. The offspring of the upper classes probably also retain their positions by attendance at special schools; notable among these is the Moscow State Institute for International Relations, which prepares students for diplomatic and related careers.[43]

Official position, especially standing in the party, has thus become immensely important as a source of satisfaction. It is a species of property, the most important kind of property where high privileges and special enjoyments, ranging from fine cars to country estates and prestige, derive not from wealth, ownership, or independent accomplishment (except in unusual cases), but from the favor of the party. Understandably, then, people cling to position, and the right to tenure seems to be increasingly recognized, in practice, as social change and the urge toward transformation come to an end. After the upheaval of Lenin's revolution and the turmoil in the first part of Stalin's reign, the party has been settling down to the exercise and enjoyment of power. Khrushchev tried to reshuffle the party and shake it up, but his decentralization failed and his splitting of the party was the last disturbing reform that was attempted. The circulation of elites by purge is no longer feasible, because there is no longer a strong drive for change or a leadership that is able to force it through.

Probably the chief objective of the Brezhnev leadership is stability, the maintenance of a condition that is approximately the best that can be devised for its beneficiaries. A major preoccupation, more important than economic growth, is the avoidance of a new purge, and the best guarantee of the safety of each is the immunity of all. Khrushchev liked at least to talk of trust in the people, but the motto of his followers is trust in cadres, and the Brezhnev regime demands less and rewards more. The Soviet elite is like a club that may be exclusive in admissions but that seldom pushes members out. It is a cruel thing to punish a longtime colleague even though he may be losing his powers of concentration, especially inasmuch as, in Soviet society, he has nowhere else to go; and everyone in authority has an interest in the principle that positions are for keeps. For the superiors, it is like turning a faithful old servant out into the cold; for equals, the loss of one is a threat to all.

One reason for low productivity in Soviet industry is the high degree of job security; it is so difficult to fire someone (unless he is politically marked) that managers seldom try. Likewise, membership in the club of Soviet authority seems highly secure, without legal guarantees, as long as one is loyal and does not offend the powers above; even under Khrushchev the dismissal of a local party secretary required elaborate excuses and months of maneuvering.[44] Stability has increased remarkably since then. The attrition rate of provincial (obkom) buro members was 63 percent in 1958/59 to 1965, but only 35 percent in 1965/66−71.[45] In 1973, 30 percent of obkom buro membership had been in place for more than ten years, compared with 15 percent in 1962—64.[46] Turnover rates in the obkom buros were reduced by more than half in less than a decade, 1960–64 to 1969–73. The changes that are made involve mostly internal rotation; less than 6 percent of appointments went to persons who had never held comparable positions.[47] In 1974, report-and-election conferences left 149 out of 150 provincial (krai and oblast) first secretaries in office, and in the preceding three years, only three had been dismissed, all of non-Russian nationality.[48]

As a result, it is becoming more difficult for a youth to climb the career ladder.[49] The Politburo members in 1951, on the average, had been party members for fourteen years before they entered the Central Committee; the members in 1971 had taken twenty-two years, on the average, to cover the same distance.[50]

The higher ranks of the party are increasingly clublike and positions are more stable. Some people stay at one post for decades. For example, B. P. Beshchev became Deputy Minister of Railroads in 1944 and Minister in 1948; he was still in that post in 1977. Andrei Gromyko became Deputy Foreign Minister in 1946, at the age of thirty-seven, when the system was more fluid. He became Foreign Minister in 1957, and still held that position in 1977, having far outlasted all his colleagues of major powers. Such fixity of tenure is regarded as a positive achievement, favoring expertise.[51] In the upper ranks, officials often move as in musical chairs. For example, in 1972 the Ukrainian premier, V. V. Schcherbitsky, took Shelest's place as first secretary, and the Ukrainian chairman, A. P. Liashko, took Schcherbitsky's place as premier; moreover, the first deputy chairman, S. Stetsenko, took (at least provisionally) Liashko's seat as chairman. The stability of the Politburo since Khrushchev has been remarked on already. It is also true that within the Politburo, members are not shifted from one department to another, as occurs in the reshuffles of Western cabinets. Each member thus has an opportunity to become identified with his clientele, whom he will presumably protect.

Fixity in positions is synonymous with aging, and the Leninist youth movement has become a gerontocracy. Lenin was the oldest major figure in his party, at age forty-seven, when the revolution was made. The average age of Bolshevik delegates to the Congress of Soviets in November 1917 (those who answered questionnaires) was twenty-nine.[52] In 1927 the average age of party members was less than thirty, and Stalin kept the leadership youthful through his purges. In 1939, at the Eighteenth Congress, only 20 percent of the delegates were forty or over, and only 3 percent were over fifty.[53] The latter Stalin years were characterized by stability and aging, however, and Khrushchev's shake-ups only checked, but did not reverse, the trend. In 1939 the Soviet elite was among the youngest to rule a modern state; by 1959 it was among the oldest. At the Twenty-First Congress (1959), the proportion of delegates over forty had risen to 79 percent. The same men stayed around; 81 percent of the 1939 delegates had entered the party in 1921–29; twenty years later, 53 percent of delegates came from the same group.[54] Recent congresses have ceased reporting in detail on the age composition either of the congress or of the party.

The aging of the top rank is shown by the age progression of the Central Committee as it has been formed at recent congresses. The members averaged 49 years old in 1952, 51 in 1956, 52 in 1961, 56 in 1966 and 60 in 1976.[55] New voting members in 1976 averaged 55.[56] In 1961 one-quarter of the candidate members were holdovers; in 1971 half of them were. The members of the Politburo in 1966 averaged 57.5 years of age, in 1971 they averaged 61 years, and in 1976 the average age was 66 years. Brezhnev, who was 70 at the end of 1976, was the youngest of the four top figures at that time, including Podgorny (73), Kosygin (72), and Suslov (74). Brezhnev apparently feels more comfortable with old men than with their potential replacements.[57] He has expressed a need to advance new cadres, but has done little of it, and turnover in the Politburo has brought little rejuvenation. The changes made at the Twenty-Fifth Congress lowered the average age by less than three months. Rarely, perhaps never, have Politburo members been retired solely because of age, and opportunities to bring in fresh blood have often been rejected. For example, Semichastny, who was ousted because of his affiliation with Shelepin, was replaced by Andropov, who was a decade older; and when Grechko died at the age of 70, he was replaced by 68-year-old Ustinov as Minister of Defense. Ripeness of years is accepted; on being decorated after his 70th birthday, Kirilenko said, "It is good that in our country this is considered only middle age."[58]

Such aging of the Politburo, by nearly a year for every calendar year, obviously cannot continue for very long. Yet it is difficult to foresee a way out. The superannuated oligarchs are not likely to remove themselves willingly or to welcome as their new leader someone who is capable of dismissing them. Yet, as the system operates, they have the power to prevent changes. It would seem that only something like a coup (although perhaps disguised) can renew the top layer. Here the Soviet system is at a disadvantage in comparison with the tsarist one. Now there is no autocrat to discharge a ministry that has overstayed its welcome, and no young heir waits in the wings for the decease of the old tsar.

The Soviet leader is thus surrounded by a group of elder statesmen who must feel themselves approximately his equals and whom he can get rid of only with great difficulty, if at all. They are generally more interested in checking the power of the leader than in giving him unrestricted powers. At the same time, it is harder for him to build up the unconditionally dedicated following he must have to operate arbitrarily in the Soviet system. The office of General Secretary confers not so much power as the means of building power. But however much power the General Secretary may build, it is certain to be far less than Stalin enjoyed. He is no longer very free to reward by promotions, since positions only gradually become vacant. He cannot demote freely without the concurrence of his colleagues, who are in principle opposed to demotion. Furthermore, the ruthless, ignorant men whom Stalin raised to do his bidding are no longer available, or they are no longer welcome. Everyone in the upper levels of the hierarchy has been there a long time and has acquired a higher education, which gives self-confidence if not breadth of vision. Authority, after all, is supposedly based on mastery of Marxism-Leninism, and there must be hundreds in the party who are more sophisticated in that discipline than Brezhnev. ''Trust in cadres'' comes naturally when all have been through the same schools and have climbed the career ladders together, but it means a restricted leader; without the power of purge, there is no real dictator.

That such a man as Brezhnev has been built up as the guiding genius of the proletariat and the joy of all hearts does not mean very much. Flattery and sycophancy are characteristic of all authoritarian systems, and the Soviet system is no exception. Praise costs nothing, and the cadres are doubtless more willing to exalt the leader when they are convinced he is not going to hurt them. The party needs a paternal figure at its head, a symbol of its unity and a focus of loyalty beyond the shadowy reality of the organization. The party also needs a final decision maker, who must be generally respected and accepted, particularly to settle personnel questions; it is impractical to decide all such matters in the Politburo. In the sanctity of party unity, which is the foundation of party supremacy, all must ultimately bow to the same personality, who in turn can trust his subordinates not because of any real belief in their loyalty or because of their fear of him, but because he is an essential part of a structure that benefits all its components. Only if there is great dissatisfaction are his subordinates likely to combine against him; it is likely that Khrushchev could have remained into his dotage if he had been content with a less active role.

For these reasons, Brezhnev appears to be powerful in doing what the party wants. He never fights the machine or his fellow oligarchs. Unlike the American president, the General Secretary can at any given time make only minor changes in his government, and he has to clear policy with a cabinet he cannot change. Consequently, he can become gradually more influential through the cumulative effect of his influence over appointments, but he can embark on no bold initiatives in either foreign or domestic policies. To push anything very hard might well draw down his limited stock of power.

A further result of this broad development is the increasing facelessness of the leadership. It is undesirable for the oligarchs to project themselves as charismatic personalities in a system where popular appeal would be dangerous. At the same time, able and dynamic men arouse distrust and are probably sidetracked from the career ladder. Shelepin's potentialities caused his downfall. Hence many who were just below the top under both Khrushchev and Brezhnev have come across as mere names, faceless nonentities, for example, Kirichenko, Saburov, Beliaev, Mazurov and Grishin, In part, their personalities are deliberately screened; in part they are absorbed by the enveloping system and the desirability of everyone's thinking and acting alike.

A further consequence is the tendency of the leader to work through a private secretariat that he can staff and command freely; these aides correspond somewhat to the White House staff that American presidents prefer because its members are not responsible to Congress and are not subject to civil-service regulation. Brezhnev built up his private office far beyond its stature under Khrushchev; in it he has included general assistant G. Sukhanov, E. Samotekin for domestic policies, A. Aleksandrov-Agentov for agriculture, and A. Blatov and K. Rusakov for foreign policy.[59]

There is another result that is somewhat anomalous for the proletariat in its struggle with the class enemy; the personality of the leader emerges chiefly in his contacts with the capitalist world. In his native surroundings, Brezhnev is something of a gray symbol who speaks in the language of Central Committee resolutions, a figure with only a formal and official existence. On his tours abroad or in conversations with foreign visitors, however, he appears to be a thorough politician who is fairly humorous and folksy, warmly greeting individuals and crowds. At home, his family and private life are nonexistent; abroad, he speaks freely of his fairly modest apartment, his fondness for hunting, even his minor vices.

Behind these reasons for the constriction of the real power of the leader—his inability to move or change the system on which he rests—lies the basic fact that the impetus of the revolution, the mission of changing society, cannot endure forever. The big emotional drive was directed at overturning the old order. The personalities of Stalin and Khrushchev were forged under the weight of tsardom; for the present rulers that is almost impersonal history. New structures were long ago put together and they have gradually hardened. The faith that once moved the party has become desiccated, and the letter has replaced the spirit. Lenin's works have ceased to be a message and have been turned into a scripture; in 1975 Soviet scholars began work on a multivolume concordance to his writings, cataloguing every word and phrase.

Ideology has been cultivated and elaborated,[60] but it is formalistic, containing far more mental conditioned reflex than emotion; indeed, it is not far from sanctified and traditionalized collective hypocrisy. As the Spanish Communist leader remarked in a demonstration of independence, the party cultivates an irrelevant doctrine like a fossilized church.[61] It is calcified to a high degree; over the entire post-Stalin period there has been virtually no change in the "class" emphasis in school histories.[62]

The revolutionary spirit outlasted the disillusionment of the postponement of utopia and the retreat of the 1920s, and it was revived to some extent in Stalin's transformations. It was blighted by the purges, but they would not have been possible without persistent genuine faith in the party and its mission. Something of the party's faith in its glorious cause was revived by the ordeal of the Second World War, the vindication of that cause by the greatest of victories, and the concomitant rejuvenation and revitalization of the party. Khrushchev was perhaps led by his wartime experiences to attempt to renew the vision and the inspiration, but his utopianism was pallid and has been virtually abandoned. The Brezhnev regime seems to have no explicit vision of the future, only a vague and largely meaningless promise of improvement.

Philosophical discussion, which was banned under Stalin and mildly re-animated under Khrushchev, has again subsided. *Voprosy filosofii* ("Questions of Philosophy") was little more than a sterile propaganda journal in 1974 and after, with articles like those in *Kommunist*. After Khrushchev's rather feeble efforts to update ideology—such shifts of emphasis as peaceful coexistence, the victory of socialism by economic superiority, and the state of the whole people—his successors have reverted to arid fundamentalism and clichés about proletarianism in arrant conflict with the privileges of the elite. Instead of utopianism, there has been an effort to idealize the status quo of "developed socialism" that has been scientifically perfected by a regime that disallows social science.[63] Inapplicable doctrines are simply ignored, not refuted or replaced. The principal dogma is the infallibility of the party, which is regarded as blameless and virtuous despite its past leaders.

If the tenets of Bolshevism are ossified, the ideology is increasingly being fleshed out with ideas that are extraneous to Marxism. Communism since the mid-1930s has been merging into the Russian nationalistic-messianic tradition, revolutionary-equalitarian change has been yielding to the sense of power, and military themes are being woven into, and are often used to cover up, Marx-ist ideology. Wartime heroism and glory are being cultivated with undimin-ished intensity thirty years after the end of hostilities. Lenin has become the god of the state, less the author of change than a symbol of permanence and order.

It is probably fair to say that Marxism-Leninism has become generally discredited; it is now used by the party mostly as a means for the slightly esoteric communication of ideas that cannot be conveyed in plain speech—much as "proletarian internationalism" is the code term for Soviet domination in discussion with foreign parties.[64] Marxism is essentially a doctrine of change, and it can be retained only in a morally deformed state where change is not desired. The Brezhnev regime has stressed the essentially conservative values of military valor, dedication and discipline, and Soviet patriotism, as well as the apotheosis of Lenin, and the historical tradition, rather than the future promise. Yet it has looked away somewhat from the revolution itself and has had little to say about most of Soviet history—the eras of Stalin and Khrushchev—except the war years.* Informally, and in part covertly, the party has brought another conservative element into its ideology, anti-Zionism or anti-Semitism, which is presently woven into anti-capitalism as it was in the tsarist empire.

It is difficult to envision a solution to the problem of an obsolete and ever more irrelevant ideology. To impose changes would evidently require dictatorial power in the hands of a strong-willed reformer, indeed, a new revolutionary leader, but nothing of the kind is in prospect. The leader's works are quoted, but he is bound by the fixed canon; he has nothing of importance to say, and everyone knows that his words will be buried as soon as he leaves the scene. Yet the party-state needs a functional ideology in order to maintain reasonable vigor.

Just as there is no ideological drive and no drive for change, there are no issues that evoke a passionate commitment—political criticism is left to outsiders and dissenters. Virtually no controversies are evident within the party, even when speeches are examined by the kremlinologist's microscope; all is controlled and orderly. Even under Stalin party congresses meant something; now they have become mere displays of unanimity. Party bigwigs divide not along the lines of policy differences, but, so far as they form any discernible groups, by personal association—it is important not that someone agrees with Brezhnev but that he was with the Brezhnev group in Dnepropetrovsk.[65] There is no evidence of consistent groups of hawks and doves in the Politburo, and there is no more talk of "dogmatists" and "revisionists" in the party, no principled divisions of any kind in the philosophic uniformity of cadres who have been trained to a common perspective and moved by little idealism.

There seem to be loose lobbies in the Brezhnev system, such as the military, the police, the advocates of heavy industry, the party apparat, and the ministerial bureaucrats, but the only pressures seem to be those of self-interest. The alliances fluctuate, and groups are more capable of defending their positions than of pushing any positive programs. If there are contrary tendencies toward the slackening or tightening of controls, none of them push hard or far; confrontation is avoided, and so far as it exists, it is kept quiet. The compromises that are reached involve policies less than persons, and an individual may be entrusted with the execution of a policy that is contrary to his own.[66] Groups are held together by mutual advantage; political progress depends upon the members of the collective helping one another, and a shift to another group makes a person seem disloyal. The principle is loyalty to the party. Again stability is more important than change, harmony is preferred to movement.

Fixity of personnel is almost equivalent to fixity of policy; to embark on new programs usually requires putting new people in charge. Since there is no great drive to change, in any case, the settled party rulership has become remarkably

---

*In Brezhnev's 1967 speech for the fiftieth anniversary of the Soviet state, he skipped more than four-fifths of Soviet history.

conservative. Even formal change comes very hard. Khrushchev proposed in January 1959 that the 1936 "Stalinist" constitution be replaced. Three years later, in April 1962, a drafting commission was formed, and it was reconstituted under the chairmanship of Brezhnev after Khrushchev's fall. Nothing was revealed of the debates or proposals, but the new constitution was promised for the fiftieth anniversary of the revolution in 1967, as well as several times since then. It was finally unveiled in June 1977 in connection with Brezhnev's assumption of the presidency, and the changes it made were almost entirely declarative or cosmetic. In 1935 Stalin decided on a new constitution to reflect his achievements, and it was produced in a few months. In another minor way, the party finds itself paralyzed in replacing the symbols of the Stalin era. The words of the national anthem hailing Stalin were dropped in 1956; twenty-one years later, the commission produced verses almost unchanged except for dropping the name of Stalin.[67]

Similarly, basic dogmas live on. The old priority of heavy industry has become increasingly irrelevant in the age of plastics and computers, but it has been retained ever since Stalin put it in place in his First Five Year Plan. There was some wavering in 1953 and again under Khrushchev, but since his political demise the policy has been repeatedly reaffirmed. According to Kosygin at the Twenty-Fifth Congress, heavy industry at that time accounted for 73 percent of industrial production, the same proportion as five years before, and it is scheduled to be no less five years later. Apparently, to permit the Soviet economy to become consumer oriented would be too threatening to important sectors of the party.

Agriculture is also locked into the system of huge centralized and politically directed collective and state farms. There have been many suggestions for the devolution of management to more practical units and for better incentives for smaller groups of farmers, and experiments using such changes have demonstrated startling increases in output. Soviet leaders, like Western agronomists, must know that the collective farm system is a serious brake on productivity, just as the old peasant village commune had become at the beginning of this century. Nevertheless, the village commune was retained for political reasons (until it was attacked by the Stolypin reforms after the 1905 revolution), and the collective farm is untouchable today for political reasons.

The cultural scene is also frozen, with only marginal relaxation of censorship and of the required adherence to the canons of socialist realism, and there are no positive new directions. Andrei Zhdanov, the architect of Stalin's postwar ideological repressions and his crackdowns on contacts with the West, received high posthumous honors on his eightieth birthday in March 1976, as though the party were nostalgic for the more potent regimen of 1947–48. There has recently been less cultural freedom than there was in 1965 or 1956.[68] Again, as in tsarist days, creativity in art or literature seems to imply an antiregime posture.

In complete contrast to the 1920s, the interesting Soviet works are hostile, or at least critical.

In any realm, the party watchdogs distrust initiative and spontaneity, which they believe might erode sacrosanct authority. It is dangerous to do a good job, even under official auspices, if this reflects on powerful interests. This was the melancholy experience of I. N. Khudenko, who was authorized in November 1960 by the Council of Ministers to set up an experimental collective farm with payment of brigades according to the results achieved. Under an incentive system, the cost of grain was reduced severalfold, wages were increased fourfold, and the profits per worker increased even more. The success was written up in several papers and journals. In response, the minister of agriculture of Kazakhstan closed the farm, made sundry criminal charges, and brought about the imprisonment of Khudenko and his chief associate.[69]

Since change is unwelcome, the system rests its legitimacy increasingly on tradition, the momentum of the going concern, and the inability or unwillingness of most people—especially those in positions of influence—to demand change. The Soviet citizen, knowing only the present political system, educated to it and submerged in it, can hardly conceive of anything very different. Even its critics and opponents are generally convinced that whatever its faults, the Soviet regime represents socialism, or public ownership of the means of production; hence it is basically of a superior order and cannot be opposed. People grumble but accept the rulership.[70] The bureaucrats who run the economy, the press, the Writers' Union, and the scientific institutes apparently like things the way they are. The workers do not mind if the intellectuals are kept under pressure in the name of socialism, and the party democratically makes some concessions, mostly but not entirely concessions of form, to the less educated. The Soviet way is in harmony with traditional Russian political culture: the fear of invasion and of anarchy, the xenophobia, the sense of the necessity of authority, the modest expectations and small demand for social mobility, the low valuation of the individual, and the underlying inferiority complex vis-a-vis the West.

The party prefers consent and conciliation, but it ultimately relies on force. There are many means of compulsion—threats and harassment, unfavorable publicity, loss of career standing or of position, expulsion from housing or from principal cities, irregular manhandling, and the like—that suffice to deter all but the most resolute dissidents and to convince nearly everyone that it is pointless to fight the system. For those who persist, the security forces employ sterner measures; the number of political prisoners in labor camps, mostly those of minority nationality or religious protesters, has been estimated at around ten thousand, while several hundred are confined in psychiatric wards.[71] Although these numbers are small in comparison to those in the Stalin era, they suffice largely to silence the opposition.

Meanwhile the party grows closer to the order-keeping forces. In no other sector of the population is the percentage of party members so high.[72] The KGB has been bathed in favorable publicity in the post-Khrushchev years; its head, who did not even sit in the Central Committee under Khrushchev, has been a member of the Politburo since 1973. Prior to the Twenty-Fifth Congress, KGB officials were made chiefs of Georgia and Azerbaidzhan and members of the politburos of Azerbaidzhan, Belorussia, Kazakstan, Lithuania, Tadzhikistan, the Ukraine, and Uzbekistan. The military has also gained more prominence and a greater voice in inner circles.[73] The military is not only the ultimate guarantor of order and the unity of the Soviet Union, but a prime instrument of propaganda and indoctrination at home, the basic force for maintaining dominion over East Europe, the chief means of influence in the Third World, and the strongest claim to the respect of the West.

The party has thus settled into place as the monolithic edifice of power, but its ability to work its will has decreased as its will has withered, and its authority is crumbling around the edges. Police repression is arbitrary, but like the official ideology, it lacks real conviction, hesitates a little in the face of public opinion at home and abroad, and is only partially effective. An opposition movement has grown up that is small but well publicized and determined.[74] For a tiny sector of the intelligentsia, repugnance for the established order has become a matter of principle. Like the tsarist state, the Soviet order must seemingly live with intellectual dissidence, and it risks embittering without crushing. The nonconformists are of many shades, from neo-Stalinists and neo-Leninists to Russians and other nationalists, advocates of civil rights, and a few liberal democrats.[75] Physically they are impotent, and they are far better known (as are Andrei Sakharov and Alexander Solzhenitsyn) in the West than in their homeland; still, they are catalytic, as well as symptomatic of the further decadence of Marxist-Leninist orthodoxy.

Doubtless more worrisome to the party is the deterioration of its capacity to regulate. Lawbreaking is rampant in the overregimented economy (this has also occurred in Western states when bureaucracies have tried to regulate more than they can properly oversee). Gray and black markets prosper and account for a substantial fraction—a fifth or a fourth—of the economy; they are indeed necessary for its reasonably smooth functioning.[76] Consumption of hard liquor has risen steadily for many years,[77] and Academician Strumilin estimated that half of the vodka drunk is home brew.[78]

Since the rewards for civil servants have become less service to the cause for its own sake and more material gain, minor officials seem increasingly to use their authority over permits, powers of inspection, and so on, for personal benefits; corruption is rampant. Multimillion-ruble frauds are reported from time to time, especially in the Caucasus; that they are seldom reported in Russian areas probably indicates the absence of reporting rather than the absence of fraud. Such defalcations—such as incidences of private factories operating on stolen materials—could not occur without the complicity of many well-placed party people.

Up to the latter 1960s it could plausibly be asserted that the energies of the party were concentrated on economic development. Now these energies have decreased; they seem to be concentrated more on retention than on creation, and the results are modest. The shortfalls of Soviet agriculture are familiar; less well known is the fact that prior to 1880 Russia was the world's premier grain exporter, and it remained a close second to the United States from 1880 until the eve of the revolution.[79] There are perennial deficits and faults of planning, (production of unneeded goods, autarky of ministries and enterprises, interminable delays in construction, poor utilization of labor and machinery, and the like), and these are no longer compensated by a high growth rate. The supply of consumer goods is improved chiefly by import.

Even one of the most lauded of Soviet achievements, medical care, seems to have suffered, since patients who are able to do so pay for private attention. Crime grows along with alcoholism.[80] In Sakharov's assessment, which may be overly bitter but would have been unlikely a decade or so ago, "What is hidden is a sea of human misery, difficulties, animosities, cruelty, profound fatigue, and indifference—things that have accumulated for decades and are undermining the foundations of society."[81]

In a dynamic world in which to stand still is to regress, the party seems fixed in its patterns of power and belief. It is aging at a time when renovation is indispensable, and it is losing morale when high morale is required to avoid putrefaction. The question is whether the system can break out of its mold without destroying itself.

At best, this would be a formidable task, but the Soviet system imposes difficulties upon itself. Pervasive secrecy makes it very hard for anyone outside the most privileged core, perhaps even for those within, to think seriously about major problems. Soviet negotiators at the SALT talks knew less about Soviet weaponry than did their American counterparts, because military secrets are not for civilians.[82] Under Khrushchev a little light was shed on political affairs, but the Brezhnev government has covered itself with a Stalin-style screen.

Information about the shortcomings of the system not only is not published; it is probably gathered only partially. Even if the Politburo members really desired to inform themselves objectively about their country (they have occasionally been reported to seek straight facts on foreign questions), it is nearly impossible for them to do so. The party rejects, and must reject, objectivity in principle, and the hierarchic system is opaque to the passage of truth from bottom to top. The party lays claim to scientific management, basing its legitimacy upon its supposed knowledge; yet it does not permit any study of the operation of society—no political science or sociology is permitted in the Soviet Union except for limited researches that are intended to serve party purposes.

On the one hand, any individual's thoughts about problems are burdened by a mass of ideological myths that are drummed into him from nursery school on; hardly anyone can fully free himself from them even though he may turn against the party. In addition, there is a tremendous quantity of useless but distracting information or what is put forward as information. According to an economist, "Thousands of statisticians, economists, and planners, plus an uncounted number of supporting personnel, are spending millions of rubles cranking out useless figures."[83] The other side of the picture is that there is minimal feedback. It is impossible for the absolute despot to learn much about his realm, because everyone is above all concerned with pleasing him. In the Soviet system, it is in no one's interest to ferret out truths about the political system and to think deeply on them.

Nothing may be brought forward that reflects on the primary dogma of the right of the party to rule. The fact that troubles may be caused by unchecked power cannot be recognized. Indeed, the mechanisms and rights of power, and the entirety of the political processes of decision making and of ascension to the top not only in the present but also in the past, are beyond the purview of discussion. It cannot even be asked how a bloody Stalin or a hare-brained Khrushchev (or other reprobated leaders, such as Bukharin or Beria) came to the top.* No legitimate discussion is allowed of any political question in the Soviet context, from the reasons for holding elections to the frequency of meetings of the Central Committee. It is only assumed that those who are in power at any time are worthy.

The crux of the problem may be as follows: those who might possibly be able to effect change, the oligarchs at the summit (it is by no means certain that they could in fact really reform the system) have a very strong personal interest in mantaining the structure as is, which may well be the only way it can be maintained. Even if they were prepared to sacrifice their own positions, their thinking has been so compressed by their indoctrination and their careers that they would not be likely to frame appropriate questions. On the other hand, those outside who are in a better position to perceive a need for change and who might gain, or at least would not lose, by it, are kept as powerless as the party can manage.

Withal, the party system is cunningly contrived and very strong. There is no visible threat to its magnificent supremacy, even though economic growth should cease or a few intellectuals should become more unruly. The succession question obviously bears down, however; it must soon become acute, and it may well

---

*Not a single work on Stalin has appeared in the Soviet Union since his death. Lazitch, *Le rapport Khrouchtchev*, p. 43.

shake the fundaments of the party. Modern medicine enables men to hang on to their power into deeper senility; it is better able to keep them alive than to keep their minds fresh. Communist states have no new or good solutions to the age-old problem of transferring power in authoritarian regimes, and the problem is potentially graver in more centralized systems.[84]

In the past, the succession raised conflicts and questions; but after Lenin, Stalin, and Khrushchev, a younger group was prepared to take the reins. In Khrushchev's case, particularly, it was possible simply to subtract him and to leave in charge those who had managed during his travels. Stalin had his heir apparent in Malenkov, and Khrushchev had his in Brezhnev. But to prepare a succession is to raise a rival. Stalin was strong enough to resist his successor, and Khrushchev thought he was, but Brezhnev apparently is not. The top leadership is wearing out together, conspiring to avoid replacement, but it must sooner or later give way.[85] The longer it can postpone the day, the more tumultuous the transition is likely to be, and the greater the possibility of release of long-repressed tensions and contradictions. Meanwhile, the system can take no steps to prepare; it can no more talk about the problem than the people of imperial China could discuss the death of the emperor.

Conclusion

The Party Transformed and the Same

The Communist Party of the Soviet Union proudly claims today to be the selfsame organization that was begun by Lenin as the Bolshevik faction of the Russian Social Democratic Workers' Party, the party that found its strength in 1917, made a sweeping revolution, fought a civil war, and transformed the land under Stalin. The membership has undergone much flux, and four men have stood over the party, but there has always been organizational continuity. A series of Central Committees have summoned congresses, which have sanctioned new Central Committees to carry forward the work of the party, and the Politburo (Presidium) and the apparatus of the Secretariat have always depended formally on the properly constituted Central Committee. The thread of continuity was somewhat thinned when Stalin dispensed with congresses and the Central Committee for long years, and there was a break in legality upon the death of Stalin, when a self-appointed group with the support of the security forces called itself the Presidium and named a new government. Nevertheless, the new Presidium was nearly equivalent to the old Politburo that was dissolved by Stalin in his enlarged Presidium.

Despite this continuity, the Communist party has evolved, by many small steps and a few leaps, into an organization that is virtually the opposite of what it was at its inception. The Brezhnev party differs from Lenin's prerevolutionary movement quite as much as an aging man differs from a neonate. Lenin's party was a tiny group, with a few tens or hundreds of full-time party workers and a few thousand members; it has become a massive organization with approximately sixteen million members, scores of millions if affiliates are counted, and hundreds of thousands of professionals. It began as a simple and informal group; it is now extremely highly structured and formal. It was fluid, with frequent reelections and a high rate of turnover in its leadership; its apparat has become fixed and frozen. It was a youth movement, fighting custom and traditions; even through the 1920s the Bolsheviks were setting the young people against the older generation. Now it is a party of the mature led by the elderly, and it wishes youth to be conformist and obedient to the norms it lays down. When there were few educated women and the mores consigned women to the home, it brought many women into political activity and a few into high places. Now, when there are many educated women and it is taken for granted that women work, they are almost entirely excluded from high politics.

The crucial metamorphosis came, of course, as the outsiders shouting at the gate became the masters of the fortress. A clique of revolutionaries, who previously could hardly hope to do more than annoy the mighty tsarist government, became themselves the rulers, and even more than governors, the virtual owners of the immense state and its wealth and power. As men who had achieved their chief goal, the radicals turned conservative. For years after 1917, they tried to think of themselves as path breakers of a still greater revolution, but the revolutionary spirit was gradually cast off. Khrushchev was the last seriously to seek to revive the mission of broader change; now nothing remains of that mission except a hope, like that of any powerful state, for greater influence abroad. Correspondingly, the Marxist vision and its dedication to the oppressed have yielded to privilege for the elite and their loyalty to their organization.

A less obvious and less readily understandable reversal is that a party that was in large part inspired by resentment against Russian domination of the empire, a party that depended heavily on the support of oppressed minorities and a large fraction of whose leadership was Jewish, has become an essentially Russian organization with strong notes of anti-Semitism in its outlook. The party has become Russian at the center and top because it rules an empire in which Russians are the central and dominant nationality. In the new Soviet state, non-Russians became the internationalists and agitators against whom Stalin's "socialism in one country" was directed, or they were separatists, whose desire for autonomy conflicted with the power of the center in Moscow.

In the processes of first building and then maintaining a new bureaucratic state, the Russians became increasingly the rulers, as they had been for generations. Russian military men and bureaucrats were on the spot, they were the more reliable adherents of the Moscow-based regime, and they were called upon to make sure that the Caucasus, the Ukraine, and Central Asia remained faithful to Moscow. Russianization of the party progressed even under Stalin, the Georgian, who purged the old revolutionaries and minority nationalists. It has since advanced. Russian publications are dominant even in areas of non-Russian population; 85 percent of the periodical circulation in the USSR is Russian. According to recent figures, 61 percent of party membership is Russian, a solid majority and considerably more than the Russian proportion of the population (about 50 percent), and the domination of Russians in the apparatus is much stronger.[1] The core of the party apparatus, the Secretaries of the Central Committee and its section chiefs, have for many years been almost purely Russian, diluted only by a few near-Russians, Ukrainians, or Belorussians. The security police is also strongly Russian; in the minority republics the real, if not the nominal, boss of the KGB is Russian. Lenin decried "Great Russian chauvinism"; his latter-day successors combat all "bourgeois nationalism" except Russian. In brief, the party has become in many ways quite like its onetime antagonist, the government it originally set about destroying.

Despite these profound reversals in the character of the party, there are equally strong continuities. The party began as an educated group that looked down upon the workers but claimed to speak for them. After some proletarianization under Stalin, the party leadership is today a highly, although narrowly, educated elite that speaks and rules in the name of workers who live far below them. The early Leninist movement also represented a breaking away from the general Western orientation of the Russian intelligentsia, a movement that was basically contrary to Western ("bourgeois") society and values, to the commercial, individualistic, libertarian outlook that had grown up over the centuries in Western Europe. The party remains contrary in philosophy and approach to what is still described as the rotten Western capitalistic world; it derives support from popular distrust of the Westernized intellectuals. The party was and is an elitist organization that presents itself as representative of the masses.[2]

The party was and is anti-Western in spirit because it was designed to achieve power under Russian conditions, and it is dedicated to maintaining that power under conditions that remain fundamentally unchanged. This power orientation represents the party's fundamental continuity. At first, change was on the agenda as a means to power; now change is no longer necessary, but has instead become a threat to power, so it is off the agenda; the goal of rulership is constant. The party began as an exclusive, semiconspiratorial, secretive organization that demanded philosophical conformity, obedience, and dedication from its members in return for the satisfactions of belonging to the vanguard organization, including opportunities for political activism, and promises of power. This description still applies, although the promises of power are now firmer. The party has always mixed idealism with cynicism and ambition, although the mix has now changed, to the benefit of careerism. As soon as the party acquired control of the government, it was able to offer material benefits, and it has increasingly done so; however, the party's rewards have always been more psychological than material. It was and is fundamentally a political rather than an administrative or economic organization; the leadership of the party remains always with the maneuverers and bosses, not the managers or technocrats.[3] Party leaders may have technical training, but they have generally spent their lives in straight party work.

The party can be understood only as a scheme for first the acquisition, then the maintenance of power by a strong-willed and able minority. Its great purpose is not a particular program for the improvement of society—Lenin himself was apparently quite uncertain what his postrevolutionary order should be—but, as Conquest put it, an effort to keep power in the hands of a self-chosen few and to conceal that fact.[4]

To achieve this purpose, there is a guiding nucleus at the center, a kind of holy fellowship, headed by a more or less dictatorial leader—the party has functioned under single heads with varying personalities or oligarchies with equal effectiveness. Beneath the sovereign core, the party apparatus and the general membership serve as a sort of transmission belt of power, and the auxiliary organizations of the party, most importantly the administrative and economic bureaucracies, the Komsomol, and the trade unions, carry out the will of the party to move the society as it desires. The party as a whole is something of a facade for the rule of the elite, just as the system of supposedly elected soviets is a facade for the rule of the party.

The system may be compared to a set of interlocking wheels, wherein the tiny but supremely powerful wheel in the center turns the larger wheels of the Central Committee, the central apparatus, the council of ministers, and so forth. The central party bureaucracy in turn moves the lower apparatus, which (to follow only one line in the diffusion of power) directs the mass party membership, which in turn guides other organizations and the people as a whole.

In this scheme, power, responsibility, and privileges decrease as one moves down and away from the central nucleus. As a means of government, this design has the weakness of minimizing feedback, admitting a flow upward of only limited information and very little influence. But it has psychological strength and great stability, and it seems to tend to restore itself when strained. Each layer knows that its position depends upon the unity of the whole, and each layer below the summit knows that it must accept subordination in return for domination. The inner circle at the top acknowledges a leader, even a bloody Stalin, to whom it bows and who receives disproportionate adulation, because of its awareness that the rulership needs a focus and its fear that to attack him would endanger unity and party rule. The party apparatus is expected to be unconditionally loyal to directives from above; in return it exercises great power and perquisites. The ordinary party members work under superior direction and have the compensation of elite status with respect to nonparty folk. Even though he may not live much better than his nonparty neighbors, the party man can congratulate himself on his closer relationship with the powers of society. He is flattered, furnished with information that is denied to the masses, consulted about minor matters, called upon to watch over other citizens, and largely immune from criticism, even from prosecution for crimes unless the party turns its back on him. He belongs to the elect of society.

The party is a very large group indeed to enjoy elite status, but there is a still larger rulership, that of the Russians over their empire. They may not gain much materially from their dominant position—although it is not inconceivable that political advantage translates into economic benefit, and it is certainly easier for Russians than for Central Asians to get high-ranking jobs—but the psychological rewards are incontestable. The basic culture is Russian; non-Russians are outsiders to the heritage of Peter the Great, Pushkin, Alexander I, Lenin, and so on. The basic language is Russian; non-Russians have access to much less, and usually poorer, literature, broadcasts, and cinema, and to have significant careers, they must operate in a foreign language. Positions of real power are held by Russians (with the assistance of some Ukrainians and White Russians), who are the real rulers in minority republics as well as Slavic lands. The Russians are the prime "builders of communism," the heirs of the empire that has expanded in the past five hundred years to cover a sixth of the earth's land, an empire annexation to which was, in the tsarist as in the modern Soviet interpretation, liberation.

Since the Second World War, the Russian dominion has been extended over half a dozen countries of Eastern Europe. That this dominion contributes significantly to the Soviet economy is doubtful, but its importance for the feelings of the Russians is enormous. It represents a vindication of the October Revolution, which finally spread beyond the country of its origin. In the ideological picture, the revolution must go forward, as Trotsky required, even though there may be indefinite delay, as Stalin postulated, and expansion is taken as proof of correctness. To state the same thing in different words, Russian rule over the formerly independent countries of Eastern Europe is a vindication of Russianism and a welcome reversal; peoples who formerly regarded themselves as superior to the Russians, to whom the Russians had to admit some cultural inferiority, now have to look up to, or at least obey, their eastern neighbor.

Before 1917 Russians generally accepted the autocracy as the only way to hold the empire together, that is, to maintain the status of the ruling people. Now they are called upon to accept the rule of the party and its ideology for the same reason. There is no easily conceivable way the dominion could be held without the party, its devices, its organization, and its philosophic rationale. A few, such as Sakharov, may think in terms of union in freedom, as did some liberals before the revolution, but these are insubstantial and implausible dreams. To the contrary, the fear is very real that to attack the party means to invite anarchy and disorder, risking the hard-won gains of the past generation, or of several centuries.[5]

The unequal relationship between the Russians and the smaller peoples living around them is thus a principal factor in assuring the hegemony of the party and adherence to the Marxist-Leninist creed, which justifies the priority of "class," that is, party interests over nationality. Other inequalities—of party over people, of apparatus over party, and of the central core over the apparatus—contribute to the grandiose political structure, but the inequality of nationalities has a special importance. It is part of the landscape on which the political edifice is built. The rest is artificial and could conceivably be torn down. The numerical preponderance of the Russians and their situation, surrounded by a large number of weaker nationalities, would invite domination (which would have to be somehow philosophically rationalized and sustained by organization and force) even if it did not already exist.

Marxist-Leninist party supremacy thus has a firm foundation in political reality. Yet it lacks intrinsic stability and is wearing out the advantages gained through the revolution, renewal and the inspiration of elites. There is, as pointed out by Bertram Wolfe, a "law of diminishing dictators."[6] Through the sequence of Lenin, Stalin, Khrushchev, and Brezhnev, each leader has been less imposing than his predecessor, and the distrust of able and energetic men, plus the compressive tendencies of the system, indicate that the sequence will probably continue. There is also a "law of revolutionary reversal": unless it brings freedom, a revolution inevitably reverts toward the prerevolutionary condition. Stalin was in the tradition of Peter the Great, and his successors, it increasingly seems, are in the tradition of Peter's successors. The great times not only of change, but also of order, are behind. Russians are not only nostalgic for Lenin because he promised a new order and brought equality and dignity for the ordinary people; they are nostalgic for Stalin because he kept the petty bosses from cheating.[7] The new rulers are the uninspired consumers of a revolution made by others; those who come after will not even have been tempered by the war.

A ruling class thus develops, perhaps becoming a ruling caste that, having worn out its function of social renewal, has nowhere to go and becomes increasingly irrational and parasitic. It may be taken as axiomatic that a closed elite will turn power to enjoyment, its selfishness being hedged only by idealism. Nothing serves to revive withered idealism; after it is exhausted, privileges and abuses of power become customary, and the rulership can be expected to care increasingly for itself and its own. Achievement is measured in perquisites. Positions become property, valued for usufruct. The example is contagious, and those on top can hardly change it. Perhaps they do not care to, because they also are beneficiaries of the system and to attempt any material change might be dangerous.

Perhaps, also, those on top know little of what goes on in their system. There is no independent criticism, and those who might criticize are dependent on those whom they would be criticizing. In any case criticism risks being taken as disloyalty to the system, the unforgivable sin. Routine prevails, and there is no emergency to shock the system into action. Its very effectiveness prevents the challenges that might lead to the changes necessary to sustain vigor. Moreover, as the system loses its dynamism and the purposeful spirit that animated its beginnings, change becomes more threatening and difficult.

This situation leads the party to a profound dilemma. To keep its hold, to save all that it has built, it must continue to draw from the West the techniques of modern material power, while upholding an anti-Western and unmodern absolutist political structure. It may be that today, as a century or so ago, the domain (which means not Russia strictly speaking but the empire) can be governed only as an isolated autocracy.[8] But an isolated autocracy is not consonant with the prevalent trends of this century. Either civilization goes backward—held back by political failures above all—or the Russian empire must one day adapt to the modern world.

Figures on the Party

TABLE 1

PARTY MEMBERSHIP

	Members	Candidates	Total
1905	8,400	none	8,400
1907	46,000	none	46,000
1917 (March)	24,000	none	24,000
1917 (October)	350,000	none	350,000
1918 (March)	390,000	none	390,000
1919 (March)	350,000	none	350,000
1920 (March)	611,978	not counted	611,978
1921 (March)	732,521	not counted	732,521
1922	410,430	117,924	528,354
1923	381,400	117,700	499,100
1924	350,000	122,000	472,000
1925	440,365	361,439	801,804
1926	639,652	440,162	1,079,814
1927	786,288	426,217	1,212,505
1928	914,307	391,547	1,305,854
1929	1,090,508	444,854	1,535,362
1930	1,184,651	493,259	1,677,910
1931	1,369,406	842,819	2,212,225
1932	1,769,773	1,347,477	3,117,250
1933	2,203,951	1,351,387	3,555,338
1934	1,826,756	874,252	2,701,008
1935	1,659,104	699,610	2,358,714
1936	1,489,907	586,935	2,076,842
1937	1,453,828	527,869	1,981,697
1938	1,405,879	514,123	1,920,002

TABLE 1

Party Membership (Cont.)

	Members	*Candidates*	*Total*
1939	1,514,181	792,792	2,306,973
1940	1,982,743	1,417,232	3,399,975
1941	2,490,479	1,381,986	3,872,465
1942	2,155,336	908,540	3,063,876
1943	2,451,511	1,403,190	3,854,701
1944	3,126,627	1,791,934	4,918,561
1945	3,965,530	1,794,839	5,760,369
1946	4,127,689	1,383,173	5,510,862
1947	4,774,886	1,277,015	6,051,901
1948	5,181,199	1,209,082	6,390,281
1949	5,334,811	1,017,761	6,352,572
1950	5,510,787	829,396	6,340,183
1951	5,658,577	804,398	6,462,975
1952	5,853,200	854,339	6,707,539
1953	6,067,027	830,197	6,897,224
1954	6,402,284	462,579	6,864,863
1955	6,610,238	346,867	6,957,105
1956	6,767,644	405,877	7,173,521
1957	7,001,114	493,459	7,494,573
1958	7,296,559	546,637	7,843,196
1959	7,622,356	616,775	8,239,131
1960	8,017,249	691,418	8,708,667
1961	8,472,396	803,430	9,275,826
1962	9,051,934	839,134	9,891,068
1963	9,581,149	806,047	10,387,196
1964	10,182,916	839,453	11,022,369
1965	10,811,443	946,726	11,758,169
1966	11,548,287	809,021	12,357,308
1967	12,135,103	549,030	12,684,133
1968	12,484,836	695,389	13,180,225
1969	12,958,303	681,588	13,639,891
1970	13,395,253	616,531	14,011,784
1971	13,745,980	626,583	14,372,563
1972	14,109,432	521,857	14,631,289
1973	14,330,525	490,506	14,821,031
1974	14,493,524	532,391	15,025,915
1976 (March)	15,058,017	636,170	15,694,187

Sources: *Partinaia zhizn* 14 (July 1973): 9–10, and 10 (May 1976): 13. The latter is translated in *Current Digest of the Soviet Press* 28 (September 29, 1976): 1–5.

Notes: There was no systematic count of party members until 1922. In the figures for 1907 are included only members of the Bolshevik party represented at the Fifth (London) Congress.

TABLE 2

CPSU: Ethnic Composition

Nationality	1946		1961		1965		1967		1973		1976	
USSR	5,513,649	100.0	9,626,700	100.1	11,758,200	100.0	12,684,133	100.1	14,821,031	100.0	15,638,891	100.0
Russians	3,736,165	67.8	6,116,700	63.5	7,335,200	62.4	7,846,292	61.9	9,025,363	60.9	9,481,536	60.6
Ukrainians	667,481	12.1	1,412,200	14.7	1,813,400	15.4	1,983,090	15.6	2,369,200	16.0	2,505,378	16.0
Belorussians	114,799	2.1	287,000	3.0	386,000	3.3	424,360	3.3	521,544	3.5	563,408	3.6
Georgians	61,467	1.1	170,400	1.8	194,300	1.7	209,196	1.6	291,550	2.0	321,458	2.1
Armenians	92,354	1.7	161,200	1.7	187,900	1.6	200,605	1.6	254,667	1.7	282,471	1.8
Kazakhs	107,910	2.0	149,200	1.5	181,300	1.5	199,196	1.6	246,214	1.7	259,520	1.7
Uzbeks	55,448	1.0	142,700	1.5	193,600	1.6	219,196	1.7	212,122	1.4	232,223	1.5
Azerbaidzanis	3,704	0.1	106,100	1.1	141,900	1.2	162,181	1.3	96,558	0.7	106,967	0.7
Lithuanians	2,913	0.1	42,800	0.4	61,500	0.5	71,316	0.6	59,434	0.4	67,707	0.4
Latvians	8,408	0.1	33,900	0.4	44,300	0.4	49,559	0.4	61,755	0.4	65,116	0.4
Tadzhiks	14,039	0.3	32,700	0.3	41,900	0.4	46,593	0.4	46,049	0.3	49,542	0.3
Kirgiz	13,757	0.2	27,300	0.3	35,000	0.3	39,053	0.3	58,668	0.3	63,611	0.4
Turkmen	100,449	1.8	27,300	0.3	32,400	0.3	35,781	0.3	225,132	1.5	234,253	1.5
Moldavians	12,675	0.2	26,700	0.3	40,300	0.3	46,593	0.3	44,218	0.4	48,021	0.3
Estonians	7,976	0.1	24,400	0.3	33,900	0.3	37,705	0.3	46,424	0.3	49,739	0.3
Others	514,104	9.3	866,100	9.0	1,035,300	8.8	1,113,263	8.8	1,262,133	8.5	1,294,022	8.4

SOURCES: *Partinaia zhizn* 10 (May 1973): 18, and 14 (July 1976): 16; Ellen Mickiewicz, *Handbook of Soviet Social Science Data* (New York: Free Press, 1973).

NOTE: "Others" include all nationalities not represented by a Soviet republic; 294,744 Jews, and 300,714 Tatars were the largest components in 1976.

TABLE 3

WOMEN IN THE PARTY

Year	Number	%
1920	45,297	7.4
1926	128,807	11.9
1930	219,338	13.1
1934	395,763	14.7
1939	333,821	14.5
1946	1,033,115	18.7
1952	1,276,560	19.0
1956	1,414,456	19.7
1961	1,809,688	19.5
1966	2,548,901	20.6
1971	3,195,556	22.2
1973	3,412,029	23.0
1976	3,793,859	24.3

SOURCES: *Partinaia zhizn* 10 (May 1973): 18, and 14 (July 1976): 17.

TABLE 4

CPSU MEMBERSHIP: AGE

Year	Under 25	% of Total	26–40	% of Total
1927	303,126	25	739,628	61
1965	823,072	7	5,526,339	47
1967	634,207	5	5,898,122	47
1973	834,166	6	4,590,733	38

Year	41–50	% of Total	Over 50	% of Total
1927	133,376	11	36,375	3
1965	2,939,542	25	2,469,216	21
1967	3,247,138	25	2,904,666	23
1973	4,329,005	29	3,967,127	27

SOURCES: *Partinaia zhizn* 10 (May 1973): 19; Mickiewicz, p. 164. Figures for 1976 have not been published.

TABLE 5

CPSU Membership: Social Position

Year	Workers	% of Total	Peasants (Collective Farmers)	% of Total	White Collar and Others	% of Total
1922	234,589	44.4	141,071	26.7	152,694	28.9
1923	224,096	44.9	128,269	25.7	146,735	29.4
1924	207,680	44.0	135,936	28.8	128,384	27.2
1925	454,623	56.7	212,478	26.5	134,703	16.8
1926	613,334	56.8	279,672	25.9	186,808	17.3
1927	668,256	55.1	331,096	27.3	213,454	17.6
1928	741,725	56.8	229.041	22.9	265,088	20.3
1929	942,712	61.4	333,174	21.7	259,476	16.9
1930	1,095,675	65.3	338,937	20.2	243,296	14.5
1937	2,398,263	32.0	1,296,561	17.3	3,799,749	50.7
1946	1,865,126	33.8	1,023,903	18.6	2,621,833	47.6
1952	2,162,059	32.2	1,206,668	18.0	3,338,812	49.8
1956	2,291,455	32.0	1,227,767	17.1	3,654,299	50.9
1961	3,146,135	33.9	1,632,847	17.6	4,496,844	48.5
1966	4,675,879	37.8	1,999,138	16.2	5,682,291	46.0
1971	5,759,379	40.1	2,169,437	15.1	6,443,747	44.8
1973	6,037,771	40.7	2,169,764	14.7	6,613,496	44.6
1976	6,509,312	41.6	2,169,813	13.9	6,959,766	44.5

SOURCES: Mickiewicz, p. 165; *Partinaia zhizn* 14 (July 1976): 15.

TABLE 6

Local Party Organs

	1971	1976
Central Committees of Union Republics	14	14
Krai Committees	6	6
Oblast Committees	142	148
City Committees equated with Oblast Committees (Moscow and Kiev)	1	2
Okrug Committees	10	10
City Committees	759	813
City District Committees	448	571
Village District Committees	2,810	2,857
Primary Party Organizations	369,695	390,387
Shop Party Organizations	352,871	400,388
Party Groups	443,233	528,894

SOURCE: *Partinaia zhizn* 14 (July 1976): 18–19.

TABLE 7

Educational Level of Party Members

Year	Higher	Incomplete Higher	Secondary	Incomplete Secondary	Primary	None
			Number and Percentage			
1927	9,614.0	—	104,714.0	—	720,203.0	309,522.0
%	0.8		9.1		63.0	27.1
1939	127,751.0	45,603.0	289,185.0	314,058.0	1,062,859.0	467,517.0
%	5.5	2.0	12.5	13.6	46.1	20.3
1946	404,167.0	120,981.0	1,284,924.0	1,356,029.0	1,894,939.0	449,822.0
%	7.3	2.2	23.3	24.6	34.4	8.2
1952	597,538.0	188,157.0	1,486,469.0	1,854,125.0	2,107,872.0	473,378.0
%	8.9	2.8	22.2	27.6	31.4	7.1
1956	801,384.0	256,856.0	1,593,505.0	2,127,862.0	2,036,745.0	357,169.0
%	11.2	3.6	22.2	29.6	28.4	5.0
1961	1,226,145.0	278,806.0	2,427,837.0	2,649,114.0	2,394,836.0	299,088.0
%	13.2	3.0	26.2	28.6	25.8	3.2
1966	1,934,567.0	315,366.0	3,816,180.0	3,402,057.0	2,889,138.0	—
%	15.7	2.5	30.9	27.5	23.4	—
1971	2,819,642.0	337,995.0	4,932,958.0	3,573,368.0	2,708,600.0	—
%	19.6	2.4	34.3	24.9	18.8	—
1973	3,209,605.0	328,493.0	5,344,433.0	3,406,208.0	2,532,292.0	—
%	21.6	2.2	36.1	23.0	17.1	—
1976	3,808,000.0	383,000.0	6,022,000.0	3,175,000.0	2,251,000.0	—
%	24.3	2.5	38.5	20.3	14.4	—

SOURCES: *Partinaia zhizn* 10 (May 1973): 16, and 14 (July 1976): 15. For 1927, persons with incomplete higher education counted as "secondary"; with incomplete secondary education counted as "primary."

Women in the Party

Although the liberation of women was not closely related logically to Marxist dialectics and economic materialism, it was stressed by Engels and became a prominent thesis of Social Democracy in the last part of the nineteenth century. Equality of women was also a Populist passion in nineteenth-century Russia, and women, such as Vera Figner and Yekaterina Breshkovskaia, were conspicuous in the Russian revolutionary movement. It was taken for granted that the socialist revolution meant liberation for women and equality of the sexes.[1]

The Bolsheviks entirely subscribed to this general leftist aspiration, and women, from Krupskaya and Stasova down, were prominent in the movement. Lenin typically wrote, "Unless women are brought to take an independent part not only in political life generally but also in daily and universal public service, it is no use talking about full and stable democracy, let alone socialism."[2]

In the revolution, women were rather conspicuous among the Bolsheviks, although they had no leader comparable to Maria Spiridonova, the most outstanding Left Socialist Revolutionary. In 1921 Alexandra Kollontai became the most effective advocate of the Workers' Opposition, but after the revolution Bolshevik women were mostly consigned to special women's organizations.[3]

Since the first agitated years, the party has been run by men. Only eighty-four women have come into the approximately forty-six hundred high party positions to which appointments have been made since 1917.[4] Women are strongly represented in the powerless soviets; the considerable uniformity in the proportion of females in the various organizations—about 35 to 45 percent in the local soviets and 30 to 40 percent in the union republic and the Soviet Union supreme soviets—indicates that quotas are used.[5] The percentage of women in the Central Committee was around 7 percent up to the revolution, had fallen to zero by the end of the civil war, was back to about 3 percent by 1928, had sunk near zero again by 1941, and since 1952 has been around 2 to 3 percent, never higher than 4 percent. Thus it has decreased in times of crisis and reached a modest token level in quieter periods; tokenism is also indicated by the fact that female Central Committee members seldom remain in those positions long. Of the fourteen women who were members of the Central Committee in 1971, six were there in honorary capacities as outstanding workers;[6] similarly, women in local soviets are seldom party leaders.[7]

About one-third of local party secretaries and a few district (raion) secretaries are women, but they have hardly ever been oblast secretaries. In recent years, there has been only one woman minister, Yekaterina Furtseva; as Khrushchev's protégé she was also the only woman to have served (briefly) on the Secretariat and the Politburo (she became a candidate in February 1956 and was a full member from June 1957 to October 1961). In 1973 one woman, I. R. Rakhimova, was a republic secretary in Tadzhikistan; she was presumably thus elevated to encourage the emancipation of Moslem women and their participation in the work force.

It is a paradox that at present, when there are very many educated women, they are less prominent in the directorate of Soviet society than they were when they were few and the Bolsheviks were fighting the antifeminist mores of the tsarist state. This paradox is a tribute to the essentially conservative, authoritarian political environment produced by the radical revolution.

Notes

1. THE RUSSIAN DISCONTENT

1. This is a thesis of Robert Wesson's, presented in *The Russian Dilemma* (New Brunswick, N.J.: Rutgers University Press, 1974).

2. On the Russian autocratic tradition, see Tibor Szamuely, *The Russian Tradition*.

3. Leopold Haimson, *The Russian Marxists and the Origins of Bolshevism*, p. 6.

4. As observed by Adam B. Ulam in *The Bolsheviks*, p. 38.

5. Isaiah Berlin, "Foreword," to *Roots of Revolution*, by Franco Venturi, p. xv.

6. Cited in Robert W. Tucker, ed., *The Lenin Anthology* (New York: W. W. Norton, 1975), pp. xxx–xxxi.

7. Letter to Kugelman of October 1, 1868, cited in *A Documentary History of Communism*, ed. Robert V. Daniels, p. xxvii.

8. Berlin, "Foreword," p. xiv.

9. Haimson, *Russian Marxists*, p. 10.

10. Szamuely, *Russian Tradition*, pp. 314–18.

11. Deborah Hardy, "Tkachev and the Marxists," *Slavic Review* (March 1970): 22–34.

12. Haimson, *Russian Marxists*, p. 18.

13. Ronald Hingley, *The Nihilists* (New York: Delacorte Press, 1967), p. 57.

2. LENIN'S PARTY: FORMATION AND WAITING

1. For an extended commentary on the Western background of Marxism-Leninism, see Edmund Wilson, *To the Finland Station* (Garden City, N.Y.: Doubleday, 1947).

2. Karl Marx, "First Draft of the Reply to V. I. Zasulich's Letter," in Karl Marx and Frederick Engels, *Selected Works in Three Volumes* (Moscow: Progress Publishers, 1970), vol. 3, pp. 152–53.

3. Leopold H. Haimson, *The Russian Marxists and the Origins of Bolshevism*, pp. 21–23.

4. Alan K. Wildman, *The Making of a Workers' Revolution: Russian Social Democracy, 1891–1903* (Chicago: University of Chicago Press, 1967), pp. 5–7.

5. Adam B. Ulam, *The Bolsheviks*, p. 99.

6. There are biographies by Adam B. Ulam, Bertram Wolfe, Louis Fischer, David Shub, and others. For an official treatment, see P. N. Pospelov, chief ed., *Vladimir Ilich Lenin: Biography* (Moscow: Izd. politicheskoi literatury, 1972). For a strongly antimythical biography, see Stefan T. Possony, *Lenin: The Compulsive Revolutionary* (Chicago: Henry Regnery, 1964).

7. Soviet writing portrays Lenin as totally Russian. Louis Fischer, *The Life of Lenin*, p. 4.

8. Bertram D. Wolfe, *Three Who Made a Revolution*, p. 75.

9. For his youth, see Nikolai Valentinov, *The Early Years of Lenin* (Ann Arbor: University of Michigan Press, 1969).

10. Nadezhda K. Krupskaya, *Reminiscences of Lenin*, vol. 1, p. 23.

11. Wolfe, *Three Who Made a Revolution*, p. 85.

12. Ulam, *Bolsheviks*, p. 107.

13. Nadezhda Krupskaya, *Memories of Lenin* (New York: International Publishers, 1930), vol. 1, p. 2.

14. Robert H. McNeal, *Bride of the Revolution*, p. 9.

15. V. I. Lenin, "What is to Be Done," in V. I. Lenin, *Selected Works in Three Volumes* (Moscow: Progress Publishers, 1970), vol. 1, p. 263.

16. Wildman, *Making of Workers' Revolution*, pp. 176−77.

17. Rolf H. W. Theen, *Lenin: Genesis and Development of a Revolutionary* (Philadelphia: J. B. Lippincott, 1973), p. 100.

18. Krupskaya, *Memories*, p. 60.

19. V. I. Lenin, "What is to Be Done," in *A Documentary History of Communism*, ed., Robert V. Daniels, vol. 1, pp. 12−13.

20. Ibid., p. 14.

21. Ibid., pp. 16−17.

22. Krupskaya, *Reminiscences*, p. 65.

23. Lenin, "What is to Be Done," in *Selected Works*, p. 217.

24. Wildman, *Making of Workers' Revolution*, p. 252.

25. Ibid., pp. 232−33.

26. Ulam, *Bolsheviks*, p. 73.

27. Robert H. McNeal, ed., *Resolutions and Decisions of the Communist Party of the Soviet Union 1898−1964*, vol. 1, p. 41.

28. Leonard Schapiro, *The Origin of the Communist Autocracy*, p. 12.

29. Leon Trotsky, *Lenin*, p. 48; Fischer, *Life of Lenin*, p. 515.

30. Isaac Deutscher, *The Prophet Armed*, pp. 89−90.

31. For an account of the rise of Bolshevism from a Menshevik viewpoint, see Theodore Dan, *The Origins of Bolshevism*.

32. Adam B. Ulam, *Stalin*, p. 50.

33. Robert V. Daniels, *The Conscience of the Revolution*, p. 15.

34. David Shub, *Lenin*, p. 369.

35. McNeal, *Resolutions and Decisions*, p. 42.

36. Barrington Moore, Jr., *Soviet Politics—The Dilemma of Change* (Cambridge: Harvard University Press, 1950), p. 50.

37. Pospelov, *Lenin*, p. 106.

38. Deutscher, *Prophet Armed*, p. 45.

39. Wildman, *Making of Workers' Revolution*, pp. 243−44.

40. Oskar Anweiler, *The Soviets*, p. 31.

41. Cited in Edward H. Carr, *Socialism in One Country 1924−1926*, p. 127.

42. On the Russian moral-philosophical roots of Bolshevism, see Nicolas Berdyaev, *The Origins of Russian Communism*.

43. Carr, *Socialism in One Country*, p. 17. For a treatment that emphasizes the distance between Bolshevism and Western culture, see Stuart R. Tompkins, *The Triumph of Bolshevism: Revolution or Reaction* (Norman, Okla.: University of Oklahoma Press, 1967).

44. Haimson, *Russian Marxists*, p. 192.

45. Krupskaya, *Reminiscences*, p. 20.

46. Leonard Schapiro, *The Communist Party of the Soviet Union*, pp. 22, 69.

47. On the 1905 revolution, see Sidney Harcave, *First Blood: The Russian Revolution of 1905* (New York: Macmillan, 1964).

48. Deutscher, *Prophet Armed*, p. 125.

49. Anweiler, *Soviets*, pp. 38−46.

50. Daniels, *Conscience of the Revolution*, p. 36.

51. Deutscher, *Prophet Armed*, p. 158.

52. Ulam, *Bolsheviks*, pp. 218, 230.

53. On the social origins and distribution of the party membership at this time, see David Lane, *The Roots of Russian Communism*.

54. Schapiro, *Communist Party*, p. 68.

55. Robert H. McNeal, *The Bolshevik Tradition: Lenin, Stalin, Khrushchev* (Englewood Cliffs, N.J.: Prentice-Hall, 1963), p. 22.

56. Marc Ferro, *The Russian Revolution of February 1917* (Englewood Cliffs, N.J.: Prentice-Hall, 1972), pp. 325−26.

57. Haimson, *Russian Marxists*, p. 218.

58. Harold Shukman, *Lenin and the Russian Revolution* (London: B. T. Batsford, 1966), p. 126; McNeal, *Bolshevik Tradition*, p. 22.

59. Krupskaya, *Reminiscences*, p. 181.

60. Daniels, *Conscience of the Revolution*, p. 18.

61. Possony, *Lenin*, p. 99.

62. Krupskaya, *Reminiscences*, p. 166.

63. Daniels, *Conscience of the Revolution*, p. 23.

64. Tompkins, *Triumph of Bolshevism*, pp. 292−93.

65. William H. Chamberlin, *The Russian Revolution 1917−1921*, vol. 1, p. 54.

66. Cited in Bertram D. Wolfe, *An Ideology in Power: Reflections on the Russian Revolution* (New York: Stein and Day, 1969), p. 167.

67. McNeal, *Bolshevik Tradition*, p. 13.

68. Fischer, *Life of Lenin*, p. 63.

69. Lane, *Roots of Russian Communism*, p. 35.

70. Schapiro, *Communist Party*, p. 73.

71. Lane, *Roots of Russian Communism*, p. 44.

72. Possony, *Lenin*, p. 110.

73. Daniels, *Conscience of the Revolution*, p. 33.

74. Ulam, *Bolsheviks*, p. 7.

75. Shub, *Lenin*, p. 133.

76. Ibid., p. 122.

77. David Anin, "Lenin and Malinovsky," *Survey* 21 (Autumn 1975): 148.

78. Ibid., pp. 146−47, 151.

79. Fischer, *Life of Lenin*, p. 84.

80. Possony, *Lenin*, p. 152.

81. Ulam, *Stalin*, p. 126.

82. As remarked by Alexander Solzhenitsyn in *Lenin in Zurich* (New York: Farrar, Strauss and Giroux, 1976), p. 8.

83. Wolfe, *Ideology in Power*, p. 113.

84. Schapiro, *Origin of Communist Autocracy*, p. 18.

85. Krupskaya, *Reminiscences*, p. 293.

86. Possony, *Lenin*, p. 185.

87. For the atmosphere, see Solzhenitsyn, *Lenin in Zurich*.

88. Krupskaya, *Reminiscences*, p. 304.

89. V. I. Lenin, "Principles Involved in the War Issue" (originally published December 1916), in V. I. Lenin, *Collected Works* (Moscow: Foreign Languages Publishing House, 1963), vol. 23, p. 157.

90. Cited in Shub, *Lenin*, pp. 152–53.

91. Stephen F. Cohn, "Bukharin, Lenin, and the Theoretical Foundations of Bolshevism," *Soviet Studies* 21 (April 1970), 446–48.

92. Lenin, "Lecture on the 1905 Revolution" (originally published January 22, 1917), in V. I. Lenin, *Collected Works* (Moscow: Foreign Languages Publishing House, 1963), vol. 23, p. 253.

3. CONQUEST OF POWER

1. Evgenii A. Evtushenko, *Autobiografiia* (London: Flegon Press, 1964), p. 46.

2. Alexander Kerensky, *Russia and History's Turning Point*, p. 147.

3. Marc Ferro, *The Russian Revolution of February 1917* (Englewood Cliffs, N.J.: Prentice-Hall, 1972), p. 25.

4. Kerensky, *Russia*, pp. 174–76.

5. Stefan T. Possony, *Lenin*, pp. 198–201.

6. George Katkov, *Russia 1917*, pp. 222–23; Katkov, "A Pro-Monarchist Theory of Conspiracy," in *The Russian Revolution*, ed. Virgil D. Medlin (Hinsdale, Ill: Dryden Press, 1974), pp. 65–66; Possony, *Lenin*, pp. 193–201.

7. *Pravda*, April 3 (16), 1917; Lenin, *Collected Works*, vol. 23, p. 301.

8. Oskar Anweiler, *The Soviets*, p. 104.

9. Kerensky, *Russia*, p. 233.

10. Robert H. McNeal, ed., *Resolutions and Decisions of the Communist Party of the Soviet Union 1898–1964*, vol. 1, pp. 198–99.

11. Frank A. Golder, *Documents of Russian History 1914–1917*, pp. 287–88.

12. Ibid., p. 319.

13. William H. Chamberlin, *The Russian Revolution 1917–1921*, vol. 1, pp. 86–87.

14. Ibid., p. 88.

15. D. A. Longley, "The Divisions in the Bolshevik Party in March 1917," *Soviet Studies* 24 (July 1972): 62.

16. T. H. Rigby, *Communist Party Membership in the U.S.S.R.*, pp. 59, 63.

17. Roy A. Medvedev, *Let History Judge*, p. 8.

18. Anweiler, *Soviets*, p. 148.

19. Cited in David Shub, *Lenin*, p. 184.

20. V. I. Lenin, *Selected Works in Three Volumes* (Moscow: Progress Publishers, 1970), vol. 2, pp. 43–48.

21. Ibid., p. 44.

22. Rigby, *Communist Party Membership*, p. 61.

23. Kerensky, *Russia*, p. 244.

24. McNeal, *Resolutions and Decisions*, p. 199.

25. Leonard Schapiro, *The Origin of the Communist Autocracy*, p. 45.

26. Anweiler, *Soviets*, p. 177.

27. Sergei P. Melgunov, *The Bolshevik Seizure of Power*, p. xviii.

28. For details of this adventurous time, see Shub, *Lenin*, pp. 218–21.

29. George Katkov, "German Foreign Office Documents on Financial Support to the Bolsheviks in 1917," *International Affairs* 32 (April 1956): 184.

30. Z. A. B. Zeman and W. B. Scharlau, *The Merchant of Revolution*, pp. 227–28.

31. Many documents are reproduced in Z. A. B. Zeman, *Germany and the Revolution in Russia 1915–1918.*

32. Katkov, *Russia 1917*, p. 100.

33. Kerensky, *Russia*, p. 263.

34. Louis Fischer, *The Life of Lenin*, p. 133.

35. David Anin, "Lenin and Malinovsky," *Survey* 21 (Autumn 1975): 150.

36. *The Letters of Lenin* (Westport, Conn.: Hyperion Press, 1973), p. 416.

37. Possony, *Lenin*, pp. 78–80.

38. Leon Trotsky, *Lenin*, p. 339.

39. To be found especially in Zeman and Scharlau, *Merchant of Revolution*.

40. Zeman and Scharlau, *Merchant of Revolution*, pp. 90–92.

41. Shub, *Lenin*, p. 137.

42. Zeman and Scharlau, *Merchant of Revolution*, p. 152.

43. For a graphic account of Lenin's relations with German agents, see Solzhenitsyn, *Lenin in Zurich* (New York: Farrar, Strauss and Giroux, 1976) pp. 129–81.

44. Zeman and Scharlau, *Merchant of Revolution*, pp. 162–65.

45. Katkov, *Russia 1917*, pp. 76, 97.

46. Fischer, *Life of Lenin*, p. 111.

47. For details of Bolshevik contacts in Scandinavia, see Michael Futrell, *Northern Underground* (London: Faber and Faber, 1963).

48. Stuart A. Tompkins, *The Triumph of Bolshevism: Revolution or Reaction* (Norman, Okla.: University of Oklahoma Press, 1967), p. 269.

49. Zeman and Scharlau, *Merchant of Revolution*, pp. 250–51.

50. Zeman, *Germany*, p. 70.

51. Ibid., p. 94.

52. Robert H. McNeal, *The Bolshevik Tradition: Lenin, Stalin, Khrushchev* (Englewood Cliffs, N.J.: Prentice-Hall, 1975), p. 36.

53. Leonard Schapiro, *The Communist Party of the Soviet Union*, p. 41.

54. Adam B. Ulam, *Bolsheviks*, p. 327.

55. Rigby, *Communist Party Membership*, p. 60.

56. Anweiler, *Soviets*, p. 110.

57. Isaac Deutscher, *The Prophet Armed*, p. 288.

58. Simon Liberman, *Building Lenin's Russia*, p. 74.

59. Robert V. Daniels, *The Conscience of the Revolution*, p. 30.

60. Melgunov, *Bolshevik Seizure of Power*, p. xvii; G. T. Robinson, *Rural Russia under the Old Regime* (New York: Macmillan, 1949), pp. 230–31.

61. I. N. Steinberg, *In the Workshop of the Revolution*, p. 38.

62. Melgunov, *Bolshevik Seizure*, p. 4.

63. Ibid., p. 12.

64. On this party, see Oliver H. Radkey, *The Agrarian Foes of Bolshevism: Promise and Default of the Russian Socialist Revolutionaries February to October 1917* (New York: Columbia University Press, 1958).

65. John Plamenatz, *German Marxism and Russian Communism* (London: Longmans, Green, 1954), p. 236.

66. Daniels, *Conscience*, p. 29.

67. Rodney Barfield, "Lenin's Utopianism: State and Revolution," *Slavic Review* 30 (March 1971): 45−56.

68. Stephen F. Cohen, "Bukharin, Lenin, and the Theoretical Foundations of Bolshevism," *Soviet Studies* 21 (April 1970): 456.

69. For the thesis that Bolshevism is an expression of Russian national (essentially peasant) character, see Nicholas Vakar, *The Taproot of Soviet Society* (New York: Harper and Bros., 1962).

70. Schapiro, *Origin of Communist Autocracy*, p. 349.

71. John Reed, *Ten Days that Shook the World* (New York: International Publishers, 1934), p.1.

72. Rigby, *Communist Party Membership*, pp. 63−64.

73. Anweiler, *Soviets*, p. 184.

74. Ibid., p. 177.

75. Schapiro, *Origin of Communist Autocracy*, p. 170.

76. Norman E. Saul, "Lenin's Decision to Seize Power: The Influence of Events in Finland," *Soviet Studies*, 24 (April 1973): 499:502.

77. V. I. Lenin, "The Crisis has Matured," (originally published September 29 [October 12], 1917) in V. I. Lenin, *Collected Works* (Moscow: Foreign Languages Publishing House, 1963), vol. 26, pp. 74−77.

78. Lenin, "Letter to Central Committee Members" (originally published October 24 [November 6], 1917), in Lenin, *Collected Works*, vol. 26, pp. 234−35.

79. Anweiler, *Soviets*, p. 191.

80. Martin McCauley, ed., *The Russian Revolution and the Soviet State 1917−1921*, p. 121.

81. Myron W. Hedlin, "Zinoviev's Revolutionary Tactics in 1917," *Slavic Review* 23 (March 1975): 19−43.

82. Robert V. Daniels, *A Documentary History of Communism*, p. 115.

83. Adam B. Ulam, *Stalin*, p. 156.

84. Melgunov, *Bolshevik Seizure*, p. 11.

85. Fischer, *Life of Lenin*, p. 137.

86. Robert V. Daniels, *Red October*, pp. 122−25.

87. For the modern Soviet version of the events of October, see P. N. Sobolev et al., *History of the October Revolution* (Moscow: Progress Publishers, 1965).

88. Daniels, *Red October*, pp. 149−50; Steinberg, *Workshop of Revolution*, p. 42.

89. Robert V. Daniels, "A Gamble Won by Default," in *Russian Revolution*, ed. Medlin p. 168.

90. D. N. Collins, "A Note on the Numerical Strength of the Red Guard in October 1917," *Soviet Studies* 24 (October 1972): 270−80.

91. For the atmosphere from the Bolshevik side, see Reed, *Ten Days*.

92. David R. Jones, "The Officers and the October Revolution," *Soviet Studies* 27 (April 1976): 207−23.

93. As observed by Ulam in *Bolsheviks*, p. 270.

94. Jacob Walkin, *The Rise of Democracy in pre-Revolutionary Russia*, p. 220.

95. As he remarked, in Kerensky, *Russia*, p. 403.

96. Daniels, *Red October*, p. 153.

97. As contended in Daniels, "A Gamble Won by Default," in *Russian Revolution*, ed. Medlin, p. 167.

98. Reed, *Ten Days*, p. 11.

99. Given in McCauley, *Russian Revolution*, p. 124.

100. Reed, *Ten Days*, p. 126.

101. For these decrees, see Golder, *Documents*, pp. 605−25.

102. Such as Albert R. Williams, *Through the Russian Revolution* (New York: Monthly Review Press, 1967: originally published in 1920).

103. Cited by Steinberg, *Workshop of Revolution*, p. 12.

104. Deutscher, *Prophet Armed*, pp. 322−23.

105. Leon Trotsky, *My Life*, p. 342.

106. Ibid., p. 341.

107. Chamberlin, *Russian Revolution*, p. 324.

108. Rigby, *Communist Party Membership*, p. 66.

109. Chamberlin, *Russian Revolution*, p. 323.

110. Schapiro, *Origin of Communist Autocracy*, p. 173.

111. Cited by Simon Liberman, *Building Lenin's Russia*, p. 60.

112. Trotsky, *Lenin*, p. 120.

113. Schapiro, *Origin of Communist Autocracy*, p. 50.

114. Steinberg, *Workshop of Revolution*, p. 58.

115. G. H. Leggett, "Lenin, Terror, and the Political Police," *Survey* 21 (Autumn 1975): 157−61.

116. Trotsky, *Lenin*, p. 123.

117. Lenin, "How to Organize Competion" (originally published December 24−27, 1917 [January 6−9, 1918]), in Lenin, *Collected Works*, vol. 26, p. 414.

118. Steinberg, *Workshop of Revolution*, p. 145.

119. Fischer, *Life of Lenin*, pp. 138−39.

120. Melgunov, *Bolshevik Seizure*, p. 188.

121. Schapiro, *Origin of Communist Autocracy*, p. 150.

122. Ibid., p. 136.

123. For example, by Fischer in *Life of Lenin*, p. 213.

124. McNeal, *Bolshevik Tradition*, p. 49.

125. Schapiro, *Origin of Communist Autocracy*, p. 104.

126. *Letters of Lenin*, pp. 372−73.

127. Lenin, *Selected Works*, p. 43.

128. Lenin, "Speech on the National Question," in Lenin, *Selected Works*, p. 137.

129. Zeman, *Germany*, p. 85.

130. Ibid., pp. 94−95.

131. Zeman and Scharlau, *Merchant of Revolution*, p. 243.

132. Deutscher, *Prophet Armed*, p. 401.

133. Georg von Rauch, *A History of Soviet Russia*, 5th ed. (New York: Praeger, 1967), pp. 98−99.

134. Ulam, *Bolsheviks*, p. 438.

135. Trotsky, *Lenin*, p. 130.

136. Liberman, *Building Lenin's Russia*, pp. 30−31.

137. Paul C. Roberts, ''War Communism: A Re-examination,'' *Slavic Review* 29 (June 1970): 238−61.

138. Cited by Plamenatz, *German Marxism*, p. 262.

139. G. H. Leggett, ''Lenin, Terror,'' *Survey* 21 (Autumn 1975): 168−69.

140. Ulam, *Stalin*, p. 175.

141. Leggett, ''Lenin, Terror,'' p. 174.

142. Ulam, *Stalin*, p. 173.

143. Liberman, *Building Lenin's Russia*, p. 14.

144. McCauley, *Russian Revolution*, pp. 151−52.

145. Ibid., p. 148.

146. Ibid., p. 165.

147. Lenin, *Collected Works*, vol. 31, p. 294.

148. Rigby, *Communist Party Membership*, pp. 68−69.

149. Schapiro, *Communist Party*, p. 237.

150. Ibid., p. 241.

151. McNeal, *Bolshevik Tradition*, p. 56.

152. Trotsky, *My Life*, p. 343.

153. Ulam, *Bolsheviks*, p. 453.

154. Janice Ali, ''Aspects of the RKP (b) Secretariat, March 1919 to April 1922,'' *Soviet Studies* 26 (July 1974): 398.

155. T. H. Rigby, ''The Soviet Politburo: A Comparative Profile, 1951−1971,'' *Soviet Studies* 24 (July 1972): 3.

156. Leonard Schapiro, ''The General Department of the CPSU,'' *Survey* 21 (Summer 1975): 54.

157. Rigby, *Communist Party Membership*, p. 77.

158. Ibid., p. 81.

159. Schapiro, *Communist Party*, p. 258.

160. Fischer, *Life of Lenin*, p. 121.

161. Ulam, *Stalin*, p. 199.

162. Lenin, ''Contribution to the History of the Question of the Dictatorship of the Proletariat'' (originally published October 20, 1920), in Lenin, *Collected Works*, vol. 31, p. 353.

4. LIQUIDATION OF DISSENT

1. Leon Trotsky, *The Revolution Betrayed* (Garden City, N.Y..: Doubleday, 1937), pp. 89−90.

2. Moshe Lewin, *Lenin's Last Struggle*, p. 27.

3. William H. Chamberlin, *The Russian Revolution 1917−1921*, pp. 436−39.

4. Leonard Schapiro, *The Origin of the Communist Autocracy*, p. 301.

5. Robert V. Daniels, ed., *A Documentary History of Communism*, pp. 204−06.

6. Ivar Spector, *An Introduction to Russian History and Culture*, 5th ed. (Princeton: Van Nostrand, 1969), p. 371.

7. Oskar Anweiler, *The Soviets*, p. 249.

8. Simon Liberman, *Building Lenin's Russia*, p. 70.

9. Lenin, *Collected Works* (Moscow: Foreign Languages Publishing House, 1963), vol. 33, p. 40.

10. Ibid., p. 282.

11. Isaac Deutscher, *The Prophet Armed*, p. 493.

12. Edward H. Carr, *The Bolshevik Revolution, 1917–1923*, vol. 2, p. 213.

13. Robert Conquest, *The Great Terror*, p. 25.

14. Schapiro, *Origin of Communist Autocracy*, p. 294.

15. Ibid., p. 220.

16. Texts in Daniels, *Documentary History*, pp. 208–10.

17. T. H. Rigby, *Communist Party Membership in the U.S.S.R.*, pp. 96–97.

18. Trotsky, *Revolution Betrayed*, p. 46.

19. Edward H. Carr, *The Interregnum 1923–1924*, pp. 268–69.

20. Nikita S. Khrushchev, *Khrushchev Remembers*, p. 87.

21. Edward H. Carr, *Socialism in One Country 1924–1926*, pp. 36–37.

22. Lewin, *Lenin's Last Struggle*, pp. 35–37.

23. Lenin, "To the Fourth Congress of the Communist International," in Lenin, *Collected Works*, vol. 33, p. 428.

24. Leon Trotsky, *My Life*, p. 471.

25. Louis Fischer, *The Life of Lenin*, p. 80.

26. Trotsky, *My Life*, p. 475.

27. As suggested by Adam B. Ulam in *Stalin*, p. 208.

28. V. I. Lenin, *Collected Works* (Moscow: Foreign Languages Publishing House, 1963), vol. 33, p. 257.

29. Robert Conquest, *The Great Terror*, p. 20.

30. Adam B. Ulam, "Lenin's Last Phase," *Survey* 21 (Winter 1975), 155–58.

31. Rigby, *Communist Party Membership*, pp. 108–109.

32. Lenin, "Notes on the National Question," in V. I. Lenin, *Selected Works in Three Volumes* (Moscow: Progress Publishers, 1970), vol. 3, p. 753.

33. Lewin, *Lenin's Last Struggle*, p. 54.

34. Isaac Deutscher, *Stalin*, p. 237.

35. Lenin, *Collected Works*, vol. 45, pp. 607–08.

36. Ibid., p. 607.

37. Trotsky, *My Life*, p. 484.

38. For text, see Daniels, *Documentary History*, pp. 223–24; Lenin, *Collected Works*, vol. 36, pp. 594–96.

39. Robert H. McNeal, *Bride of the Revolution*, p. 242.

40. As remarked by John Plamenatz in *German Marxism and Russian Communism* (London: Longmans, Green, 1954), p. 248.

41. As observed by Liberman in *Building Lenin's Russia*, p. 71.

42. As observed by Bertram D. Wolfe in *An Ideology in Power: Reflections on the Russian Revolution* (New York: Stein and Day, 1969), p. 167.

43. Robert H. McNeal, *The Bolshevik Tradition: Lenin, Stalin, Khrushchev* (Englewood Cliffs, N.J.: Prentice-Hall, 1963), p. 47.

44. Louis Fischer, *The Life of Lenin*, pp. 430–31.

45. Roy A. Medvedev, *Let History Judge*, p. 19.

46. Biographies include: Nikolaus Basseches, *Stalin* (London: Staples Press, 1952); Isaac Deutscher, *Stalin: A Political Biography* (New York: Oxford University Press, 1966); Joseph Hingley, *Stalin: Man and Legend* (New York: McGraw-Hill, 1974); Harford M. Hyde, *Stalin: The History of a Dictator* (New York: Farrar, Strauss, and Giroux, 1971); Boris Souvarine, *Stalin: A*

Critical Survey of Bolshevism (New York: Longmans, Green, 1939); Robert C. Tucker, *Stalin as a Revolutionary 1879—1929* (New York: Norton, 1973); Adam B. Ulam, *Stalin: The Man and His Era* (New York: Viking, 1973).

47. Francis B. Randall, *Stalin's Russia: An Historical Reconsideration* (New York: Free Press, 1965), p. 18.

48. McNeal, *Bolshevik Tradition*, p. 88.

49. Medvedev, *Let History Judge*, p. 17.

50. Especially by Tucker, *Stalin as Revolutionary*.

51. Deutscher, *Stalin*, p. 19.

52. Ulam, *Stalin*, p. 17.

53. Medvedev, *Let History Judge*, pp. 4—5.

54. For documents, see Martin McCauley, ed., *The Russian Revolution and the Soviet State 1917—1921*, p. 151.

55. Trotsky, *My Life*, p. 50.

56. For a survey, see Robert V. Daniels, "Stalin's Rise to Dictatorship, 1922—1929" in *Politics in the Soviet Union*, Alexander Dallin and Alan F. Westin, eds. (New York: Harcourt, Brace, and World, 1966).

57. Khrushchev, *Khrushchev Remembers*, pp. 26—27.

58. Trotsky, *My Life*, p. 500.

59. Rigby, *Communist Party Membership*, p. 519.

60. Ibid., p. 137.

61. Abdurakhman Avtorkhanov, *Stalin and the Soviet Communist Party*, pp. 53—54.

62. As detailed by Avtorkhanov in Ibid., pp. 55—56, 63—64.

63. Trotsky, *My Life*, p. 514.

64. Carr, *Interregnum*, p. 352.

65. Lenin, "Notes of a Publicist," in V. I. Lenin, *Collected Works*, vol. 33, p. 210.

66. Medvedev, *Let History Judge*, p. 38.

67. Robert V. Daniels, *The Conscience of the Revolution*, p. 54.

68. The theme in Trotsky, *The Revolution Betrayed: What is the Soviet Union and Where is it Going* (New York: Merit Publishers, 1965).

69. Deutscher, *Stalin*, p. 292.

70. Trotsky, *My Life*, p. 477.

71. Ibid., p. 411.

72. Liberman, *Building Lenin's Russia*, p. 78.

73. Medvedev, *Let History Judge*, p. 38.

74. Trotsky, *My Life*, p. 477.

75. Ibid., p. 481.

76. Ibid., p. 477.

77. Ibid., p. 500.

78. Carr, *Interregnum*, p. 323.

79. Deutscher, *Stalin*, p. 275.

80. Trotsky, *My Life*, p. 535.

81. Carr, *Interregnum*, p. 350.

82. Cited by Carr in *Interregnum*, p. 363.

83. As Trotsky perceptively saw himself in retrospect in *My Life*, pp. 504—05.

84. McNeal, *Bride of Revolution*, p. 259; Khrushchev, *Khrushchev Remembers*, p. 46.

85. Stalin, *History of the Communist Party of the Soviet Union (Bolsheviks), Short Course* (Moscow: Foreign Languages Publishing House, 1939), pp. 356—57.

86. Trotsky, *My Life*, Chapter 45.

87. Deutscher, *Stalin*, p. 313.

5. STALINISM IN POWER

1. Robert G. Wesson, *Soviet Communes* (New Brunswick, N.J.: Rutgers University Press, 1963), pp. 97–102.

2. Abdurakhman Avtorkhanov, *Stalin and the Soviet Party*, p. 138.

3. In his Secret Speech; Howard R. Swearer, *The Politics of Succession in the U.S.S.R.*, p. 177.

4. D. J. Male, *Russian Peasant Organization before Collectivization* (Cambridge: The University Press, 1971), pp. 210–11.

5. Winston Churchill, *The Hinge of Fate* (Boston: Houghton-Mifflin, 1950), p. 498.

6. John A. Armstrong, *The Politics of Totalitarianism*, p. 6.

7. See Wesson, *Soviet Communes*, Chapter 11.

8. Robert V. Daniels, *A Documentary History of Communism*, vol. 2, p. 3.

9. Deutscher, *Stalin*, p. 334.

10. Nikita S. Khrushchev, *Khrushchev Remembers*, p. 108.

11. Robert Conquest, *The Great Terror*, pp. 44, 49–50.

12. John A. Armstrong, *Politics of Totalitarianism*, p. 9.

13. Conquest, *Great Terror*, p. 47.

14. Daniels, *Documentary History*, pp. 22–23. It is notable that in the list of invaders Stalin did not mention the Germans.

15. Leonard B. Schapiro, *The Communist Party of the Soviet Union*, p. 368.

16. Arthur Feiler, *The Experiment of Bolshevism* (London: Allen and Unwin, 1930), p. 85.

17. Armstrong, *Politics of Totalitarianism*, p. 4.

18. See, for example, John Scott, *Behind the Urals* (New York: Arno Press, 1971; originally published 1942), p. 9 passim.

19. T. H. Rigby, *Communist Party Membership in the U.S.S.R.*, pp. 183–84.

20. Feiler, *Experiment of Bolshevism*, p. 28.

21. Conquest, *Great Terror*, p. 104.

22. Armstrong, *Politics of Totalitarianism*, p. 16.

23. Roy A. Medvedev, *Let History Judge*, p. 156.

24. Khrushchev, *Khrushchev Remembers*, p. 61.

25. Svetlana Alliluyeva, *Twenty Letters to a Friend*, p. 139.

26. Conquest, *Great Terror*, p. 85.

27. Stalin, "The Right Deviation in the CPSU," in *Documentary History*, ed. Daniels, vol. 2, p. 2.

28. As shown for one region by Merle Fainsod, *Smolensk under Soviet Rule*, p. 230.

29. Especially by Conquest, *Great Terror*.

30. As postulated by Rigby in *Communist Party Membership*, p. 214.

31. Khrushchev, *Khrushchev Remembers*, p. 81.

32. Swearer, *Politics of Succession*, p. 165.

33. Daniels, *Documentary History*, p. 226.

34. Conquest, *Great Terror*, p. 154.

35. Khrushchev, *Khrushchev Remembers*, p. 94.

36. A. T. Stuchenko, in *Stalin and his Generals*, ed. Seweryn Bialer, p. 81.

37. Conquest, *Great Terror*, pp. 645–46.

38. Armstrong, *Politics of Totalitarianism*, p. 59.

39. Daniels, *Documentary History*, p. 63.

40. Conquest, *Great Terror*, p. 149.

41. John Dornberg, *Brezhnev*, p. 69.

42. Conquest, *Great Terror*, p. 632.

43. Discussed at length in Conquest, *Great Terror*, Chapter 3.

44. Alliluyeva, *Twenty Letters*, p. 31.

45. Ibid., pp. 78−79.

46. Conquest, *Great Terror*, p. 29.

47. Rigby, *Communist Party Membership*, pp. 519−20.

48. Cited in Deutscher, *Stalin*, pp. 350, 352.

49. Sheila Fitzpatrick, "Culture and Politics under Stalin: A Reappraisal," *Slavic Review* 35 (June 1976): 218.

50. June 9, 1934. Daniels, *Documentary History*, p. 40.

51. Medvedev, *Let History Judge*, p. 540.

52. Merle Fainsod, *How Russia is Ruled* (Cambridge: Harvard University Press, 1958), pp. 177−78.

53. Rigby, *Communist Party Membership*, p. 521.

54. Ibid., p. 224.

55. Khrushchev, *Khrushchev Remembers*, p. 49.

56. Ibid., p. 74.

57. Deutscher, *Stalin*, p. 381.

58. Armstrong, *Politics of Totalitarianism*, p. 114.

59. Michael Morozow, *Leonid Breschnew*, p. 74.

60. *New York Times*, December 25, 1939.

61. Georg von Rauch, *A History of Soviet Russia*, 5th ed. (New York: Praeger, 1967), p. 299.

62. S. Bialer, in *Stalin and His Generals*, ed. Bialer, p. 61.

63. N. N. Voronov, "At Supreme Headquarters," in *Stalin and His Generals*, ed. Bialer, p. 210.

64. Medvedev, *Let History Judge*, p. 458.

65. Michel Gordey, *Visa to Moscow* (New York: Knopf, 1952), p. 193.

66. Schapiro, *Communist Party*, p. 504.

67. Evgeny Evtushenko, *Autobiografiia* (London: Flegon Press, 1964), p. 24.

68. Georgii K. Zhukov, *The Memoirs of Marshal Zhukov* (New York: Delacorte Press, 1971), p. 171.

69. K. K. Rokossovskii, in *Stalin and His Generals*, ed. Bialer, pp. 38, 460−61.

70. Khrushchev, *Khrushchev Remembers*, pp. 310−11.

71. Morozow, *Breschnew*, pp. 45−46.

72. Barrington Moore, Jr., *Terror and Progress USSR: Some Sources of Change and Stability in the Soviet System* (Cambridge: Harvard University Press, 1954), p. 191.

73. Ivar Spector, *An Introduction to Russian History and Culture*, 5th ed. (Princeton: Van Nostrand, 1969), pp. 461−62.

74. Khrushchev, *Khrushchev Remembers*, p. 261.

75. As commented by Daniels in *Documentary History*, p. xlvii.

76. Evtushenko, *Autobiografiia*, p. 77.

77. Gordey, *Visa to Moscow*, p. 410.

78. Roy A. Medvedev in the *New York Times*, February 7, 1974, p. 10.

79. As suggested by Adam B. Ulam in *Stalin*, pp. 708−09.

80. Robert Conquest, *Power and Policy in the U.S.S.R.: The Study of Soviet Dynamics* (London: Macmillan, 1961), p. 96.

81. Schapiro, *Communist Party*, pp. 527−28.

82. Rigby, *Communist Party Membership*, p. 276.

83. Khrushchev, *Khrushchev Remembers*, p. 264.

84. As recounted by Albert Speer in *Inside the Third Reich* (New York: Macmillan, 1967), Chapter 7.

85. As noted by Swearer in *Politics of Succession*, p. 32.

86. Khrushchev, *Khrushchev Remembers*, p. 46.

87. Cited by Ulam in *Stalin*, p. 715.

88. Moore, *Terror and Progress*, p. 187.

89. Conquest, *Power and Policy*, p. 33.

90. Khrushchev, *Khrushchev Remembers*, p. 282.

91. T. H. Rigby, "The Soviet Politburo: A Comparative Profile," *Soviet Studies* 24 (July 1972): 3.

92. Carl A. Linden, *Khrushchev and the Soviet Leadership 1957−1964*, p. 13.

93. On the rivalry of Zhdanov with Malenkov, see Jonathan Harris, "The Origins of the Conflict between Malenkov and Zhdanov, 1939−1941," *Slavic Review* 35 (June 1936): 287−303.

94. As suggested by Morozow, *Breschnew*, p. 189.

95. According to Khrushchev in *Khrushchev Remembers*, p. 308.

96. Medvedev, *Let History Judge*, p. 557.

97. Abdurakhman Avtorkhanov, *Stalin and the Soviet Party*, p. 254.

98. Edith R. Frankel, "Literary Policy in Stalin's Last Year," *Soviet Studies* 28 (July 1976): 391−405.

99. Khrushchev, *Khrushchev Remembers*, p. 274.

100. Rigby, *Communist Party Membership*, p. 301.

101. Khrushchev, *Khrushchev Remembers*, p. 259.

102. Medvedev, *Let History Judge*, p. 557.

103. Wolfgang Leonhard, *The Kremlin since Stalin*, pp. 47−48.

104. Alliluyeva, *Twenty Letters*, p. 8; Khrushchev, *Khrushchev Remembers*, pp. 318−20.

105. *Pravda*, March 5, 1953, p. 1; Georges Bortoli, *The Death of Stalin* (New York: Praeger, 1975), p. 150.

106. As reported both by Khrushchev in *Khrushchev Remembers*, p. 322, and by Alliluyeva in *Twenty Letters*, p. 8.

6. THE KHRUSHCHEV ERA

1. Svetlana Alliluyeva, *Twenty Letters to a Friend*, p. 23.

2. Bertram Wolfe, *Khrushchev and Stalin's Ghost*, pp. 5−6.

3. Roy Medvedev, *New York Times*, February 7, 1974, p. 10.

4. Nikita S. Khrushchev, *Khrushchev Remembers*, p. 323.

5. Nikita S. Khrushchev, *Khrushchev Remembers: The Last Testament*, p. 79.

6. Alliluyeva, *Twenty Letters*, p. 11.

7. Evgenii Evtushenko, *Autobiografiia* (London: Flegon Press, 1964), p. 97.

8. Roy A. Medvedev, *Let History Judge*, p. 559.

9. Wolfgang Leonhard, *The Kremlin since Stalin*, p. 27.

10. *Pravda*, May 16, 1953.

11. Borys Lewytzkyj, *The Uses of Terror: The Soviet Secret Police 1917—1970* (New York: Coward McCann and Geoghegan, 1972), pp. 222—23.

12. Mark Frankland, *Khrushchev*, p. 27.

13. Howard R. Swearer, *The Politics of Succession in the U.S.S.R.*, p. 54.

14. Biographies include Edward Crankshaw, *Khrushchev: A Career* (New York: Viking Press, 1966); Mark Frankland, *Khrushchev* (New York: Stein and Day, 1967); Konrad Hellen, *Khrushchev: A Political Portrait* (New York: Praeger, 1961); George Paloczi-Horvath, *Khrushchev: The Making of a Dictator* (Boston: Little, Brown, 1961); Lazar Pistrak, *The Grand Tactician: Khrushchev's Rise to Power* (New York: Praeger, 1961).

15. Frankland, *Khrushchev*, p. 19.

16. Pistrak, *Grand Tactician*, pp. 31—33.

17. Khrushchev, *Khrushchev Remembers*, p. 62.

18. Ibid., pp. 108—09.

19. Frankland, *Khrushchev*, p. 57.

20. Carl A. Linden, *Khrushchev and the Soviet Leadership 1957—1964*, pp. 24—25.

21. Paloczi-Horvath, *Khrushchev*, pp. 151—53.

22. Leonhard, *Kremlin since Stalin*, p. 23.

23. John A. Armstrong, *The Politics of Totalitarianism*, p. 262.

24. Robert Conquest, *Power and Policy in the U.S.S.R.: The Study of Soviet Dynamics* (London: Macmillan, 1961), p. 243.

25. For Khrushchev's rise, see Swearer, *Politics of Succession*.

26. Conquest, *Power and Policy*, p. 126.

27. Paloczi-Horvath, *Khrushchev*, p. 164.

28. Pravda, January 24, 1955; Robert V. Daniels, ed., *A Documentary History of Communism*, vol. 2, p. 894.

29. As contended by Linden in *Khrushchev and Soviet Leadership*.

30. As argued by Paloczi-Horvath in *Khrushchev*.

31. Armstrong, *Politics of Totalitarianism*, p. 298.

32. Conquest, *Power and Policy*, p. 267.

33. Wolfe, *Khrushchev and Stalin's Ghost*, p. 32.

34. Nadezhda K. Krupskaya, *Memories of Lenin* (New York: International Publishers, 1930), vol. 2, p. 192.

35. Leonhard, *Kremlin since Stalin*, p. 105.

36. On this speech, see Wolfe, *Khrushchev and Stalin's Ghost*; Thomas H. Rigby, *The Stalin Dictatorship: Khrushchev's "Secret Speech" and Other Documents* (London: Methuen, 1968); and Branko Lazitch, *Le rapport Khrouchtcev et son histoire* (Paris: Editions du Seuil, 1976).

37. Khrushchev, *Khrushchev Remembers*, p. 353.

38. Khrushchev, *Khrushchev Remembers: The Last Testament*, p. 109.

39. Lazitch, *Le Rapport Khrouchtchev*, pp. 18—20.

40. Khrushchev, *Khrushchev Remembers*, p. 351.

41. Wolfe, *Khrushchev and Stalin's Ghost*, p. 248.

42. Khrushchev, *Khrushchev Remembers*, pp. 347—49.

43. Ibid., p. 343.

44. As suggested by Frankland in *Khrushchev*, pp. 49—50.

45. Wolfe, *Khrushchev and Stalin's Ghost*, p. 35.

46. Paloczi-Horvath, *Khrushchev*, p. 215.

47. Cited by Paloczi-Horvath in *Khrushchev*, p. 247.

48. Leonhard, *Kremlin since Stalin*, pp. 237–39.

49. On the crisis, see Roger Pethybridge, *A Key to Soviet Politics: The Crisis of the Anti-Party Group* (New York: Praeger, 1962).

50. Swearer, *Politics of Succession*, p. 230.

51. Robert Conquest, *Russia after Khrushchev*, p. 128.

52. An action he later regretted. Khrushchev, *Khrushchev Remembers: Last Testament*, pp. 17–18.

53. Frankland, *Khrushchev*, p. 142.

54. Linden, *Khrushchev and Soviet Leadership*, p. 63.

55. Ibid., p. 86.

56. Khrushchev, *Khrushchev Remembers: Last Testament*, p. 415.

57. Michel Tatu, *Power in the Kremlin*, p. 20.

58. Linden, *Khrushchev and Soviet Leadership*, p. 68.

59. Tatu, *Power in Kremlin*, p. 49.

60. Linden, *Khrushchev and Soviet Leadership*, p. 108.

61. Ibid., p. 102.

62. Tatu, *Power in Kremlin*, p. 138.

63. John Dornberg, *Brezhnev*, p. 160.

64. Tatu, *Power in Kremlin*, p. 127.

65. Ibid., p. 153.

66. Cited by Swearer in *Politics of Succession*, p. 14.

67. Concerning the vision, see Jerome M. Gilison, *The Soviet Image of Utopia* (Baltimore: Johns Hopkins University Press, 1975).

68. Gilison, *Soviet Image*, p. 5.

69. Herbert Ritvo, ed., *The New Soviet Society: Final Text of the Program of the Communist Party of the Soviet Union* (New York: New Leader, 1962), p. 12.

70. Jan F. Triska, ed., *Soviet Communism: Programs and Rules* (San Francisco: Chandler Publishing Co., 1962), p. 129.

71. For details, see Robert G. Wesson, "Volunteers and Soviets," *Soviet Studies* 15 (January 1964): 231–49.

72. Yaroslav Bilinsky, "The Communist Party of the Soviet Union," in *The Soviet Union under Brezhnev and Kosygin*, ed. John W. Strong, p. 40.

73. Ritvo, *New Soviet Society*, p. 7.

74. For a discussion, see Adam B. Ulam, *Expansion and Coexistence: Soviet Foreign Policy 1917–1973* (New York: Praeger, 1974), pp. 667–71.

75. Cited by Conquest, *Russia after Khrushchev*, p. 114.

76. B. N. Ponomarev, chief ed., *Istoriia Kommunisticheskoi Partii Sovetskogo Soiuza* (Moscow: Izd. politicheskoi literatury, 1969), p. 623.

77. Michael Morozow, *Leonid Breschnew*, p. 195.

78. Tatu, *Power in Kremlin*, p. 333.

79. Linden, *Khrushchev and Soviet Leadership*, p. 180.

80. Abraham Brumberg, "The Fall of Khrushchev," *Soviet Union under Brezhnev and Kosygin*, ed. Strong, pp. 3–4.

81. As suggested by Brumberg in "Fall of Khrushchev," p. 12. The writer Yesenin-Volpin similarly opined that such liberalization as was perceived came merely because the leaders wished to appear more civilized than Stalin and lacked his will. Conquest, *Russia after Khrushchev*, p. 48.

82. As believed by Linden, *Khrushchev and Soviet Leadership.*

83. Myron Rush, *Political Succession in the USSR*, pp. 119–20.

84. *Partinaia zhizn* 14 (July 1973): 13.

85. Concerning the middle-ranking elite in the latter 1950s, see Philip D. Stewart, *Political Power in the Soviet Union* (Indianapolis: Bobbs-Merrill, 1968).

86. Rush, *Political Succession*, p. 104.

87. Cited by Armstrong in *Politics of Totalitarianism*, p. 290.

88. As contended by George W. Breslauer in "Khrushchev Reconsidered," *Problems of Communism* 25 (September-October 1976): 18–33.

89. Khrushchev, *Khrushchev Remembers*, pp. 312–13.

90. Ellen Mickiewicz, *Soviet Political Schools* (New Haven: Yale University Press, 1967), pp. 10, 13.

91. Khrushchev, *Khrushchev Remembers: Last Testament*, p. 79.

92. Conquest, *Russia after Khrushchev*, p. 65.

93. Milton C. Lodge, *Soviet Elite Attitudes since Stalin* (Columbus: Charles Merrill, 1969).

94. Morozow, *Breschnew*, p. 214.

95. Khrushchev, *Khrushchev Remembers: Last Testament*, p. 77.

96. Ibid., p. 532.

97. Morozow, *Breschnew*, pp. 169–70.

98. Martin Page, *The Day Khrushchev Fell* (New York: Hawthorn Books, 1965), p. 28.

99. Morozow, *Breschnew*, p. 195.

100. Page, *The Day Khrushchev Fell*, pp. 25–26.

101. Ibid., p. 45.

102. *Pravda*, May 17, 1965.

7. BREZHNEV AND CONSERVATIVE COMMUNISM

1. Michael Morozow, *Leonid Breschnew*, p. 87.

2. As suggested by Morozow in *Breschnew*, p. 88.

3. T. H. Rigby, "The Soviet Leadership: Towards a Self-stabilizing Oligarchy," *Soviet Studies* 22 (October 1970): 175.

4. Grey Hodnett, "Succession Contingencies in the Soviet Union," *Problems of Communism* 24 (March-April 1975): 5.

5. *Partinaia zhizn*, October 1967, p. 55, cited by Branko Lazitch, *Le rapport Khrouchtchev et son histoire* (Paris: Editions du Seuil, 1976), pp. 42–43.

6. David Holloway, "Foreign and Defense Policy," in *The Soviet Union since the Fall of Khrushchev*, ed. Archie Brown and Michael Kaser, p. 49.

7. *Pravda*, February 21, 1965.

8. Borys Lewytzkyj, *The Uses of Terror: The Soviet Secret Police 1917–1970* (New York: Coward, McCann and Geoghegan, 1972), pp. 281–82.

9. Alec Nove, "Agriculture," in *Soviet Union*, ed. Brown and Kaser, p. 5.

10. George W. Breslauer, "Khrushchev Reconsidered," *Problems of Communism* 25 (September-October 1976): 31.

11. Michel Tatu, *Power in the Kremlin: From Khrushchev to Kosygin*, p. 465.

12. Jerry F. Hough, "The Brezhnev Era," *Problems of Communism* 25 (March-April 1976): 2.

13. Paul A. Smith, Jr., "Brezhnev's Ascent to Power," *Orbis* 15 (Summer 1971): pp. 580–81.

14. Morozow, *Breschnew*, p. 42.

15. As suggested by Robbins Burling in *The Passage of Power* (New York: Academic Press, 1974), p. 252.

16. Myron Rush, *Political Succession in the USSR*, p. 291.

17. Carl A. Linden, *Khrushchev and the Soviet Leadership 1957–1964*, p. 230.

18. Alexander Werth, *Russia: Hopes and Fears* (New York: Simon and Schuster, 1969), p. 275.

19. Morozow, *Breschnew*, p. 241.

20. John Dornberg, *Brezhnev: The Masks of Power*, p. 23.

21. Hough, "Brezhnev Era," p. 2.

22. On the congress, see Leonard Schapiro, "Keynote-Compromise," *Problems of Communism* 20 (July-August, 1971): pp. 2–8.

23. Sidney I. Ploss, "A Cautious Verdict in Moscow: The Twenty-Fourth Party Congress," *Orbis* 15 (Summer 1971): pp. 564–71.

24. Ibid., pp. 568–69.

25. T. H. Rigby, "Soviet Communist Party Membership under Brezhnev," *Soviet Studies* 28 (July 1976): p. 321.

26. Jerome M. Gilison, *The Soviet Image of Utopia* (Baltimore: Johns Hopkins University Press, 1975), p. 185.

27. Richard F. Staar, ed., *Yearbook on International Communist Affairs, 1973* (Stanford: Hoover Institution Press, 1973), p. 84.

28. *Pravda*, October 1, 1971, p. 1.

29. Yaroslav Bilinsky, "The Communist Party of the Ukraine since 1966," in *Ukraine in the Seventies*, ed. Peter J. Potichnyi (Oakville, Ont.: Mosaic Press, 1975), p. 240.

30. Lowell Tillett, "Ukrainian Nationalism and the Fall of Shelest," *Slavic Review* 34 (December 1975): 752–68.

31. Hough, "Brezhnev Era," p. 5.

32. Leon Smolinski, "Toward a Socialist Corporation: Soviet Industrial Reorganization of 1973," *Survey* 20 (Winter 1974): 24–35.

33. Hough, "Brezhnev Era," p. 3.

34. I. Yudin and Yu. Malov., "The Intelligence, Honor and Conscience of Our Era," *Partinaia zhizn* 13 (July 1976): 6.

35. Peter Frank, "The Changing Composition of the Communist Party," in *Soviet Union*, ed. Brown and Kaser, p. 97.

36. These and other recent figures on the party are taken from *Partinaia zhizn* 10 (May 1976): 13–22.

37. Cf. Alec Nove, "Is There a Ruling Class in the USSR?" *Soviet Studies* 27 (October 1975), 615–638.

38. Cf. Robert G. Kaiser, *Russia*, Chapter 4; Hedrick Smith, "How the Soviet Elite Lives," *Atlantic* 236 (December 1975): 39–50; Mervyn Matthews, "Top Incomes in the USSR," *Survey* 21 (Summer 1975): 1–27.

39. Yaroslav Bilinsky, "The Communist Party of the Soviet Union," in *Soviet Union*, ed. Brown and Kaser, p. 43.

40. Hedrick Smith, *The Russians*, p. 262.

41. A. Pravdin and Mervyn Matthews, "Inside the CPSU Central Committee," *Survey* 20 (Autumn 1974): 100.

42. Smith, "How Soviet Elite Lives," p. 49.

43. Kaiser, *Russia*, p. 181.

44. Robert Conquest, *Power and Policy in the USSR: The Study of Soviet Dynamics* (London: Macmillan, 1961), p. 75.

45. Joel C. Moses, *Regional Party Leadership and Policy-Making in the USSR* (New York: Praeger, 1974), p. 185.

46. Ibid., Table I.

47. Ibid., p. 16.

48. *Radio Liberty Dispatch*, April 1, 1974.

49. Robert E. Blackwell, Jr., "Career Development in the Soviet Obkom Elite," *Soviet Studies* 24 (July 1972): 39.

50. T. H. Rigby, "The Soviet Politburo: A Comparative Profile," *Soviet Studies* 24 (July 1972): 14.

51. Moses, *Regional Party Leadership*, p. 9.

52. Leonard B. Schapiro, *The Communist Party of the Soviet Union*, p. 173.

53. John A. Armstrong, *The Politics of Totalitarianism*, p. 331.

54. Ibid.

55. Figures prior to 1976 are given by Tatu in *Power in Kremlin*, p. 538.

56. Hough, "Brezhnev Era," p. 4.

57. Ibid., p. 6.

58. *New York Times*, October 27, 1976, p. 4.

59. Wolfgang Berner et al., eds., *The Soviet Union, 1973* (New York: Holmes and Meier, 1975), p. 12.

60. For the accepted ideology as of the beginning of the Brezhnev era, see Gustav Wetter, *Soviet Ideology Today* (New York: Praeger, 1966).

61. *New York Times*, July 7, 1976, p. 2.

62. Alfred Evans, "Trends in Soviet Secondary School Histories of the USSR," *Soviet Studies* 28 (April 1976): 224–43.

63. Staar, *Yearbook on Communist Affairs, 1973*, p. 77.

64. Peter Reddaway, "The Development of Opposition and Dissent," *Soviet Union*, ed. Brown and Kaser, p. 122.

65. Smith, *Russians*, p. 292.

66. Robert Conquest, *Russia after Khrushchev*, p. 260.

67. Kaiser, *Russia*, p. 4.

68. Archie Brown, "Political Developments," in *Soviet Union*, ed. Brown and Kaser, p. 231.

69. *Samizdat Bulletin* 31 (November 1975), citing *The Chronicle of Current Events*, no. 35.

70. Smith, *Russians*, p. 290.

71. Berner et al., *Soviet Union 1973*, pp. 4–5.

72. T. H. Rigby, *Communist Party Membership in the U.S.S.R.*, p. 511.

73. David Holloway, "Foreign and Defense Policy," *Soviet Union*, ed. Brown and Kaser, p. 73.

74. Lewis S. Feuer, "The Intelligentsia in Opposition," *Problems of Communism* 19 (November-December 1970): 1–16; Rudolf L. Tökés, *Dissent in the USSR: Politics, Ideology, and People* (Baltimore: Johns Hopkins University Press, 1975).

75. For ideologies of dissent, see Andrei Amalrik, "Ideologies in Soviet Society," *Survey* 22 (Spring 1976): 1–11.

76. Dimitri K. Simes, "The Soviet Parallel Market," *Survey* 21 (Summer 1975): 42–52.

77. Walter D. Connor, "Alcohol and Soviet Society," *Slavic Review* 30 (September 1971): 570–88.

78. *EKO*, no. 4, 1974, p. 37, cited by *Radio Liberty Bulletin*, 476/76, November 10, 1976.

79. Graham Stephenson, *Russia from 1812 to 1945* (New York: Praeger, 1970), p. 91.

80. Walter D. Connor, *Deviance in Soviet Society: Crime, Delinquency, and Alcoholism* (New York: Columbia University Press, 1972).

81. Andrei Sakharov, *My Country and the World* (New York: Alfred A. Knopf, 1975), pp. 11–12.

82. John Newhouse, *Cold Dawn: The Story of SALT* (New York: Holt, Rinehart and Winston, 1973), p. 238.

83. Vladimir G. Treml, "A Comment on Birman-Tretyakova," *Soviet Studies* 28 (April 1976): 187.

84. Burling, *Passage of Power*, pp. 251–52.

85. Grey Hodnett, "Succession Contingencies in the Soviet Union," *Problems of Communism* 24 (March-April 1975): 1–21.

CONCLUSION: THE PARTY TRANSFORMED AND THE SAME

1. John A. Armstrong, *The Politics of Totalitarianism*, pp. 276–77.

2. As observed by T. H. Rigby in *Communist Party Membership in the U.S.S.R.*, p. 38.

3. As concluded by Jeremy R. Azrael in *Managerial Power and Soviet Politics*.

4. Robert Conquest, *Russia after Khrushchev*, p. 6.

5. As observed by A. Brown, "Political Developments," in *The Soviet Union since the Fall of Khrushchev*, ed. Archie Brown and Michael Kaser, p. 266.

6. Bertram Wolfe, "Reflections on the Future of the Soviet System," *Russian Review* 26 (April 1967): 108.

7. Hedrick Smith, *The Russians*, pp. 241–48.

8. As suggested by Alec Nove in "Is There a Ruling Class in the USSR?" *Soviet Studies* 27 (October 1975): 636–37.

Appendix 2.

1. Robert H. McNeal, *Bride of the Revolution*, p. 3.

2. V. I. Lenin, "Tasks of the Proletariat in Our Revolution" (originally published April 10 [23], 1917) in V. I. Lenin, *Selected Works in Three Volumes* (Moscow: Progress Publishers, 1970), vol. 2, p. 64.

3. Adam B. Ulam, *The Bolsheviks* (New York: Macmillan, 1965), p. 525.

4. According to the compilation in Barbara Jancar, "Women and Soviet Politics," in *Soviet Society and Politics in the 1970s*, ed. Henry W. Morton and Rudolf L. Tökés (New York: Free Press, 1974), p. 155–60.

5. Donald R. Brown, *The Role and Status of Women in the Soviet Union* (New York: Teachers' College Press, 1968); Jancar, "Women and Soviet Politics," pp. 127, 146.

6. Jancar, "Women and Soviet Politics," p. 144.

7. Gail W. Lapidus, "Changing Women's Role in the USSR," in *Women in the World: A Comparative Study*, ed. Lynn B. Iglitzin and Ruth Ross (Santa Barbara, Calif.: Clio Press, 1976), p. 309.

Bibliographical Note

The Communist Party of the Soviet Union has elicited a volume of writing commensurate with its importance, with the most informative sources written in the English language. A large volume of historical records and a virtually infinite literature of commentary of varying utility have also been published in the Soviet Union. Useful guides to this writing include:

Jones, David L. *Books in English on the Soviet Union, 1917–1973*. New York: Garland Press, 1975.

Horecky, Paul L. *Russia and the Soviet Union: A Bibliographic Guide to Western-Language Publications*. Chicago: University of Chicago Press, 1965.

Horecky, Paul L. *Basic Russian Publications: An Annotated Bibliography on Russia and the Soviet Union*. Chicago: University of Chicago Press, 1962.

Many works, including some of those cited in the text, contain short bibliographies on various periods of the history of the party; the list in Leonard Schapiro's *The Communist Party of the Soviet Union* (New York: Random House, 1971) covers its history up to the 1960s.

Among other reference works, *Who Was Who in the USSR*, published by the Institute for the Study of the USSR (Metuchen, N.J.: Scarecrow Press, 1972) is exceptionally valuable. The brief *Party and Government Officials of the Soviet Union 1917–1967* by the same Institute (Metuchen, N.J.: Scarecrow Press, 1969) is handy for reference. Also useful is Jan F. Triska, ed., *Soviet Communism: Programs and Rules* (San Francisco: Chandler Publishing Co., 1962). Since the Second World War, selections from the Soviet press, including all important pronouncements, have been made available for the outside world by the *Current Digest of the Soviet Press*.

Any fairly short selection of books relevant to the party must be rather arbitrary, but the following may be noted:

Alliluyeva, Svetlana. *Twenty Letters to a Friend*. New York: Harper and Row, 1967.

Anweiler, Oskar. *The Soviets: The Russian Workers, Peasants, and Soldiers Councils 1905—1921*. New York: Pantheon Books, 1974.

Armstrong, John A. *The Politics of Totalitarianism: The Communist Party of the Soviet Union from 1934 to the Present*. New York: Random House, 1961.

Avtorkhanov, Abdurakhman. *The Communist Party Apparatus*. Chicago: Regnery, 1966.

———. *Stalin and the Soviet Communist Party*. New York: Praeger, 1959.

Azrael, Jeremy R. *Managerial Power and Soviet Politics*. Cambridge: Harvard University Press, 1966.

Berdyaev, Nicolas. *The Origin of Russian Communism*. Ann Arbor: University of Michigan Press, 1955 (originally published in 1937).

Bialer, Seweryn, ed. *Stalin and His Generals: Soviet Military Memoirs of World War II*. New York: Pegasus, 1969.

The Bolsheviks and the October Revolution: Minutes of the Central Committee of the Russian Social-Democratic Labour Party (bolsheviks) August 1917—February 1918, ed. Wieland Schulz-Keil. New York: Pluto Press, 1974.

Brown, Archie, and Kaser, Michael, eds. *The Soviet Union since the Fall of Khrushchev*. London: Macmillan, 1975.

Carr, Edward H. *The Bolshevik Revolution 1917—1923*. New York: Macmillan, 1952.

———. *The Interregnum 1923—1924*. New York: Macmillan, 1954.

———. *Socialism in One Country 1924—1926*. New York: Macmillan, 1958.

Chamberlin, William H. *The Russian Revolution 1917—1921*. 2 vols. New York: Macmillan, 1952.

Conquest, Robert. *The Great Terror: Stalin's Purge of the Thirties*. Rev. ed. New York: Macmillan, 1971.

———. *Russia after Khrushchev*. New York: Praeger, 1965.

Crankshaw, Edward. *Khrushchev: A Career*. New York: Viking Press, 1966.

Dan, Theodore. *The Origins of Bolshevism*. New York: Harper and Row, 1964.

Daniels, Robert V. *The Conscience of the Revolution: Communist Opposition in Soviet Russia*. Cambridge: Harvard University Press, 1960.

———. ed. *A Documentary History of Communism*. New York: Random House, 1960.

———. *Red October: The Bolshevik Revolution of 1917*. New York: Scribners, 1967.

Deutscher, Isaac. *The Prophet Armed: Trotsky 1879—1921*. New York: Oxford University Press, 1954.

———. *The Prophet Unarmed: Trotsky 1921—1929*. New York: Oxford University Press, 1959.

————. *Stalin: A Political Biography*. New York: Oxford University Press, 1949.

Dornberg, John. *Brezhnev: The Masks of Power*. London: André Deutsch, 1974.

Fainsod, Merle. *Smolensk under Soviet Rule*. Cambridge: Harvard University Press, 1958.

Fischer, Louis. *The Life of Lenin*. New York: Harper and Row, 1964.

Frankland, Mark. *Khrushchev*. New York: Stein and Day, 1967.

Golder, Frank A. *Documents of Russian History 1914–1917*. 1927. Gloucester, Mass.: Peter Smith, 1964.

Haimson, Leopold H. *The Russian Marxists and the Origins of Bolshevism*. Cambridge: Harvard University Press, 1955.

Kaiser, Robert G. *Russia: The People and the Power*. New York: Atheneum, 1976.

Katkov, George. *Russia 1917: The February Revolution*. New York: Harper and Row, 1967.

Kerensky, Alexander. *Russia and History's Turning Point*. New York: Duell, Sloan and Pearce, 1965.

Khrushchev, Nikita S. *Khrushchev Remembers*. Boston: Little, Brown, 1970.

————. *Khrushchev Remembers: The Last Testament*. Boston: Little, Brown, 1974.

Krupskaya, Nadezhda K. *Reminiscences of Lenin*. New York: International Publishers, 1960.

Lane, David. *The Roots of Russian Communism: A Social and Historical Study of Russian Social Democracy 1898–1907*. Assen: Van Gorcum, 1969.

Leonhard, Wolfgang. *The Kremlin since Stalin*. New York: Praeger, 1962.

Lewin, Moshe. *Lenin's Last Struggle*. New York: Vintage Books, 1970.

Liberman, Simon. *Building Lenin's Russia*. Chicago: University of Chicago Press, 1945.

Linden, Carl A. *Khrushchev and the Soviet Leadership 1957–1964*. Baltimore: Johns Hopkins University Press, 1966.

McCauley, Martin, ed. *The Russian Revolution and the Soviet State 1917–1921: Documents*. London: Macmillan, 1975.

McNeal, Robert H. *Bride of the Revolution: Krupskaya and Lenin*. Ann Arbor: University of Michigan Press, 1972.

————. *Resolutions and Decisions of the Communist Party of the Soviet Union 1898–1964*. 3 vols. Toronto: University of Toronto Press, 1974.

Medvedev, Roy A. *Let History Judge: The Origins and Consequences of Stalinism*. New York: Alfred A. Knopf, 1971.

Melgunov, Sergei P. *The Bolshevik Seizure of Power*. Edited by Sergei G. Pushkarev. Santa Barbara, Calif.: ABC-Clio, 1972.

Morozow, Michael. *Leonid Breschnew*. Stuttgart: W. Kohlhammer, 1973.

Paloczi-Horvath, George. *Khrushchev: The Making of a Dictator*. Boston: Little, Brown, 1961.

Pistrak, Lazar. *The Grand Tactician: Khrushchev's Rise to Power*. New York: Praeger, 1961.

Possony, Stefan T. *Lenin: The Compulsive Revolutionary*. Chicago: Henry Regnery, 1964.

Rabinowitch, Alexander. *The Bolsheviks Come to Power: The Revolution of 1917 in Petrograd*. New York: W.W. Norton, 1976.

Reshetar, John S., Jr. *A Concise History of the Communist Party of the Soviet Union*. Rev. ed. New York: Praeger, 1964.

Rigby, T. H. *Communist Party Membership in the U.S.S.R.* Princeton: Princeton University Press, 1968.

Rush, Myron. *Political Succession in the USSR*. New York: Columbia University Press, 1965.

Schapiro, Leonard B. *The Communist Party of the Soviet Union*. New York: Random House, 1971.

―――. *The Origin of the Communist Autocracy: Political Opposition in the Soviet State, First Phase, 1917–1922*. Cambridge: Harvard University Press, 1955.

Seaton, Albert. *Stalin as Warlord*. London: B. T. Botsford, 1976.

Seton-Watson, Hugh. *The Decline of Imperial Russia, 1855–1914*. New York: Praeger, 1952.

Shub, David. *Lenin*. Garden City, N.Y.: Doubleday, 1948.

Smith, Hedrick. *The Russians*. New York: Quadrangle/New York Times, 1976.

Staar, Richard F. (ed.). *Yearbook on International Communist Affairs*. Stanford, Ca.: Hoover Institution Press, 1966–1978.

Steinberg, I. N. *In the Workshop of the Revolution*. London: Victor Gollancz, 1955.

Strong, John W., ed. *The Soviet Union under Brezhnev and Kosygin: The Transition Years*. New York: Van Nostrand Reinhold, 1971.

Swearer, Howard R. *The Politics of Succession in the U.S.S.R.* Boston: Little, Brown, 1964.

Sworakowski, Witold S. (ed.). World Communism: A Handbook 1918–1965. Stanford, Ca.: Hoover Institution Press, 1973.

Szamuely, Tibor. *The Russian Tradition*. London: Secker and Warburg, 1974.

Tatu, Michel. *Power in the Kremlin: From Khrushchev to Kosygin*. New York: Viking Press, 1970.

Trotsky, Leon. *Lenin: Notes for a Biographer*. New York: G. P. Putnam's Sons, 1971.

―――. *My Life*. New York: Charles Scribner's Sons, 1930.

Ulam, Adam B. *The Bolsheviks*. New York: Macmillan, 1965.

―――. *Stalin: The Man and His Era*. New York: Viking Press, 1973.

Venturi, Franco. *Roots of Revolution: A History of the Populist and Socialist Movements in Nineteenth Century Russia*. London: Weidenfeld and Nicolson, 1960.

Walkin, Jacob. *The Rise of Democracy in Pre-Revolutionary Russia: Political and Social Institutions under the Last Three Czars*. New York: Praeger, 1962.

Wolfe, Bertram D. *Khrushchev and Stalin's Ghost*. London: Atlantic Press, 1957.

———. *Three Who Made a Revolution*. New York: Dial Press, 1964.

Zeman, Z. A. B. *Germany and the Revolution in Russia 1915–1918*. London: Oxford University Press, 1958.

Zeman, Z. A. B., and Scharlau, W. B. *The Merchant of Revolution: The Life of Alexander Israel Helphand (Parvus)*. London: Oxford University Press, 1965.

Index